WONDER WOMAN
Odyssey

volume one

J. MICHAEL STRACZYNSKI
PHIL HESTER
Writers

DON KRAMER
EDUARDO PANSICA
ALLAN GOLDMAN
DANIEL HDR
Pencillers

MICHAEL BABINSKI
JAY LEISTEN
RUY JOSÉ
SCOTT KOBLISH
MARLO ALQUIZA
WAYNE FAUCHER
EBER FERREIRA
Inkers

ALEX SINCLAIR
Colorist

TRAVIS LANHAM
Letterer

DON KRAMER
Original series cover

ALEX GARNER
Collection cover artist

Wonder Woman created by
William Moulton Marston

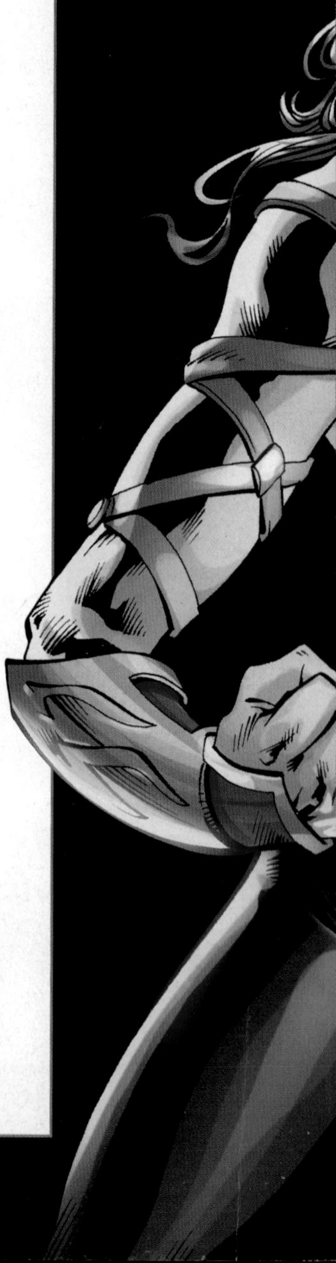

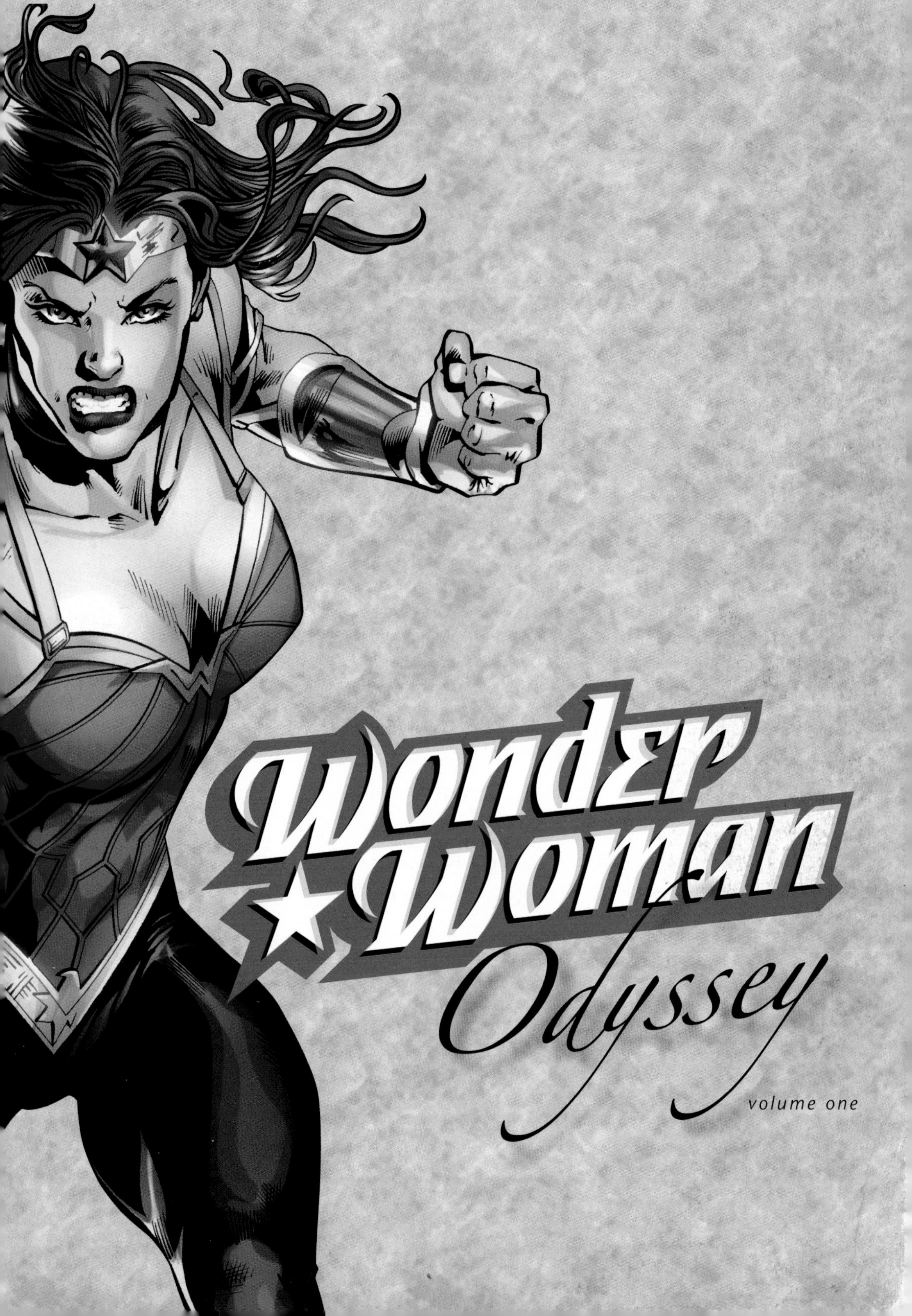

Wonder Woman Odyssey

volume one

WONDER WOMAN: ODYSSEY VOLUME ONE

Published by DC Comics. Cover and compilation Copyright © 2011 DC Comics.
All Rights Reserved.

Originally published in single magazine form in WONDER WOMAN 600-606.
Copyright © 2010, 2011 DC Comics. All Rights Reserved. All characters, their distinctive likenesses and
related elements featured in this publication are trademarks of DC Comics. The stories, characters and
incidents featured in this publication are entirely fictional.
DC Comics does not read or accept unsolicited submissions of ideas, stories or artwork.

DC Comics, 1700 Broadway, New York, NY 10019
A Warner Bros. Entertainment Company
Printed by RR Donnelley, Salem, VA, USA. 06/22/12. First Printing.
ISBN: 978-1-4012-3078-4

Library of Congress Cataloging-in-Publication Data

Straczynski, J. Michael, 1954-
Wonder Woman : odyssey volume one / writer, J. Michael Straczynski ;
pencils, Don Kramer.
    p. cm.
"Originally published in single magazine form in Wonder Woman
#600-606."
ISBN 978-1-4012-3077-7 (hardcover)
1. Graphic novels. I. Kramer, Don. II. Title. III. Title: Odyssey.
PN6728.W6S77 2011
741.5'973—dc22

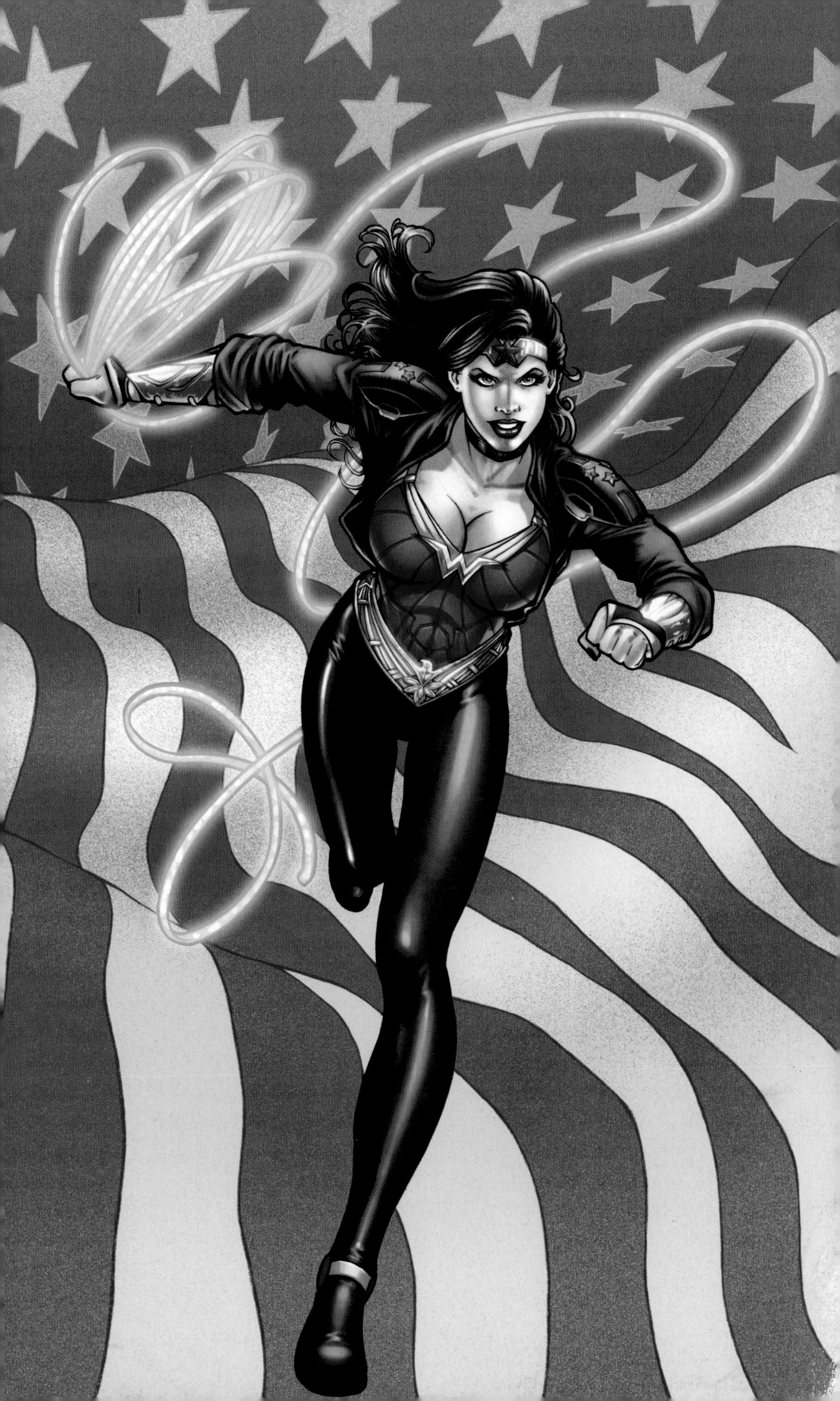

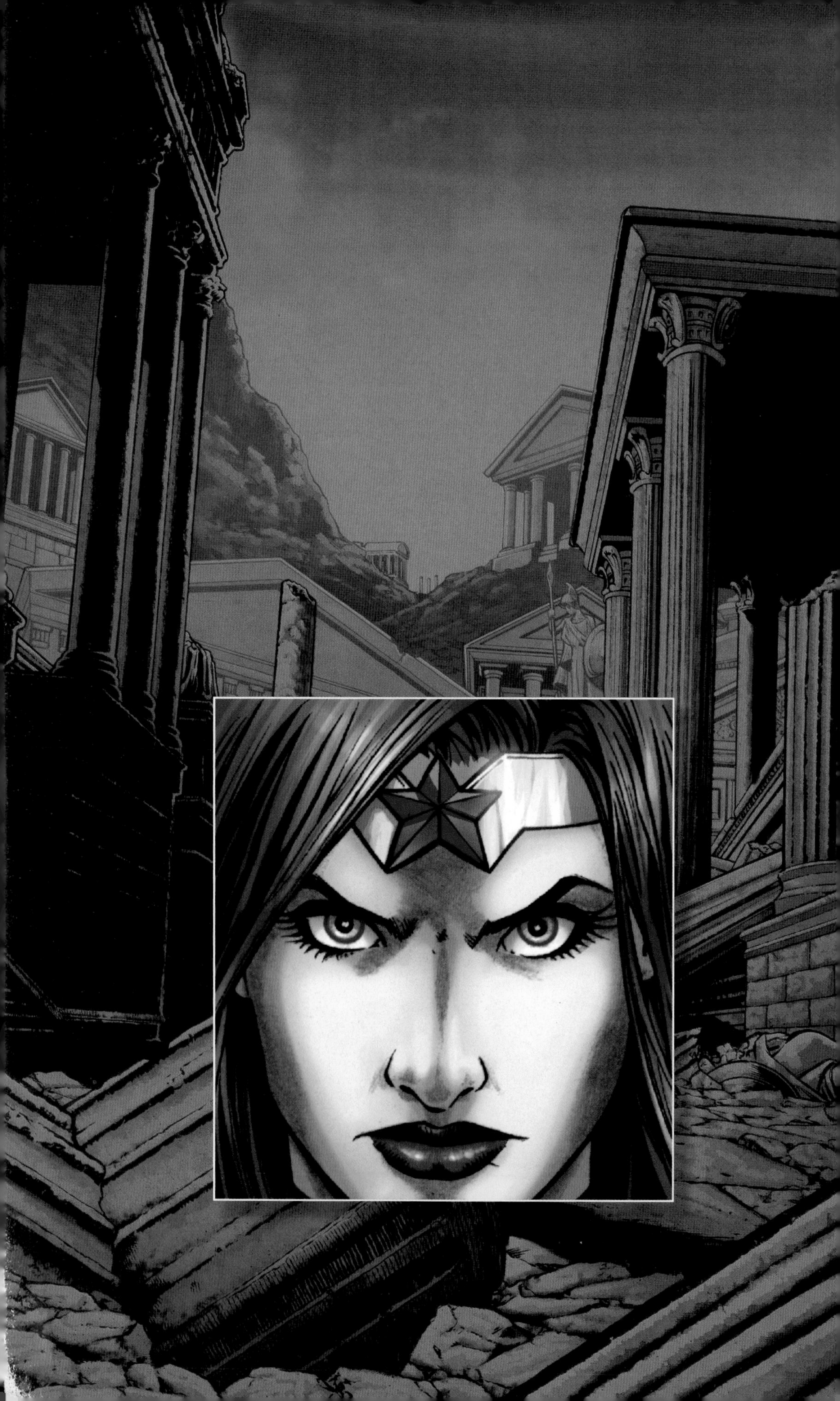

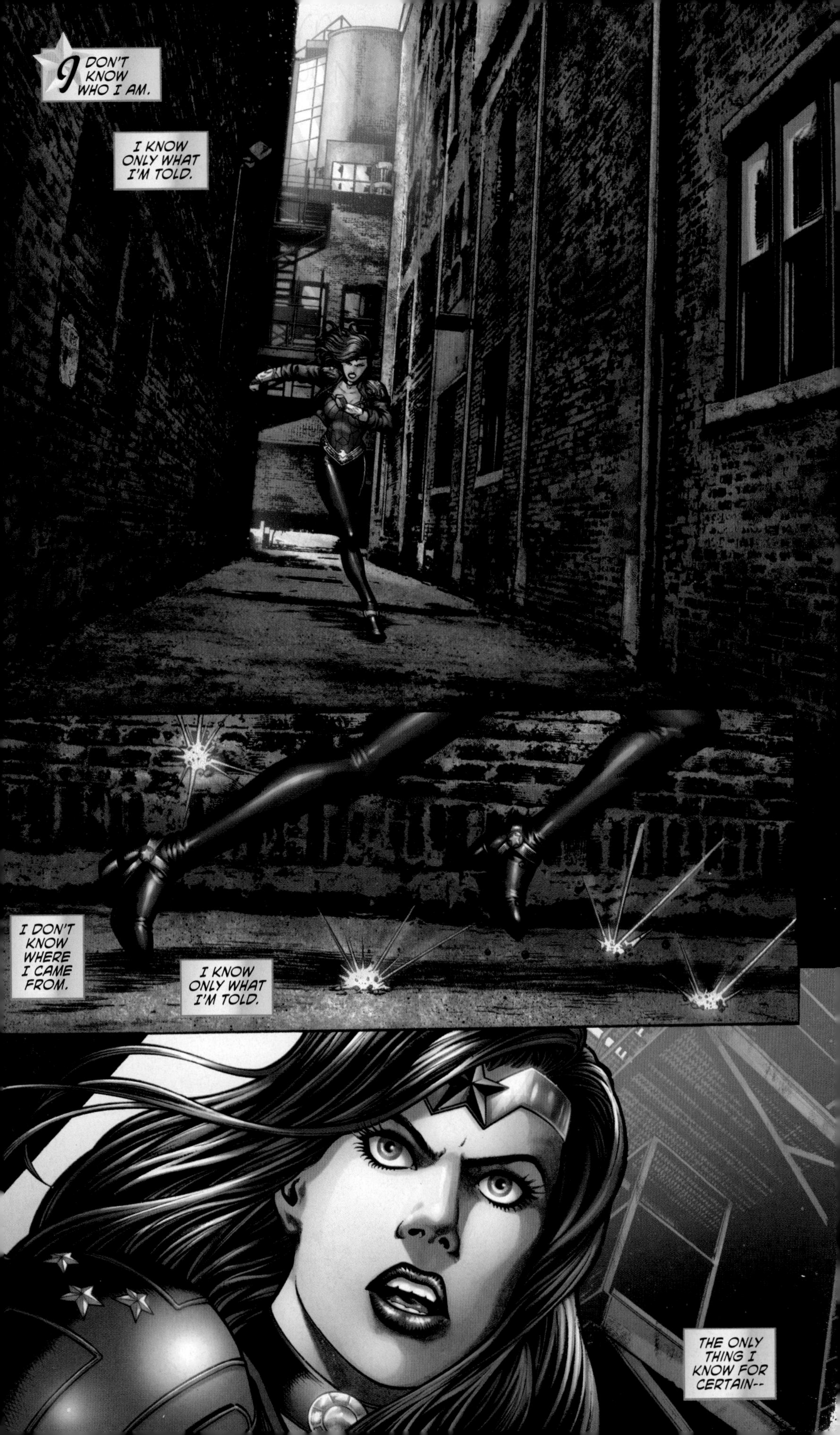
I DON'T KNOW WHO I AM.
I KNOW ONLY WHAT I'M TOLD.
I DON'T KNOW WHERE I CAME FROM.
I KNOW ONLY WHAT I'M TOLD.
THE ONLY THING I KNOW FOR CERTAIN--

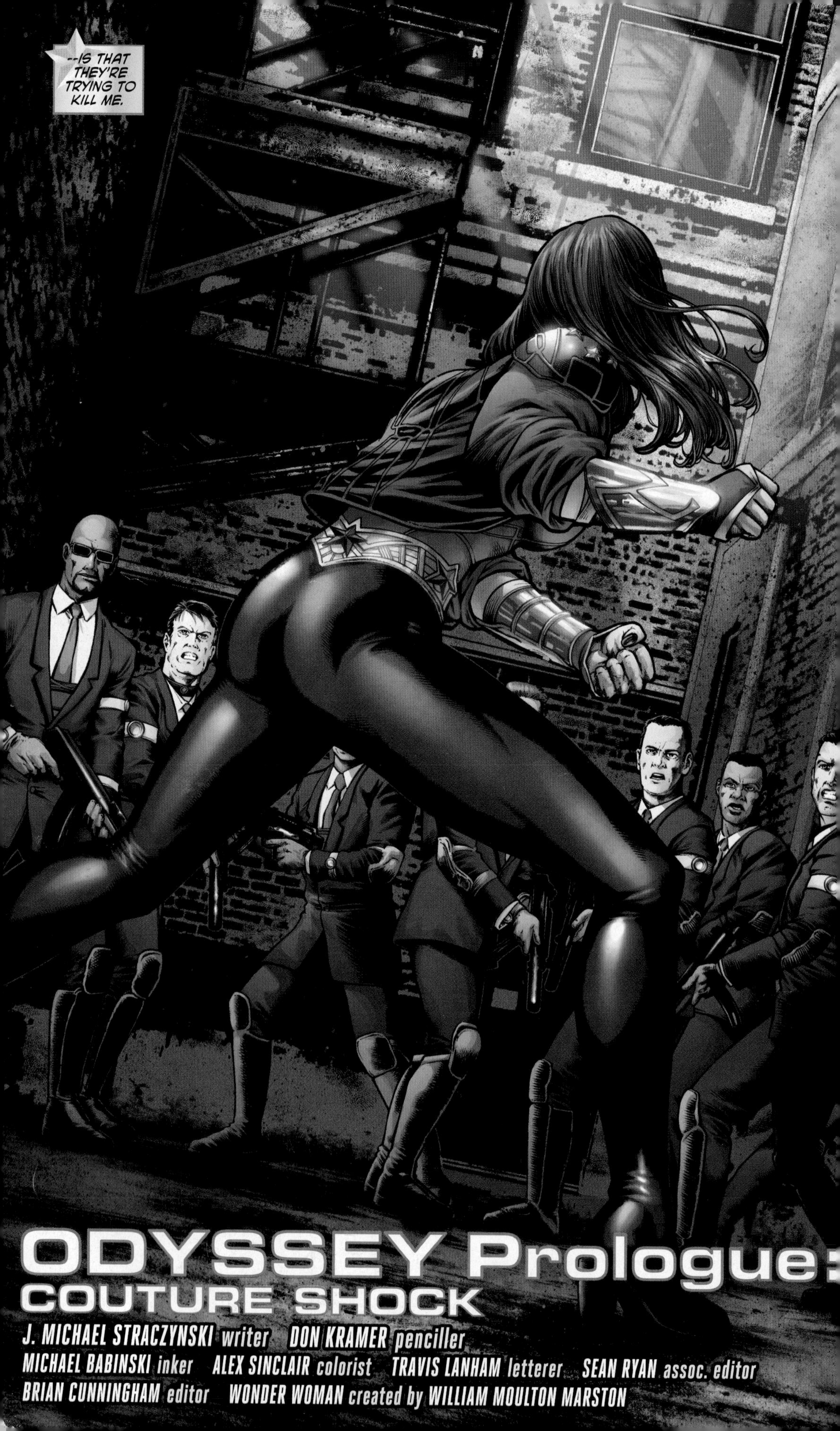
--IS THAT THEY'RE TRYING TO KILL ME.
ODYSSEY Prologue:
COUTURE SHOCK
J. MICHAEL STRACZYNSKI writer DON KRAMER penciller
MICHAEL BABINSKI inker ALEX SINCLAIR colorist TRAVIS LANHAM letterer SEAN RYAN assoc. editor
BRIAN CUNNINGHAM editor WONDER WOMAN created by WILLIAM MOULTON MARSTON

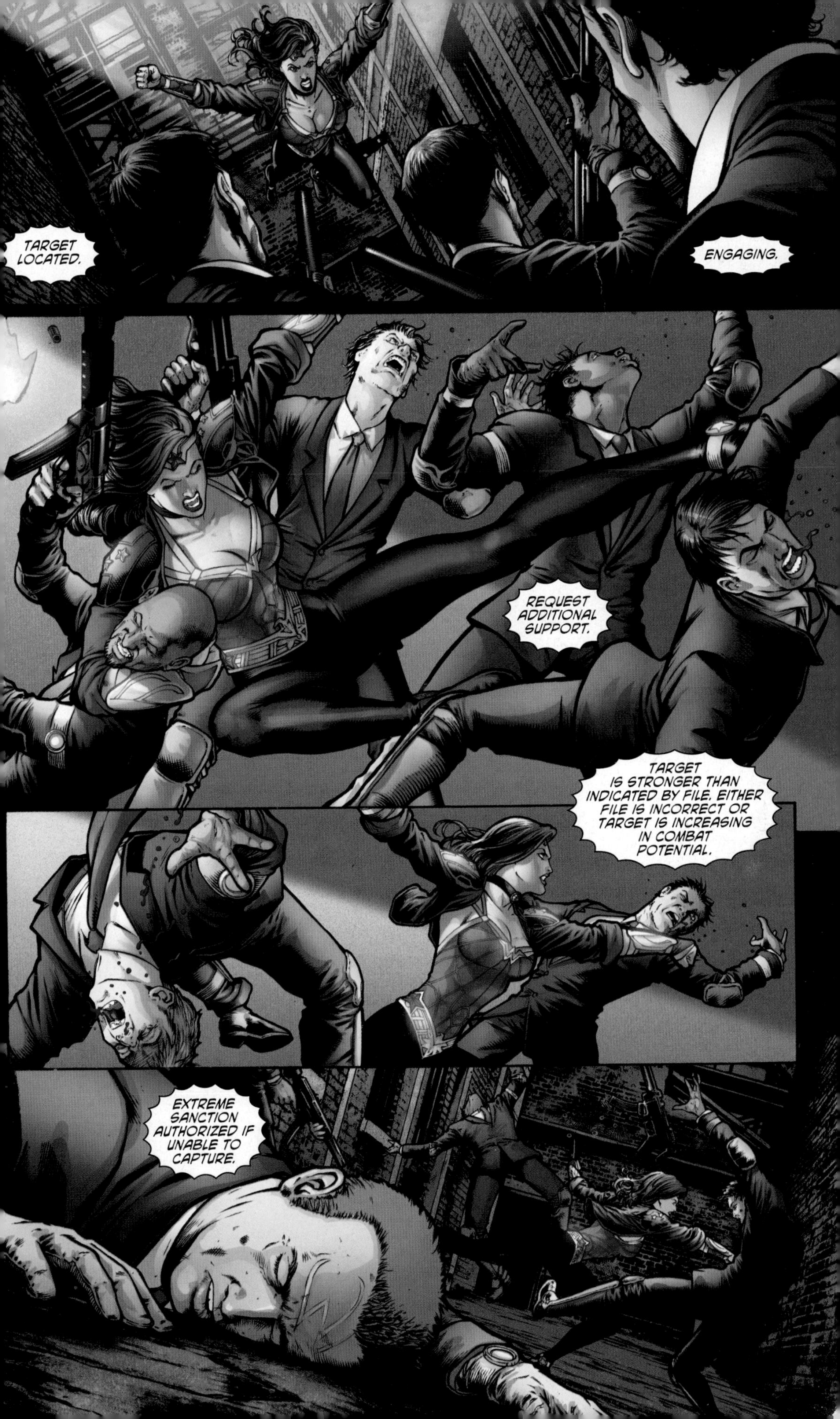
TARGET LOCATED.
ENGAGING.
REQUEST ADDITIONAL SUPPORT.
TARGET IS STRONGER THAN INDICATED BY FILE. EITHER FILE IS INCORRECT OR TARGET IS INCREASING IN COMBAT POTENTIAL.
EXTREME SANCTION AUTHORIZED IF UNABLE TO CAPTURE.

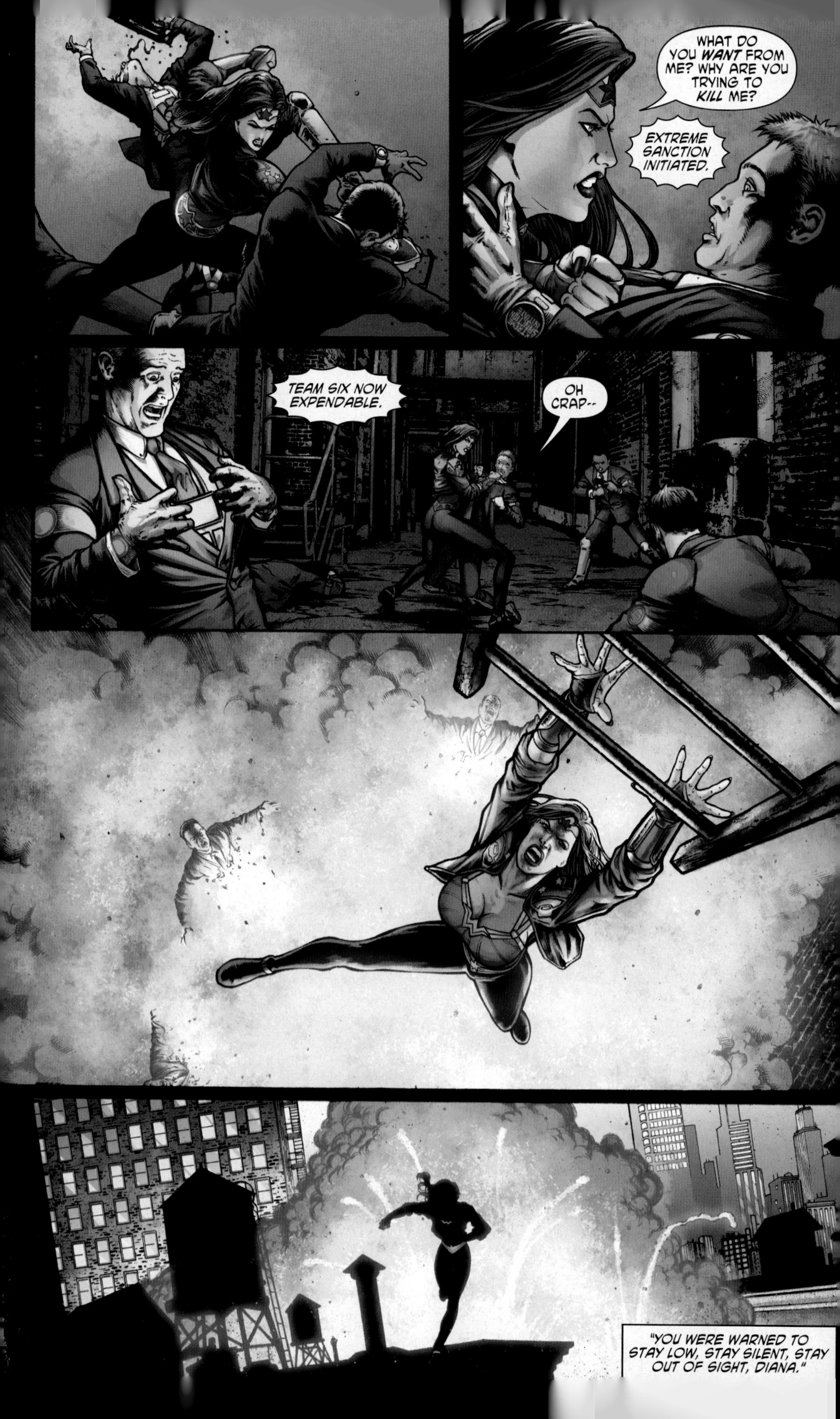

WHAT DO YOU WANT FROM ME? WHY ARE YOU TRYING TO KILL ME?
EXTREME SANCTION INITIATED.
TEAM SIX NOW EXPENDABLE.
OH CRAP--
"YOU WERE WARNED TO STAY LOW, STAY SILENT, STAY OUT OF SIGHT, DIANA."

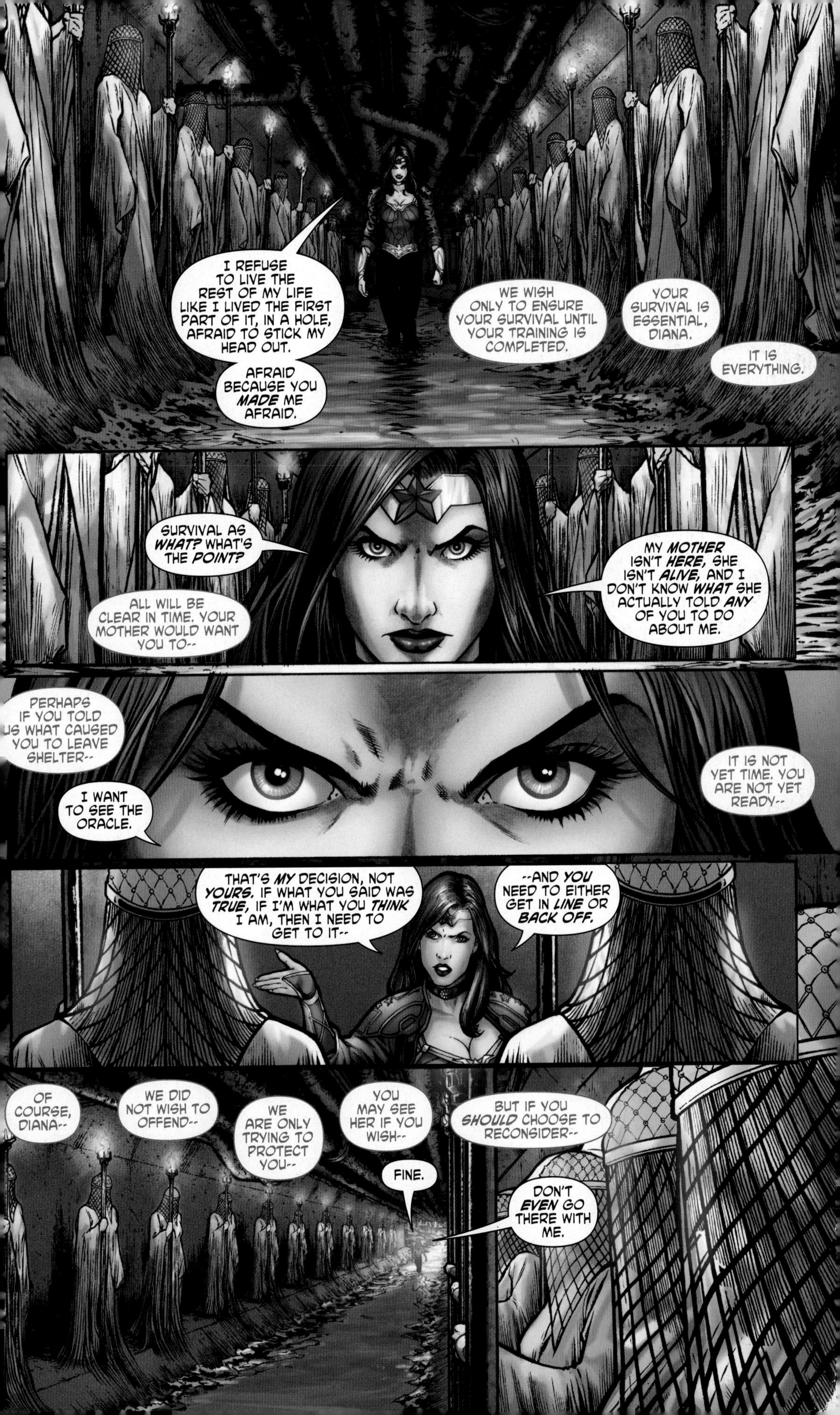
I REFUSE TO LIVE THE REST OF MY LIFE LIKE I LIVED THE FIRST PART OF IT, IN A HOLE, AFRAID TO STICK MY HEAD OUT.
AFRAID BECAUSE YOU MADE ME AFRAID.
WE WISH ONLY TO ENSURE YOUR SURVIVAL UNTIL YOUR TRAINING IS COMPLETED.
YOUR SURVIVAL IS ESSENTIAL, DIANA.
IT IS EVERYTHING.
SURVIVAL AS WHAT? WHAT'S THE POINT?
ALL WILL BE CLEAR IN TIME. YOUR MOTHER WOULD WANT YOU TO--
MY MOTHER ISN'T HERE, SHE ISN'T ALIVE, AND I DON'T KNOW WHAT SHE ACTUALLY TOLD ANY OF YOU TO DO ABOUT ME.
PERHAPS IF YOU TOLD US WHAT CAUSED YOU TO LEAVE SHELTER--
I WANT TO SEE THE ORACLE.
IT IS NOT YET TIME. YOU ARE NOT YET READY--
THAT'S MY DECISION, NOT YOURS. IF WHAT YOU SAID WAS TRUE, IF I'M WHAT YOU THINK I AM, THEN I NEED TO GET TO IT--
--AND YOU NEED TO EITHER GET IN LINE OR BACK OFF.
OF COURSE, DIANA--
WE DID NOT WISH TO OFFEND--
WE ARE ONLY TRYING TO PROTECT YOU--
YOU MAY SEE HER IF YOU WISH--
FINE.
BUT IF YOU SHOULD CHOOSE TO RECONSIDER--
DON'T EVEN GO THERE WITH ME.

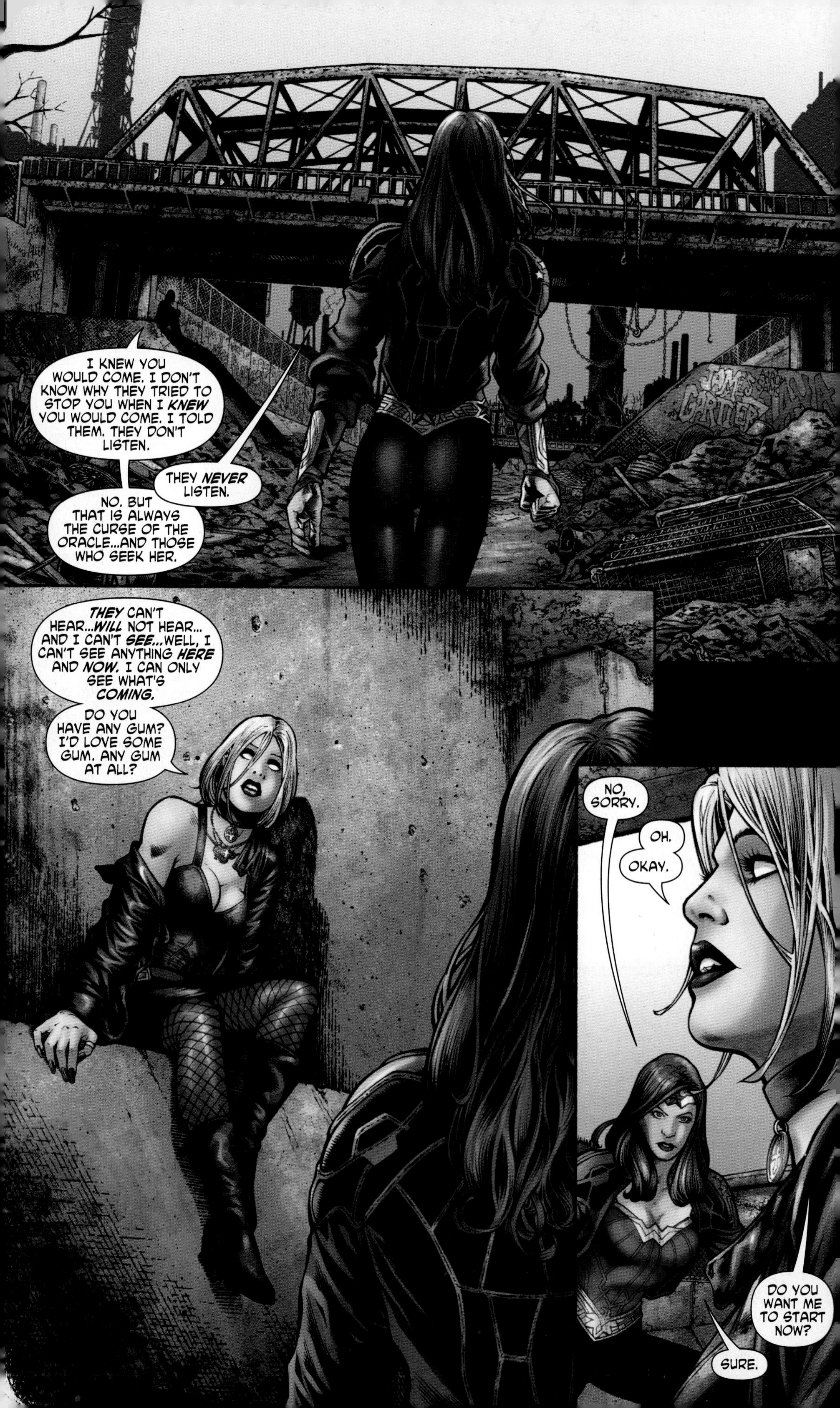

I KNEW YOU WOULD COME. I DON'T KNOW WHY THEY TRIED TO STOP YOU WHEN I *KNEW* YOU WOULD COME. I TOLD THEM. THEY DON'T LISTEN.
THEY *NEVER* LISTEN.
NO. BUT THAT IS ALWAYS THE CURSE OF THE ORACLE...AND THOSE WHO SEEK HER.
THEY CAN'T HEAR...*WILL* NOT HEAR... AND I CAN'T *SEE*...WELL, I CAN'T SEE ANYTHING *HERE* AND *NOW.* I CAN ONLY SEE WHAT'S *COMING.*
DO YOU HAVE ANY GUM? I'D LOVE SOME GUM. ANY GUM AT ALL?
NO, SORRY.
OH.
OKAY.
DO YOU WANT ME TO START NOW?
SURE.

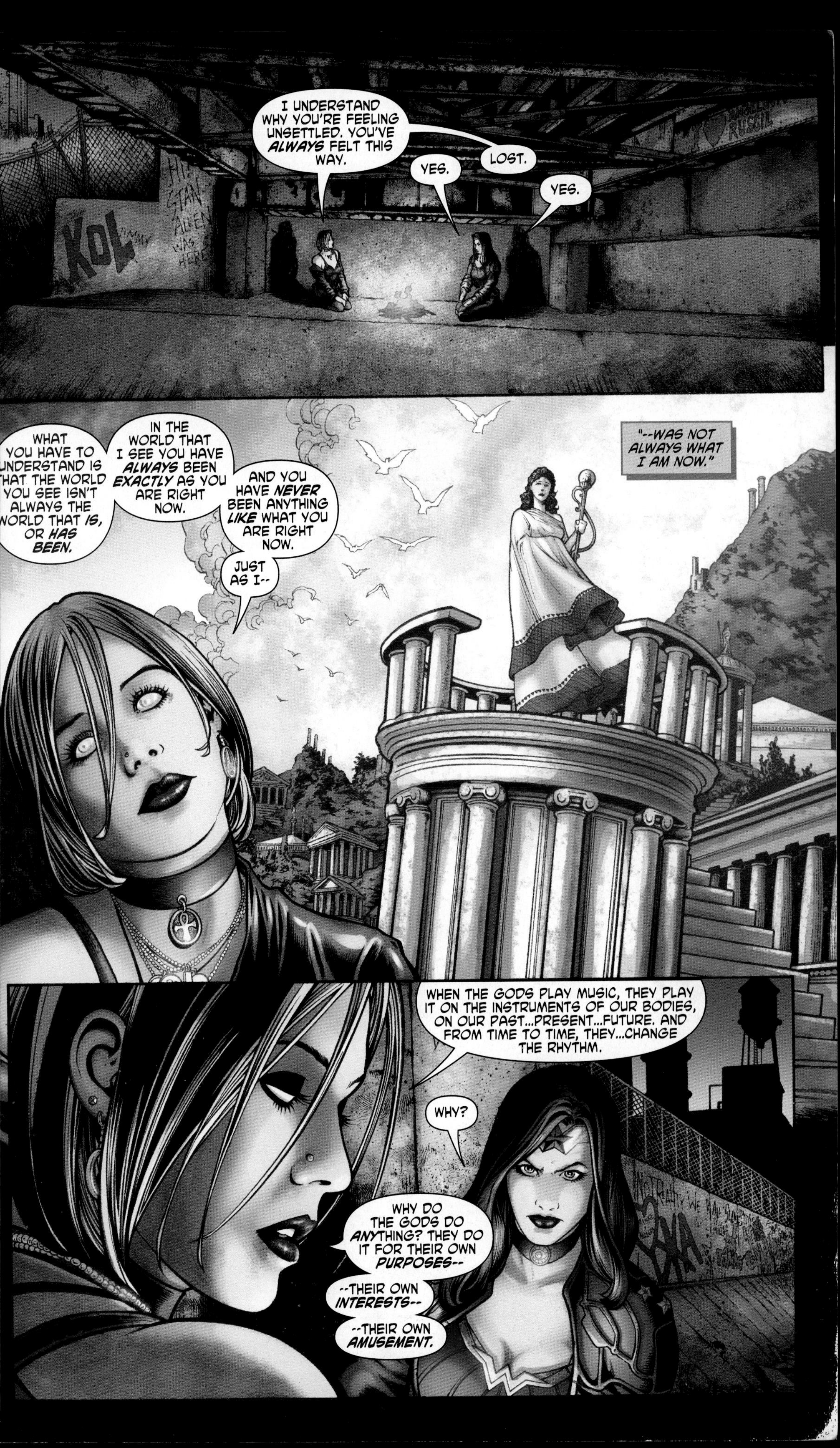
I UNDERSTAND WHY YOU'RE FEELING UNSETTLED. YOU'VE ALWAYS FELT THIS WAY.
LOST.
YES.
YES.
KOL
WHAT YOU HAVE TO UNDERSTAND IS THAT THE WORLD YOU SEE ISN'T ALWAYS THE WORLD THAT IS, OR HAS BEEN.
IN THE WORLD THAT I SEE YOU HAVE ALWAYS BEEN EXACTLY AS YOU ARE RIGHT NOW.
AND YOU HAVE NEVER BEEN ANYTHING LIKE WHAT YOU ARE RIGHT NOW.
JUST AS I--
"--WAS NOT ALWAYS WHAT I AM NOW."
WHEN THE GODS PLAY MUSIC, THEY PLAY IT ON THE INSTRUMENTS OF OUR BODIES, ON OUR PAST...PRESENT...FUTURE. AND FROM TIME TO TIME, THEY...CHANGE THE RHYTHM.
WHY?
WHY DO THE GODS DO ANYTHING? THEY DO IT FOR THEIR OWN PURPOSES--
--THEIR OWN INTERESTS--
--THEIR OWN AMUSEMENT.

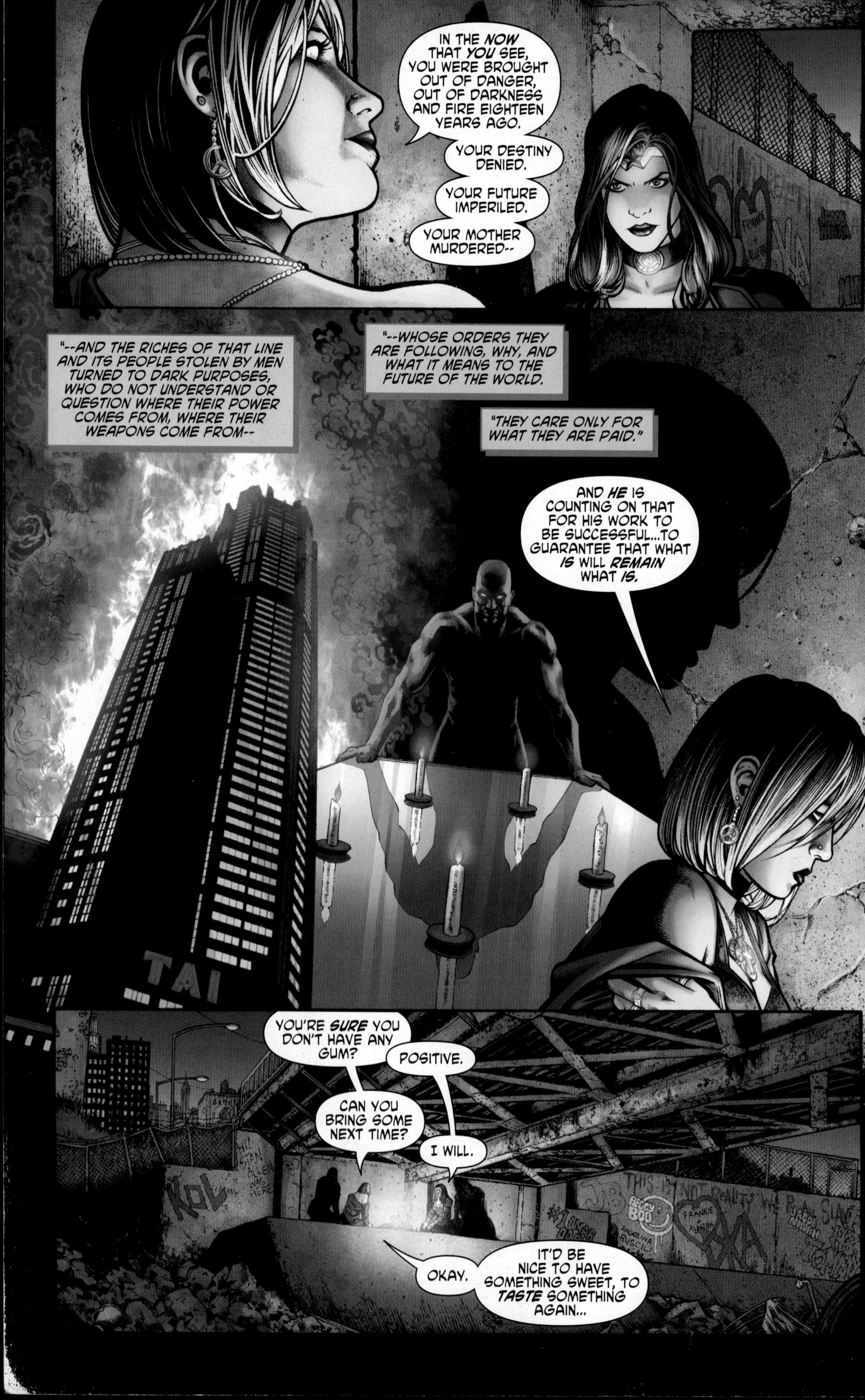
IN THE *NOW* THAT *YOU* SEE, YOU WERE BROUGHT OUT OF DANGER, OUT OF DARKNESS AND FIRE EIGHTEEN YEARS AGO.
YOUR DESTINY DENIED.
YOUR FUTURE IMPERILED.
YOUR MOTHER MURDERED--
"--AND THE RICHES OF THAT LINE AND ITS PEOPLE STOLEN BY MEN TURNED TO DARK PURPOSES, WHO DO NOT UNDERSTAND OR QUESTION WHERE THEIR POWER COMES FROM, WHERE THEIR WEAPONS COME FROM--
"--WHOSE ORDERS THEY ARE FOLLOWING, WHY, AND WHAT IT MEANS TO THE FUTURE OF THE WORLD.
"THEY CARE ONLY FOR WHAT THEY ARE PAID."
AND *HE* IS COUNTING ON THAT FOR HIS WORK TO BE SUCCESSFUL...TO GUARANTEE THAT WHAT *IS* WILL *REMAIN* WHAT *IS*.
TAI
YOU'RE *SURE* YOU DON'T HAVE ANY GUM?
POSITIVE.
CAN YOU BRING SOME NEXT TIME?
I WILL.
OKAY.
IT'D BE NICE TO HAVE SOMETHING SWEET, TO *TASTE* SOMETHING AGAIN...

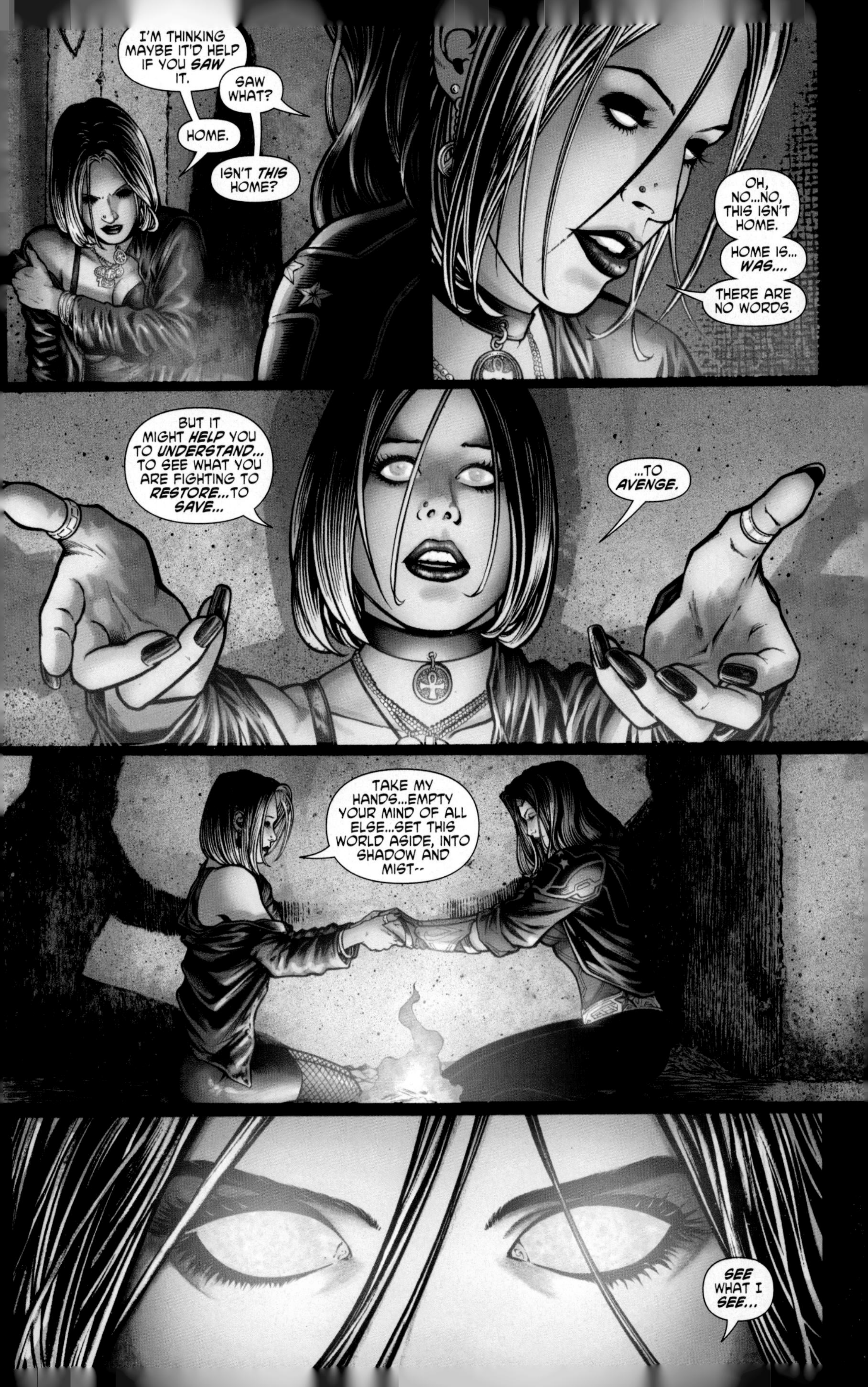
I'M THINKING MAYBE IT'D HELP IF YOU SAW IT.
SAW WHAT?
HOME.
ISN'T THIS HOME?
OH, NO...NO, THIS ISN'T HOME.
HOME IS... WAS....
THERE ARE NO WORDS.
BUT IT MIGHT HELP YOU TO UNDERSTAND... TO SEE WHAT YOU ARE FIGHTING TO RESTORE...TO SAVE...
...TO AVENGE.
TAKE MY HANDS...EMPTY YOUR MIND OF ALL ELSE...SET THIS WORLD ASIDE, INTO SHADOW AND MIST--
SEE WHAT I SEE...

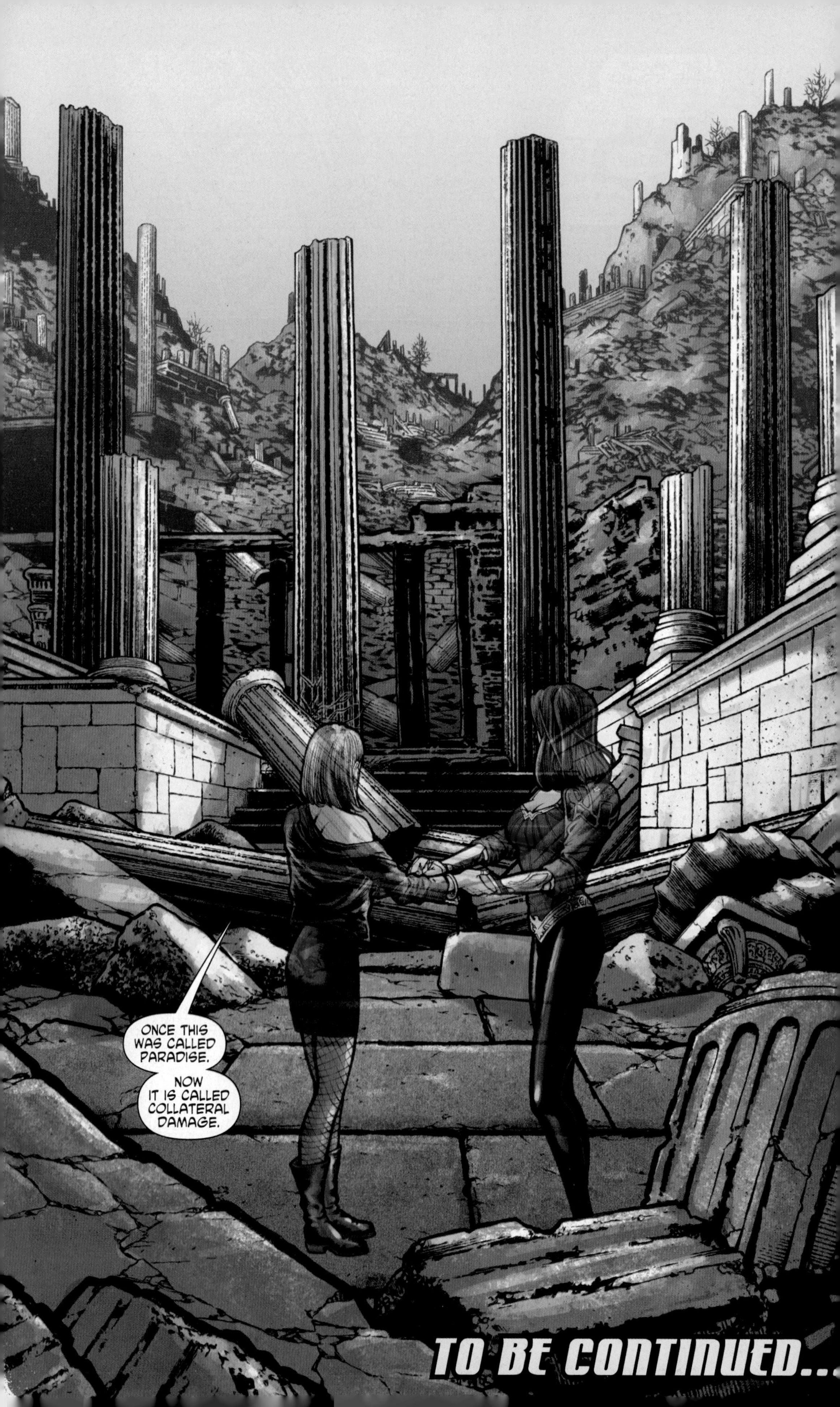
ONCE THIS WAS CALLED PARADISE.
NOW IT IS CALLED COLLATERAL DAMAGE.
TO BE CONTINUED...

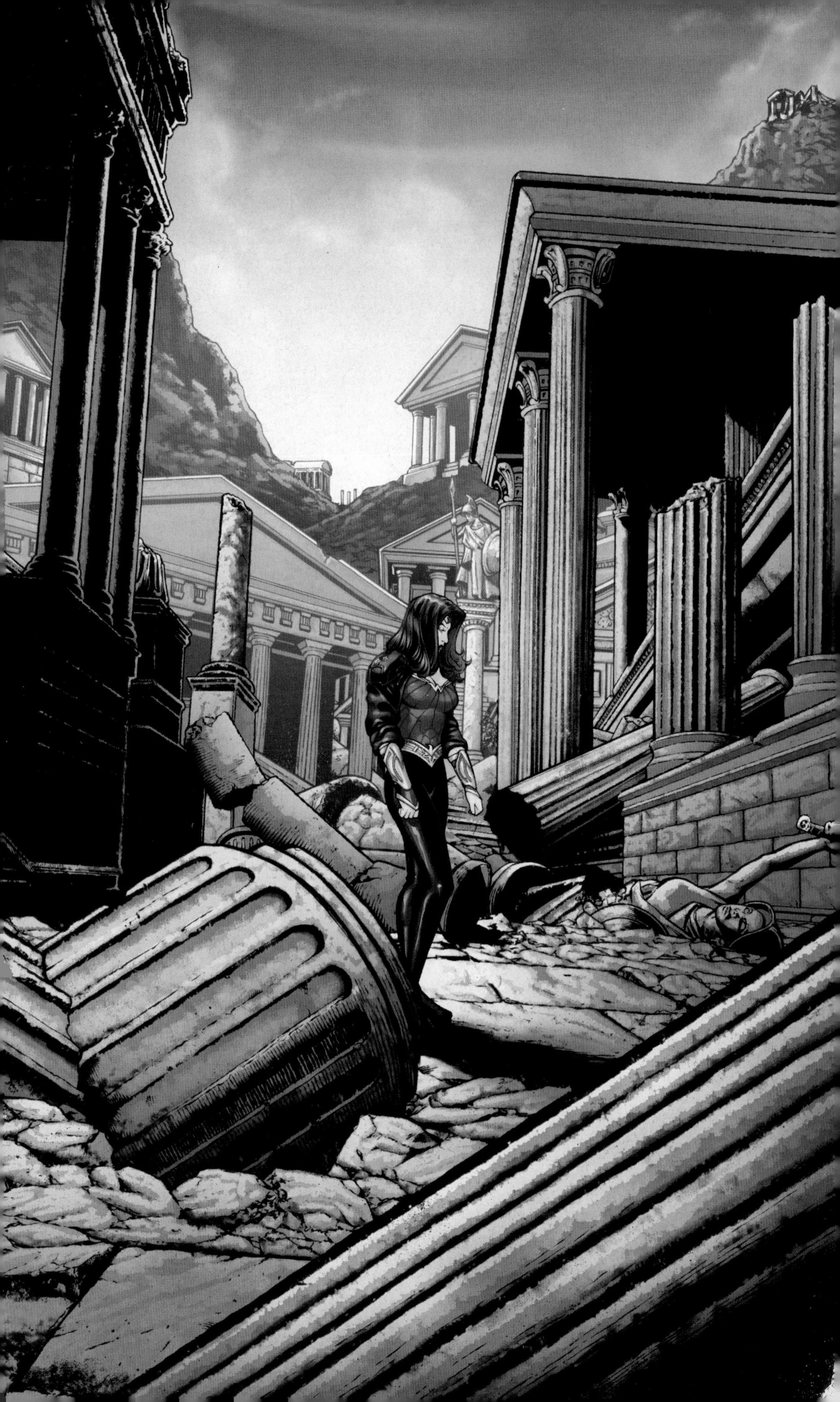

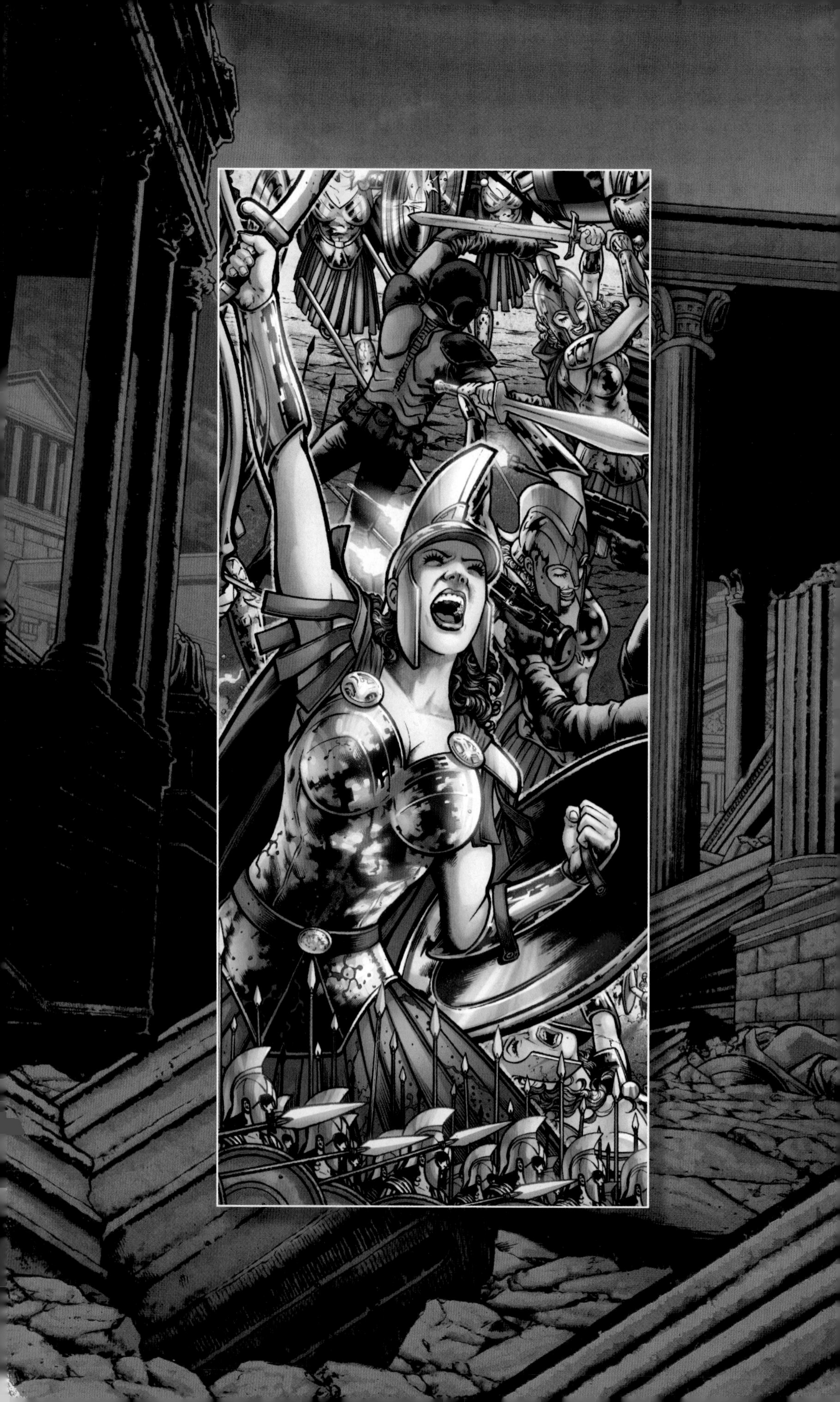

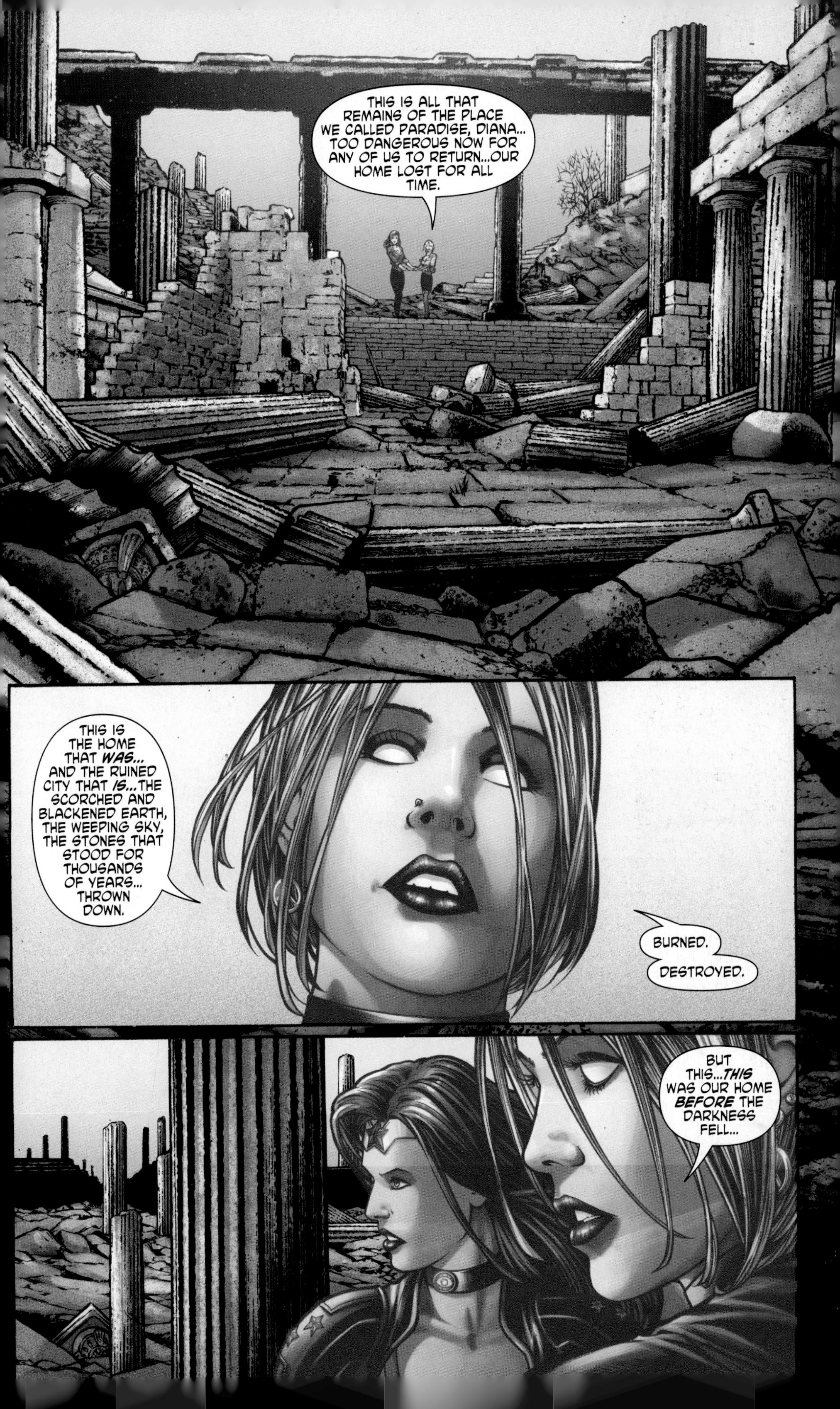

THIS IS ALL THAT REMAINS OF THE PLACE WE CALLED PARADISE, DIANA... TOO DANGEROUS NOW FOR ANY OF US TO RETURN...OUR HOME LOST FOR ALL TIME.
THIS IS THE HOME THAT *WAS*... AND THE RUINED CITY THAT *IS*...THE SCORCHED AND BLACKENED EARTH, THE WEEPING SKY, THE STONES THAT STOOD FOR THOUSANDS OF YEARS... THROWN DOWN.
BURNED.
DESTROYED.
BUT THIS...*THIS* WAS OUR HOME *BEFORE* THE DARKNESS FELL...

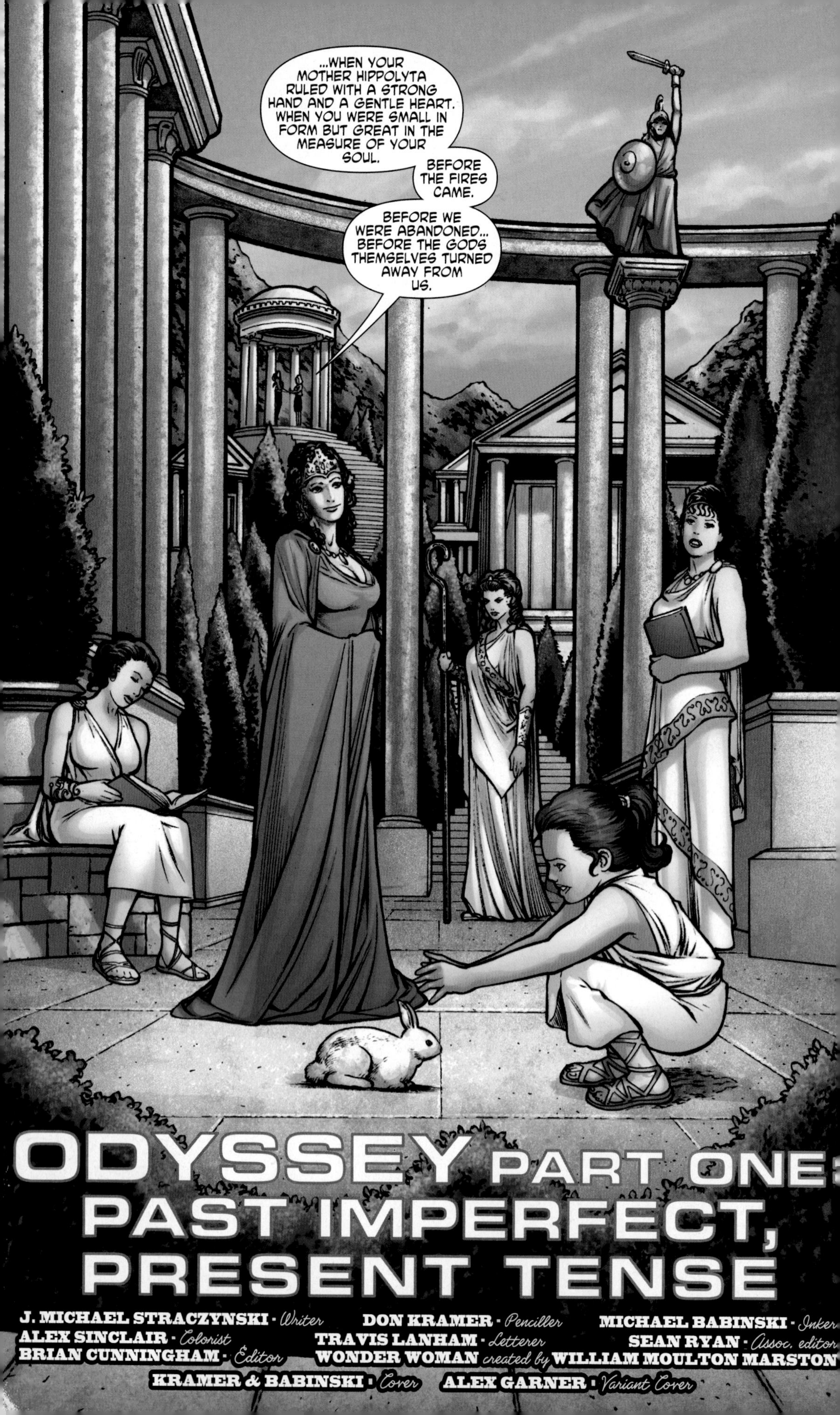
...WHEN YOUR MOTHER HIPPOLYTA RULED WITH A STRONG HAND AND A GENTLE HEART. WHEN YOU WERE SMALL IN FORM BUT GREAT IN THE MEASURE OF YOUR SOUL.
BEFORE THE FIRES CAME.
BEFORE WE WERE ABANDONED... BEFORE THE GODS THEMSELVES TURNED AWAY FROM US.
ODYSSEY PART ONE: PAST IMPERFECT, PRESENT TENSE
J. MICHAEL STRACZYNSKI - Writer
DON KRAMER - Penciller
MICHAEL BABINSKI - Inker
ALEX SINCLAIR - Colorist
TRAVIS LANHAM - Letterer
SEAN RYAN - Assoc. editor
BRIAN CUNNINGHAM - Editor
WONDER WOMAN created by WILLIAM MOULTON MARSTON
KRAMER & BABINSKI - Cover
ALEX GARNER - Variant Cover

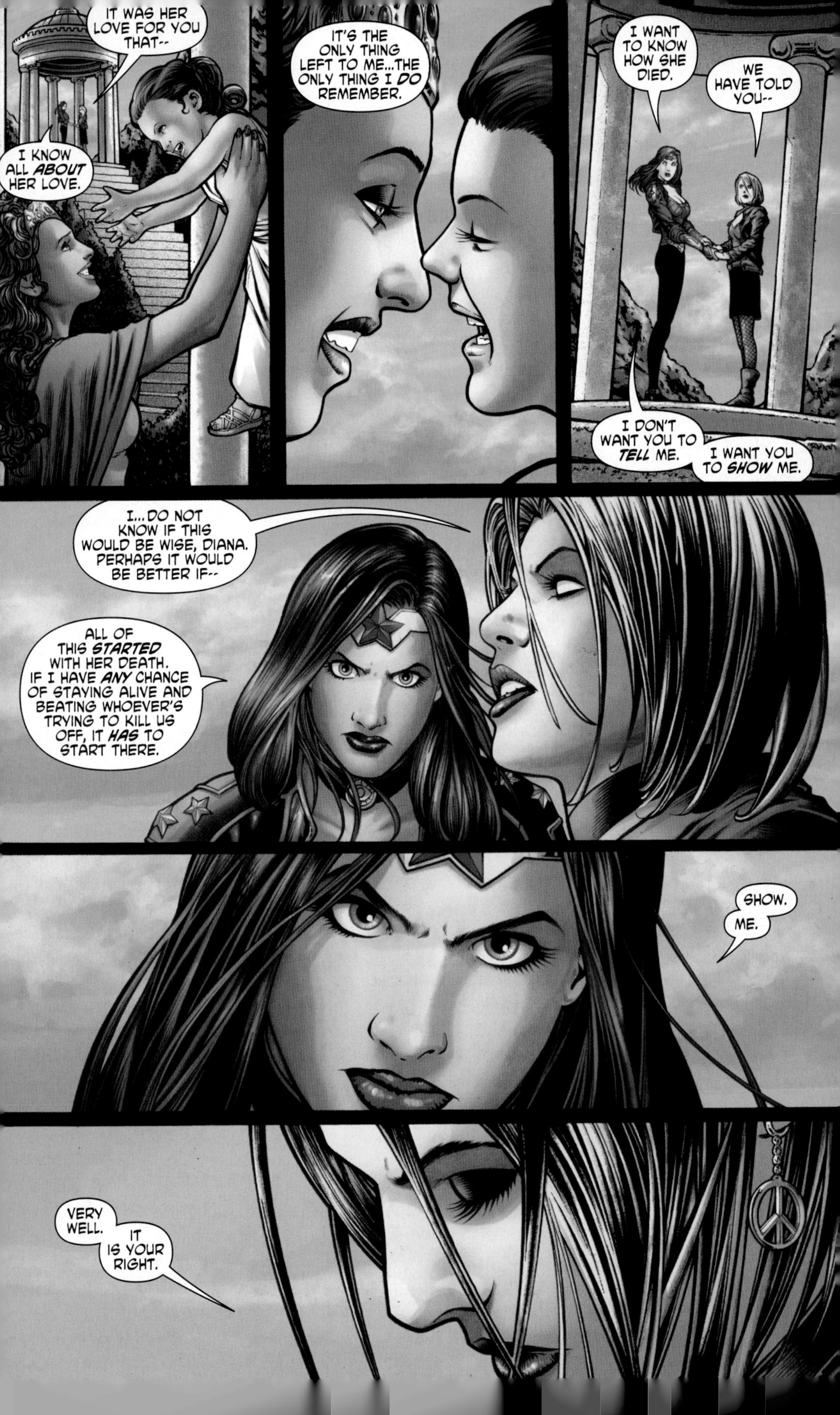
IT WAS HER LOVE FOR YOU THAT--
I KNOW ALL ABOUT HER LOVE.
IT'S THE ONLY THING LEFT TO ME...THE ONLY THING I DO REMEMBER.
I WANT TO KNOW HOW SHE DIED.
WE HAVE TOLD YOU--
I DON'T WANT YOU TO TELL ME.
I WANT YOU TO SHOW ME.
I...DO NOT KNOW IF THIS WOULD BE WISE, DIANA. PERHAPS IT WOULD BE BETTER IF--
ALL OF THIS STARTED WITH HER DEATH. IF I HAVE ANY CHANCE OF STAYING ALIVE AND BEATING WHOEVER'S TRYING TO KILL US OFF, IT HAS TO START THERE.
SHOW. ME.
VERY WELL.
IT IS YOUR RIGHT.

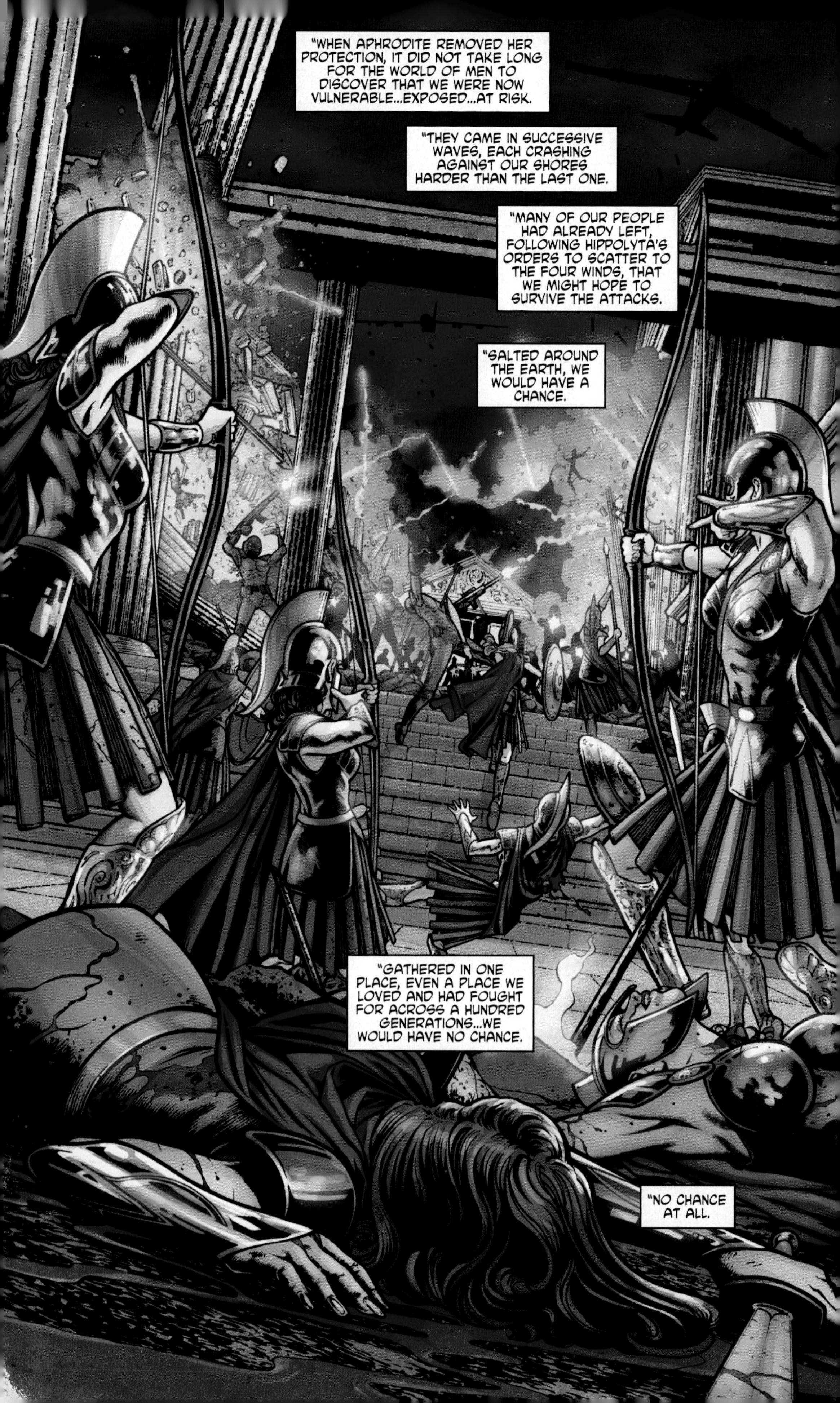
"WHEN APHRODITE REMOVED HER PROTECTION, IT DID NOT TAKE LONG FOR THE WORLD OF MEN TO DISCOVER THAT WE WERE NOW VULNERABLE...EXPOSED...AT RISK.
"THEY CAME IN SUCCESSIVE WAVES, EACH CRASHING AGAINST OUR SHORES HARDER THAN THE LAST ONE.
"MANY OF OUR PEOPLE HAD ALREADY LEFT, FOLLOWING HIPPOLYTA'S ORDERS TO SCATTER TO THE FOUR WINDS, THAT WE MIGHT HOPE TO SURVIVE THE ATTACKS.
"SALTED AROUND THE EARTH, WE WOULD HAVE A CHANCE.
"GATHERED IN ONE PLACE, EVEN A PLACE WE LOVED AND HAD FOUGHT FOR ACROSS A HUNDRED GENERATIONS...WE WOULD HAVE NO CHANCE.
"NO CHANCE AT ALL.

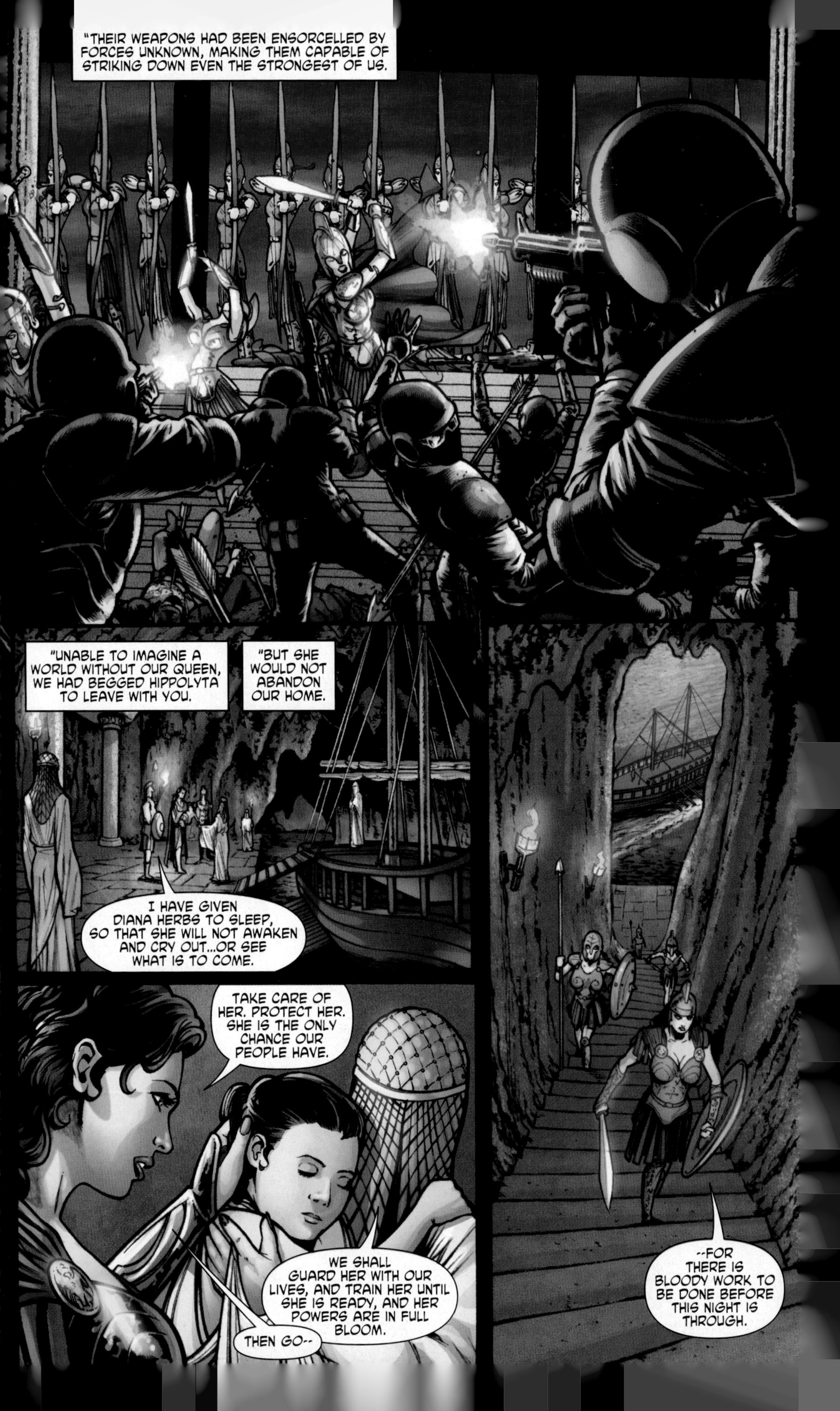
"THEIR WEAPONS HAD BEEN ENSORCELLED BY FORCES UNKNOWN, MAKING THEM CAPABLE OF STRIKING DOWN EVEN THE STRONGEST OF US.
"UNABLE TO IMAGINE A WORLD WITHOUT OUR QUEEN, WE HAD BEGGED HIPPOLYTA TO LEAVE WITH YOU.
"BUT SHE WOULD NOT ABANDON OUR HOME.
I HAVE GIVEN DIANA HERBS TO SLEEP, SO THAT SHE WILL NOT AWAKEN AND CRY OUT...OR SEE WHAT IS TO COME.
TAKE CARE OF HER. PROTECT HER. SHE IS THE ONLY CHANCE OUR PEOPLE HAVE.
WE SHALL GUARD HER WITH OUR LIVES, AND TRAIN HER UNTIL SHE IS READY, AND HER POWERS ARE IN FULL BLOOM.
THEN GO--
--FOR THERE IS BLOODY WORK TO BE DONE BEFORE THIS NIGHT IS THROUGH.

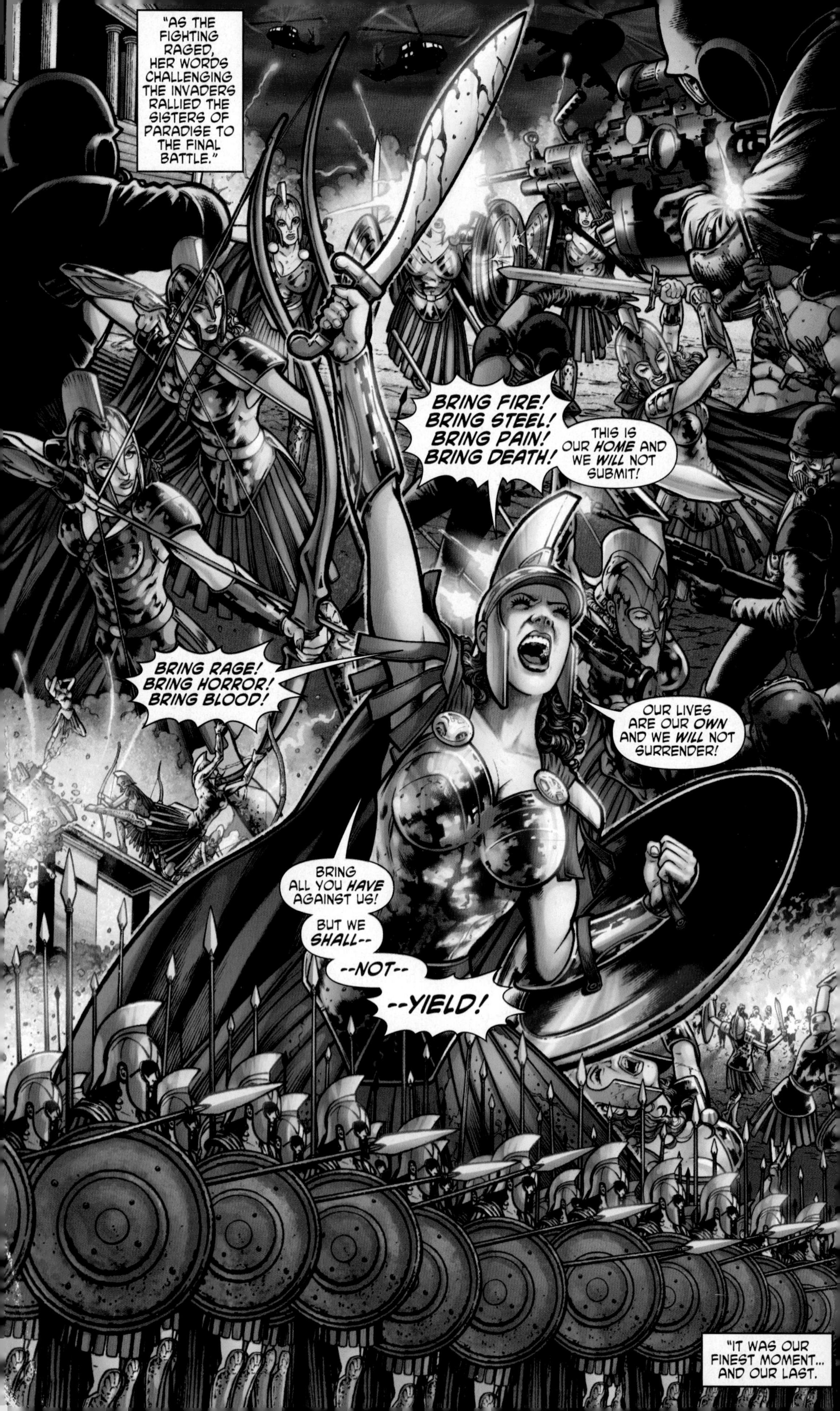
"AS THE FIGHTING RAGED, HER WORDS CHALLENGING THE INVADERS RALLIED THE SISTERS OF PARADISE TO THE FINAL BATTLE."
BRING FIRE! BRING STEEL! BRING PAIN! BRING DEATH!
THIS IS OUR HOME AND WE WILL NOT SUBMIT!
BRING RAGE! BRING HORROR! BRING BLOOD!
OUR LIVES ARE OUR OWN AND WE WILL NOT SURRENDER!
BRING ALL YOU HAVE AGAINST US!
BUT WE SHALL--
--NOT--
--YIELD!
"IT WAS OUR FINEST MOMENT... AND OUR LAST.

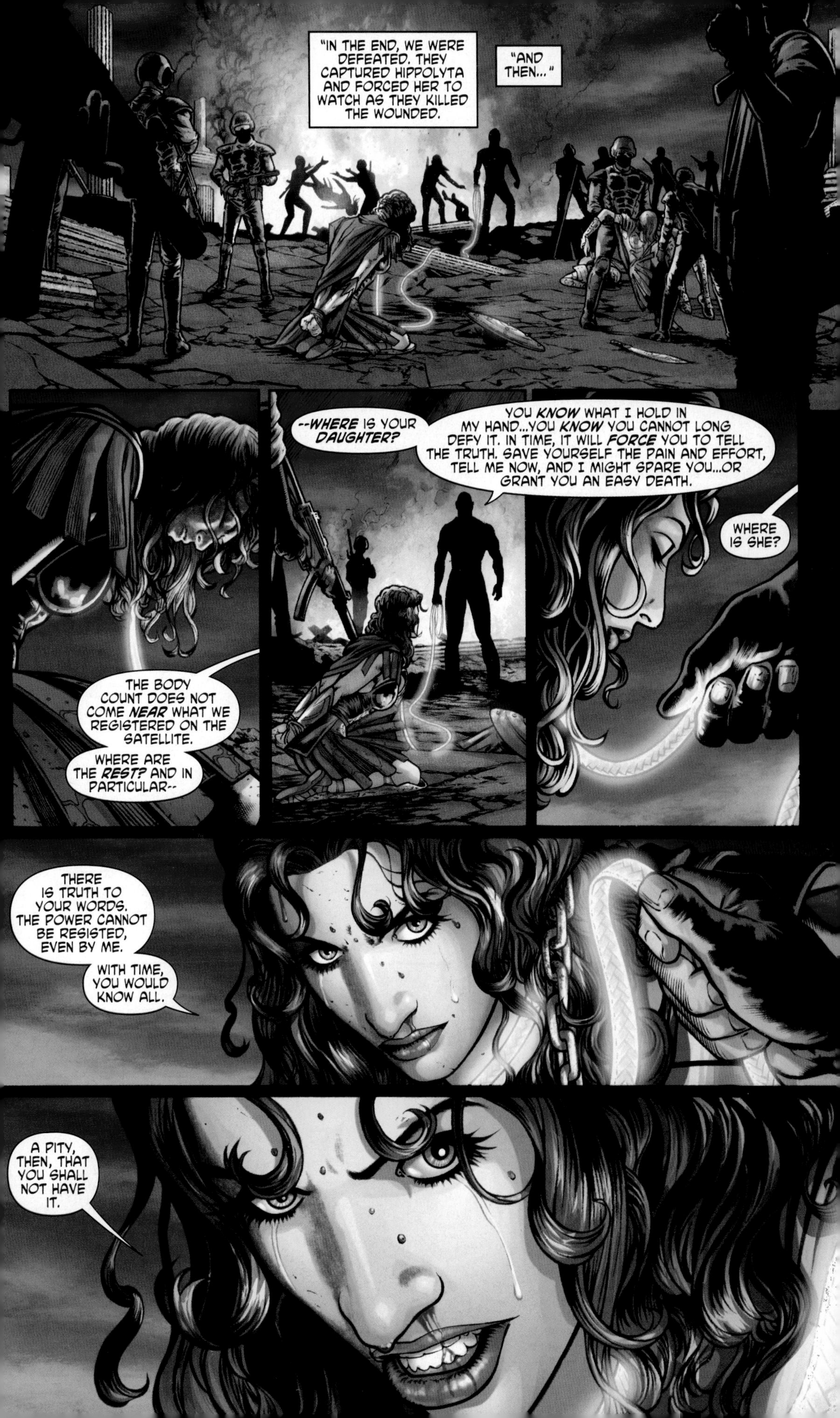
"IN THE END, WE WERE DEFEATED. THEY CAPTURED HIPPOLYTA AND FORCED HER TO WATCH AS THEY KILLED THE WOUNDED.
"AND THEN..."
THE BODY COUNT DOES NOT COME *NEAR* WHAT WE REGISTERED ON THE SATELLITE.
WHERE ARE THE *REST?* AND IN PARTICULAR--
--*WHERE* IS YOUR *DAUGHTER?*
YOU *KNOW* WHAT I HOLD IN MY HAND...YOU *KNOW* YOU CANNOT LONG DEFY IT. IN TIME, IT WILL *FORCE* YOU TO TELL THE TRUTH. SAVE YOURSELF THE PAIN AND EFFORT, TELL ME NOW, AND I MIGHT SPARE YOU...OR GRANT YOU AN EASY DEATH.
WHERE IS SHE?
THERE IS TRUTH TO YOUR WORDS. THE POWER CANNOT BE RESISTED, EVEN BY ME.
WITH TIME, YOU WOULD KNOW ALL.
A PITY, THEN, THAT YOU SHALL NOT HAVE IT.

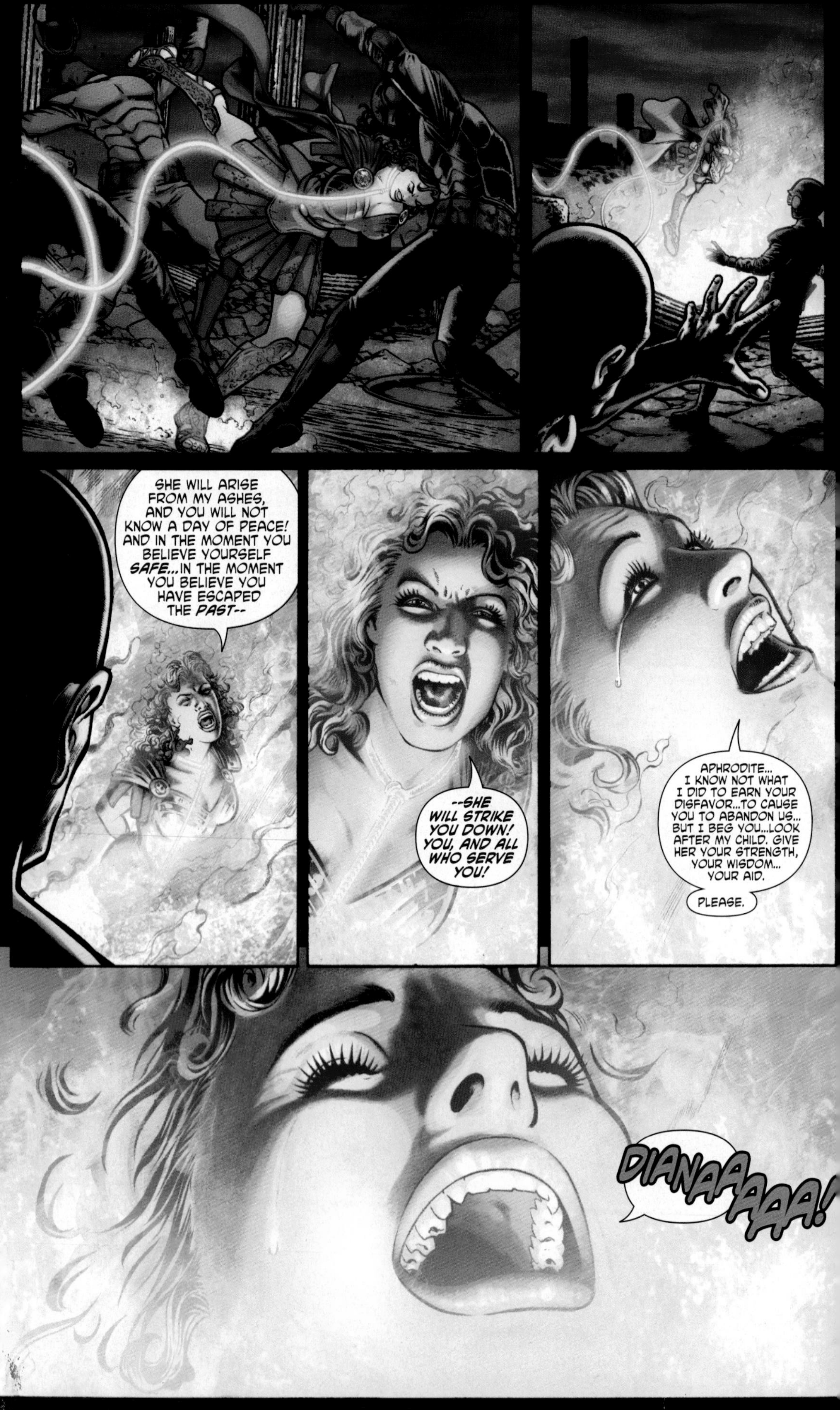
SHE WILL ARISE FROM MY ASHES, AND YOU WILL NOT KNOW A DAY OF PEACE! AND IN THE MOMENT YOU BELIEVE YOURSELF SAFE...IN THE MOMENT YOU BELIEVE YOU HAVE ESCAPED THE PAST--
--SHE WILL STRIKE YOU DOWN! YOU, AND ALL WHO SERVE YOU!
APHRODITE... I KNOW NOT WHAT I DID TO EARN YOUR DISFAVOR...TO CAUSE YOU TO ABANDON US... BUT I BEG YOU...LOOK AFTER MY CHILD. GIVE HER YOUR STRENGTH, YOUR WISDOM... YOUR AID.
PLEASE.
DIANAAAAAA!

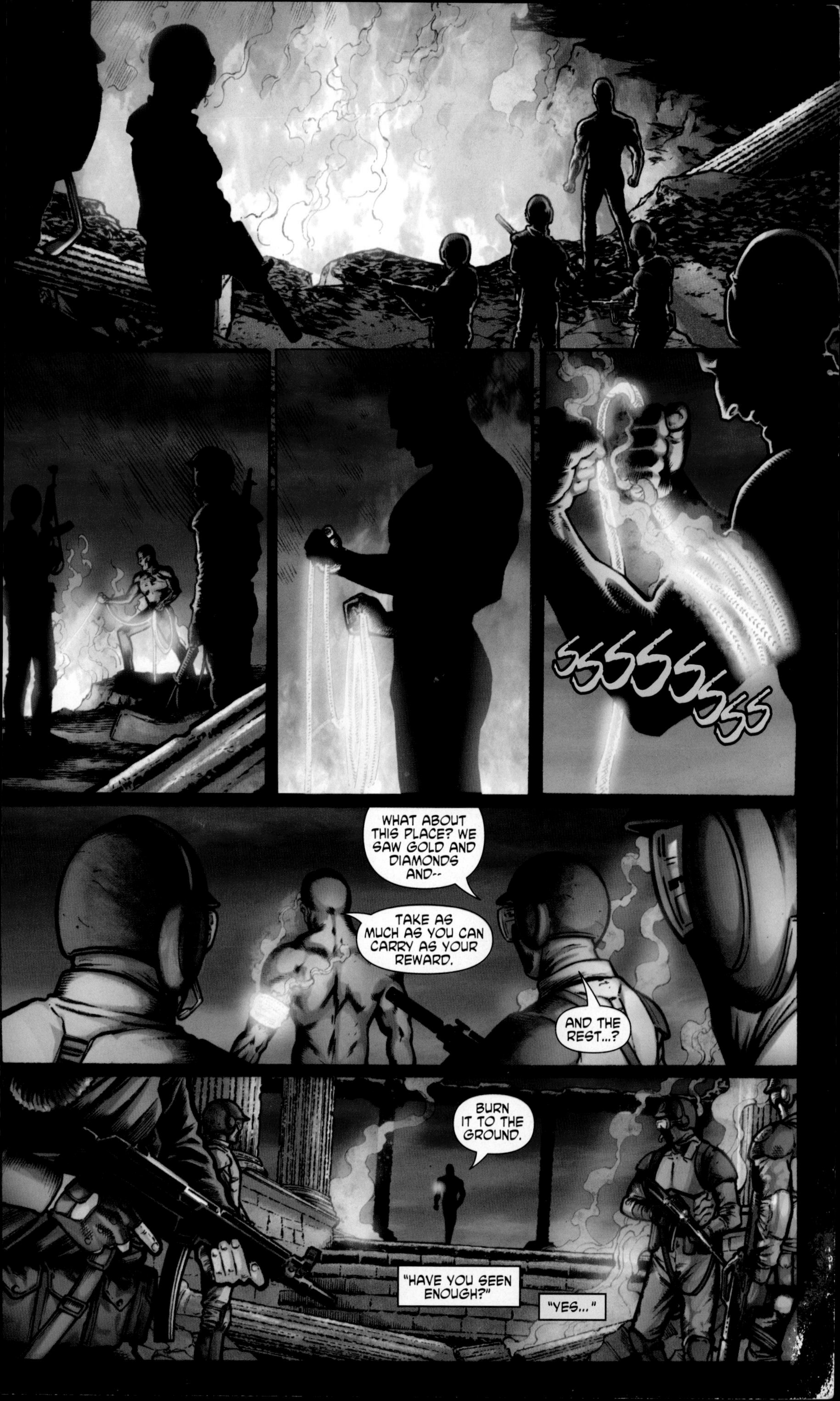
SSSSSSSSS
WHAT ABOUT THIS PLACE? WE SAW GOLD AND DIAMONDS AND--
TAKE AS MUCH AS YOU CAN CARRY AS YOUR REWARD.
AND THE REST...?
BURN IT TO THE GROUND.
"HAVE YOU SEEN ENOUGH?"
"YES..."

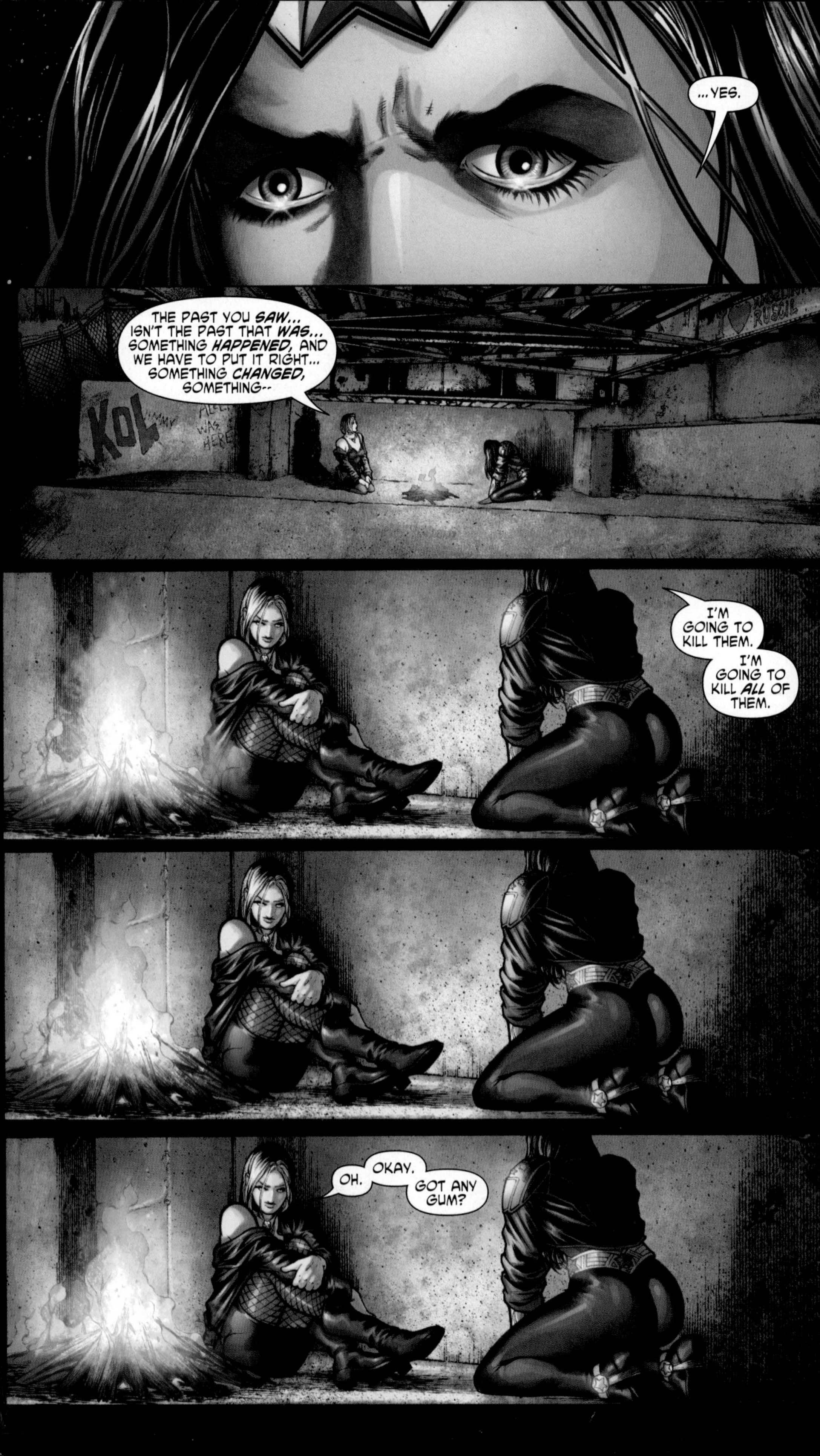
...YES.
THE PAST YOU SAW... ISN'T THE PAST THAT WAS... SOMETHING HAPPENED, AND WE HAVE TO PUT IT RIGHT... SOMETHING CHANGED, SOMETHING--
I'M GOING TO KILL THEM.
I'M GOING TO KILL ALL OF THEM.
OH.
OKAY.
GOT ANY GUM?

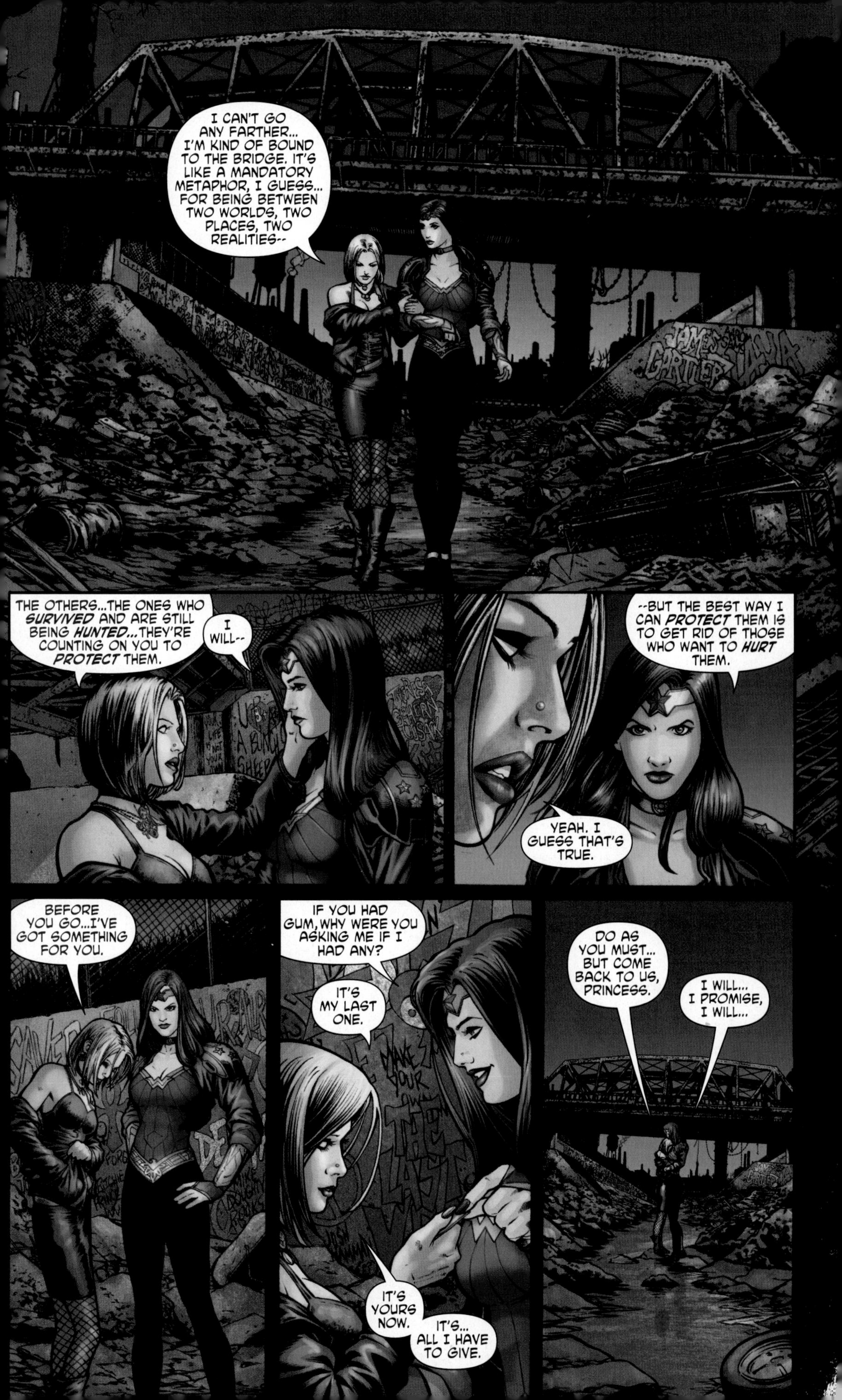
I CAN'T GO ANY FARTHER... I'M KIND OF BOUND TO THE BRIDGE. IT'S LIKE A MANDATORY METAPHOR, I GUESS... FOR BEING BETWEEN TWO WORLDS, TWO PLACES, TWO REALITIES--
THE OTHERS...THE ONES WHO SURVIVED AND ARE STILL BEING HUNTED...THEY'RE COUNTING ON YOU TO PROTECT THEM.
I WILL--
--BUT THE BEST WAY I CAN PROTECT THEM IS TO GET RID OF THOSE WHO WANT TO HURT THEM.
YEAH. I GUESS THAT'S TRUE.
BEFORE YOU GO...I'VE GOT SOMETHING FOR YOU.
IF YOU HAD GUM, WHY WERE YOU ASKING ME IF I HAD ANY?
IT'S MY LAST ONE.
IT'S YOURS NOW.
IT'S... ALL I HAVE TO GIVE.
DO AS YOU MUST... BUT COME BACK TO US, PRINCESS.
I WILL... I PROMISE, I WILL...

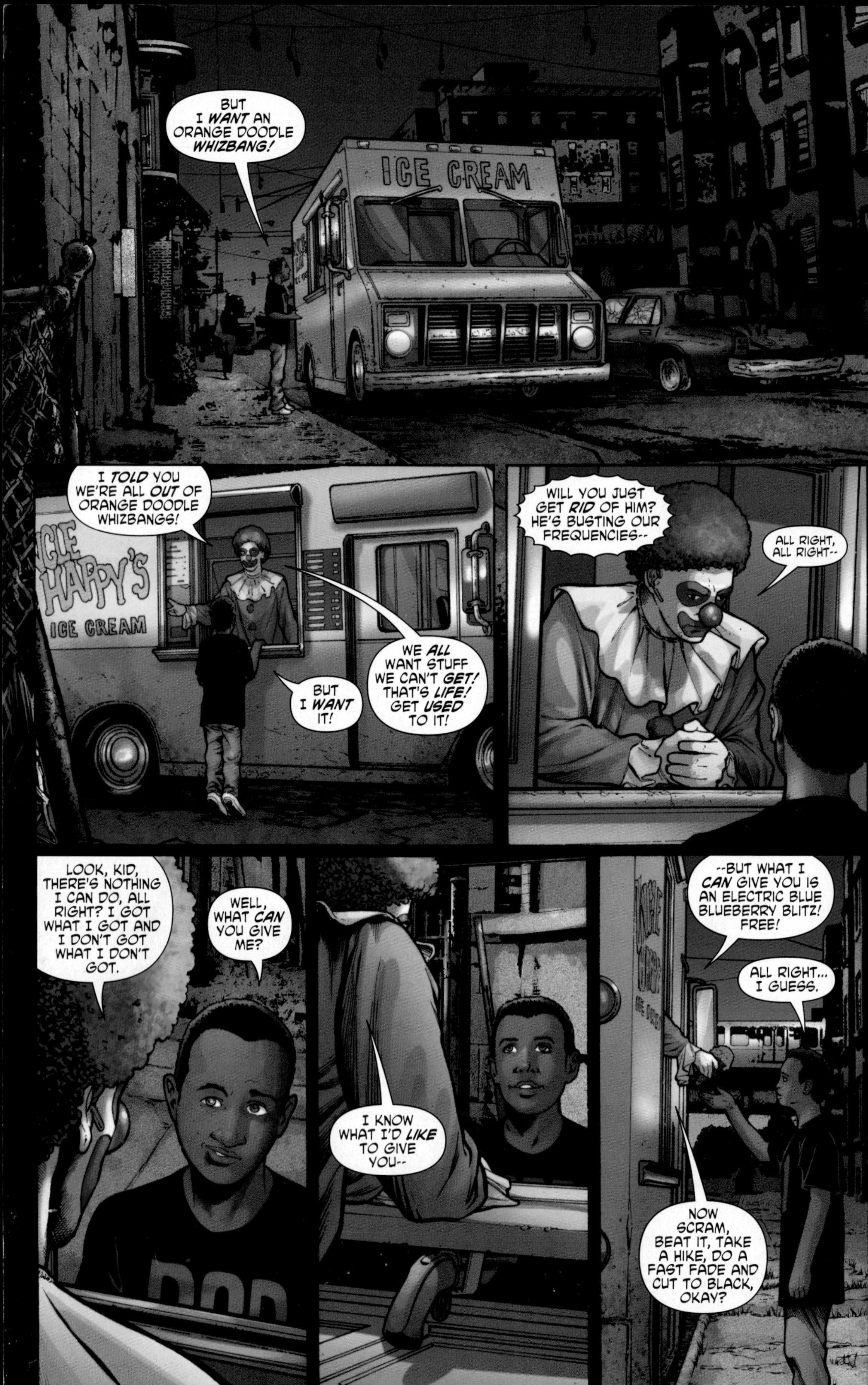
BUT I WANT AN ORANGE DOODLE WHIZBANG!
ICE CREAM
I TOLD YOU WE'RE ALL OUT OF ORANGE DOODLE WHIZBANGS!
UNCLE HAPPY'S ICE CREAM
WE ALL WANT STUFF WE CAN'T GET! THAT'S LIFE! GET USED TO IT!
BUT I WANT IT!
WILL YOU JUST GET RID OF HIM? HE'S BUSTING OUR FREQUENCIES--
ALL RIGHT, ALL RIGHT--
LOOK, KID, THERE'S NOTHING I CAN DO, ALL RIGHT? I GOT WHAT I GOT AND I DON'T GOT WHAT I DON'T GOT.
WELL, WHAT CAN YOU GIVE ME?
I KNOW WHAT I'D LIKE TO GIVE YOU--
--BUT WHAT I CAN GIVE YOU IS AN ELECTRIC BLUE BLUEBERRY BLITZ! FREE!
ALL RIGHT... I GUESS.
NOW SCRAM, BEAT IT, TAKE A HIKE, DO A FAST FADE AND CUT TO BLACK, OKAY?

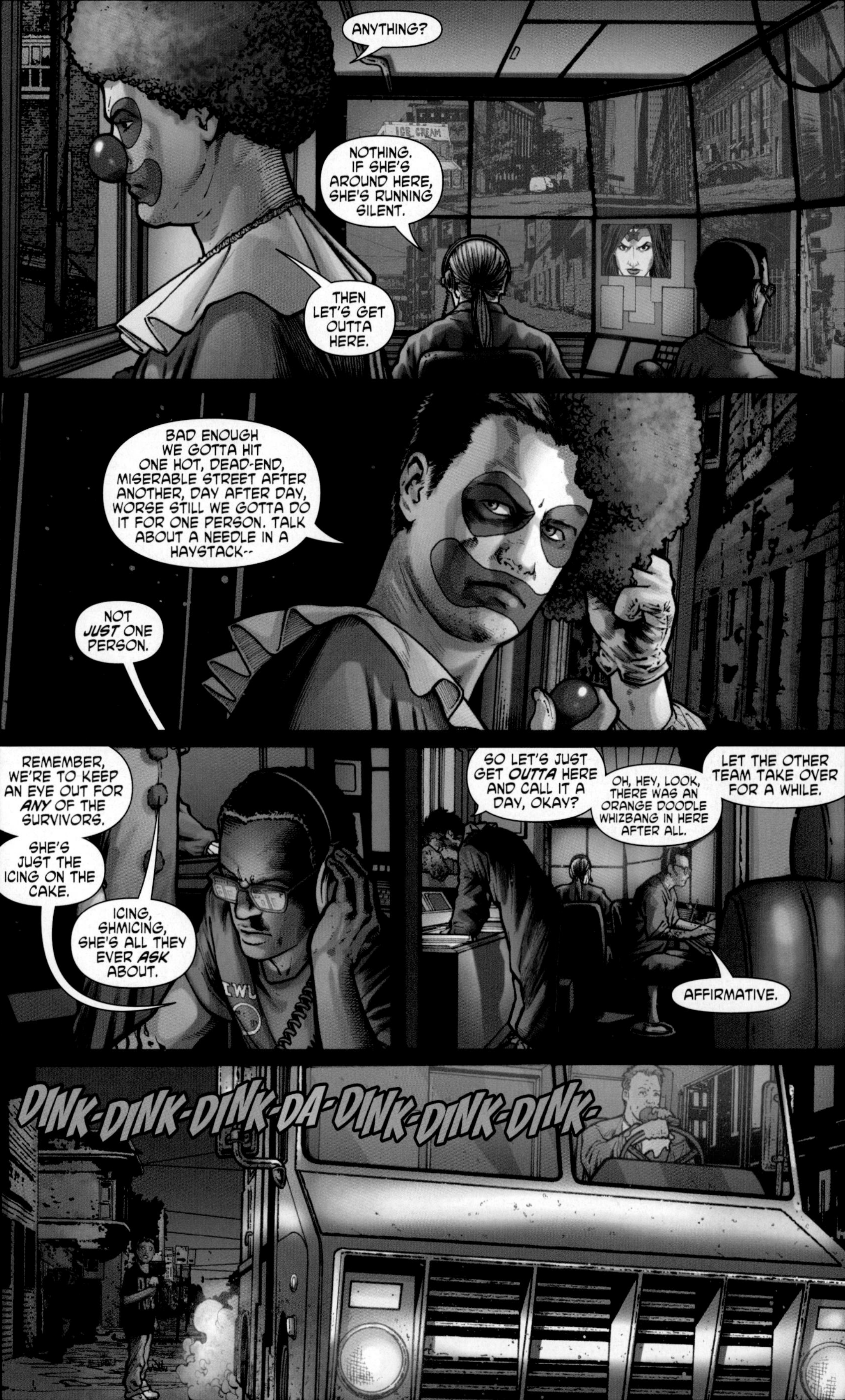
ANYTHING?
NOTHING. IF SHE'S AROUND HERE, SHE'S RUNNING SILENT.
THEN LET'S GET OUTTA HERE.
BAD ENOUGH WE GOTTA HIT ONE HOT, DEAD-END, MISERABLE STREET AFTER ANOTHER, DAY AFTER DAY, WORSE STILL WE GOTTA DO IT FOR ONE PERSON. TALK ABOUT A NEEDLE IN A HAYSTACK--
NOT *JUST* ONE PERSON.
REMEMBER, WE'RE TO KEEP AN EYE OUT FOR *ANY* OF THE SURVIVORS.
SHE'S JUST THE ICING ON THE CAKE.
ICING, SHMICING, SHE'S ALL THEY EVER *ASK* ABOUT.
SO LET'S JUST GET *OUTTA* HERE AND CALL IT A DAY, OKAY?
OH, HEY, LOOK, THERE WAS AN ORANGE DOODLE WHIZBANG IN HERE AFTER ALL.
LET THE OTHER TEAM TAKE OVER FOR A WHILE.
AFFIRMATIVE.
DINK-DINK-DINK-DA-DINK-DINK-DINK-

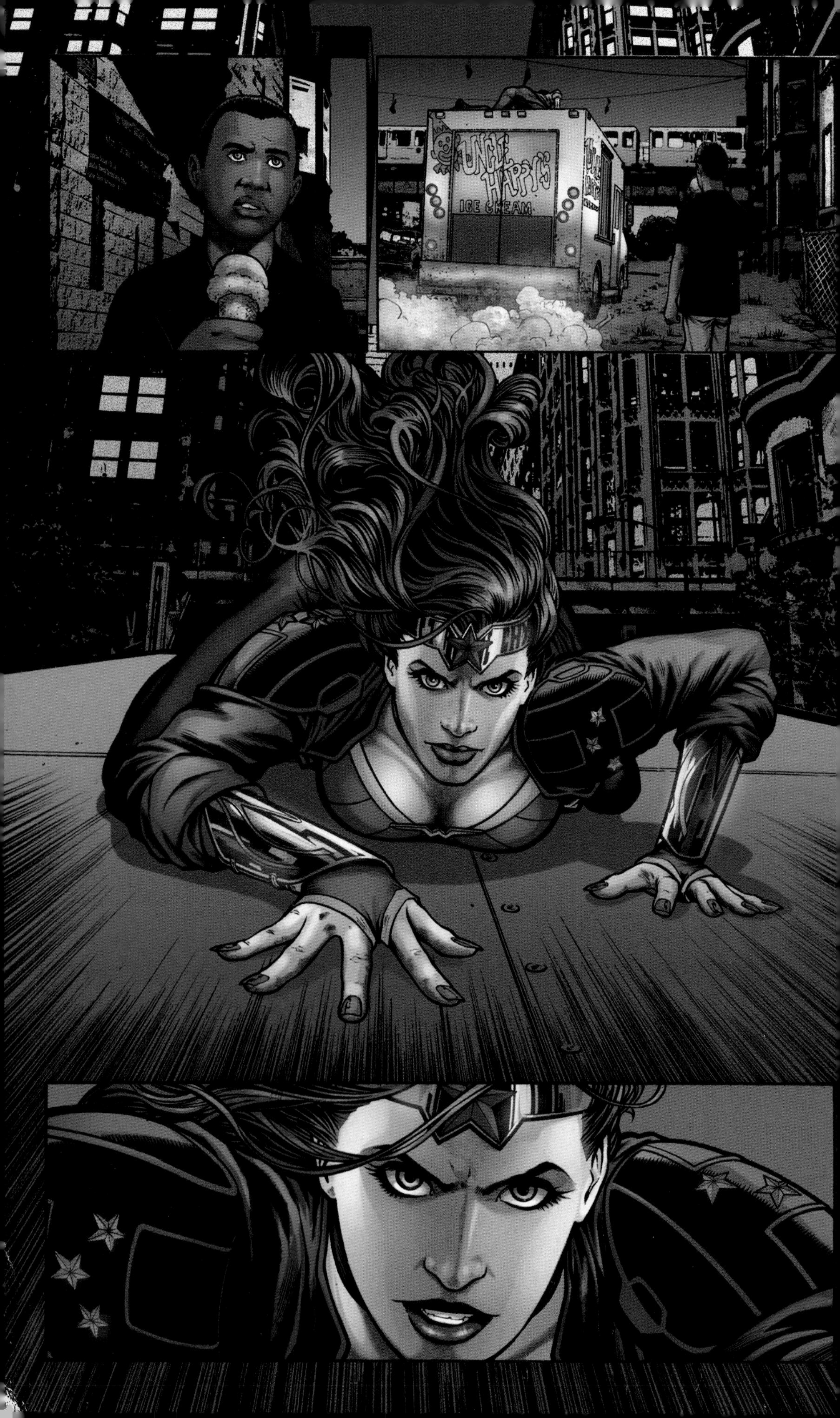
UNCLE HAPPY'S
ICE CREAM

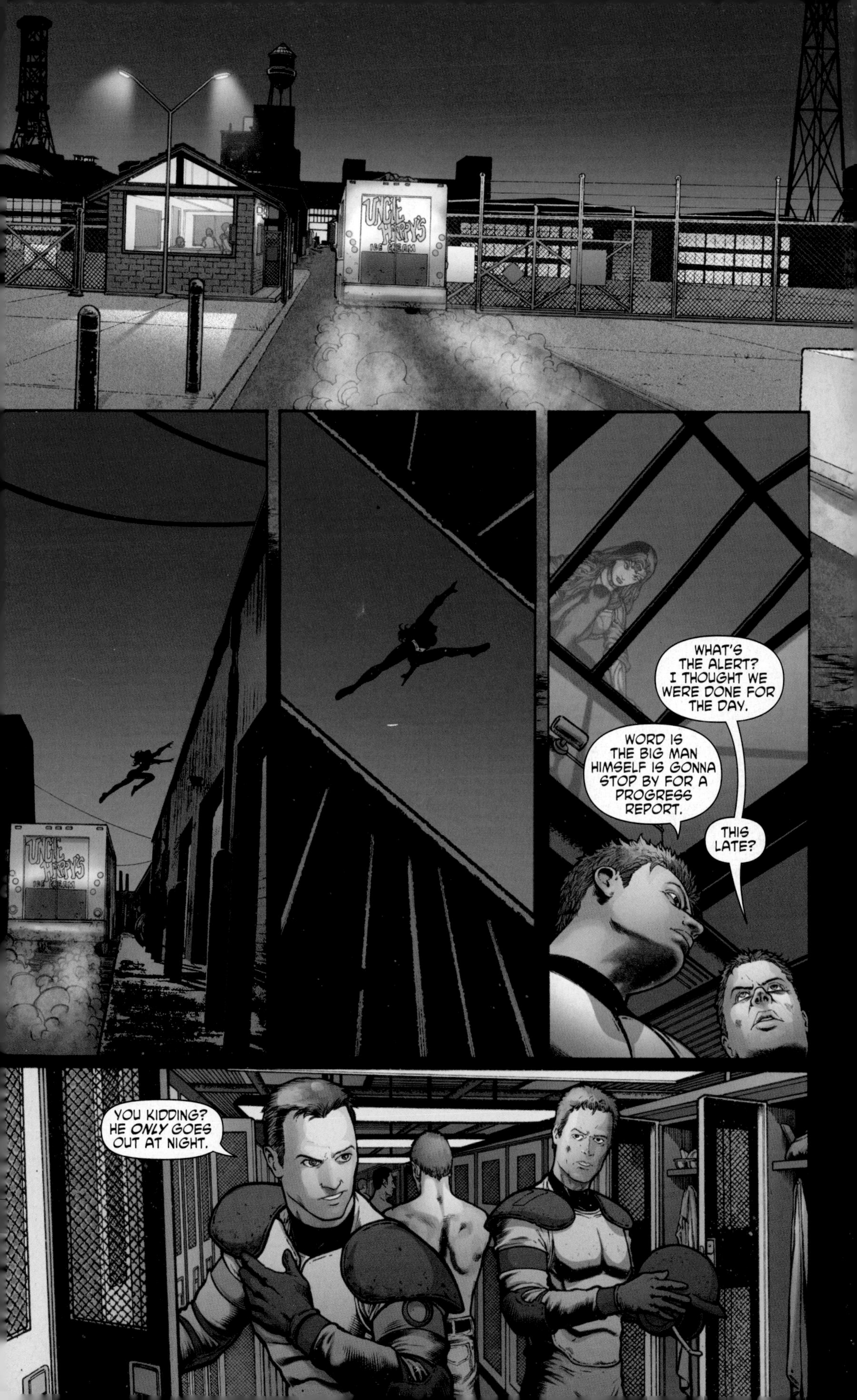
UNCLE HARPY'S ICE CREAM
WHAT'S THE ALERT? I THOUGHT WE WERE DONE FOR THE DAY.
WORD IS THE BIG MAN HIMSELF IS GONNA STOP BY FOR A PROGRESS REPORT.
THIS LATE?
YOU KIDDING? HE *ONLY* GOES OUT AT NIGHT.

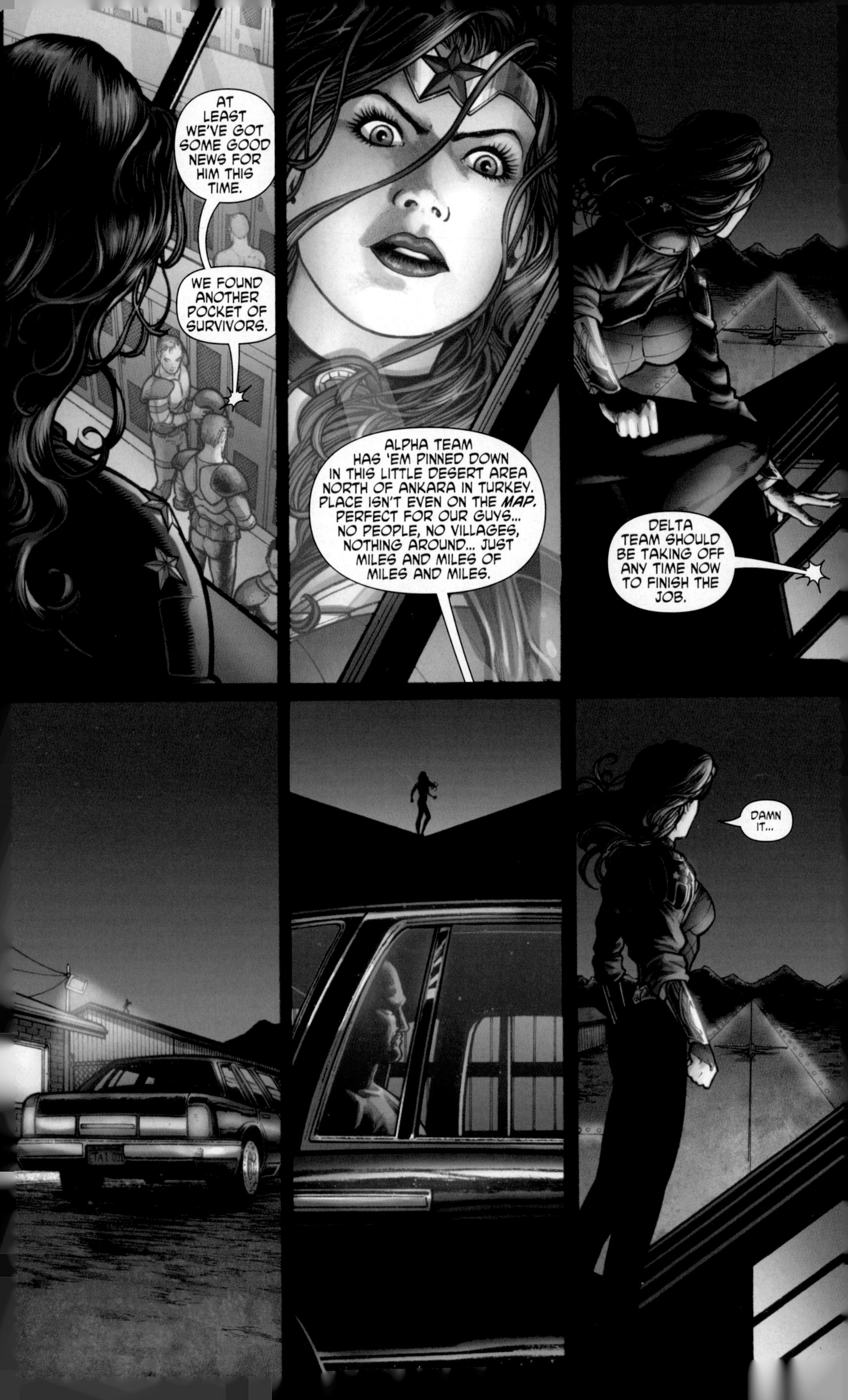
AT LEAST WE'VE GOT SOME GOOD NEWS FOR HIM THIS TIME.
WE FOUND ANOTHER POCKET OF SURVIVORS.
ALPHA TEAM HAS 'EM PINNED DOWN IN THIS LITTLE DESERT AREA NORTH OF ANKARA IN TURKEY. PLACE ISN'T EVEN ON THE *MAP.* PERFECT FOR OUR GUYS... NO PEOPLE, NO VILLAGES, NOTHING AROUND... JUST MILES AND MILES OF MILES AND MILES.
DELTA TEAM SHOULD BE TAKING OFF ANY TIME NOW TO FINISH THE JOB.
DAMN IT...

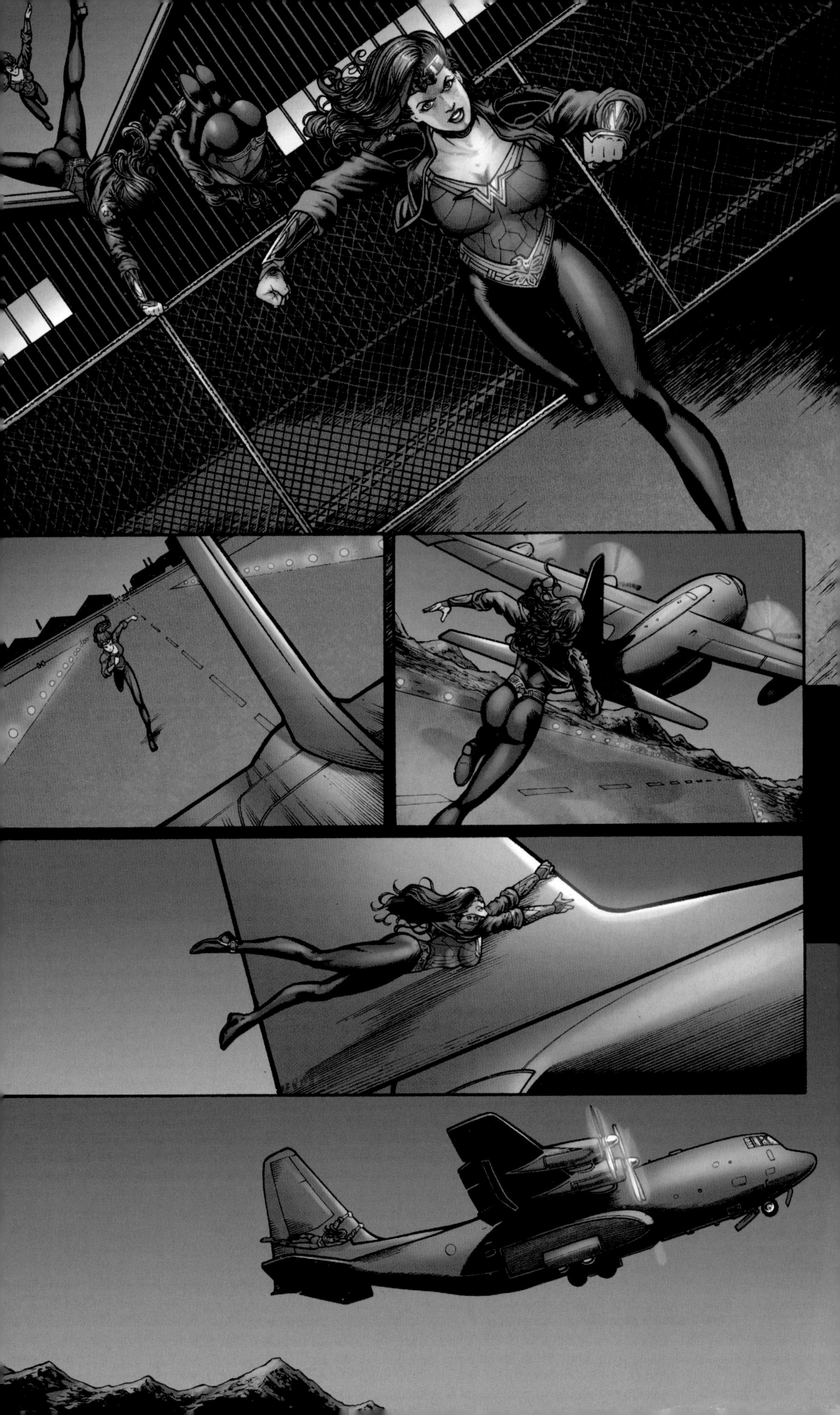

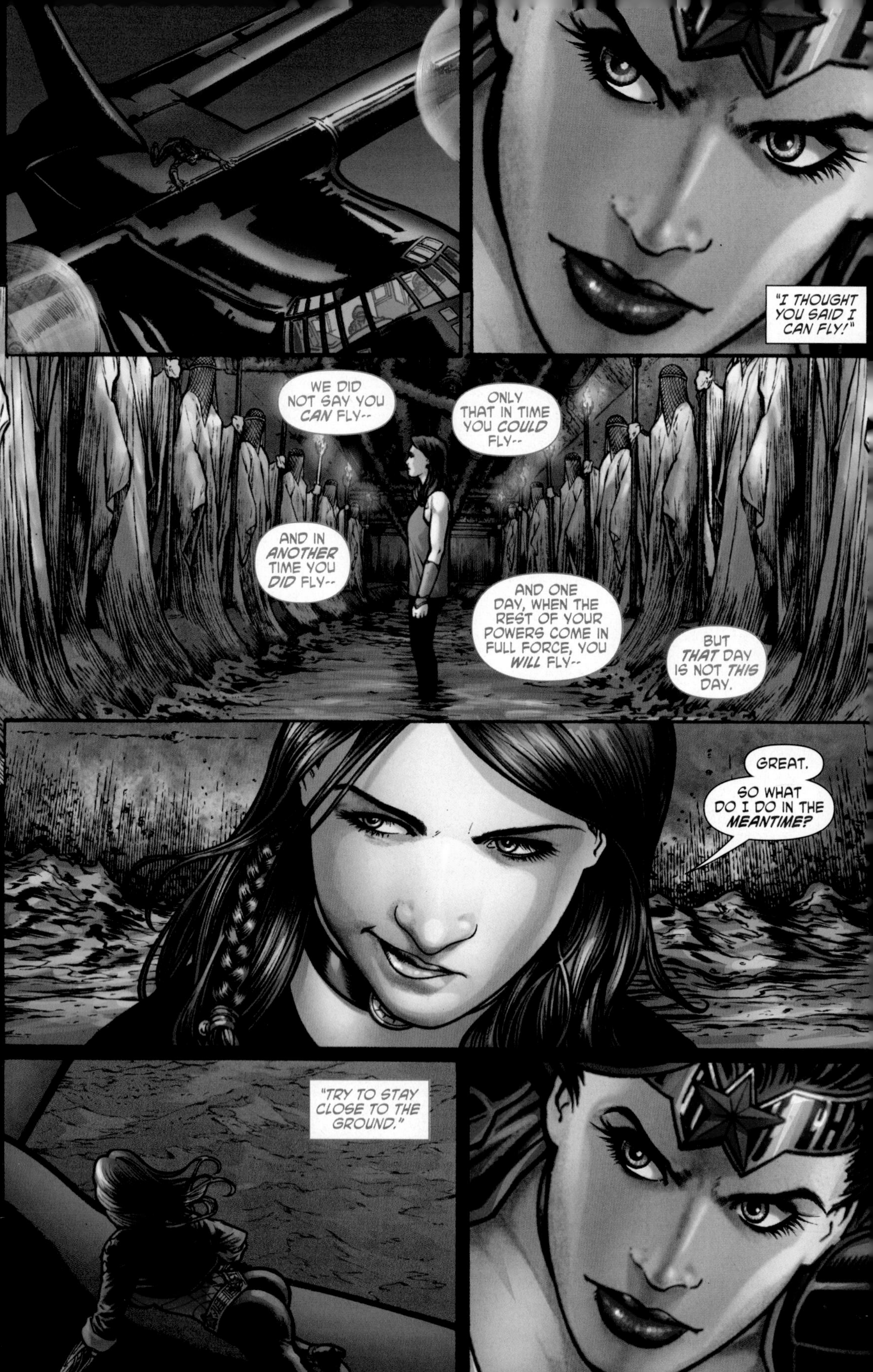
"I THOUGHT YOU SAID I CAN FLY!"
WE DID NOT SAY YOU CAN FLY--
ONLY THAT IN TIME YOU COULD FLY--
AND IN ANOTHER TIME YOU DID FLY--
AND ONE DAY, WHEN THE REST OF YOUR POWERS COME IN FULL FORCE, YOU WILL FLY--
BUT THAT DAY IS NOT THIS DAY.
GREAT.
SO WHAT DO I DO IN THE MEANTIME?
"TRY TO STAY CLOSE TO THE GROUND."

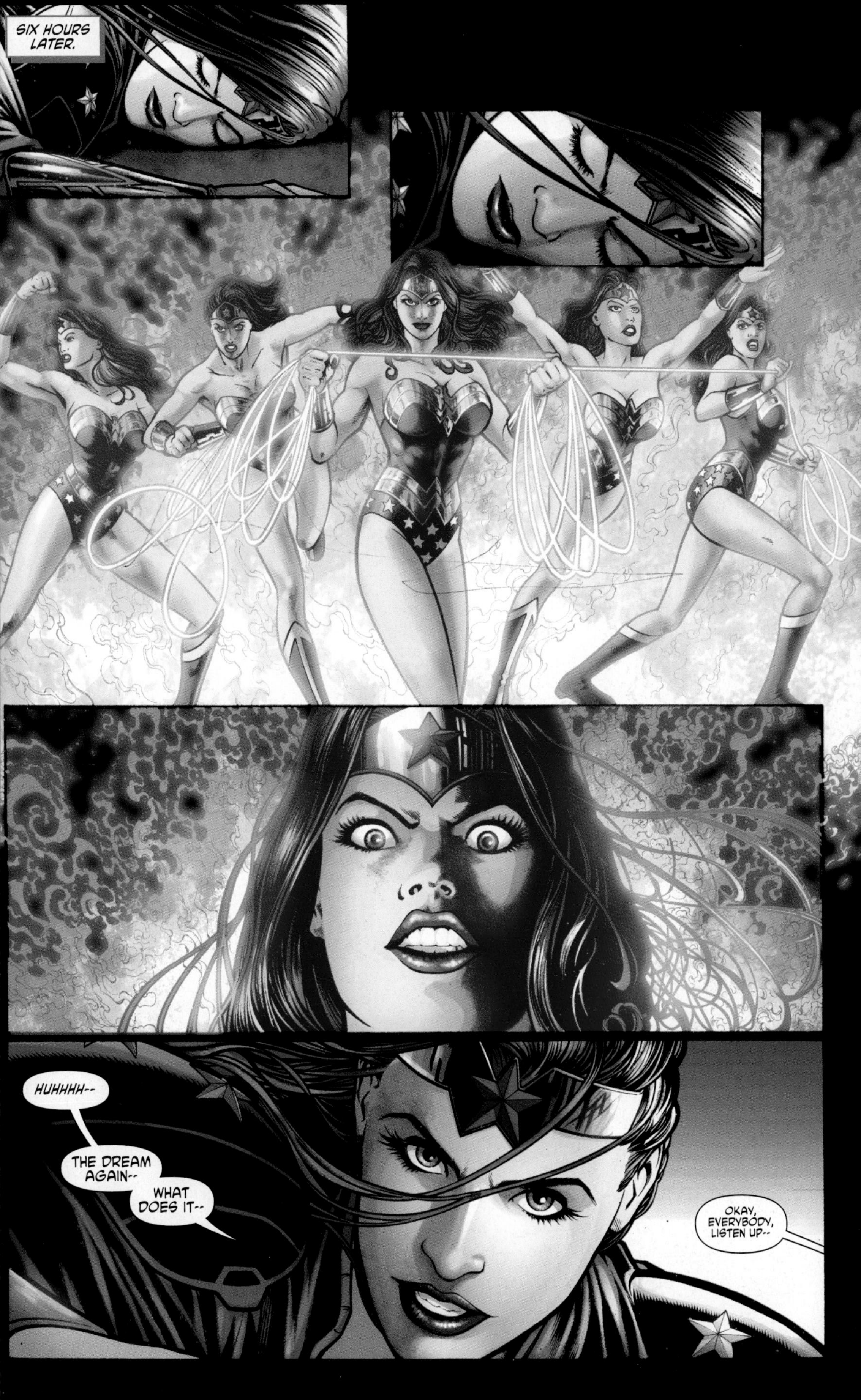
SIX HOURS LATER.
HUHHHH--
THE DREAM AGAIN--
WHAT DOES IT--
OKAY, EVERYBODY, LISTEN UP--

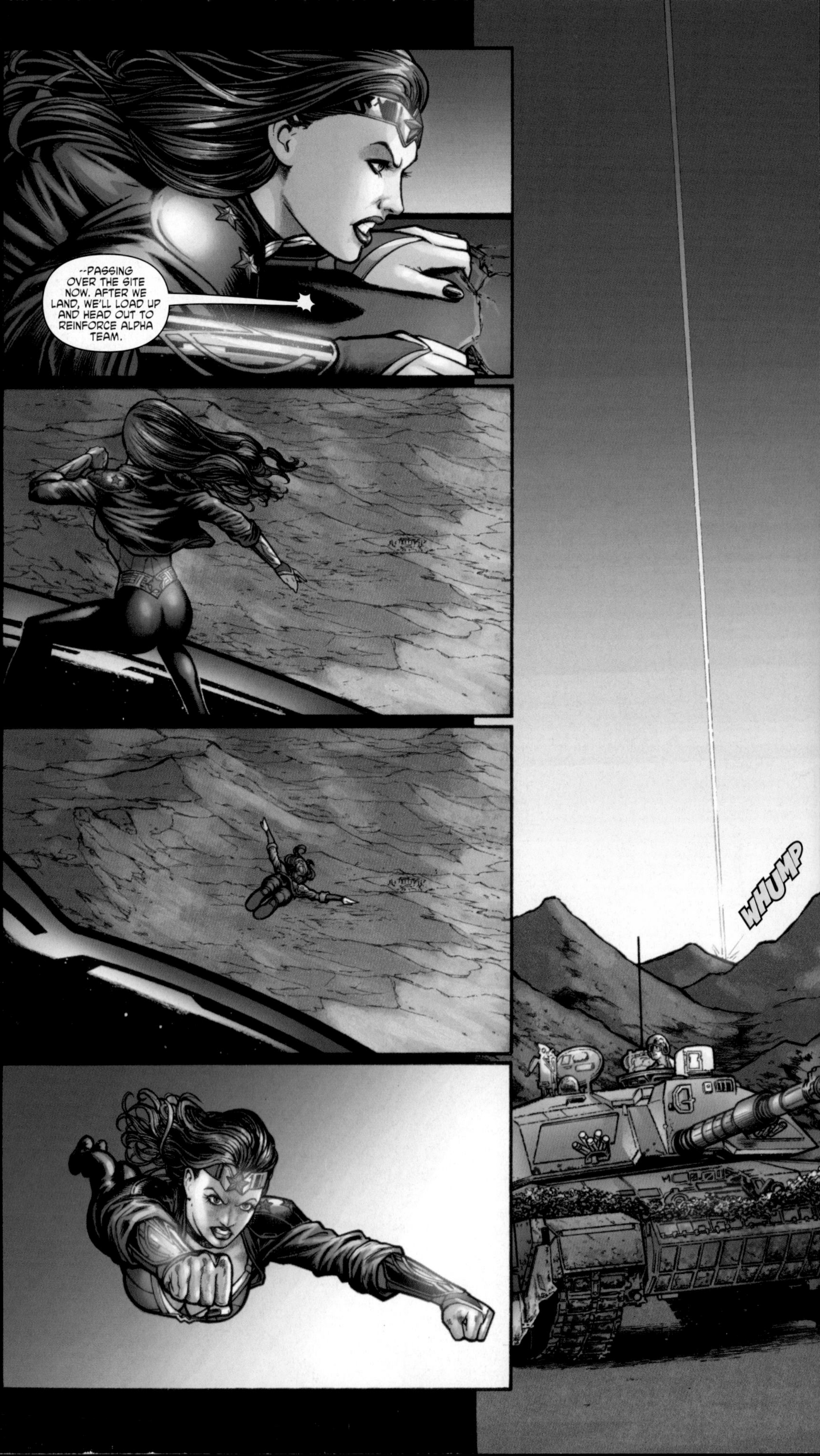
--PASSING OVER THE SITE NOW. AFTER WE LAND, WE'LL LOAD UP AND HEAD OUT TO REINFORCE ALPHA TEAM.
WHUMP

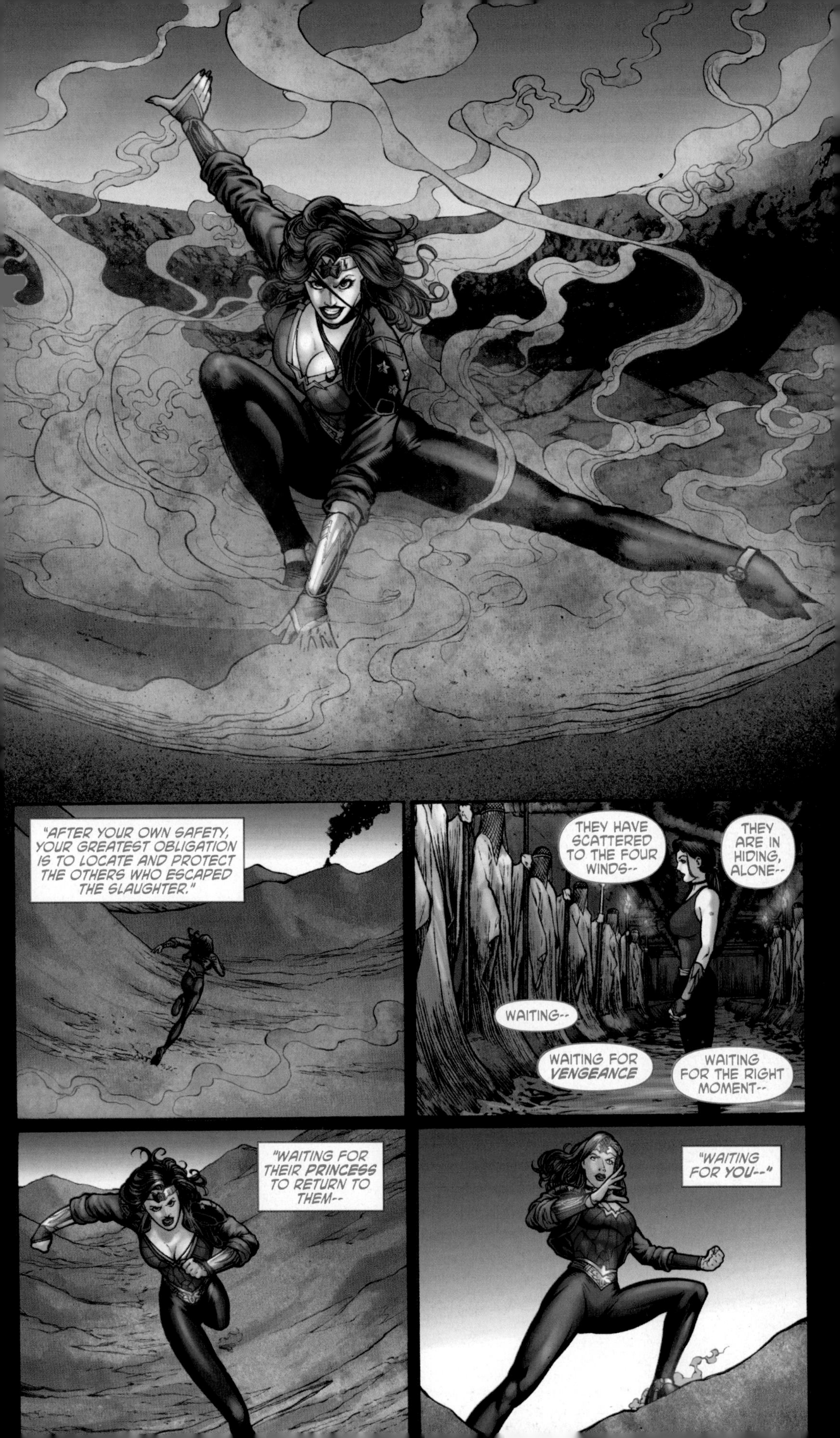
"AFTER YOUR OWN SAFETY, YOUR GREATEST OBLIGATION IS TO LOCATE AND PROTECT THE OTHERS WHO ESCAPED THE SLAUGHTER."
THEY HAVE SCATTERED TO THE FOUR WINDS--
THEY ARE IN HIDING, ALONE--
WAITING--
WAITING FOR VENGEANCE
WAITING FOR THE RIGHT MOMENT--
"WAITING FOR THEIR PRINCESS TO RETURN TO THEM--
"WAITING FOR YOU--"

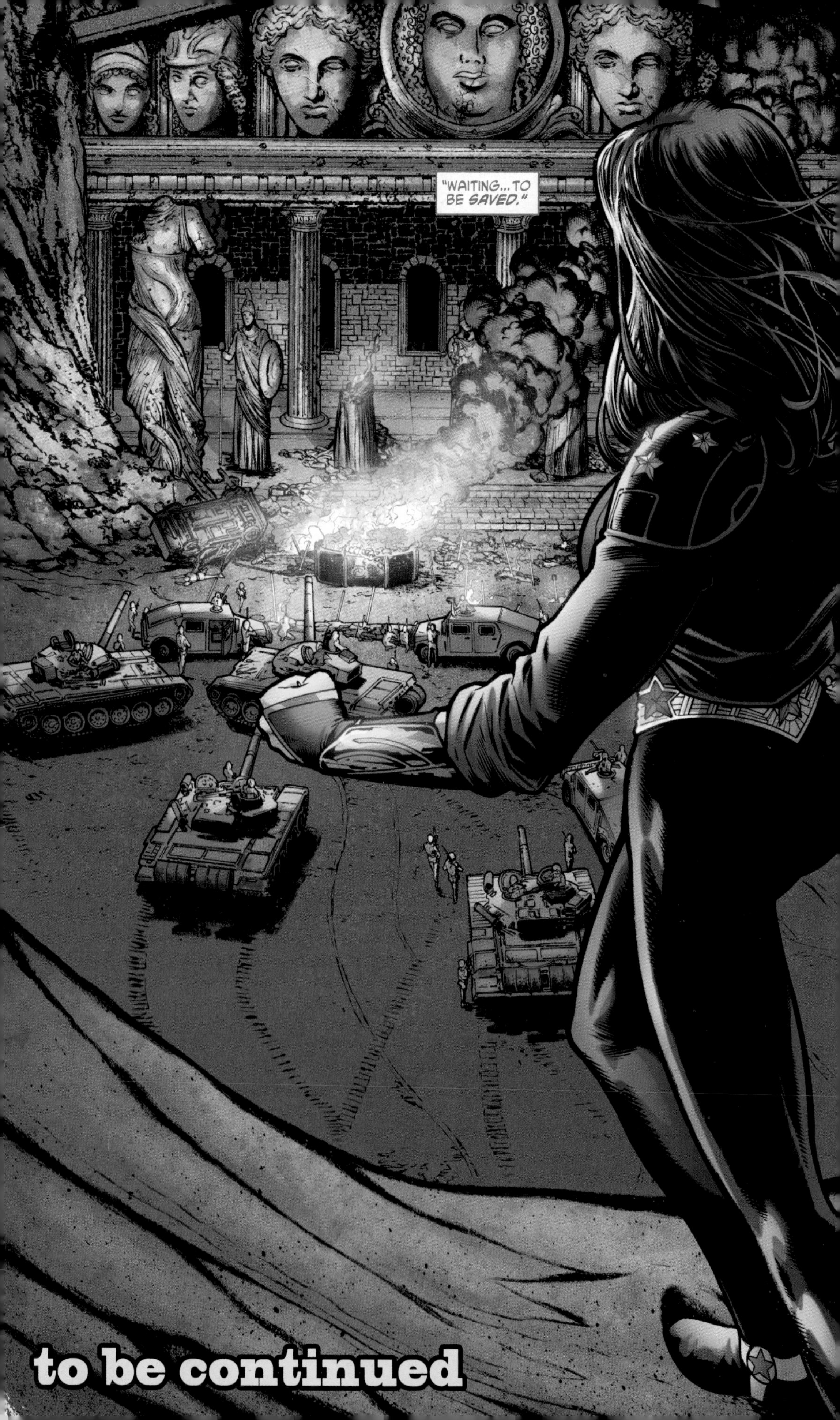
"WAITING... TO BE SAVED."
to be continued

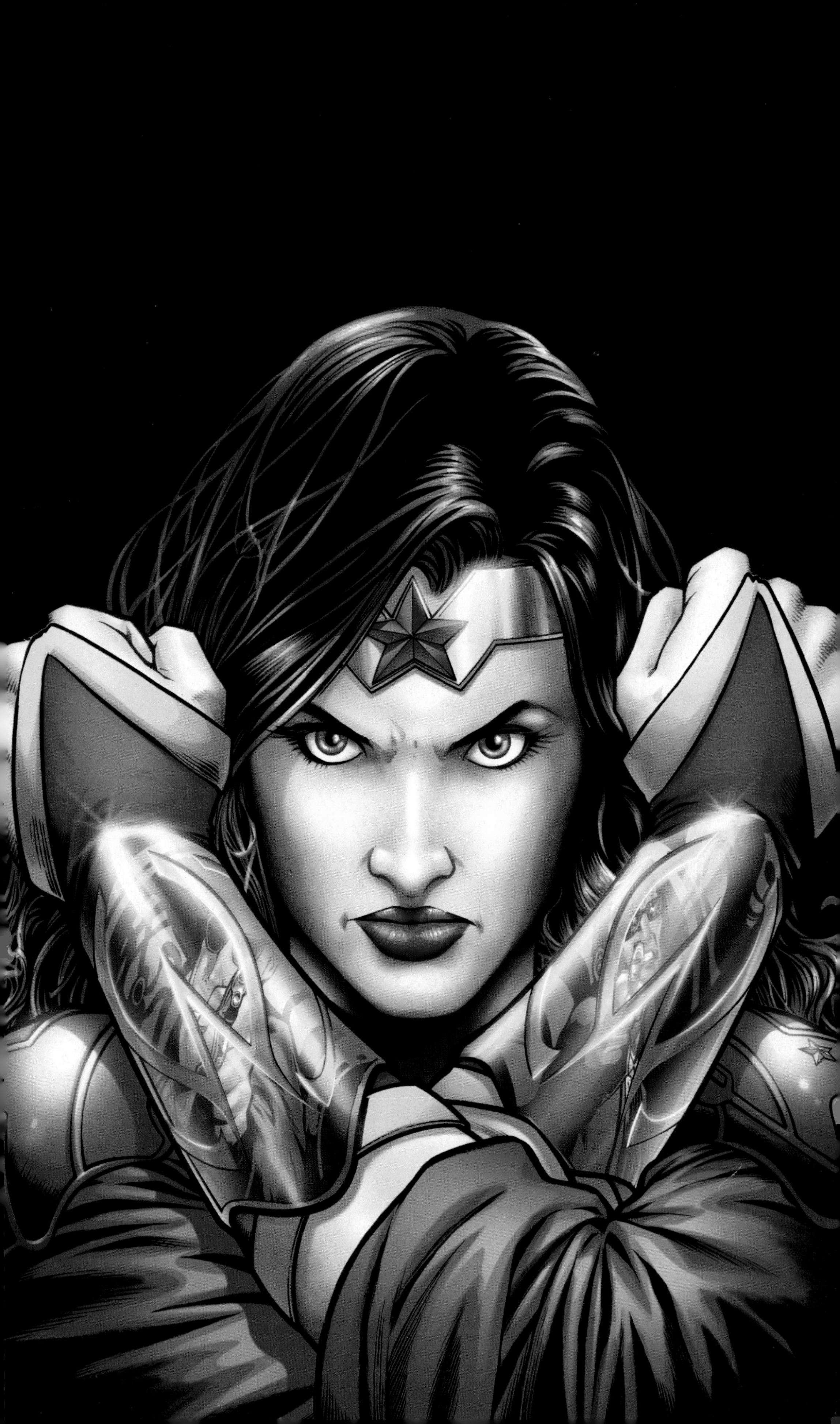

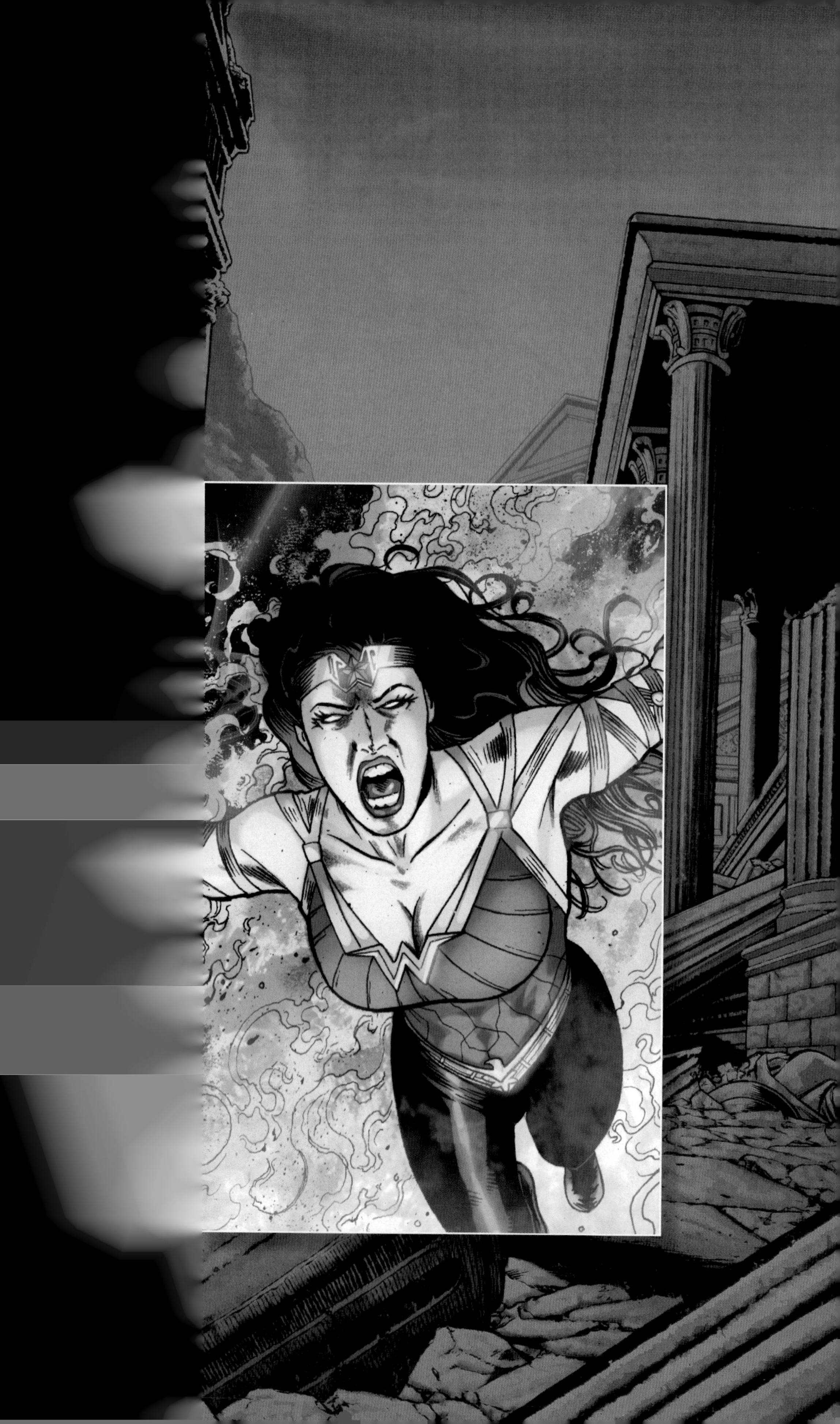

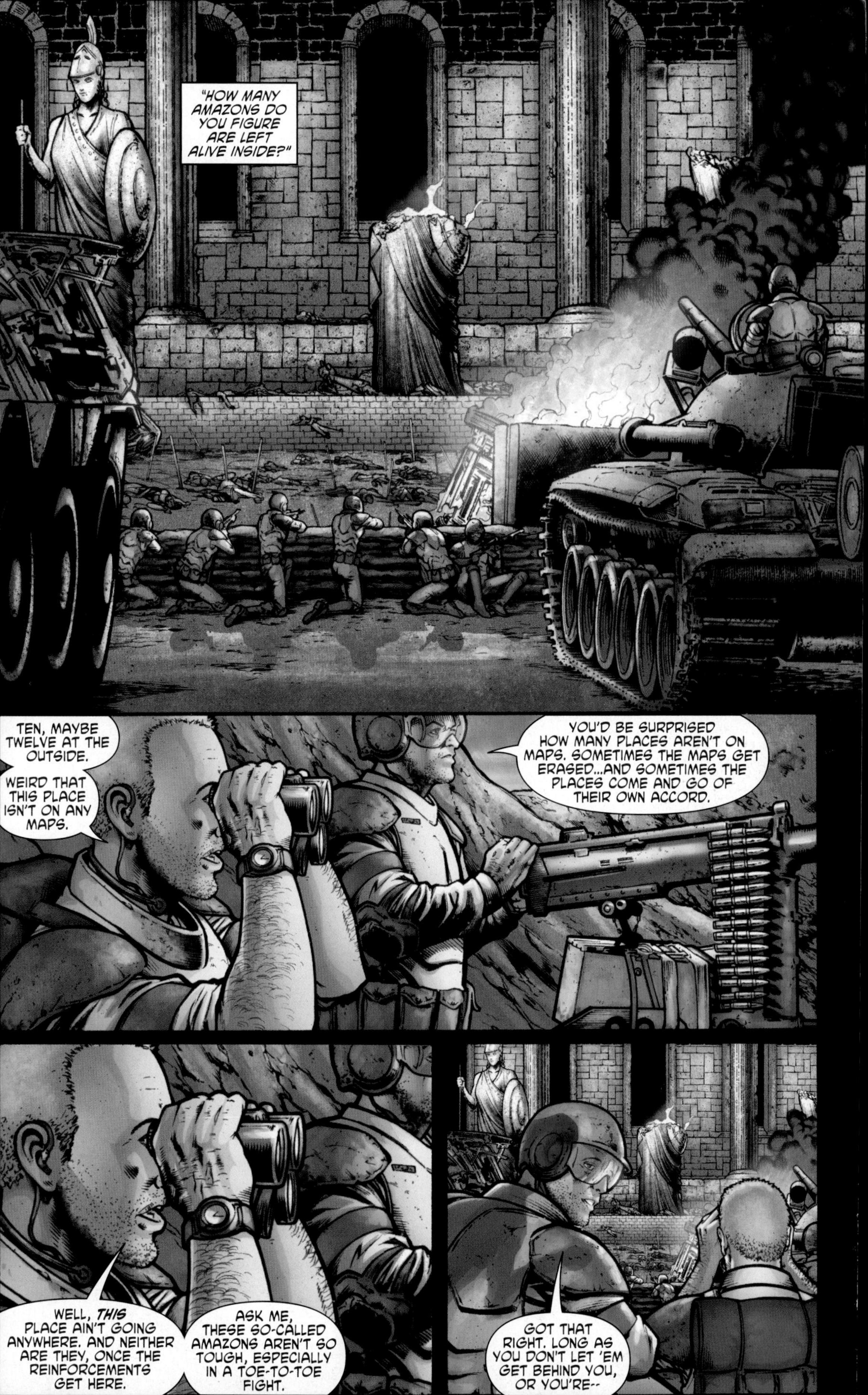
"HOW MANY AMAZONS DO YOU FIGURE ARE LEFT ALIVE INSIDE?"
TEN, MAYBE TWELVE AT THE OUTSIDE.
WEIRD THAT THIS PLACE ISN'T ON ANY MAPS.
YOU'D BE SURPRISED HOW MANY PLACES AREN'T ON MAPS. SOMETIMES THE MAPS GET ERASED...AND SOMETIMES THE PLACES COME AND GO OF THEIR OWN ACCORD.
WELL, *THIS* PLACE AIN'T GOING ANYWHERE. AND NEITHER ARE THEY, ONCE THE REINFORCEMENTS GET HERE.
ASK ME, THESE SO-CALLED AMAZONS AREN'T SO TOUGH, ESPECIALLY IN A TOE-TO-TOE FIGHT.
GOT THAT RIGHT. LONG AS YOU DON'T LET 'EM GET BEHIND YOU, OR YOU'RE--

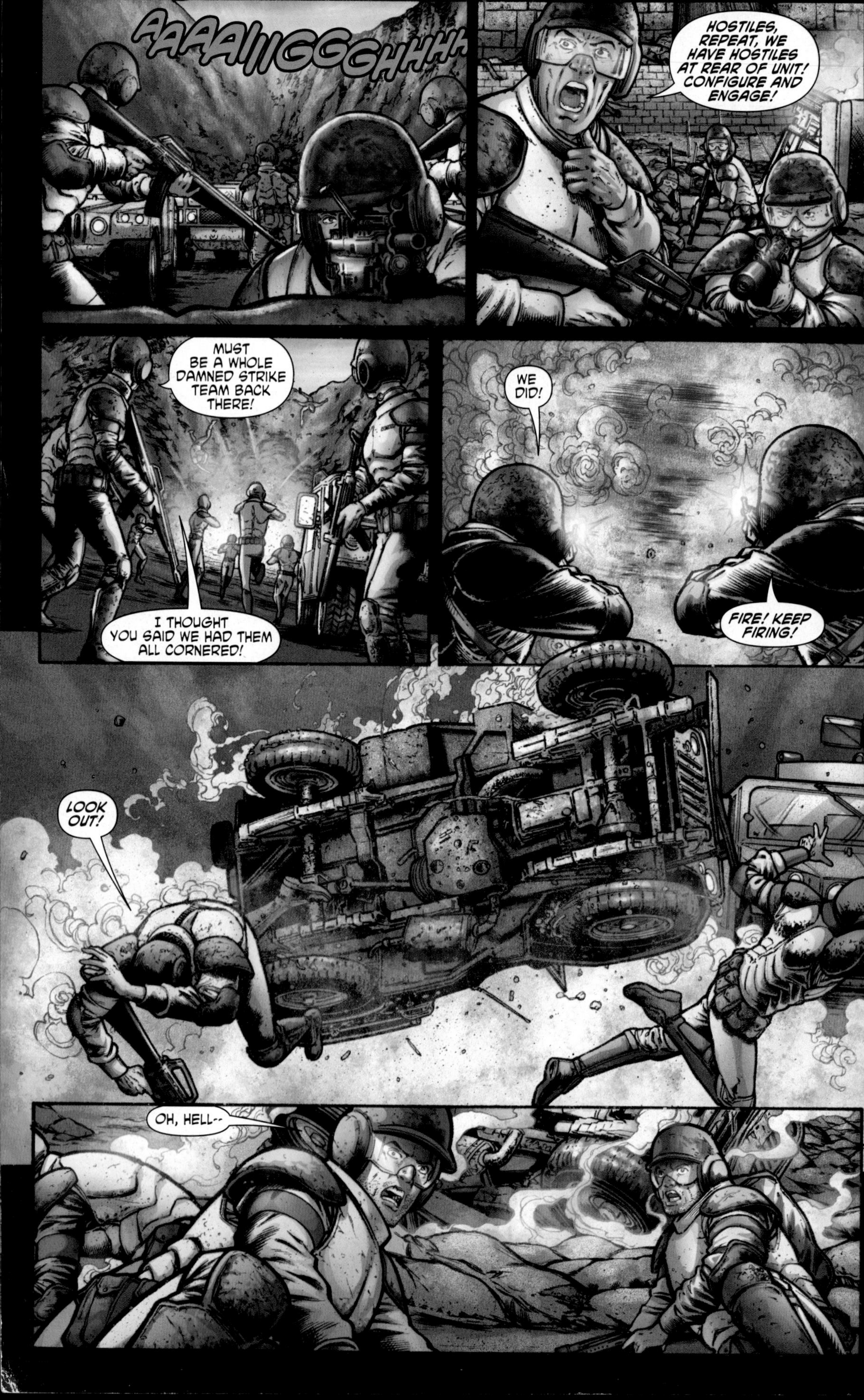
AAAAIIIGGGHHH
HOSTILES, REPEAT, WE HAVE HOSTILES AT REAR OF UNIT! CONFIGURE AND ENGAGE!
MUST BE A WHOLE DAMNED STRIKE TEAM BACK THERE!
I THOUGHT YOU SAID WE HAD THEM ALL CORNERED!
WE DID!
FIRE! KEEP FIRING!
LOOK OUT!
OH, HELL--

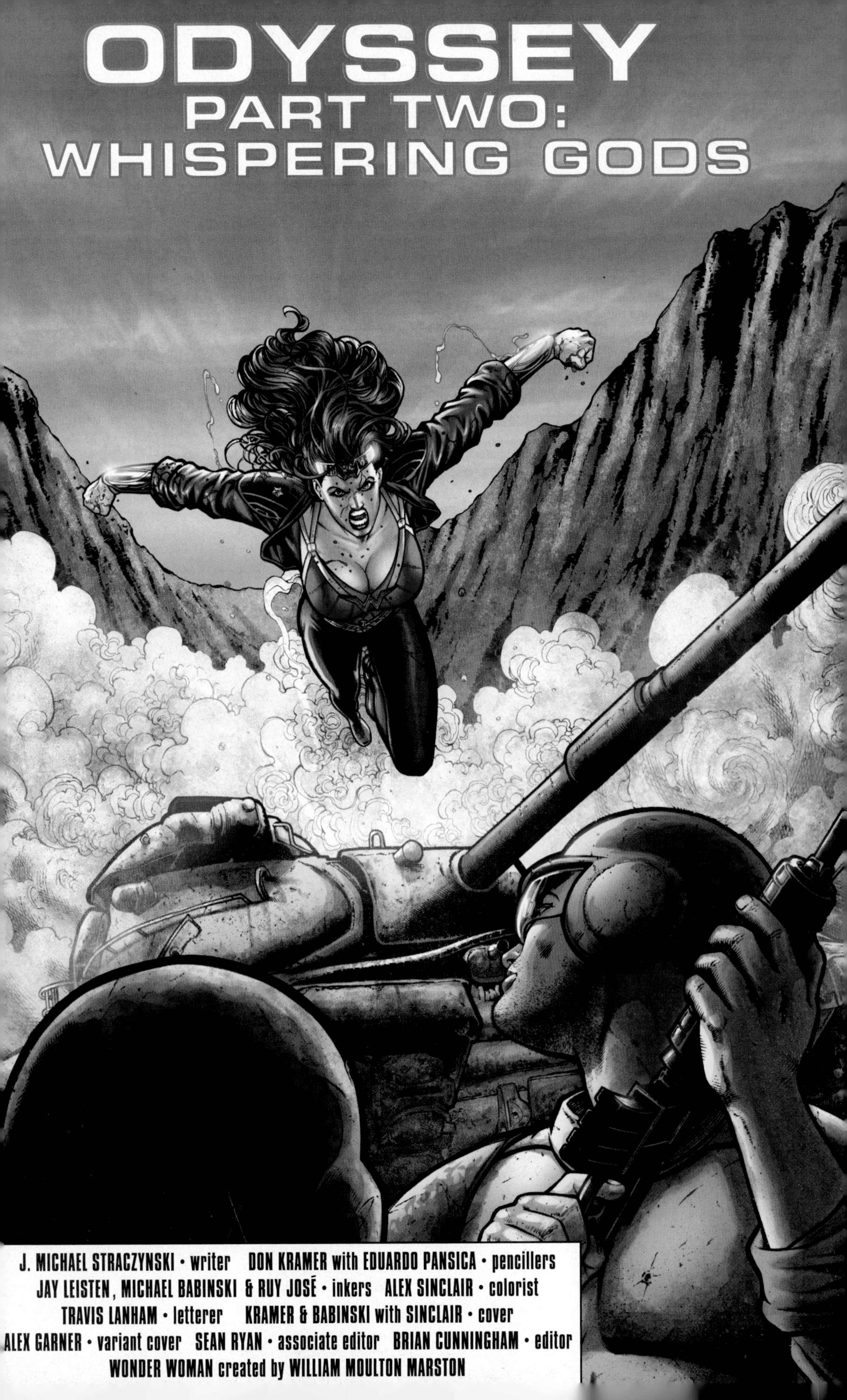

ODYSSEY
PART TWO:
WHISPERING GODS
J. MICHAEL STRACZYNSKI • writer DON KRAMER with EDUARDO PANSICA • pencillers
JAY LEISTEN, MICHAEL BABINSKI & RUY JOSÉ • inkers ALEX SINCLAIR • colorist
TRAVIS LANHAM • letterer KRAMER & BABINSKI with SINCLAIR • cover
ALEX GARNER • variant cover SEAN RYAN • associate editor BRIAN CUNNINGHAM • editor
WONDER WOMAN created by WILLIAM MOULTON MARSTON

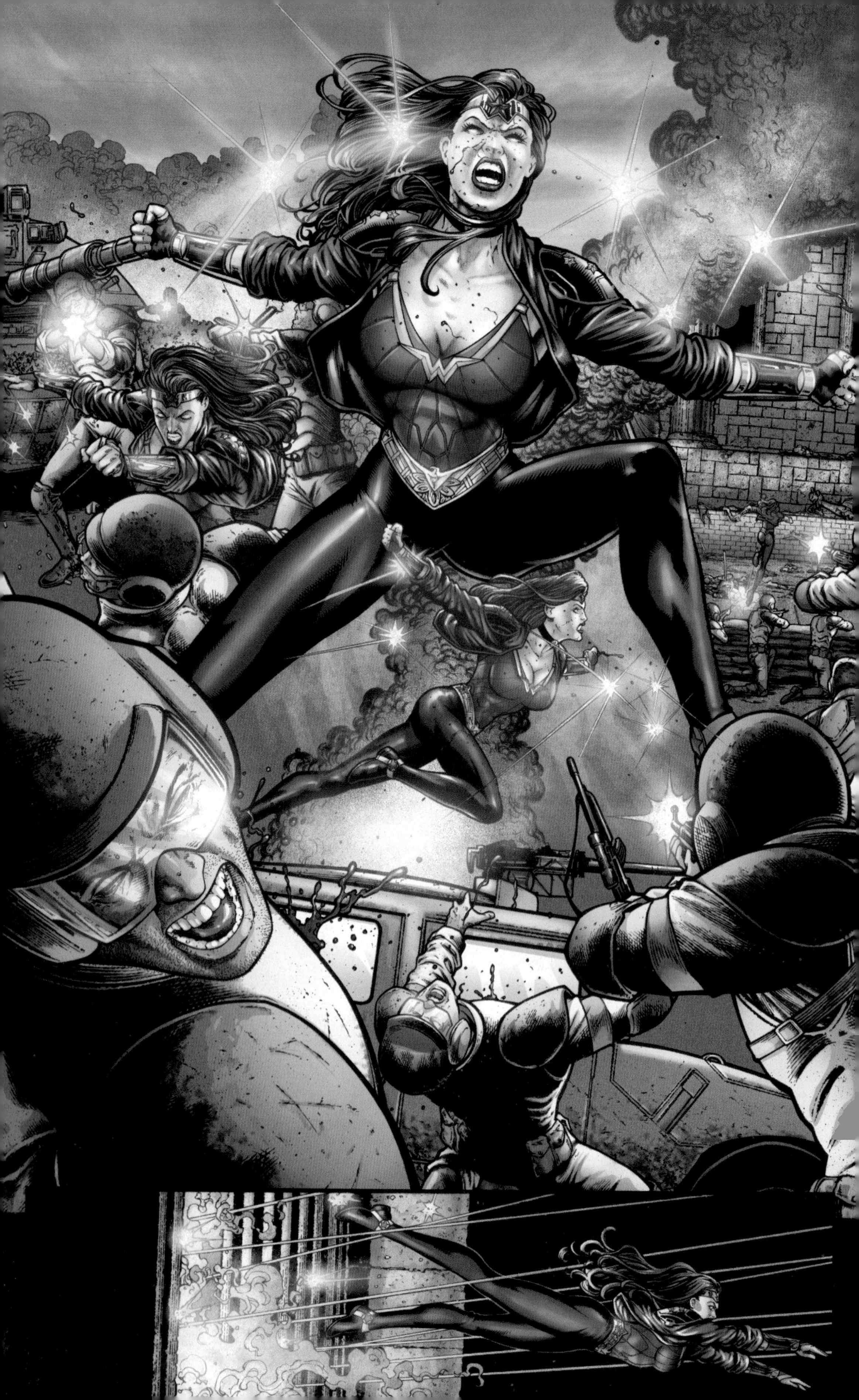

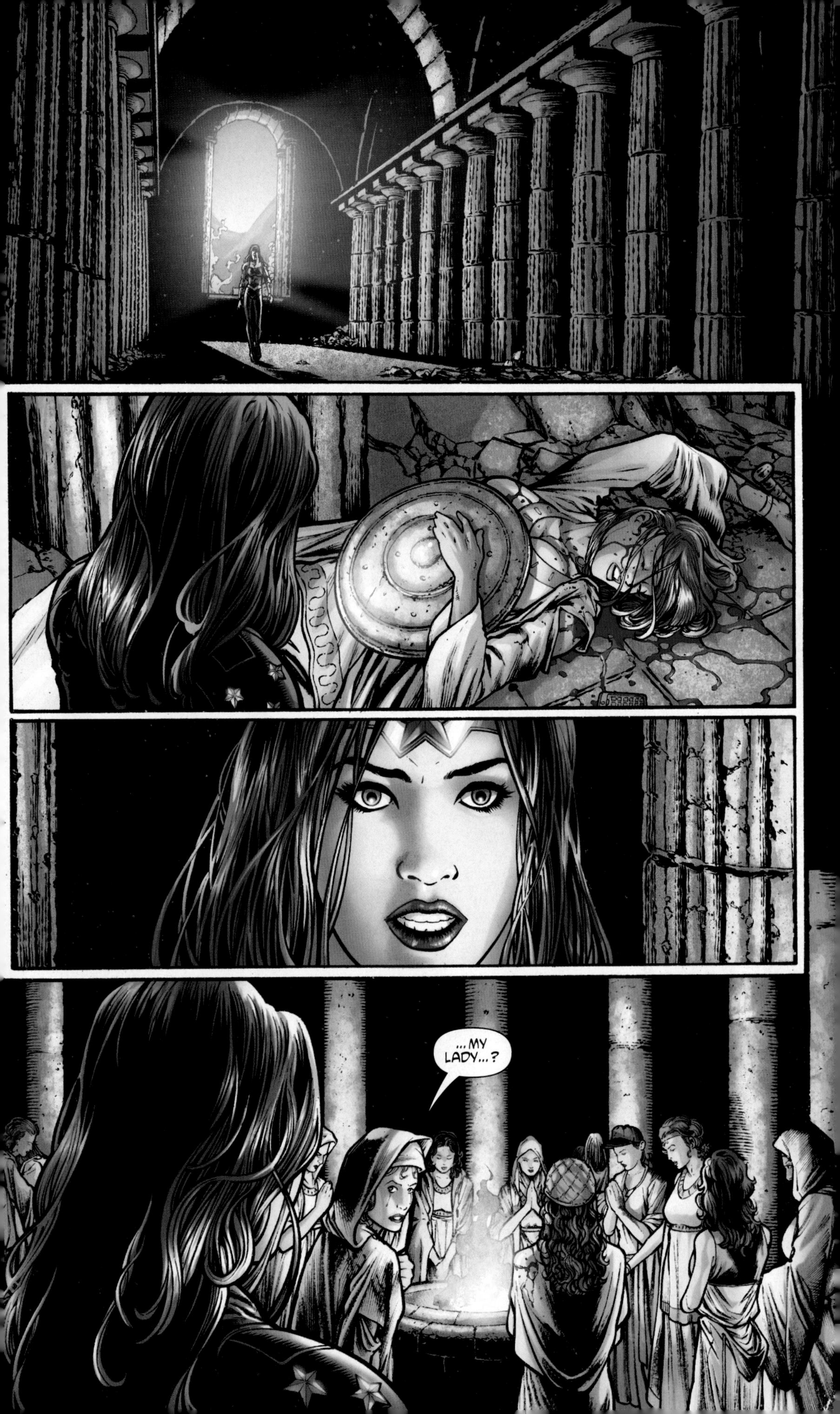
...MY LADY...?

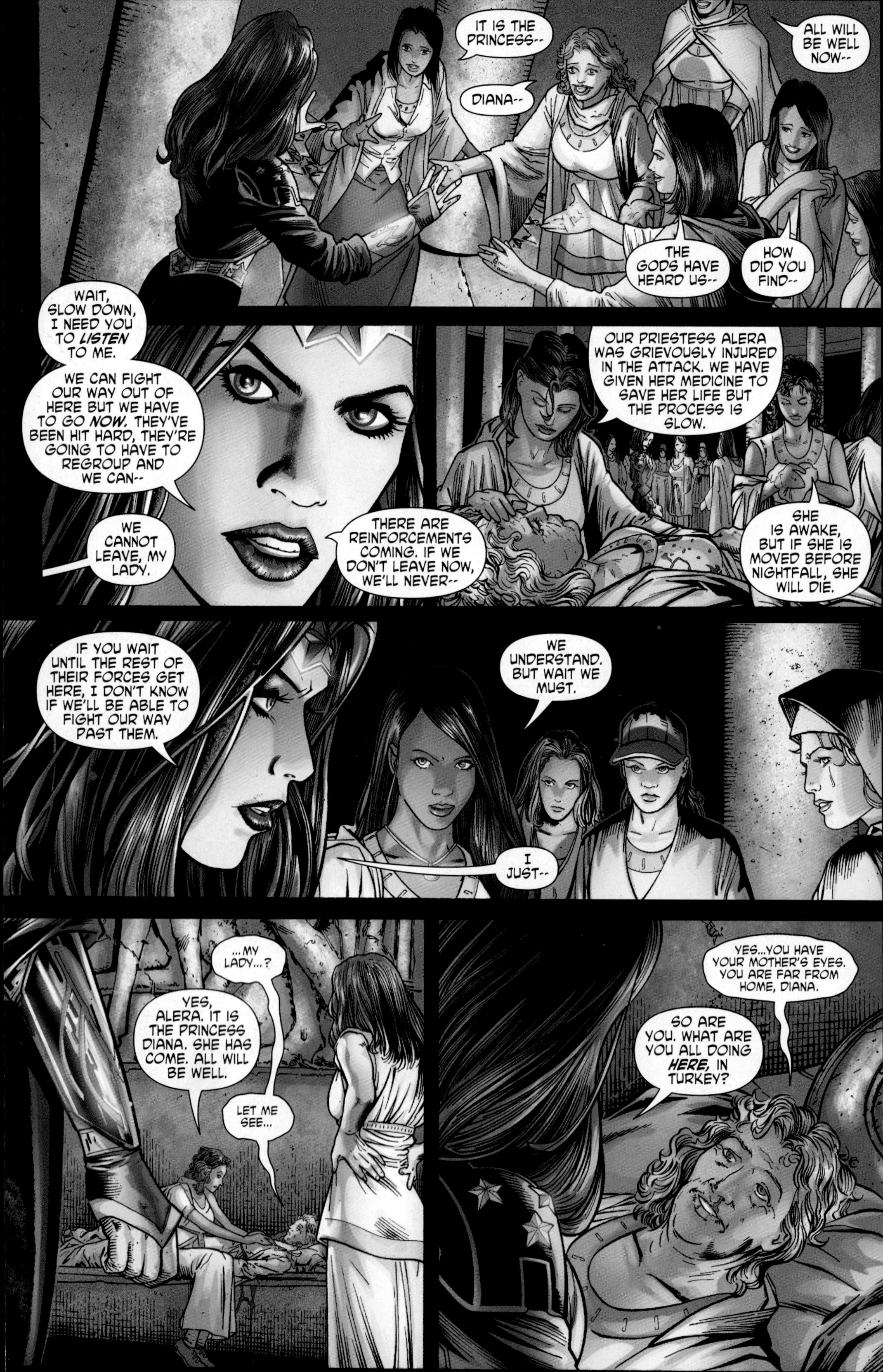
IT IS THE PRINCESS--
DIANA--
ALL WILL BE WELL NOW--
THE GODS HAVE HEARD US--
HOW DID YOU FIND--
WAIT, SLOW DOWN, I NEED YOU TO LISTEN TO ME.
WE CAN FIGHT OUR WAY OUT OF HERE BUT WE HAVE TO GO NOW. THEY'VE BEEN HIT HARD, THEY'RE GOING TO HAVE TO REGROUP AND WE CAN--
WE CANNOT LEAVE, MY LADY.
THERE ARE REINFORCEMENTS COMING. IF WE DON'T LEAVE NOW, WE'LL NEVER--
OUR PRIESTESS ALERA WAS GRIEVOUSLY INJURED IN THE ATTACK. WE HAVE GIVEN HER MEDICINE TO SAVE HER LIFE BUT THE PROCESS IS SLOW.
SHE IS AWAKE, BUT IF SHE IS MOVED BEFORE NIGHTFALL, SHE WILL DIE.
IF YOU WAIT UNTIL THE REST OF THEIR FORCES GET HERE, I DON'T KNOW IF WE'LL BE ABLE TO FIGHT OUR WAY PAST THEM.
WE UNDERSTAND. BUT WAIT WE MUST.
I JUST--
...MY LADY...?
YES, ALERA. IT IS THE PRINCESS DIANA. SHE HAS COME. ALL WILL BE WELL.
LET ME SEE...
YES...YOU HAVE YOUR MOTHER'S EYES. YOU ARE FAR FROM HOME, DIANA.
SO ARE YOU. WHAT ARE YOU ALL DOING HERE, IN TURKEY?

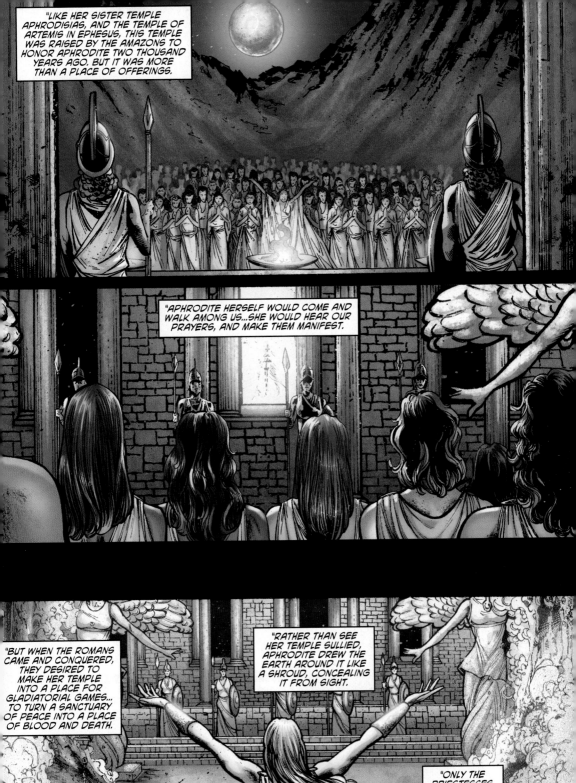

"LIKE HER SISTER TEMPLE APHRODISIAS, AND THE TEMPLE OF ARTEMIS IN EPHESUS, THIS TEMPLE WAS RAISED BY THE AMAZONS TO HONOR APHRODITE TWO THOUSAND YEARS AGO. BUT IT WAS MORE THAN A PLACE OF OFFERINGS.

"APHRODITE HERSELF WOULD COME AND WALK AMONG US...SHE WOULD HEAR OUR PRAYERS, AND MAKE THEM MANIFEST.

"BUT WHEN THE ROMANS CAME AND CONQUERED, THEY DESIRED TO MAKE HER TEMPLE INTO A PLACE FOR GLADIATORIAL GAMES... TO TURN A SANCTUARY OF PEACE INTO A PLACE OF BLOOD AND DEATH.

"RATHER THAN SEE HER TEMPLE SULLIED, APHRODITE DREW THE EARTH AROUND IT LIKE A SHROUD, CONCEALING IT FROM SIGHT.

"ONLY THE PRIESTESSES COULD SUMMON IT FORTH FROM ITS HIDING PLACE."

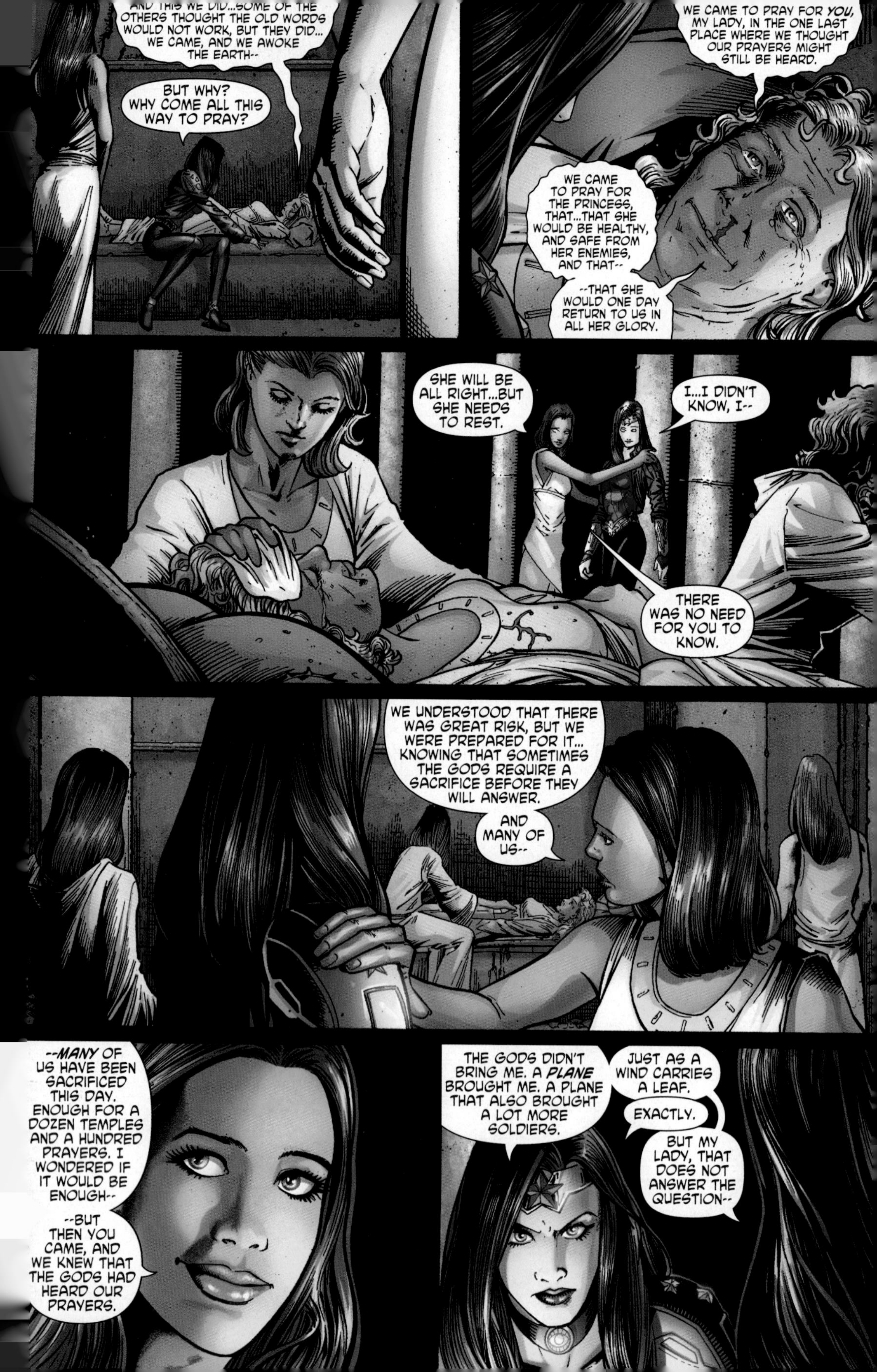
AND THIS WE DID...SOME OF THE OTHERS THOUGHT THE OLD WORDS WOULD NOT WORK, BUT THEY DID... WE CAME, AND WE AWOKE THE EARTH--
BUT WHY? WHY COME ALL THIS WAY TO PRAY?
WE CAME TO PRAY FOR *YOU*, MY LADY, IN THE ONE LAST PLACE WHERE WE THOUGHT OUR PRAYERS MIGHT STILL BE HEARD.
WE CAME TO PRAY FOR THE PRINCESS, THAT...THAT SHE WOULD BE HEALTHY, AND SAFE FROM HER ENEMIES, AND THAT--
--THAT SHE WOULD ONE DAY RETURN TO US IN ALL HER GLORY.
SHE WILL BE ALL RIGHT...BUT SHE NEEDS TO REST.
I...I DIDN'T KNOW, I--
THERE WAS NO NEED FOR YOU TO KNOW.
WE UNDERSTOOD THAT THERE WAS GREAT RISK, BUT WE WERE PREPARED FOR IT... KNOWING THAT SOMETIMES THE GODS REQUIRE A SACRIFICE BEFORE THEY WILL ANSWER.
AND MANY OF US--
--*MANY* OF US HAVE BEEN SACRIFICED THIS DAY. ENOUGH FOR A DOZEN TEMPLES AND A HUNDRED PRAYERS. I WONDERED IF IT WOULD BE ENOUGH--
--BUT THEN YOU CAME, AND WE KNEW THAT THE GODS HAD HEARD OUR PRAYERS.
THE GODS DIDN'T BRING ME. A *PLANE* BROUGHT ME. A PLANE THAT ALSO BROUGHT A LOT MORE SOLDIERS.
JUST AS A WIND CARRIES A LEAF.
EXACTLY.
BUT MY LADY, THAT DOES NOT ANSWER THE QUESTION--

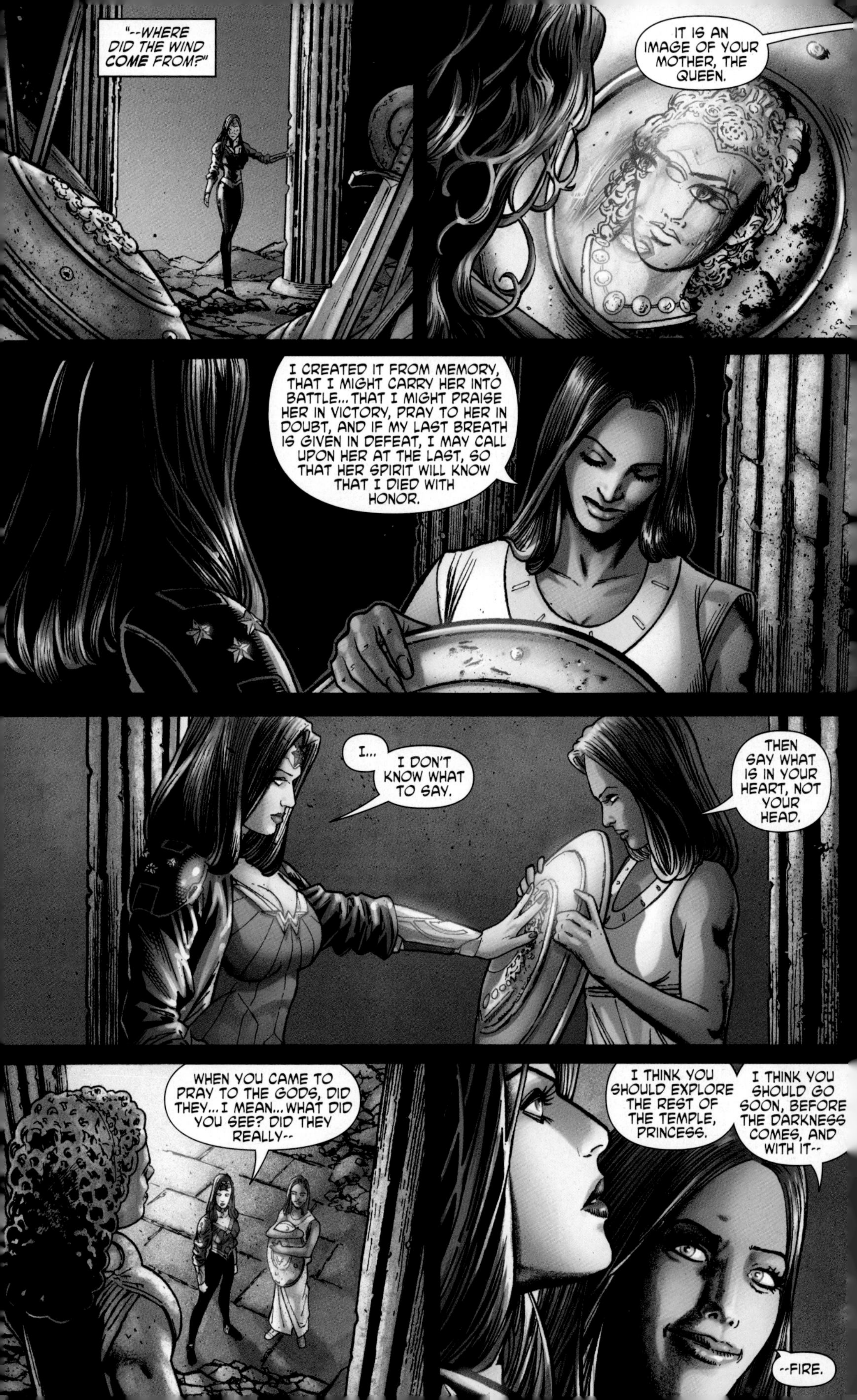
"--WHERE DID THE WIND COME FROM?"
IT IS AN IMAGE OF YOUR MOTHER, THE QUEEN.
I CREATED IT FROM MEMORY, THAT I MIGHT CARRY HER INTO BATTLE... THAT I MIGHT PRAISE HER IN VICTORY, PRAY TO HER IN DOUBT, AND IF MY LAST BREATH IS GIVEN IN DEFEAT, I MAY CALL UPON HER AT THE LAST, SO THAT HER SPIRIT WILL KNOW THAT I DIED WITH HONOR.
I...
I DON'T KNOW WHAT TO SAY.
THEN SAY WHAT IS IN YOUR HEART, NOT YOUR HEAD.
WHEN YOU CAME TO PRAY TO THE GODS, DID THEY... I MEAN... WHAT DID YOU SEE? DID THEY REALLY--
I THINK YOU SHOULD EXPLORE THE REST OF THE TEMPLE, PRINCESS.
I THINK YOU SHOULD GO SOON, BEFORE THE DARKNESS COMES, AND WITH IT--
--FIRE.

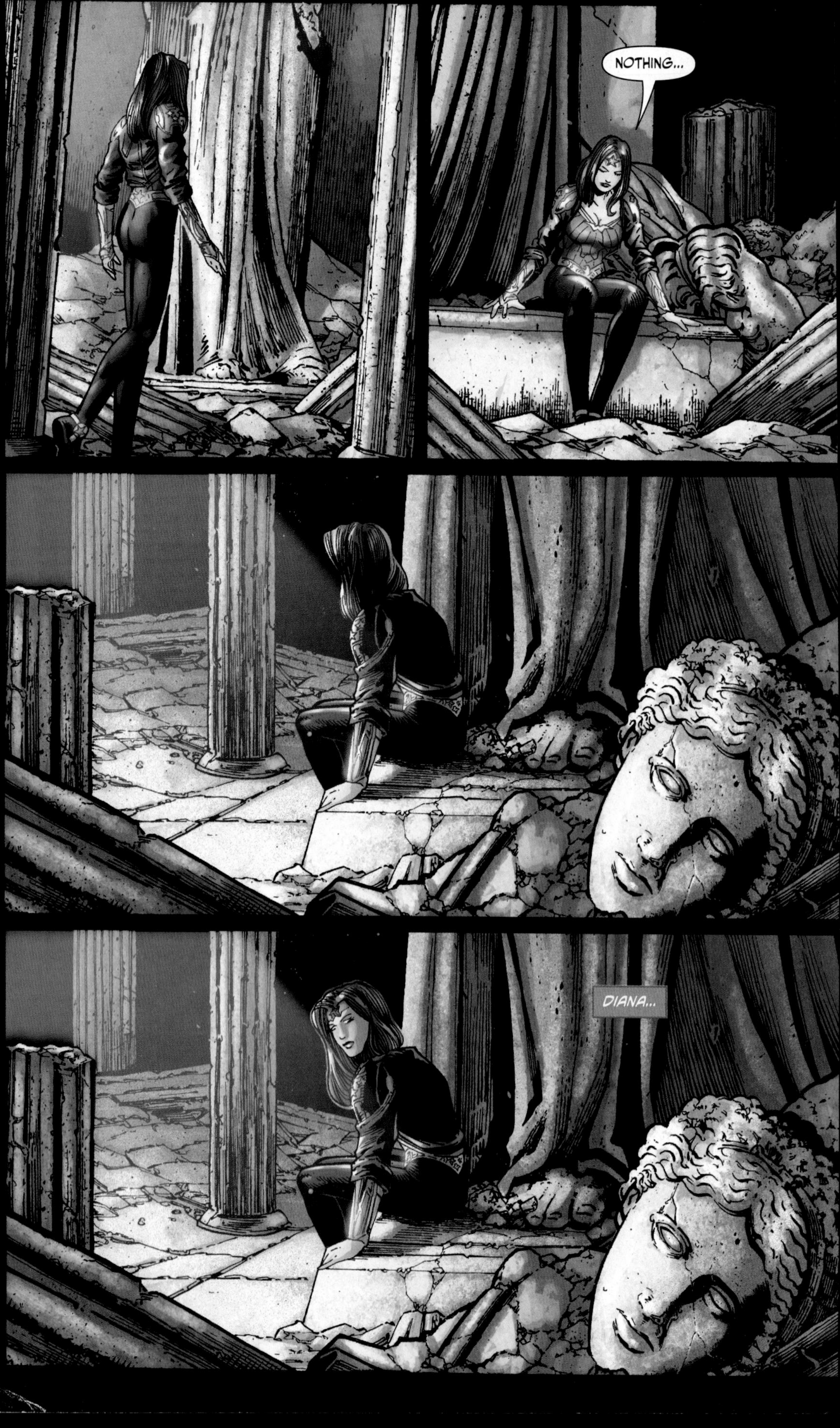
NOTHING...
DIANA...

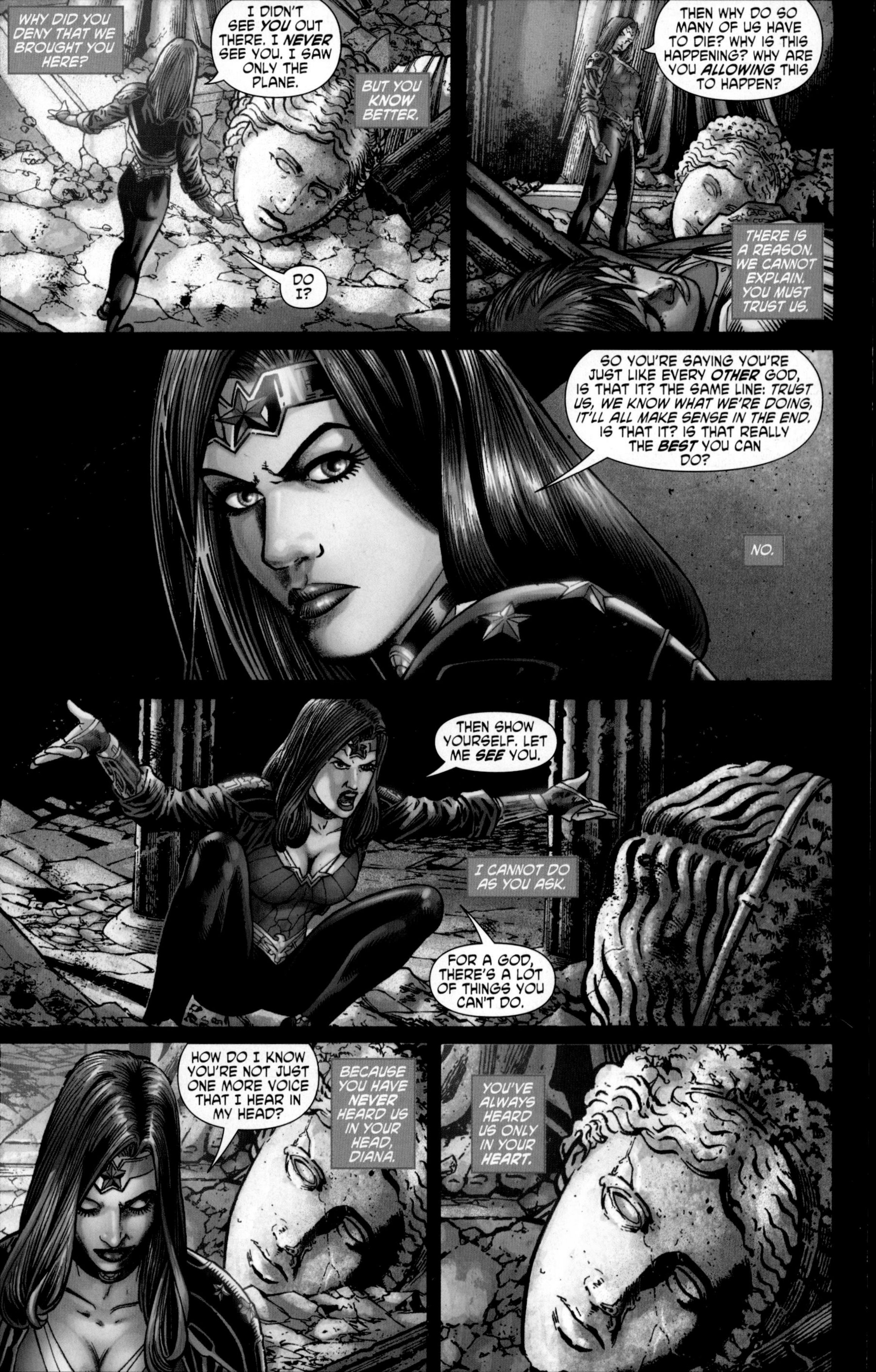
WHY DID YOU DENY THAT WE BROUGHT YOU HERE?
I DIDN'T SEE YOU OUT THERE. I NEVER SEE YOU. I SAW ONLY THE PLANE.
BUT YOU KNOW BETTER.
DO I?
THEN WHY DO SO MANY OF US HAVE TO DIE? WHY IS THIS HAPPENING? WHY ARE YOU ALLOWING THIS TO HAPPEN?
THERE IS A REASON. WE CANNOT EXPLAIN. YOU MUST TRUST US.
SO YOU'RE SAYING YOU'RE JUST LIKE EVERY OTHER GOD, IS THAT IT? THE SAME LINE: TRUST US, WE KNOW WHAT WE'RE DOING, IT'LL ALL MAKE SENSE IN THE END. IS THAT IT? IS THAT REALLY THE BEST YOU CAN DO?
NO.
THEN SHOW YOURSELF. LET ME SEE YOU.
I CANNOT DO AS YOU ASK.
FOR A GOD, THERE'S A LOT OF THINGS YOU CAN'T DO.
HOW DO I KNOW YOU'RE NOT JUST ONE MORE VOICE THAT I HEAR IN MY HEAD?
BECAUSE YOU HAVE NEVER HEARD US IN YOUR HEAD, DIANA.
YOU'VE ALWAYS HEARD US ONLY IN YOUR HEART.

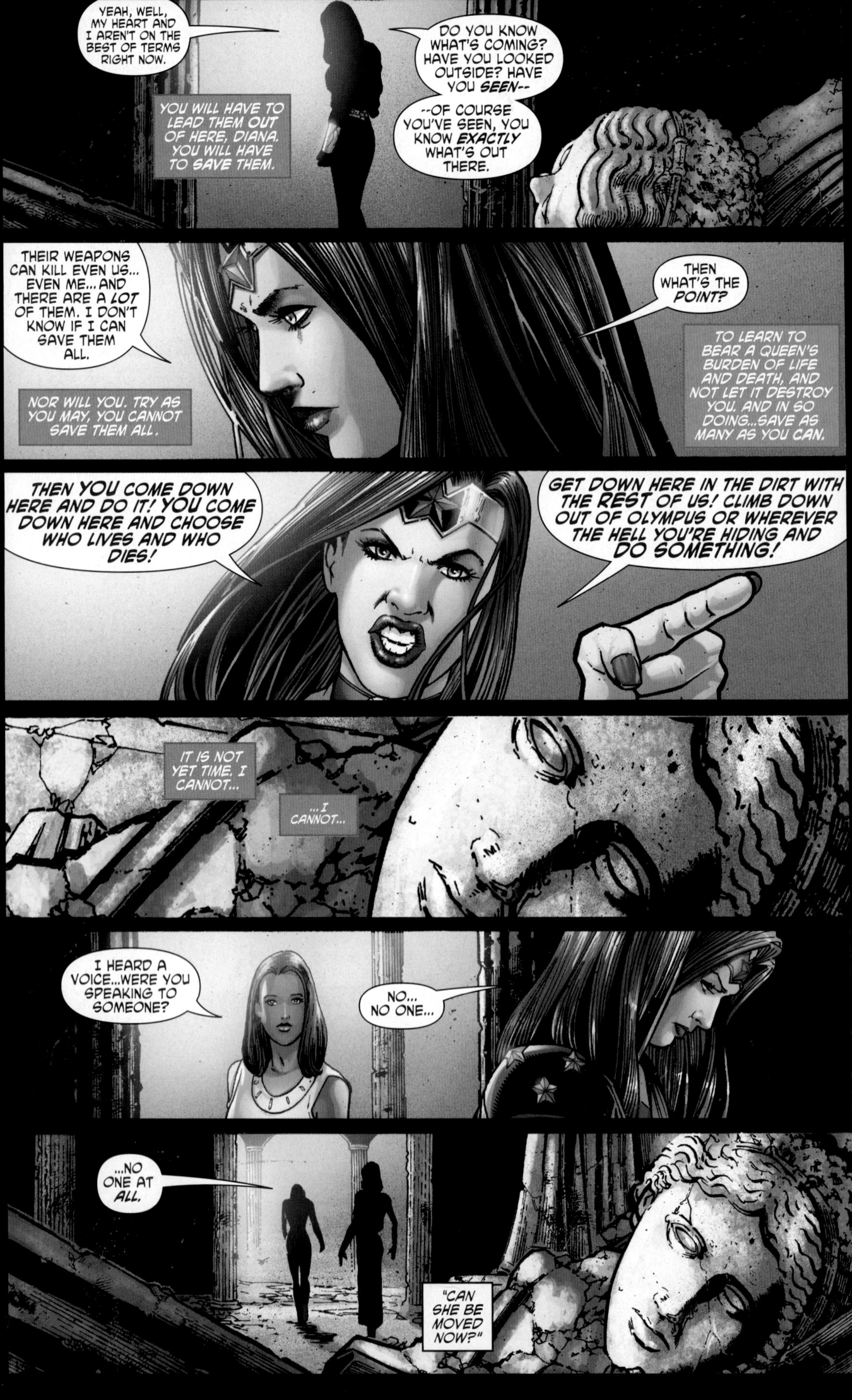
YEAH, WELL, MY HEART AND I AREN'T ON THE BEST OF TERMS RIGHT NOW.
YOU WILL HAVE TO LEAD THEM OUT OF HERE, DIANA. YOU WILL HAVE TO SAVE THEM.
DO YOU KNOW WHAT'S COMING? HAVE YOU LOOKED OUTSIDE? HAVE YOU SEEN--
--OF COURSE YOU'VE SEEN, YOU KNOW EXACTLY WHAT'S OUT THERE.
THEIR WEAPONS CAN KILL EVEN US... EVEN ME... AND THERE ARE A LOT OF THEM. I DON'T KNOW IF I CAN SAVE THEM ALL.
NOR WILL YOU. TRY AS YOU MAY, YOU CANNOT SAVE THEM ALL.
THEN WHAT'S THE POINT?
TO LEARN TO BEAR A QUEEN'S BURDEN OF LIFE AND DEATH, AND NOT LET IT DESTROY YOU. AND IN SO DOING...SAVE AS MANY AS YOU CAN.
THEN YOU COME DOWN HERE AND DO IT! YOU COME DOWN HERE AND CHOOSE WHO LIVES AND WHO DIES!
GET DOWN HERE IN THE DIRT WITH THE REST OF US! CLIMB DOWN OUT OF OLYMPUS OR WHEREVER THE HELL YOU'RE HIDING AND DO SOMETHING!
IT IS NOT YET TIME. I CANNOT...
...I CANNOT...
I HEARD A VOICE...WERE YOU SPEAKING TO SOMEONE?
NO... NO ONE...
...NO ONE AT ALL.
"CAN SHE BE MOVED NOW?"

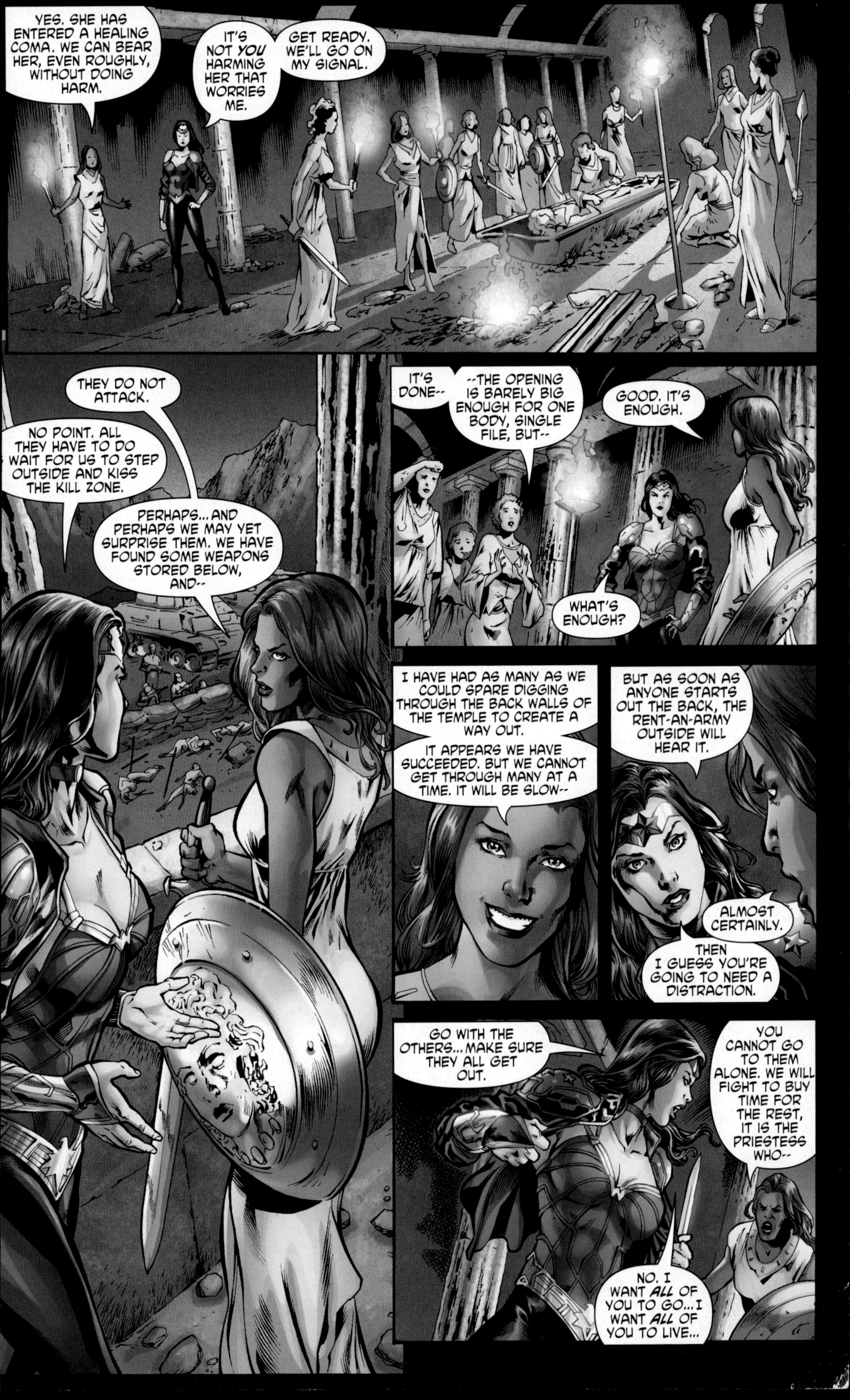
YES. SHE HAS ENTERED A HEALING COMA. WE CAN BEAR HER, EVEN ROUGHLY, WITHOUT DOING HARM.
IT'S NOT *YOU* HARMING HER THAT WORRIES ME.
GET READY. WE'LL GO ON MY SIGNAL.
THEY DO NOT ATTACK.
NO POINT. ALL THEY HAVE TO DO WAIT FOR US TO STEP OUTSIDE AND KISS THE KILL ZONE.
PERHAPS... AND PERHAPS WE MAY YET SURPRISE THEM. WE HAVE FOUND SOME WEAPONS STORED BELOW, AND--
IT'S DONE--
--THE OPENING IS BARELY BIG ENOUGH FOR ONE BODY, SINGLE FILE, BUT--
GOOD. IT'S ENOUGH.
WHAT'S ENOUGH?
I HAVE HAD AS MANY AS WE COULD SPARE DIGGING THROUGH THE BACK WALLS OF THE TEMPLE TO CREATE A WAY OUT.
IT APPEARS WE HAVE SUCCEEDED. BUT WE CANNOT GET THROUGH MANY AT A TIME. IT WILL BE SLOW--
BUT AS SOON AS ANYONE STARTS OUT THE BACK, THE RENT-AN-ARMY OUTSIDE WILL HEAR IT.
ALMOST CERTAINLY.
THEN I GUESS YOU'RE GOING TO NEED A DISTRACTION.
GO WITH THE OTHERS... MAKE SURE THEY ALL GET OUT.
YOU CANNOT GO TO THEM ALONE. WE WILL FIGHT TO BUY TIME FOR THE REST, IT IS THE PRIESTESS WHO--
NO. I WANT *ALL* OF YOU TO GO... I WANT *ALL* OF YOU TO LIVE...

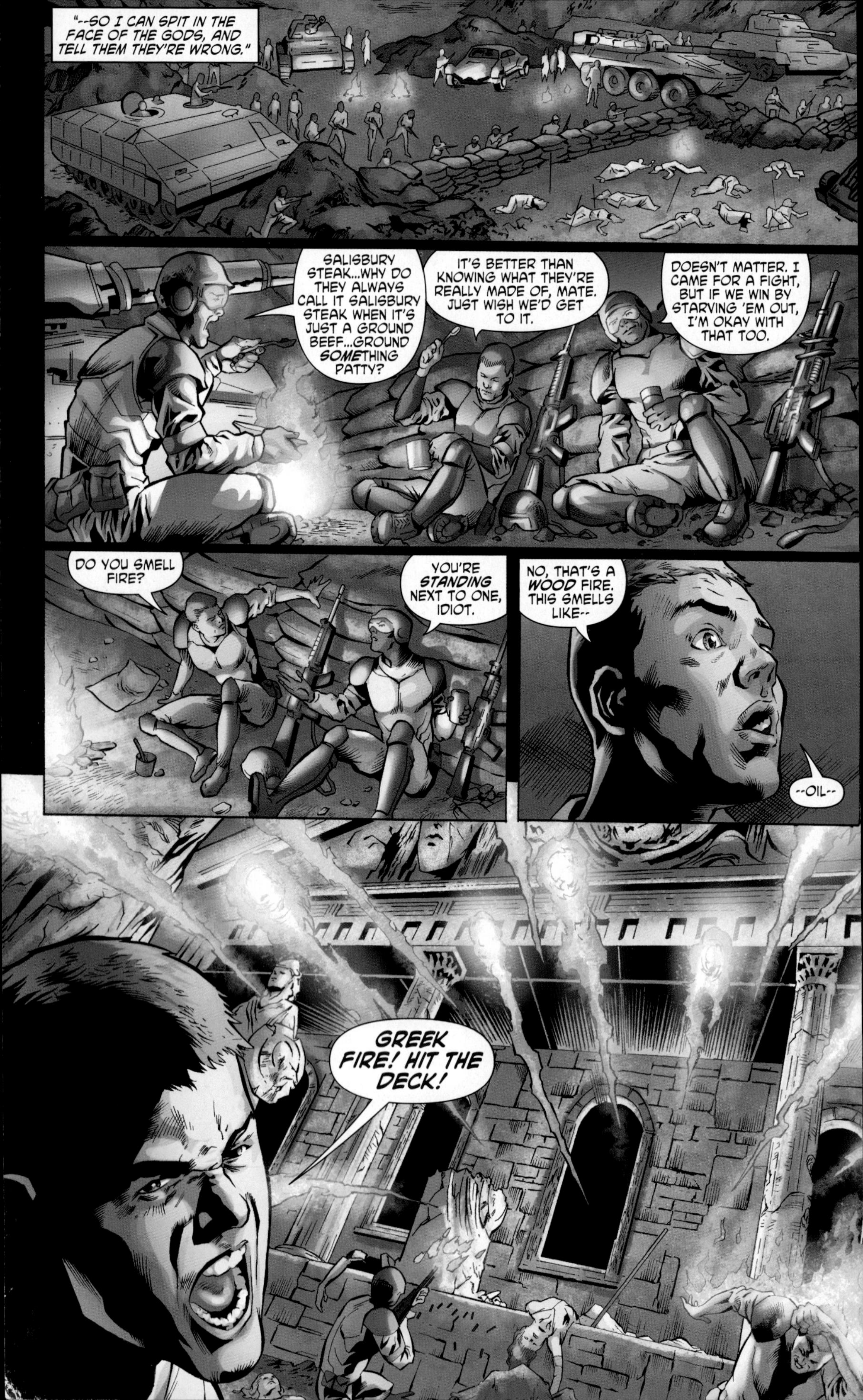
"--SO I CAN SPIT IN THE FACE OF THE GODS, AND TELL THEM THEY'RE WRONG."
SALISBURY STEAK...WHY DO THEY ALWAYS CALL IT SALISBURY STEAK WHEN IT'S JUST A GROUND BEEF...GROUND SOMETHING PATTY?
IT'S BETTER THAN KNOWING WHAT THEY'RE REALLY MADE OF, MATE. JUST WISH WE'D GET TO IT.
DOESN'T MATTER. I CAME FOR A FIGHT, BUT IF WE WIN BY STARVING 'EM OUT, I'M OKAY WITH THAT TOO.
DO YOU SMELL FIRE?
YOU'RE STANDING NEXT TO ONE, IDIOT.
NO, THAT'S A WOOD FIRE. THIS SMELLS LIKE--
--OIL--
GREEK FIRE! HIT THE DECK!

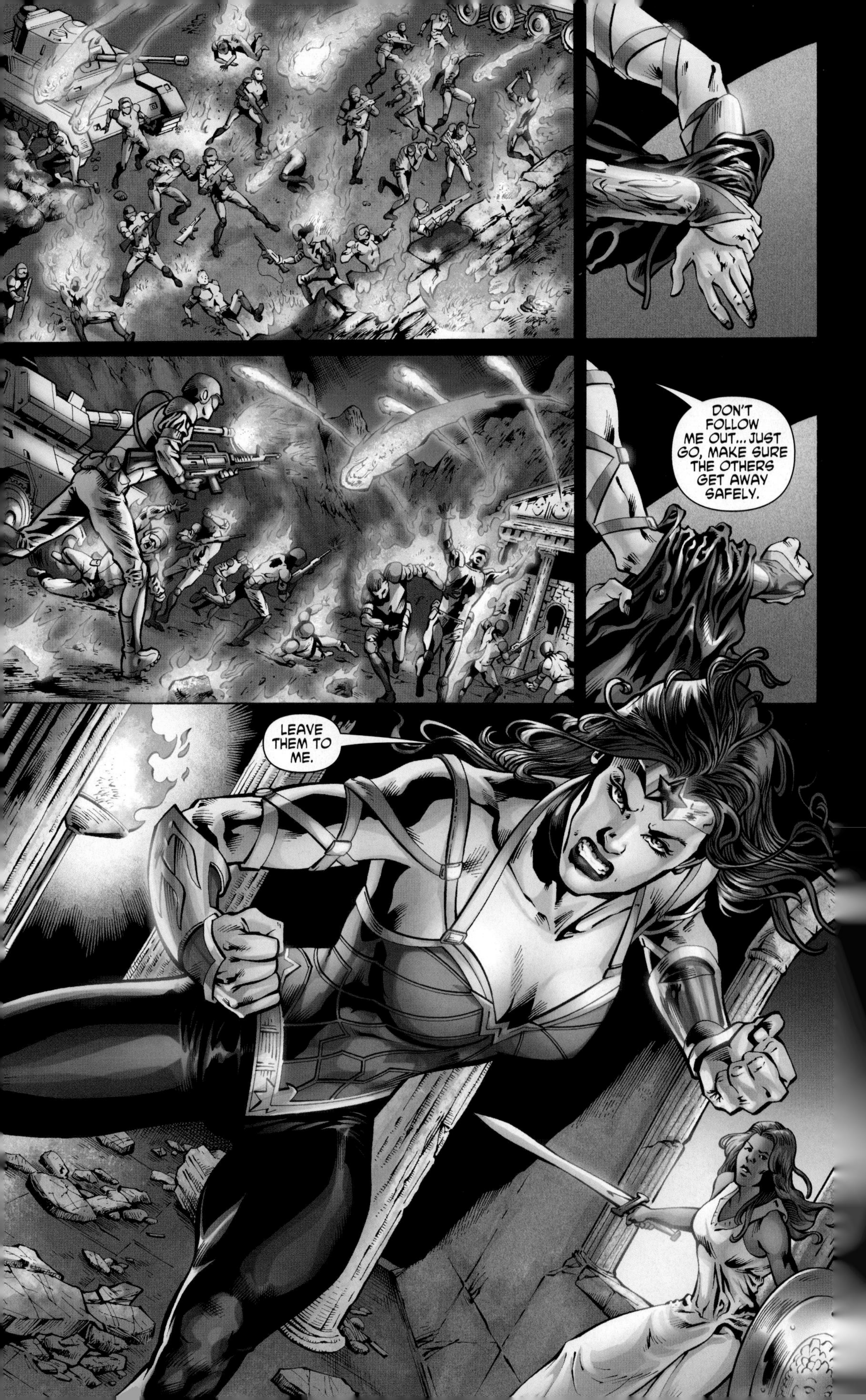
DON'T FOLLOW ME OUT... JUST GO, MAKE SURE THE OTHERS GET AWAY SAFELY.
LEAVE THEM TO ME.

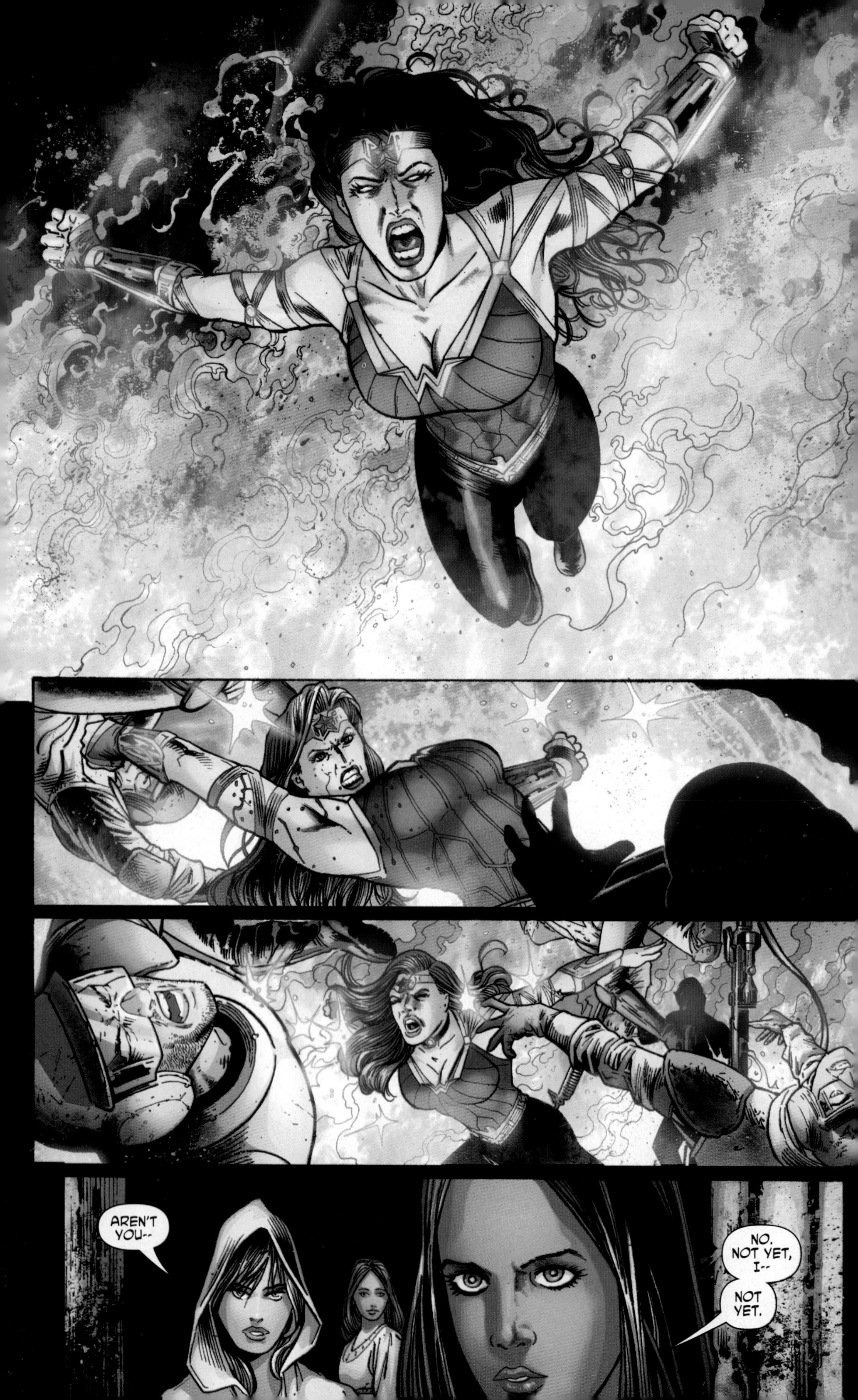

AREN'T YOU--
NO. NOT YET, I--
NOT YET.

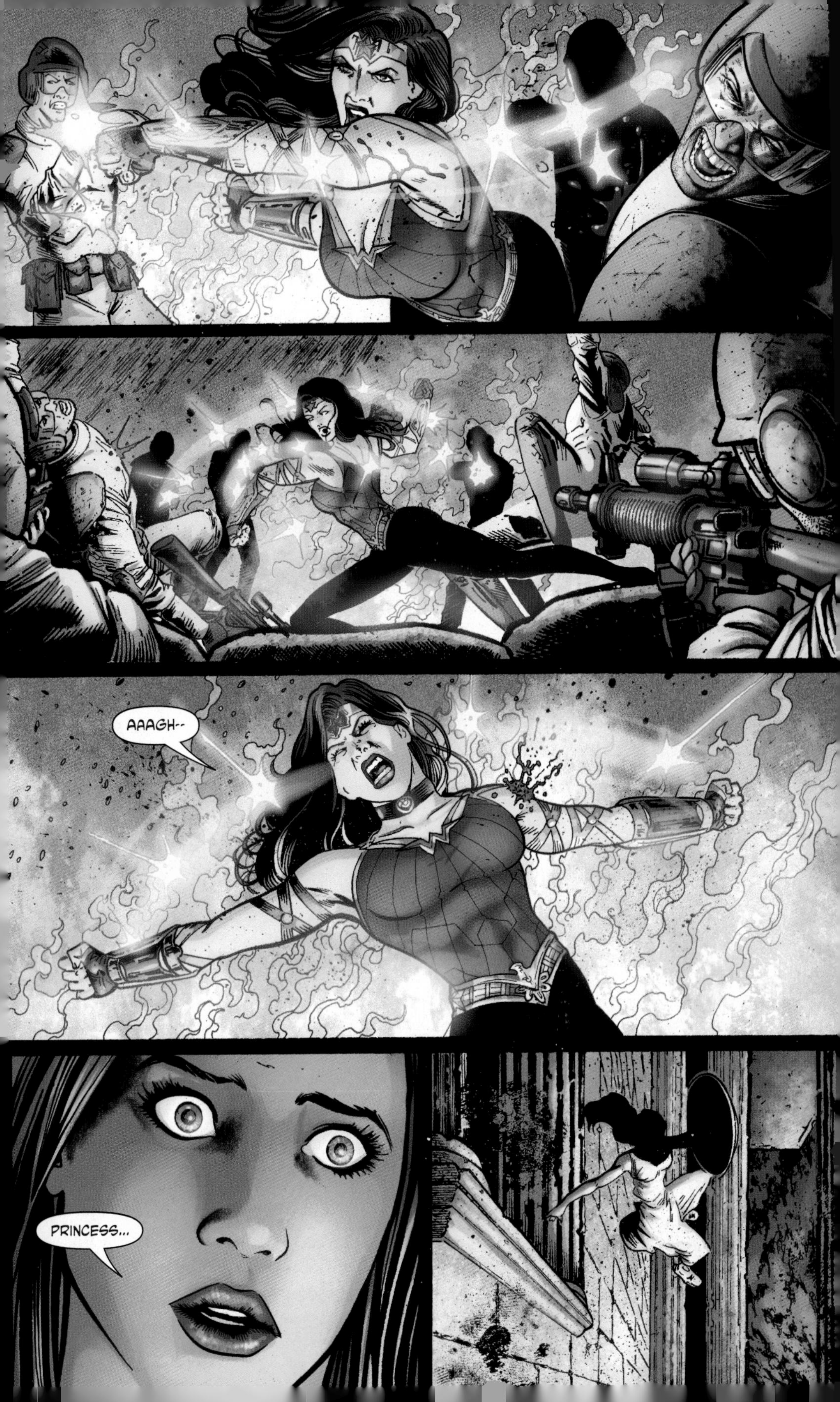
AAAGH--
PRINCESS...

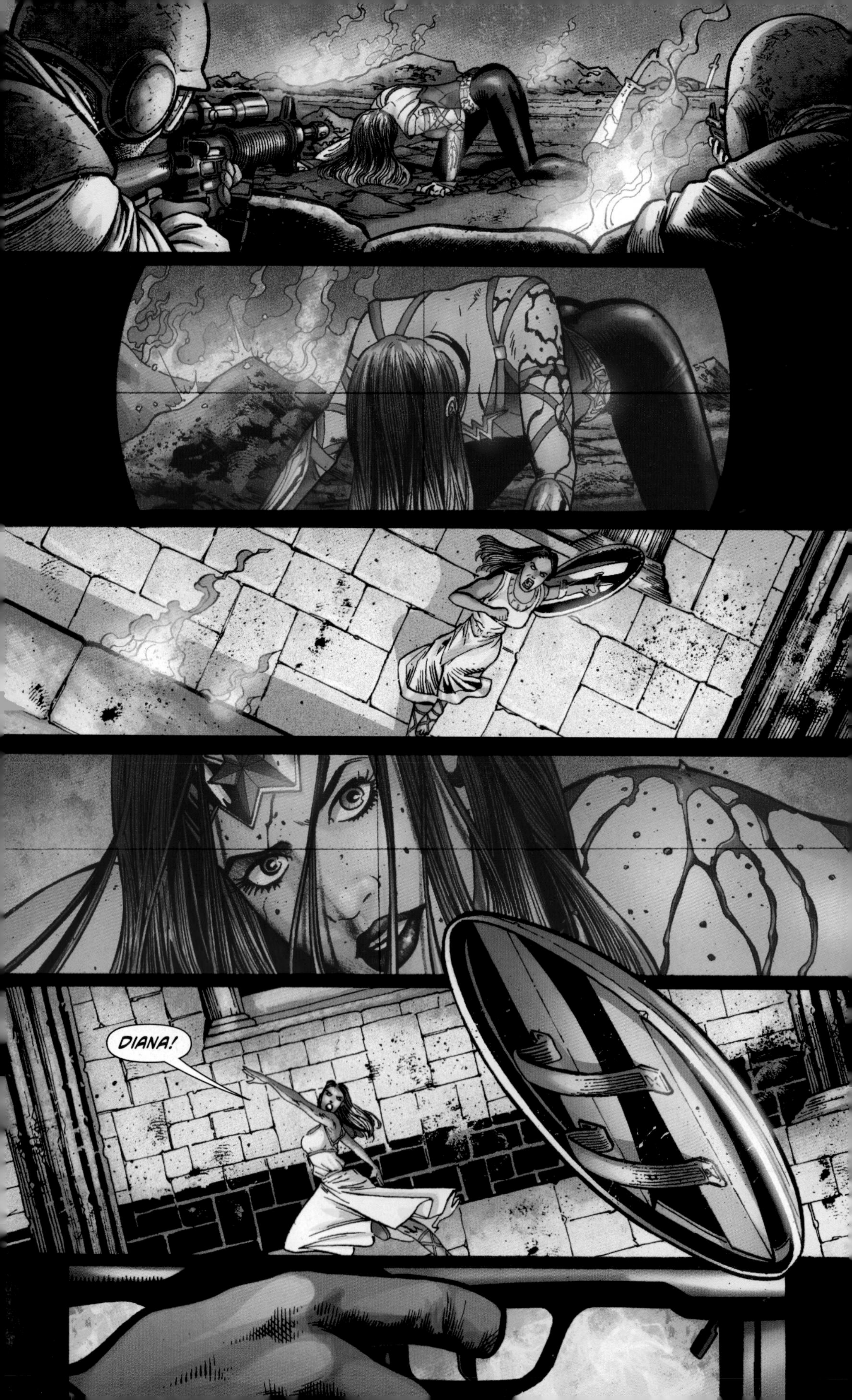
DIANA!

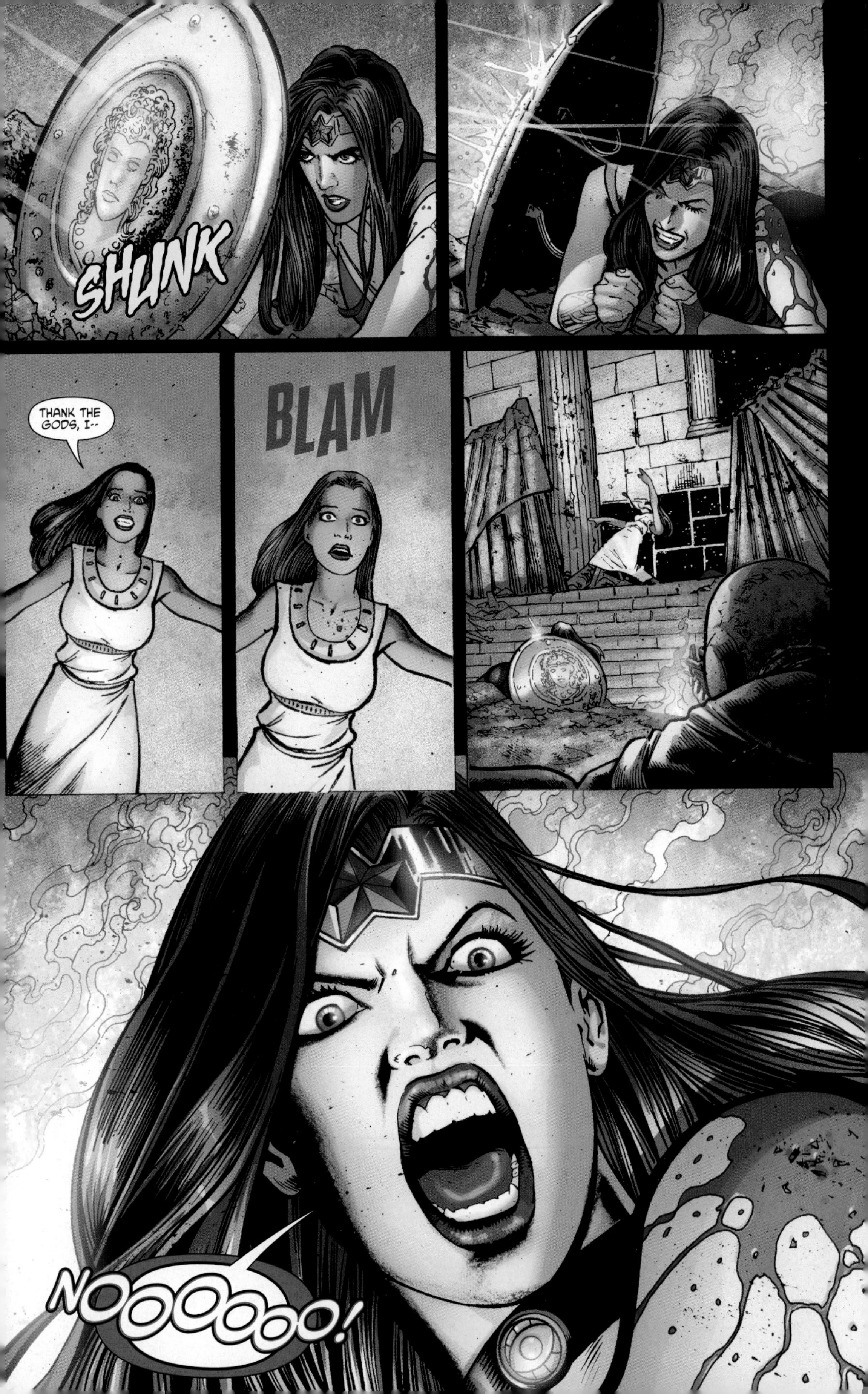
SHUNK
THANK THE GODS, I--
BLAM
NOOOOOOO!

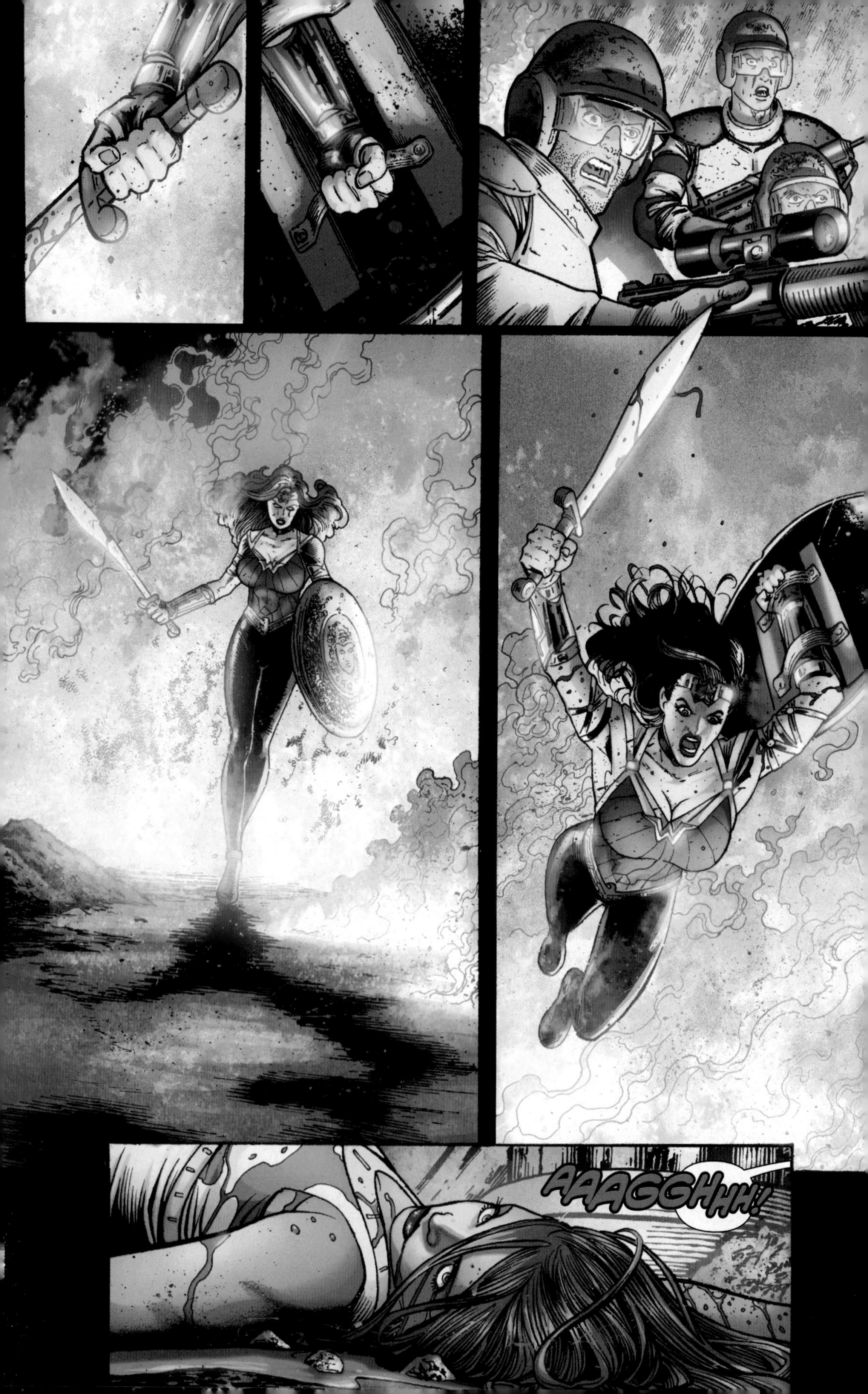
AAAGGHHHH!

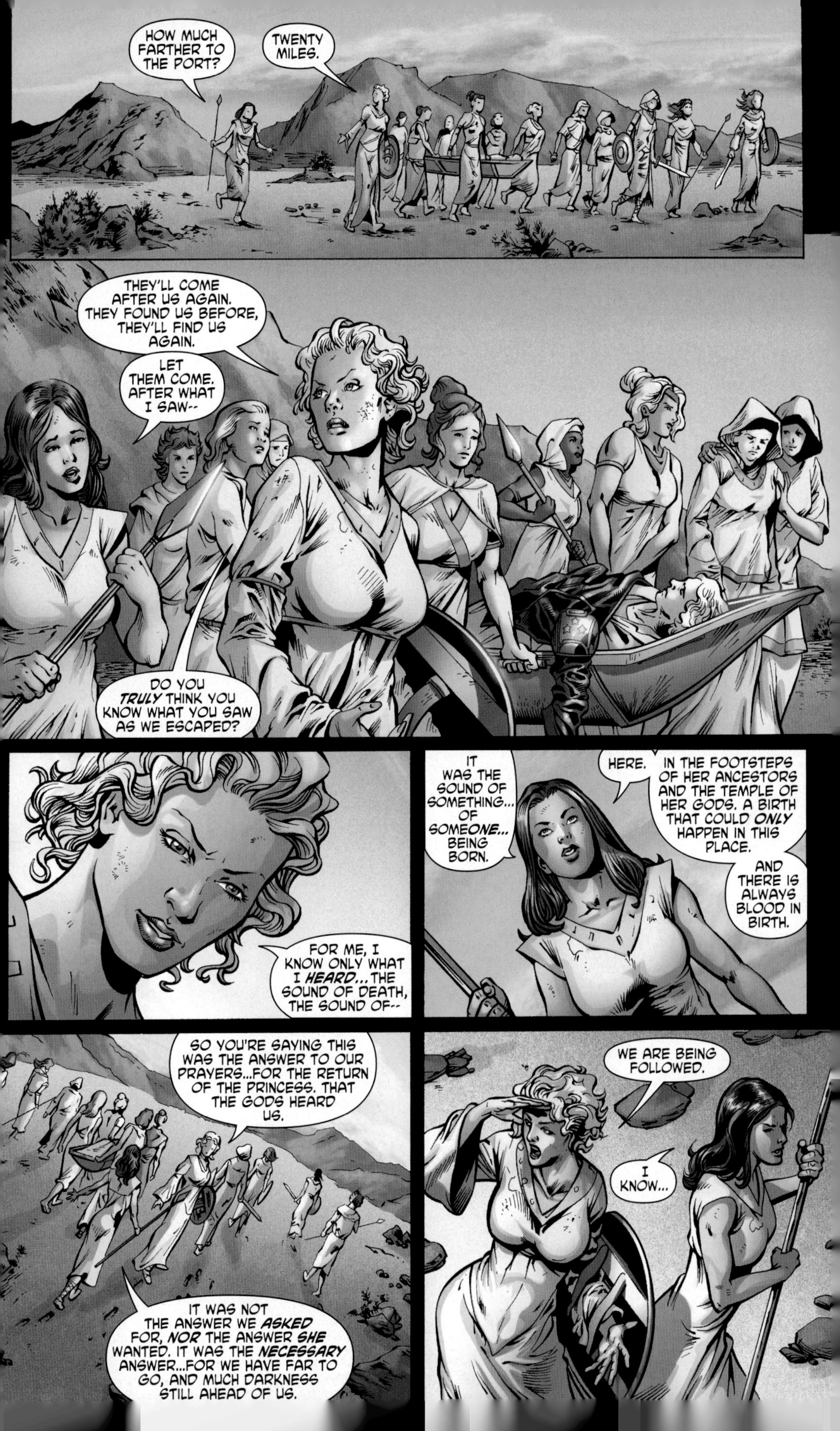

HOW MUCH FARTHER TO THE PORT?
TWENTY MILES.
THEY'LL COME AFTER US AGAIN. THEY FOUND US BEFORE, THEY'LL FIND US AGAIN.
LET THEM COME. AFTER WHAT I SAW--
DO YOU *TRULY* THINK YOU KNOW WHAT YOU SAW AS WE ESCAPED?
FOR ME, I KNOW ONLY WHAT I *HEARD*... THE SOUND OF DEATH, THE SOUND OF--
IT WAS THE SOUND OF SOMETHING... OF SOME*ONE*... BEING BORN.
HERE.
IN THE FOOTSTEPS OF HER ANCESTORS AND THE TEMPLE OF HER GODS. A BIRTH THAT COULD *ONLY* HAPPEN IN THIS PLACE.
AND THERE IS ALWAYS BLOOD IN BIRTH.
SO YOU'RE SAYING THIS WAS THE ANSWER TO OUR PRAYERS...FOR THE RETURN OF THE PRINCESS. THAT THE GODS HEARD US.
IT WAS NOT THE ANSWER WE *ASKED* FOR, *NOR* THE ANSWER *SHE* WANTED. IT WAS THE *NECESSARY* ANSWER...FOR WE HAVE FAR TO GO, AND MUCH DARKNESS STILL AHEAD OF US.
WE ARE BEING FOLLOWED.
I KNOW...

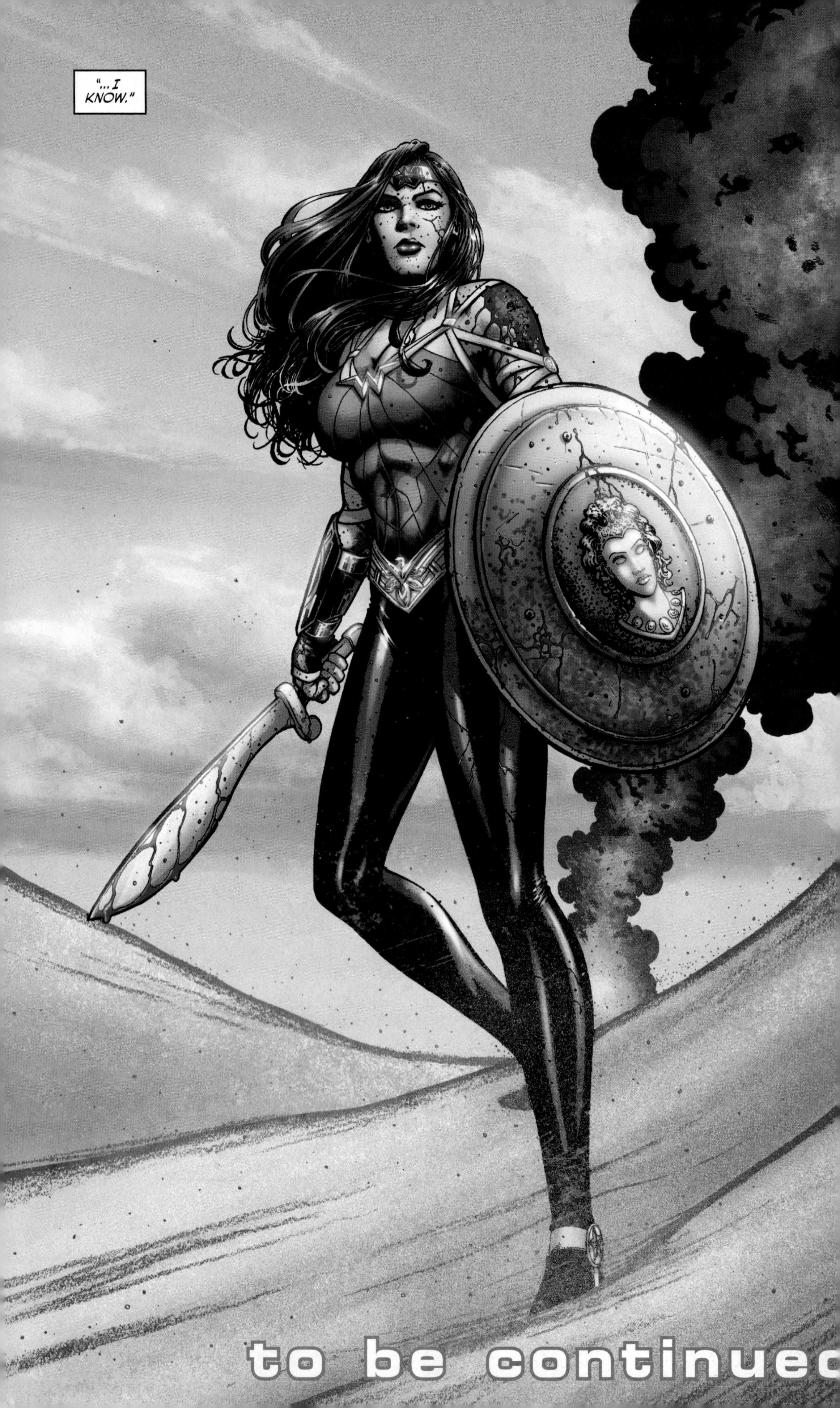
"...I KNOW."
to be continued

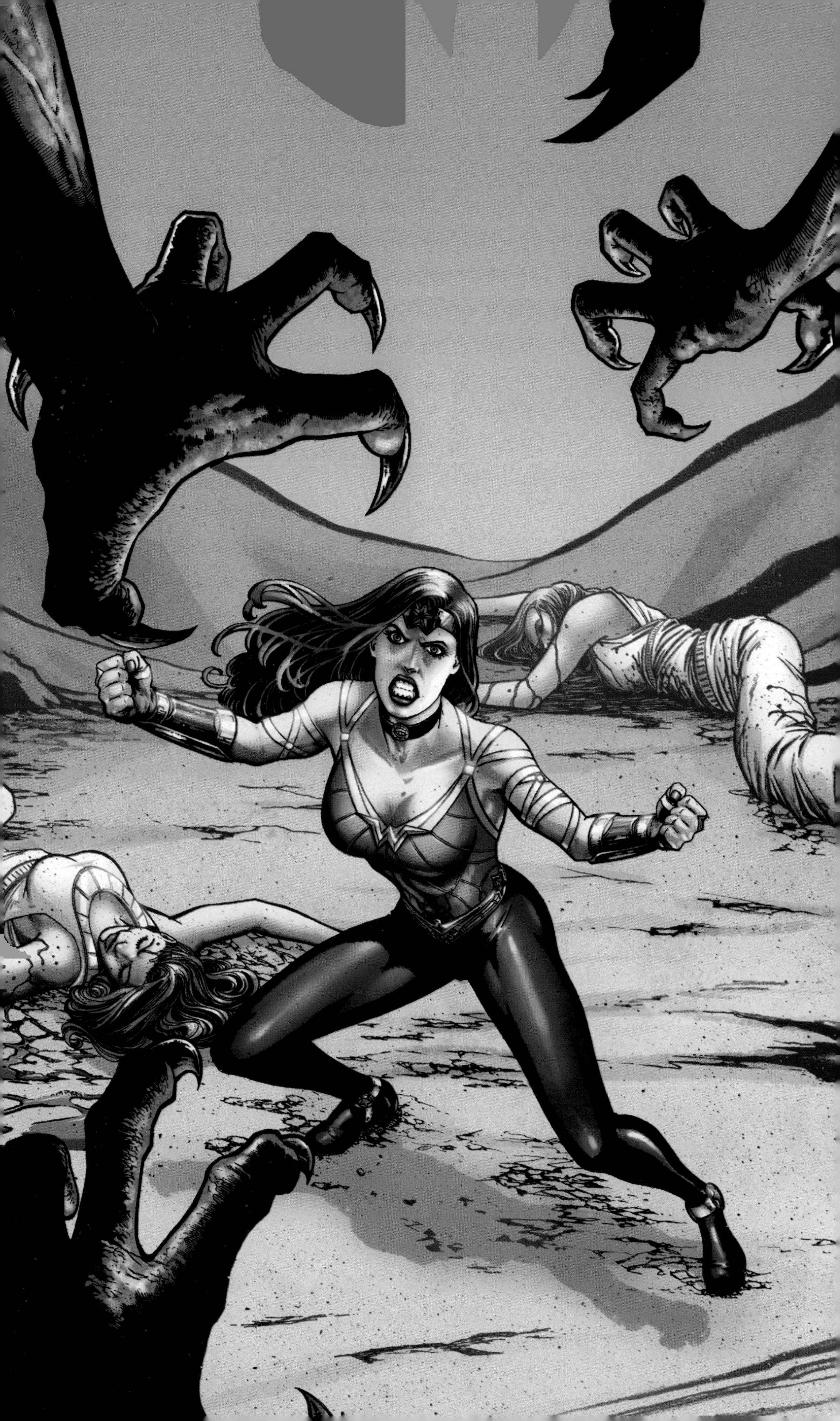

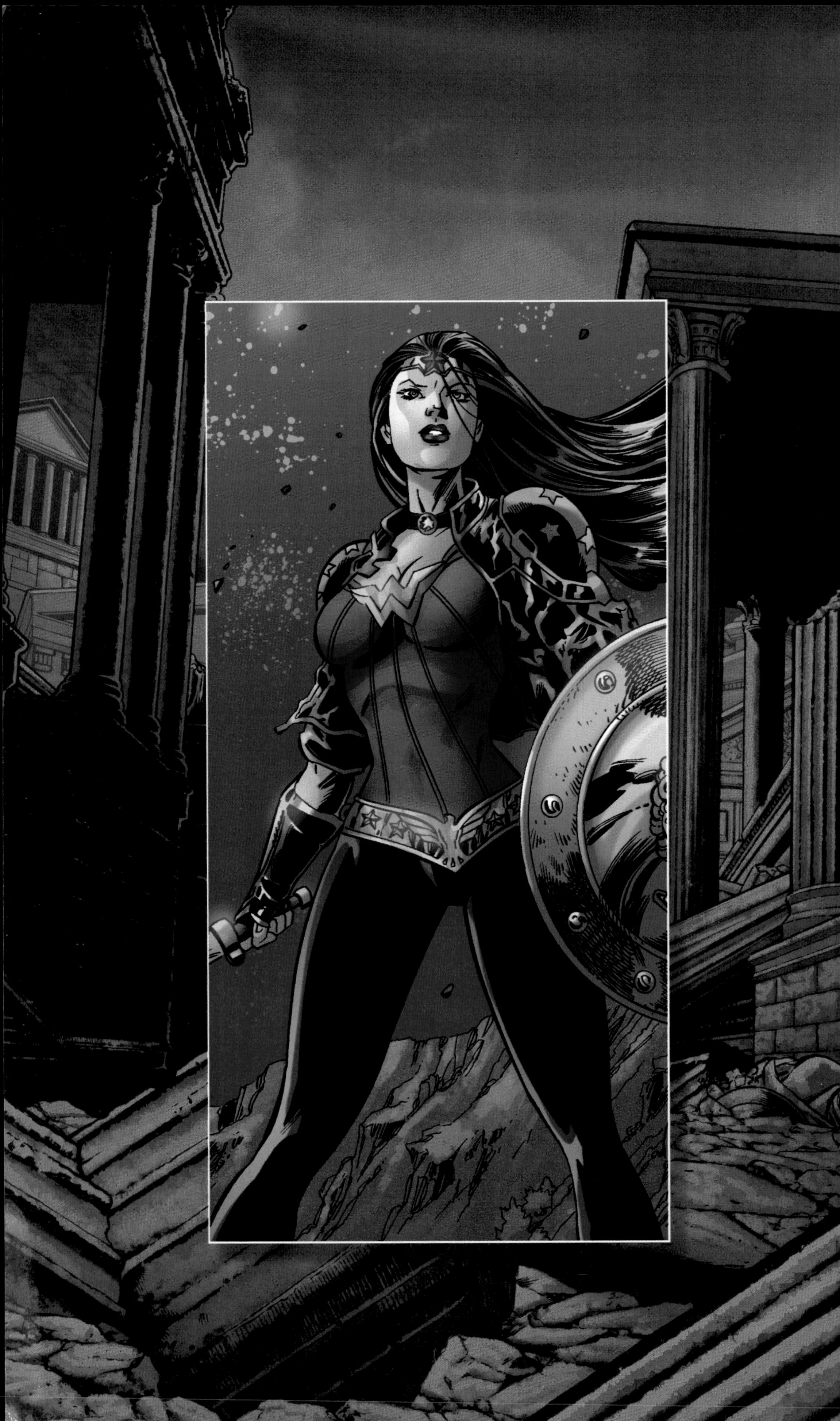

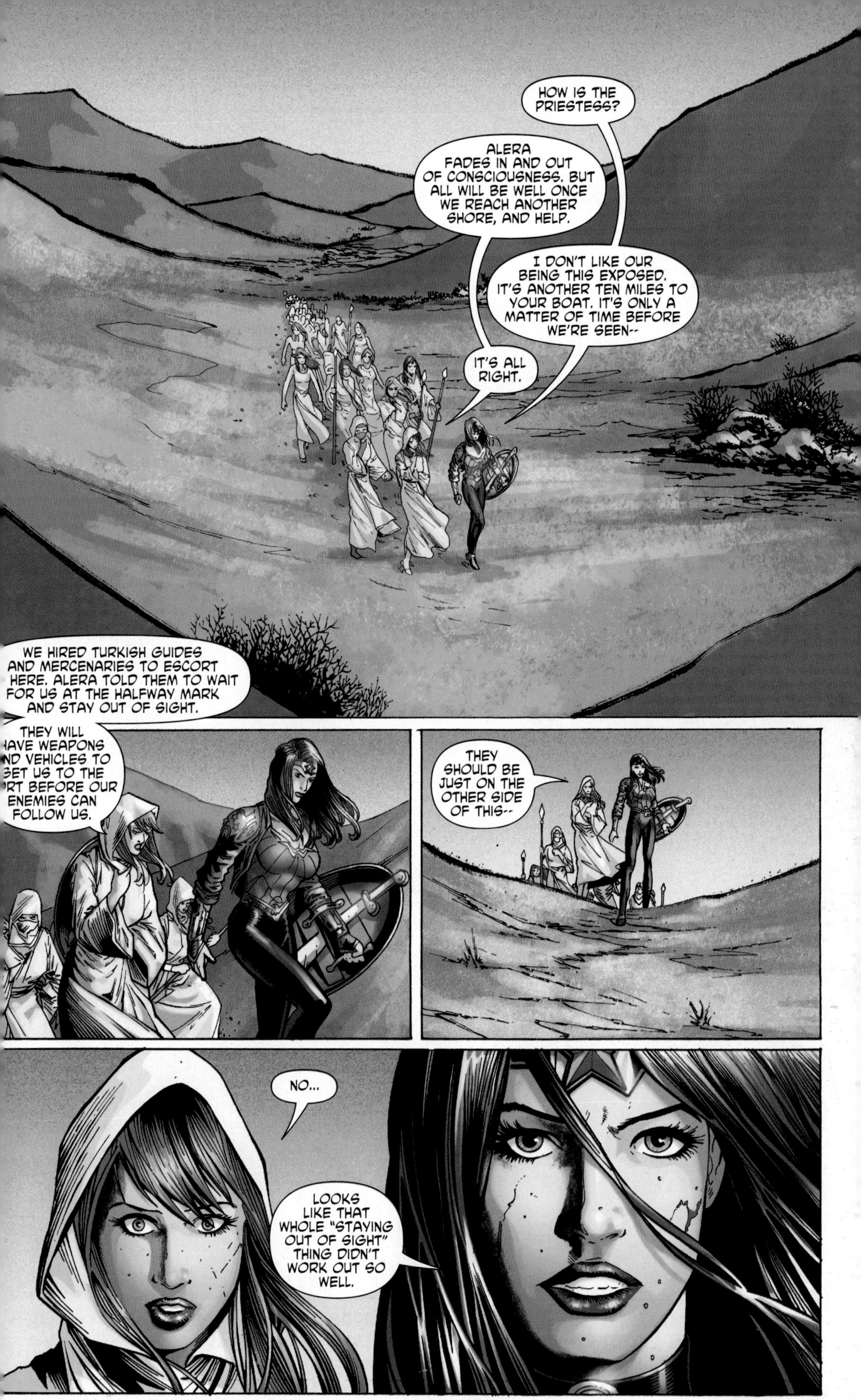
HOW IS THE PRIESTESS?
ALERA FADES IN AND OUT OF CONSCIOUSNESS. BUT ALL WILL BE WELL ONCE WE REACH ANOTHER SHORE, AND HELP.
I DON'T LIKE OUR BEING THIS EXPOSED. IT'S ANOTHER TEN MILES TO YOUR BOAT. IT'S ONLY A MATTER OF TIME BEFORE WE'RE SEEN--
IT'S ALL RIGHT.
WE HIRED TURKISH GUIDES AND MERCENARIES TO ESCORT HERE. ALERA TOLD THEM TO WAIT FOR US AT THE HALFWAY MARK AND STAY OUT OF SIGHT.
THEY WILL HAVE WEAPONS ND VEHICLES TO GET US TO THE RT BEFORE OUR ENEMIES CAN FOLLOW US.
THEY SHOULD BE JUST ON THE OTHER SIDE OF THIS--
NO...
LOOKS LIKE THAT WHOLE "STAYING OUT OF SIGHT" THING DIDN'T WORK OUT SO WELL.

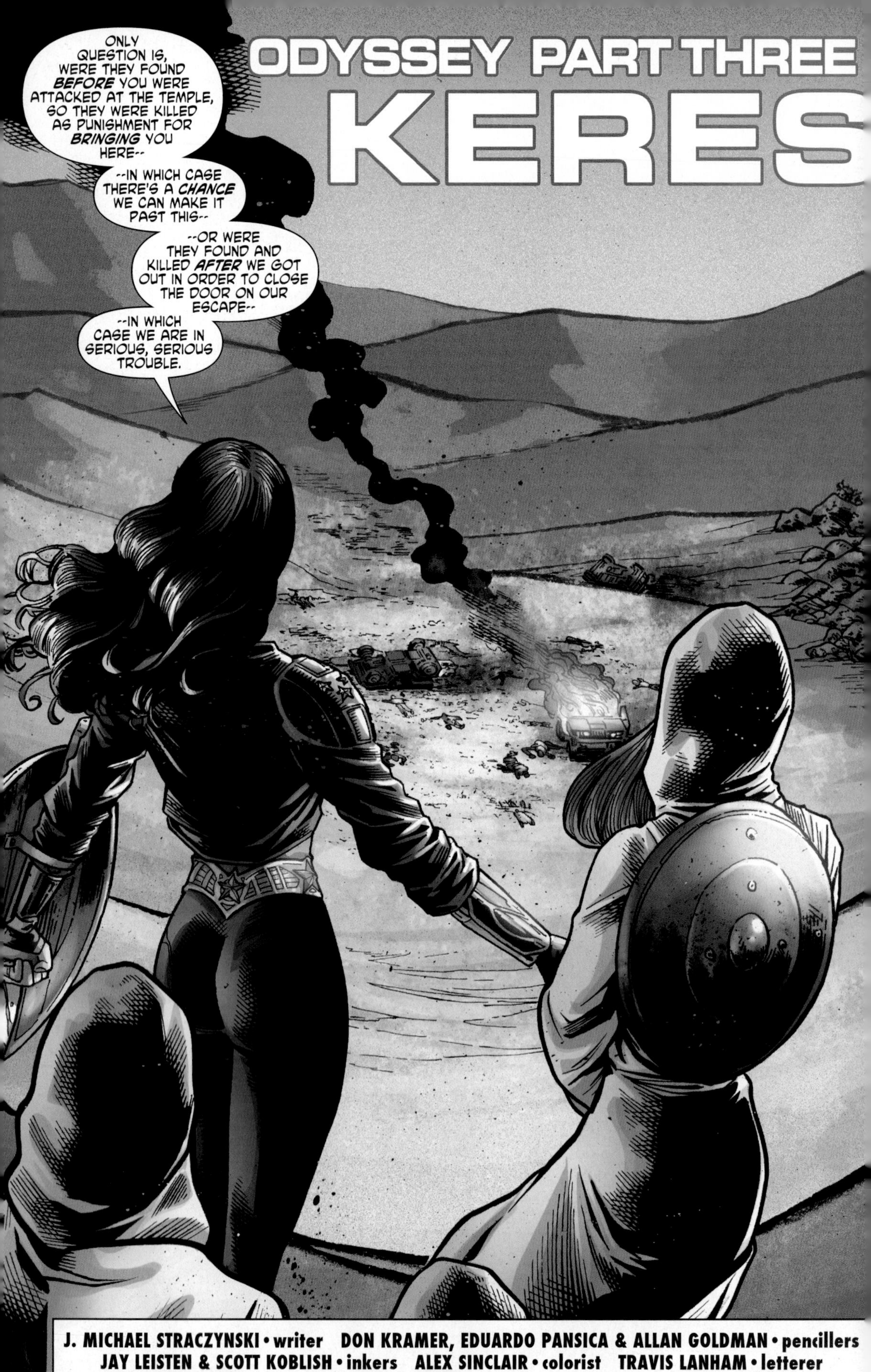

ODYSSEY PART THREE
KERES
ONLY QUESTION IS, WERE THEY FOUND BEFORE YOU WERE ATTACKED AT THE TEMPLE, SO THEY WERE KILLED AS PUNISHMENT FOR BRINGING YOU HERE--
--IN WHICH CASE THERE'S A CHANCE WE CAN MAKE IT PAST THIS--
--OR WERE THEY FOUND AND KILLED AFTER WE GOT OUT IN ORDER TO CLOSE THE DOOR ON OUR ESCAPE--
--IN WHICH CASE WE ARE IN SERIOUS, SERIOUS TROUBLE.

J. MICHAEL STRACZYNSKI • writer DON KRAMER, EDUARDO PANSICA & ALLAN GOLDMAN • pencillers JAY LEISTEN & SCOTT KOBLISH • inkers ALEX SINCLAIR • colorist TRAVIS LANHAM • letterer KRAMER with SINCLAIR • cover ALEX GARNER • variant cover SEAN RYAN • assoc. editor BRIAN CUNNINGHAM • editor WONDER WOMAN created by WILLIAM MOULTON MARSTON

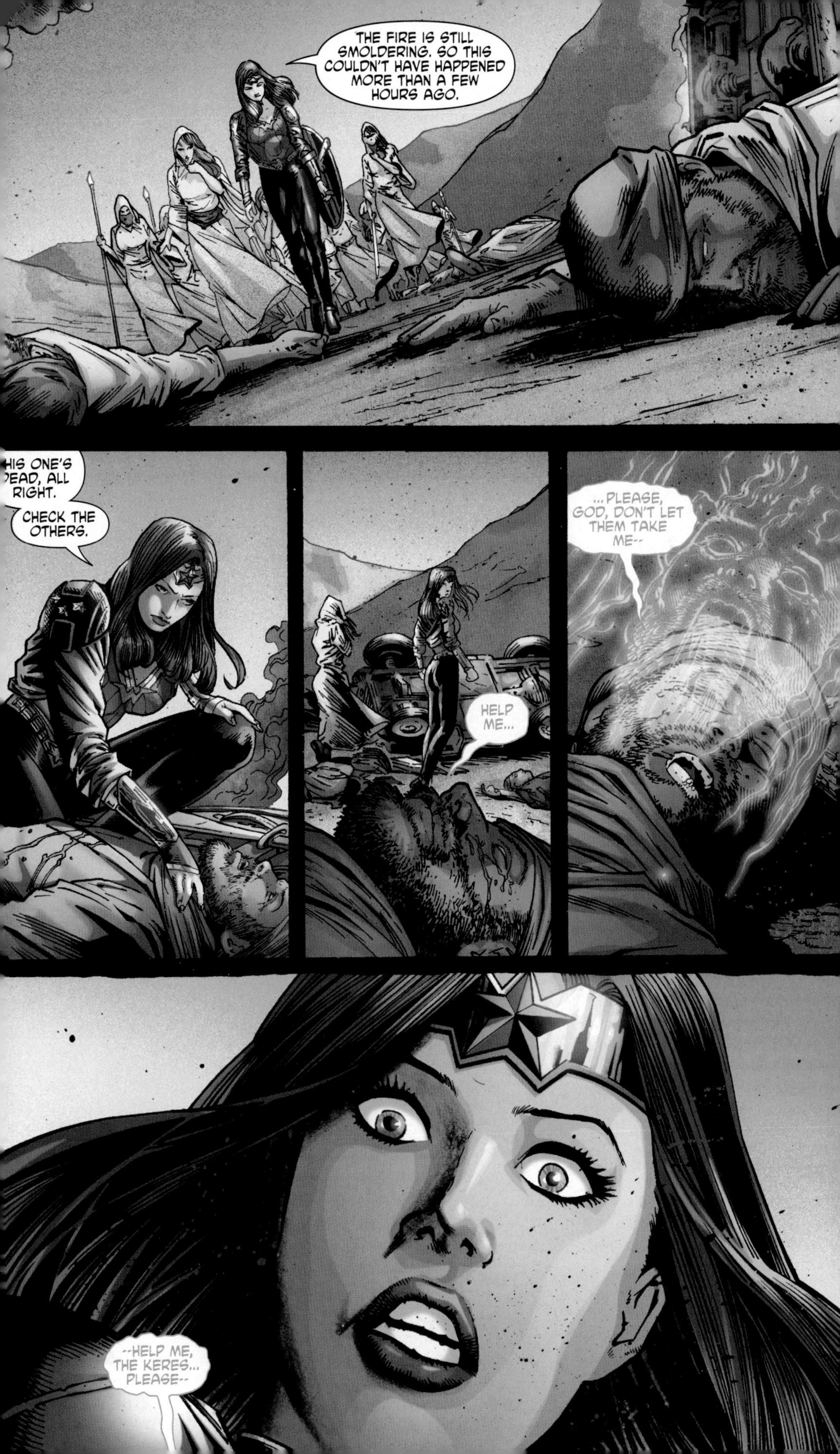
THE FIRE IS STILL SMOLDERING. SO THIS COULDN'T HAVE HAPPENED MORE THAN A FEW HOURS AGO.
HIS ONE'S DEAD, ALL RIGHT.
CHECK THE OTHERS.
HELP ME...
...PLEASE, GOD, DON'T LET THEM TAKE ME--
--HELP ME, THE KERES... PLEASE--

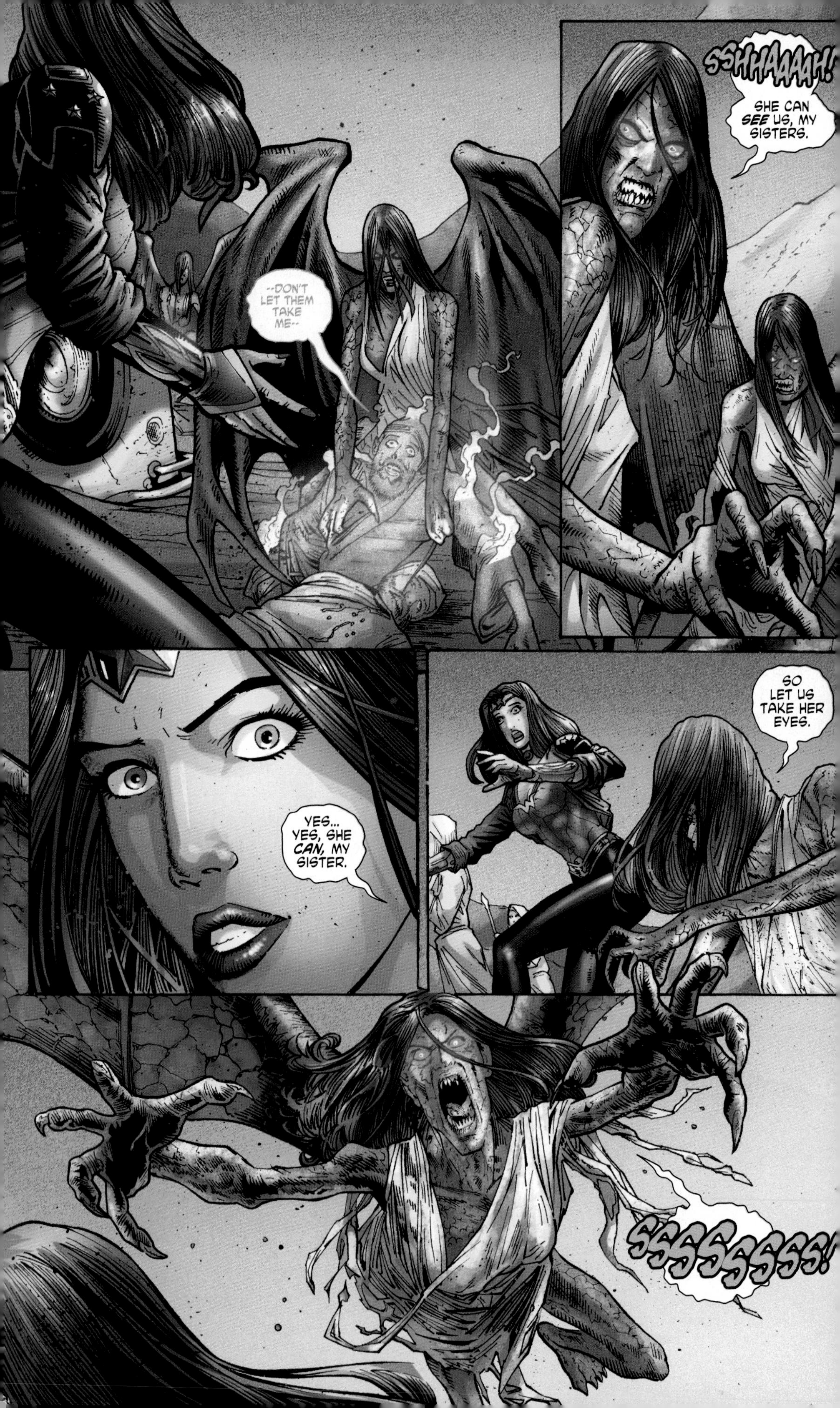
--DON'T LET THEM TAKE ME--
SSHHAAAAH!
SHE CAN SEE US, MY SISTERS.
YES... YES, SHE CAN, MY SISTER.
SO LET US TAKE HER EYES.
SSSSSSSSS!

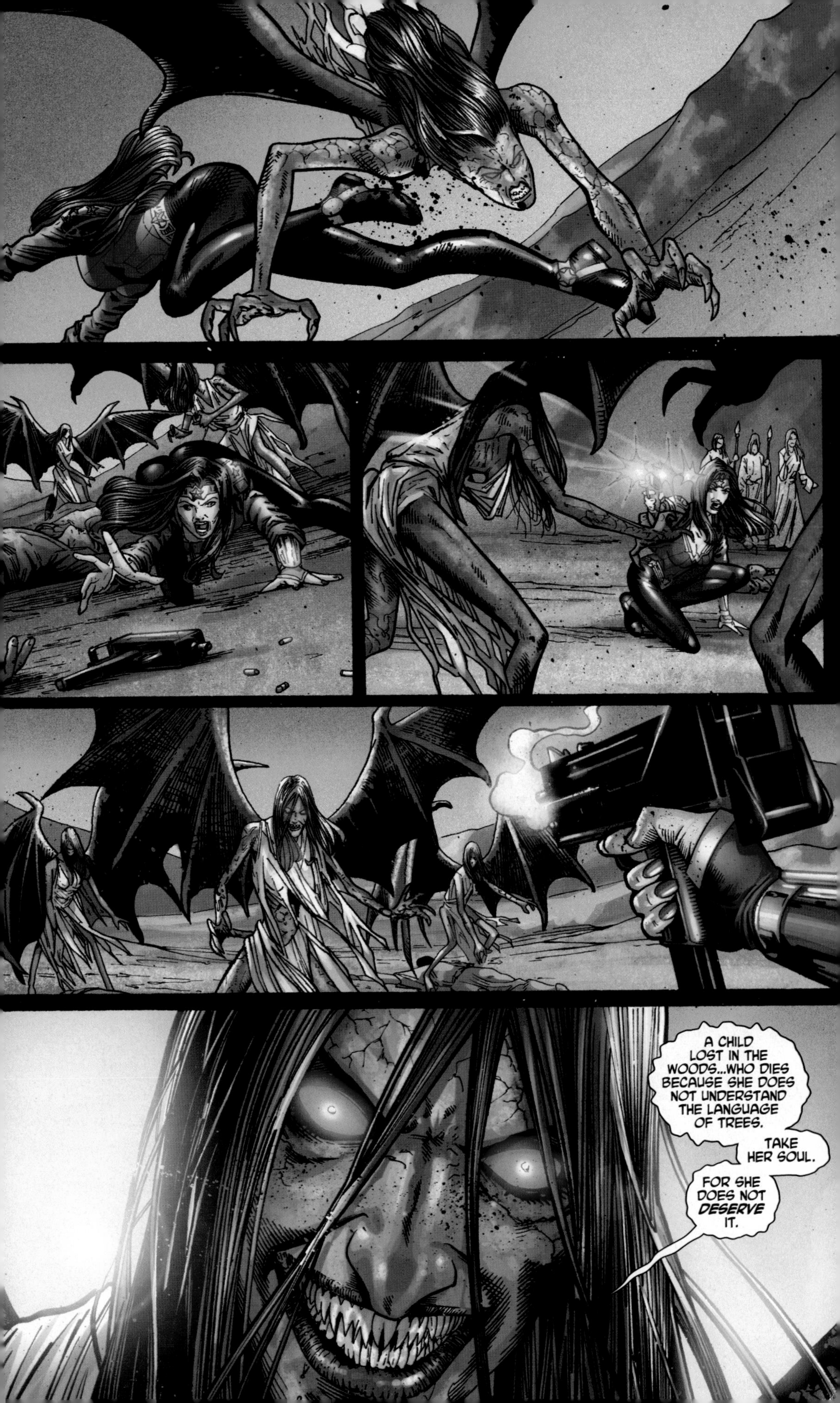
A CHILD LOST IN THE WOODS...WHO DIES BECAUSE SHE DOES NOT UNDERSTAND THE LANGUAGE OF TREES.
TAKE HER SOUL.
FOR SHE DOES NOT *DESERVE* IT.

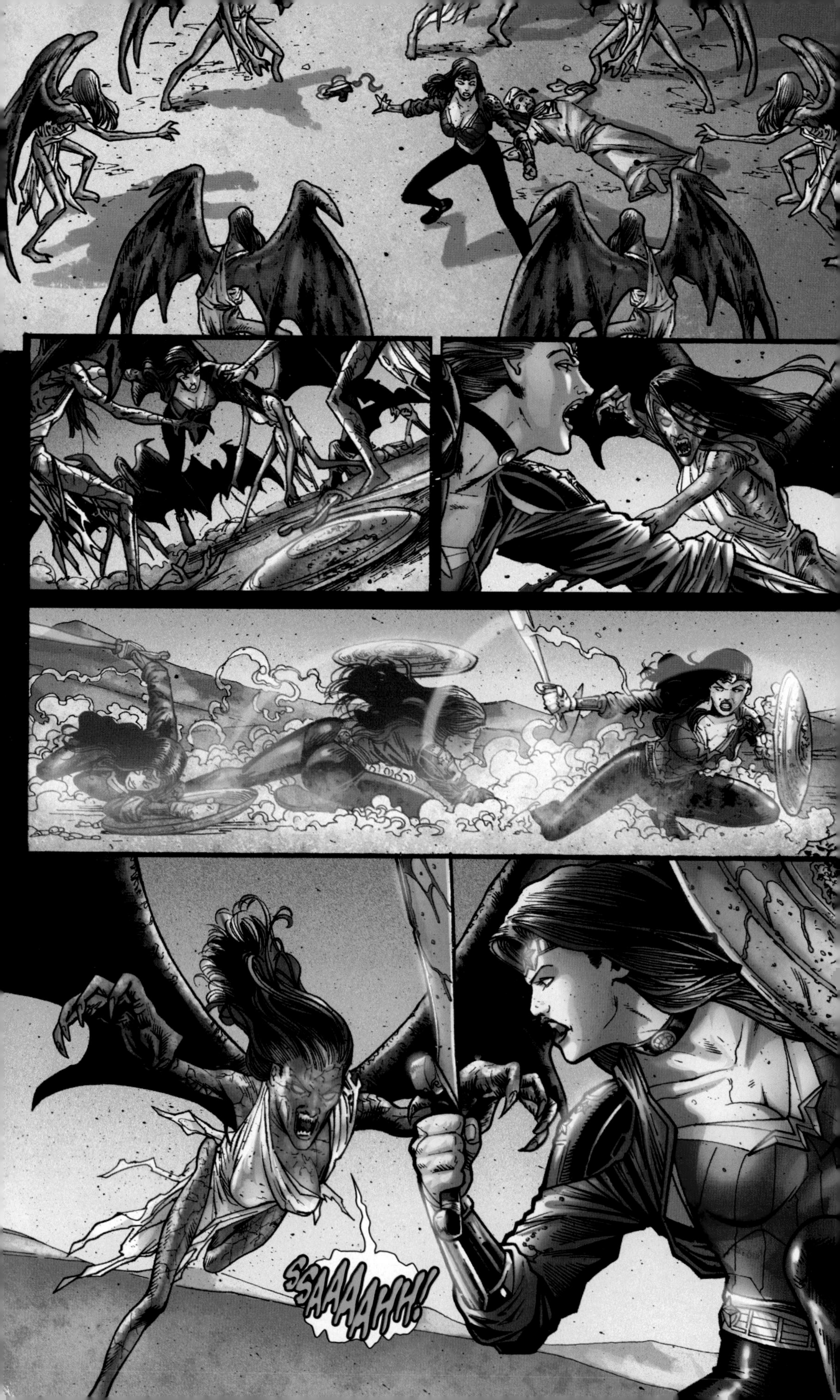
SSAAAAHH!

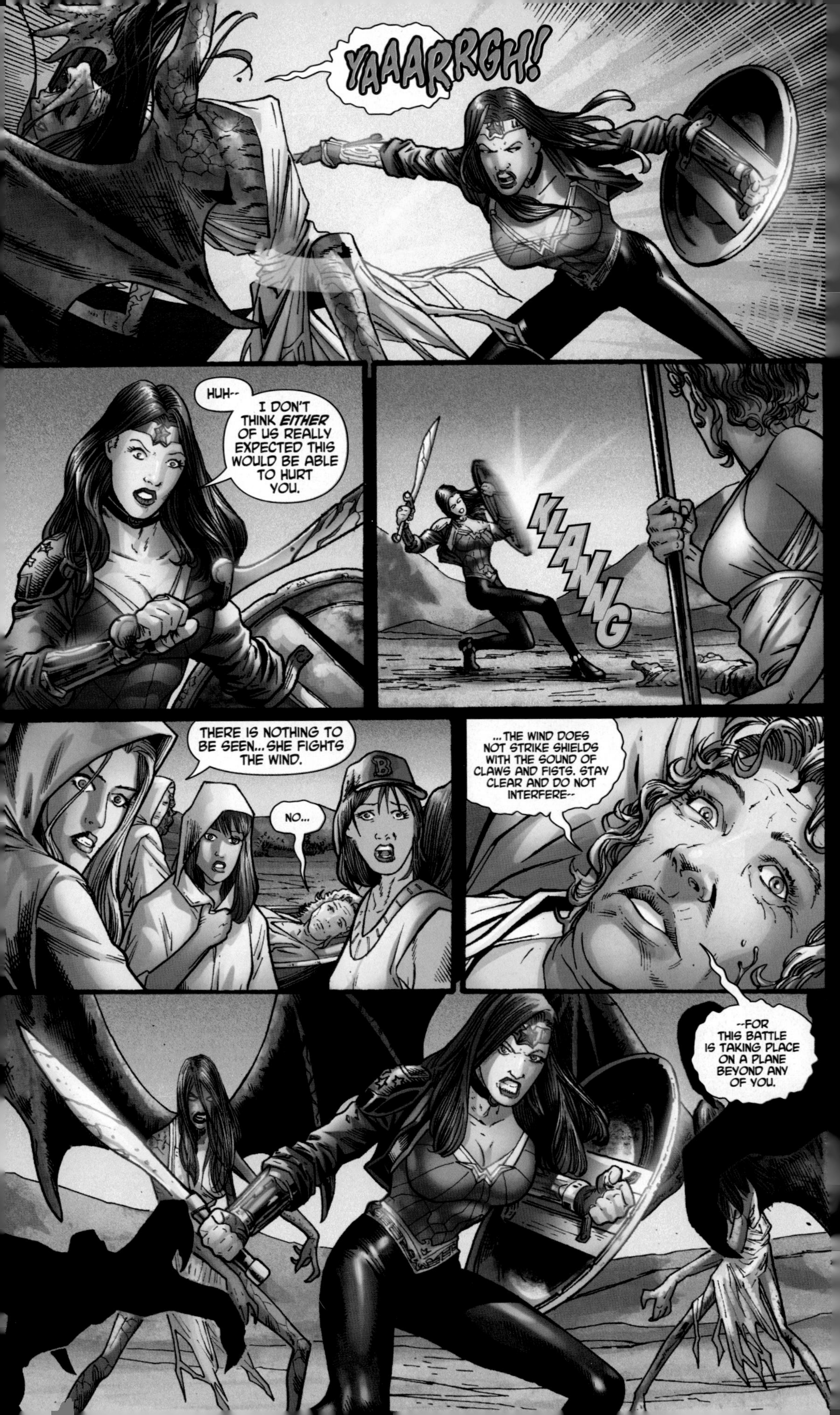
YAAARRGH!
HUH--
I DON'T THINK *EITHER* OF US REALLY EXPECTED THIS WOULD BE ABLE TO HURT YOU.
KLANNG
THERE IS NOTHING TO BE SEEN... SHE FIGHTS THE WIND.
NO...
...THE WIND DOES NOT STRIKE SHIELDS WITH THE SOUND OF CLAWS AND FISTS. STAY CLEAR AND DO NOT INTERFERE--
--FOR THIS BATTLE IS TAKING PLACE ON A PLANE BEYOND ANY OF YOU.

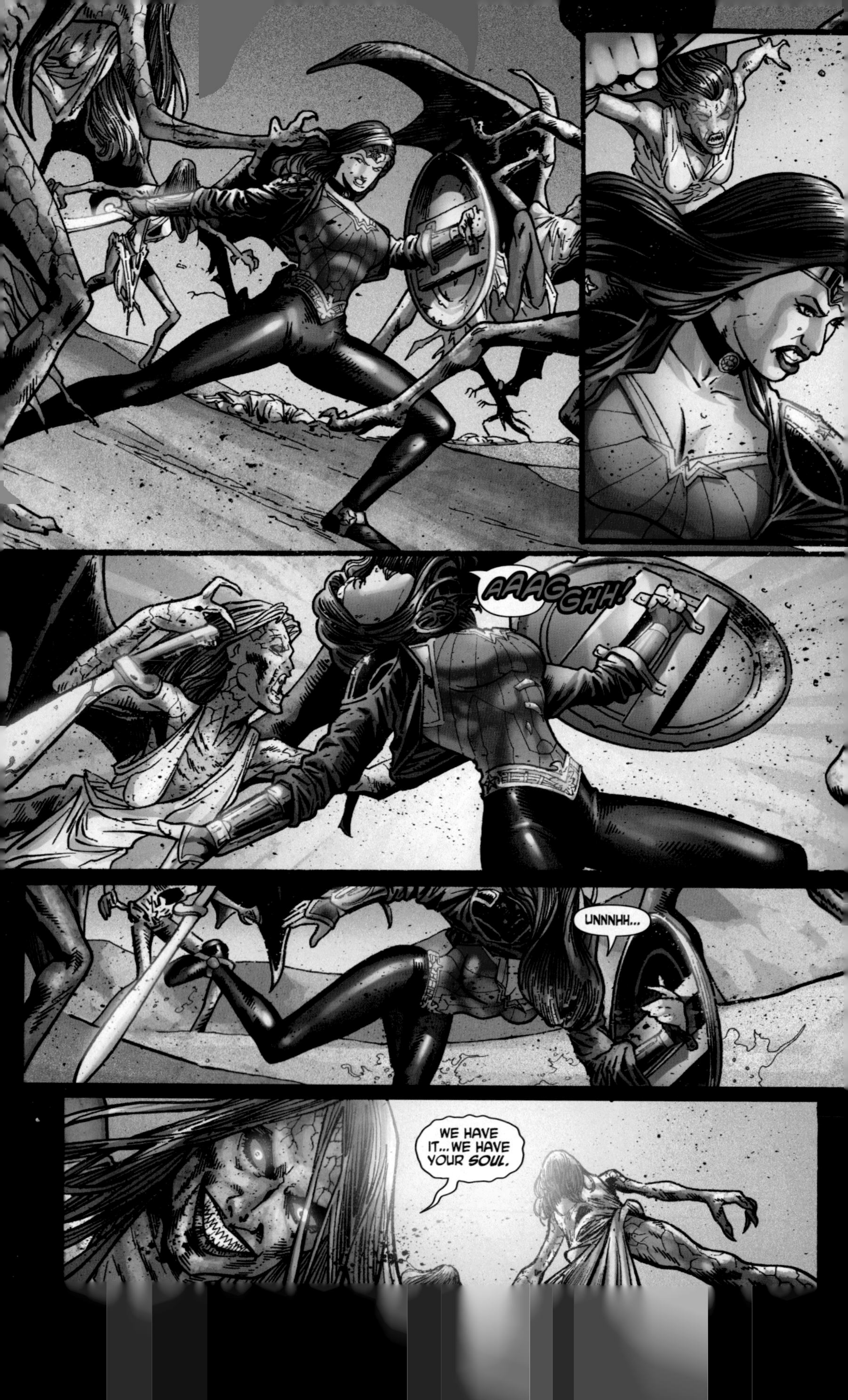
AAAGGHH!
UNNNHH...
WE HAVE IT... WE HAVE YOUR SOUL.

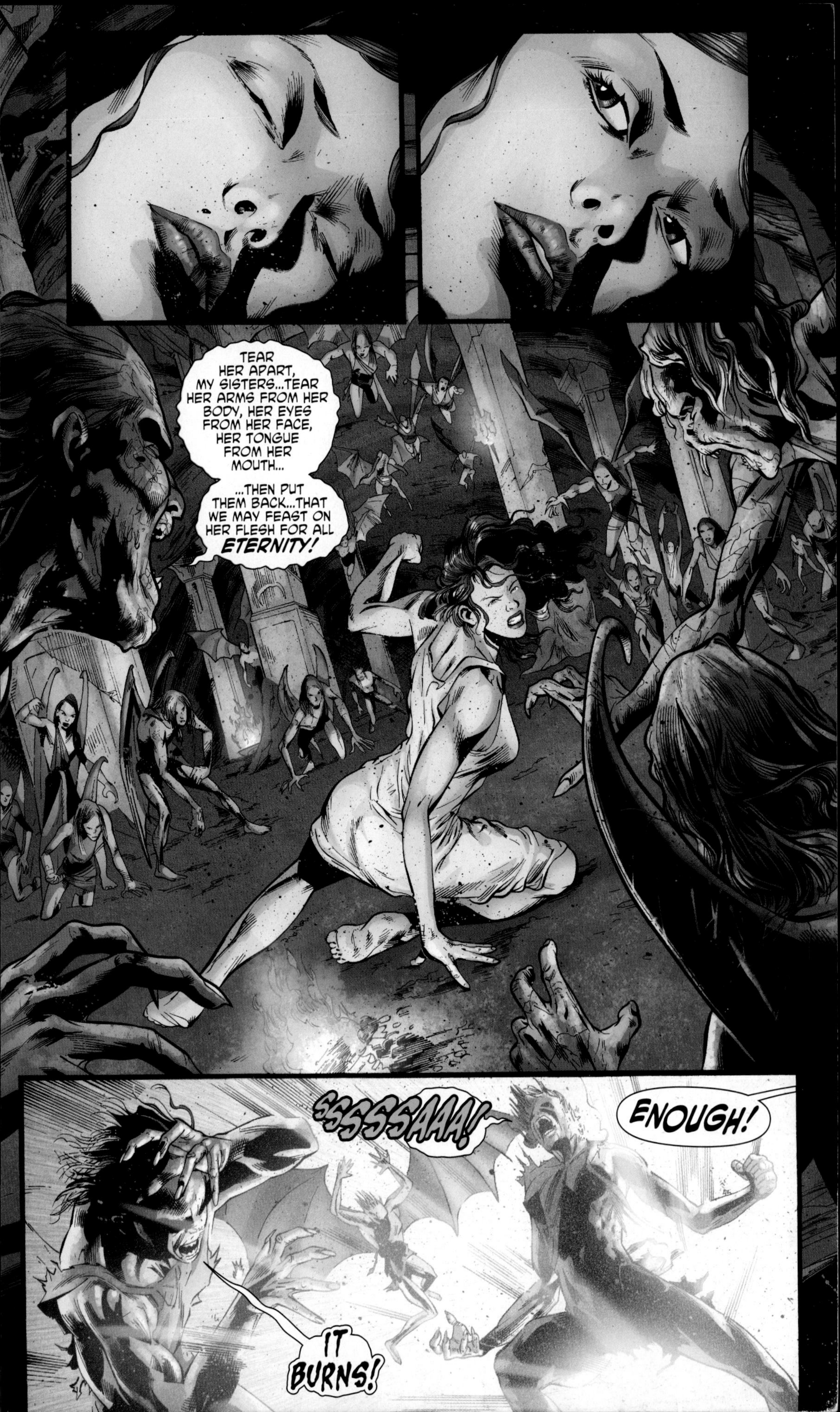
TEAR HER APART, MY SISTERS...TEAR HER ARMS FROM HER BODY, HER EYES FROM HER FACE, HER TONGUE FROM HER MOUTH...
...THEN PUT THEM BACK...THAT WE MAY FEAST ON HER FLESH FOR ALL ETERNITY!
SSSSSAAA!
ENOUGH!
IT BURNS!

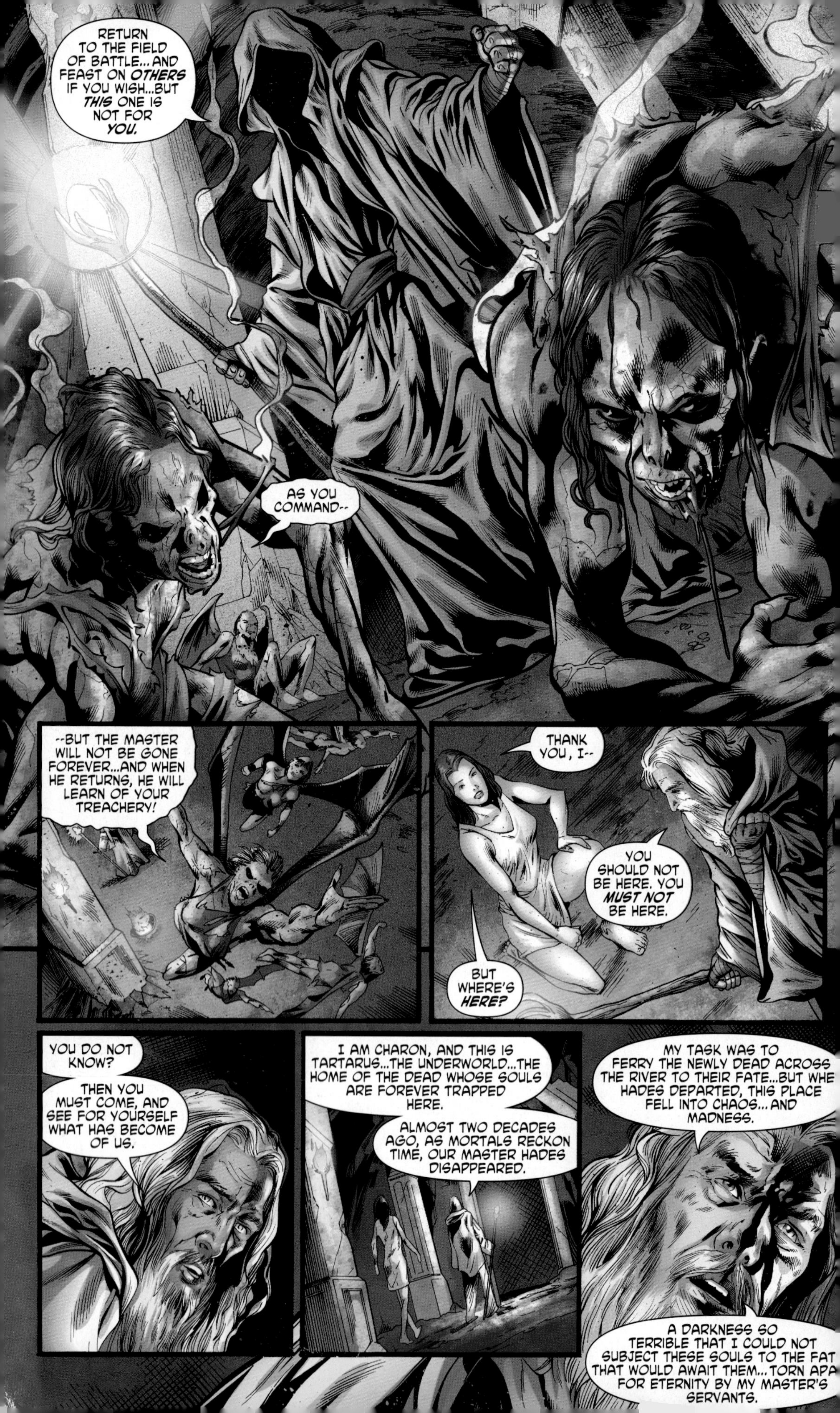
RETURN TO THE FIELD OF BATTLE...AND FEAST ON *OTHERS* IF YOU WISH...BUT *THIS* ONE IS NOT FOR *YOU.*
AS YOU COMMAND--
--BUT THE MASTER WILL NOT BE GONE FOREVER...AND WHEN HE RETURNS, HE WILL LEARN OF YOUR TREACHERY!
THANK YOU, I--
YOU SHOULD NOT BE HERE. YOU *MUST NOT* BE HERE.
BUT WHERE'S *HERE?*
YOU DO NOT KNOW?
THEN YOU MUST COME, AND SEE FOR YOURSELF WHAT HAS BECOME OF US.
I AM CHARON, AND THIS IS TARTARUS...THE UNDERWORLD...THE HOME OF THE DEAD WHOSE SOULS ARE FOREVER TRAPPED HERE.
ALMOST TWO DECADES AGO, AS MORTALS RECKON TIME, OUR MASTER HADES DISAPPEARED.
MY TASK WAS TO FERRY THE NEWLY DEAD ACROSS THE RIVER TO THEIR FATE...BUT WHE HADES DEPARTED, THIS PLACE FELL INTO CHAOS...AND MADNESS.
A DARKNESS SO TERRIBLE THAT I COULD NOT SUBJECT THESE SOULS TO THE FAT THAT WOULD AWAIT THEM...TORN APA FOR ETERNITY BY MY MASTER'S SERVANTS.

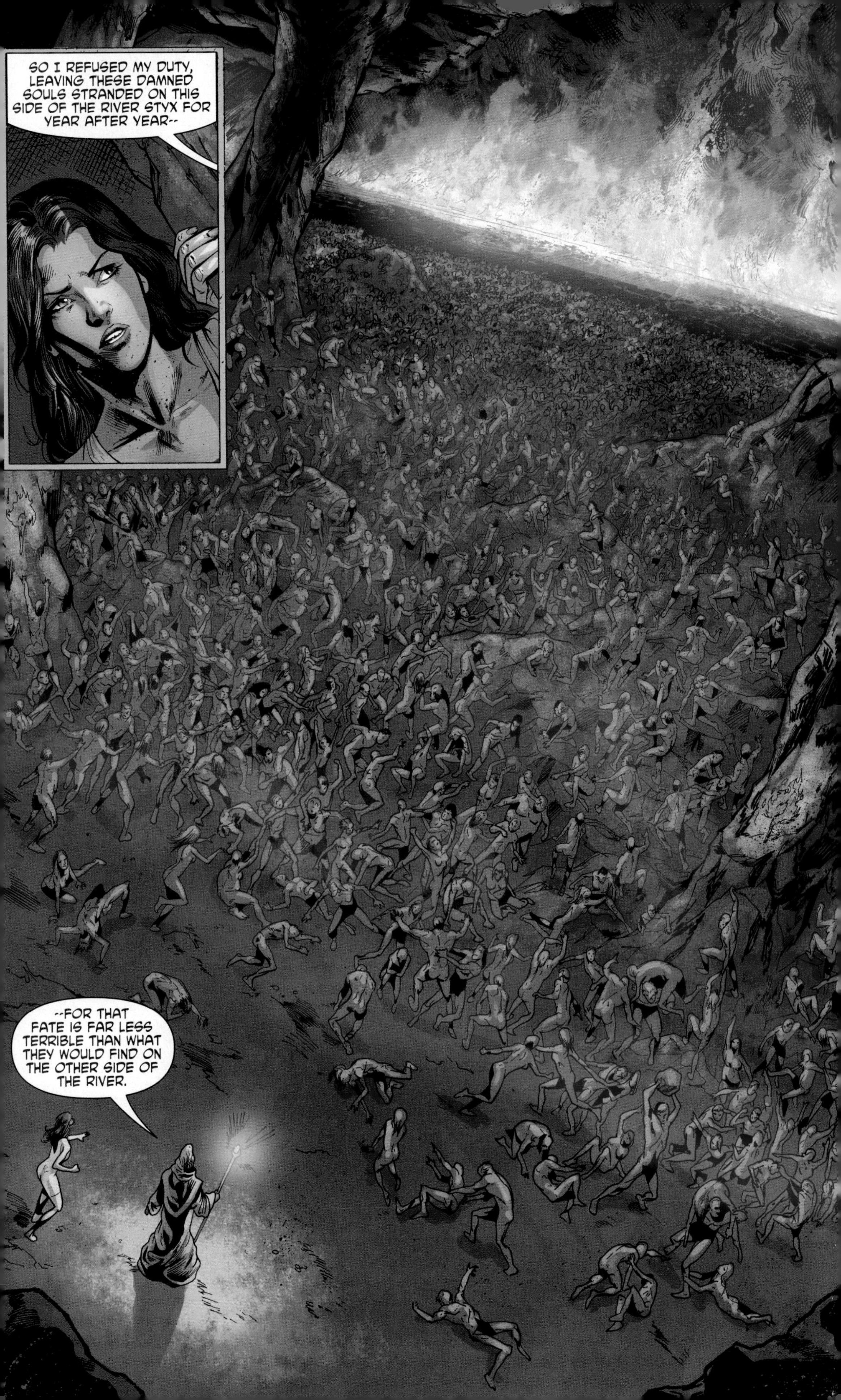
SO I REFUSED MY DUTY, LEAVING THESE DAMNED SOULS STRANDED ON THIS SIDE OF THE RIVER STYX FOR YEAR AFTER YEAR--
--FOR THAT FATE IS FAR LESS TERRIBLE THAN WHAT THEY WOULD FIND ON THE OTHER SIDE OF THE RIVER.

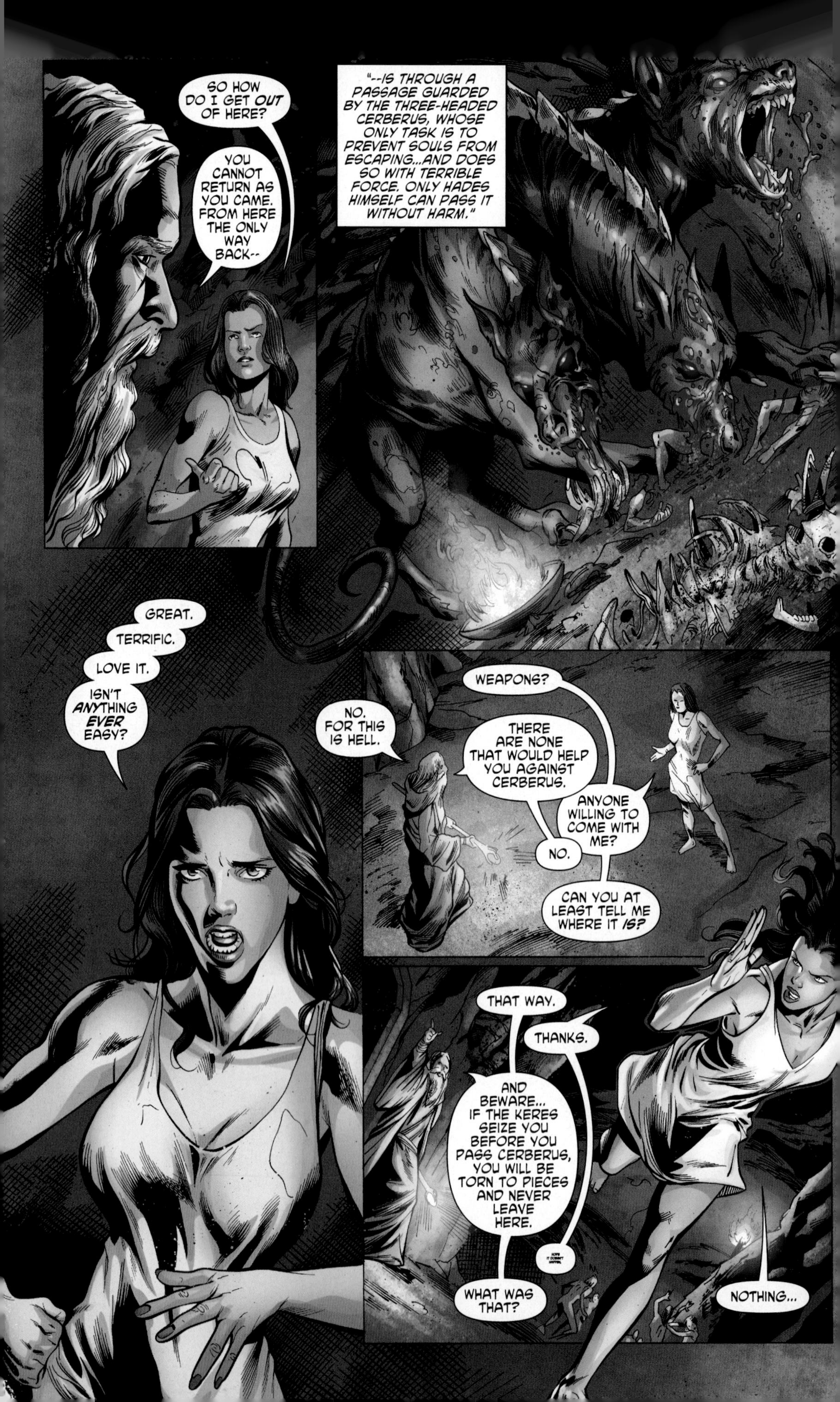

SO HOW DO I GET OUT OF HERE?
YOU CANNOT RETURN AS YOU CAME. FROM HERE THE ONLY WAY BACK--
"--IS THROUGH A PASSAGE GUARDED BY THE THREE-HEADED CERBERUS, WHOSE ONLY TASK IS TO PREVENT SOULS FROM ESCAPING...AND DOES SO WITH TERRIBLE FORCE. ONLY HADES HIMSELF CAN PASS IT WITHOUT HARM."
GREAT.
TERRIFIC.
LOVE IT.
ISN'T ANYTHING EVER EASY?
WEAPONS?
THERE ARE NONE THAT WOULD HELP YOU AGAINST CERBERUS.
NO. FOR THIS IS HELL.
ANYONE WILLING TO COME WITH ME?
NO.
CAN YOU AT LEAST TELL ME WHERE IT IS?
THAT WAY.
THANKS.
AND BEWARE... IF THE KERES SEIZE YOU BEFORE YOU PASS CERBERUS, YOU WILL BE TORN TO PIECES AND NEVER LEAVE HERE.
WHAT WAS THAT?
NOTHING...

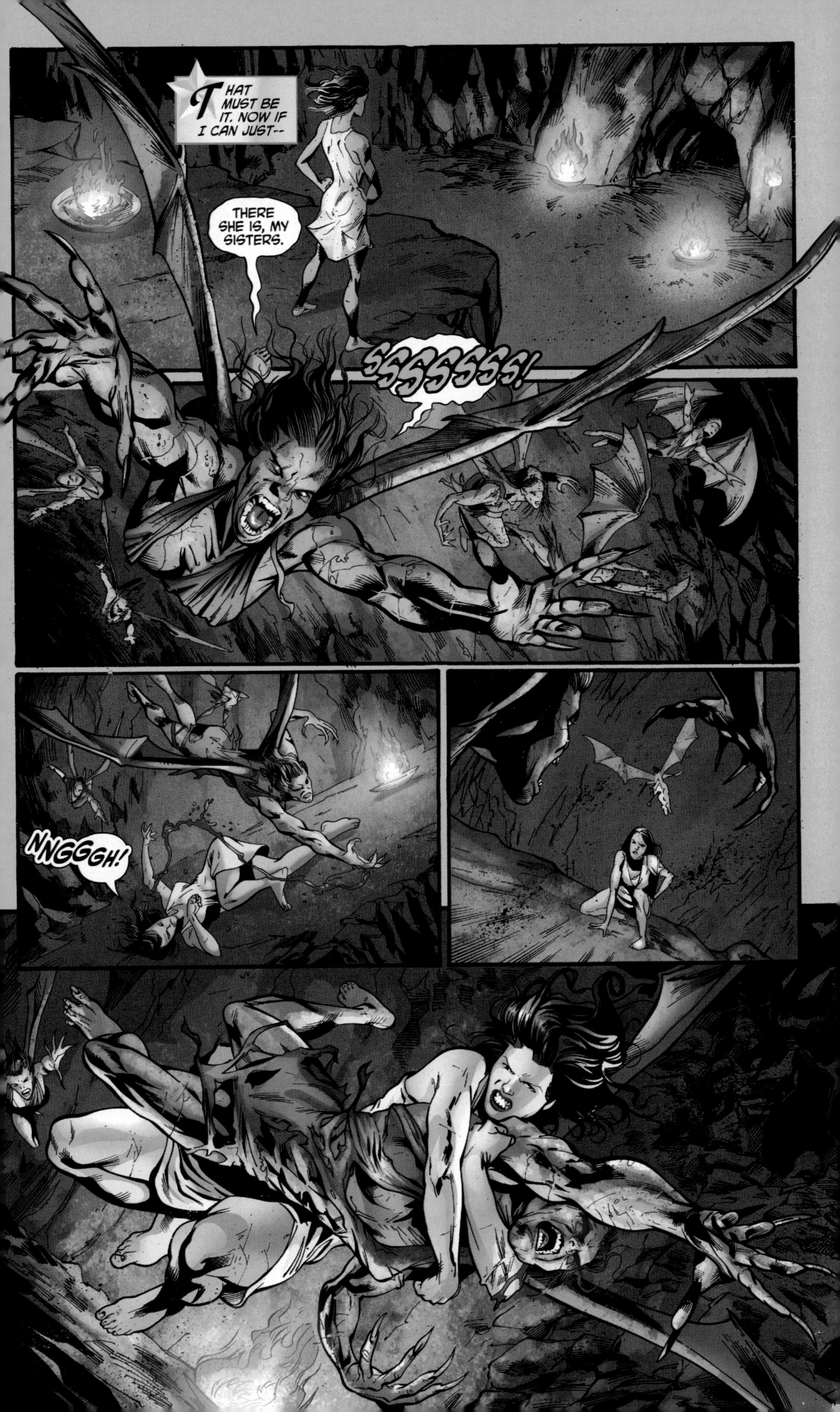
THAT MUST BE IT. NOW IF I CAN JUST--
THERE SHE IS, MY SISTERS.
SSSSSSSS!
NNGGGH!

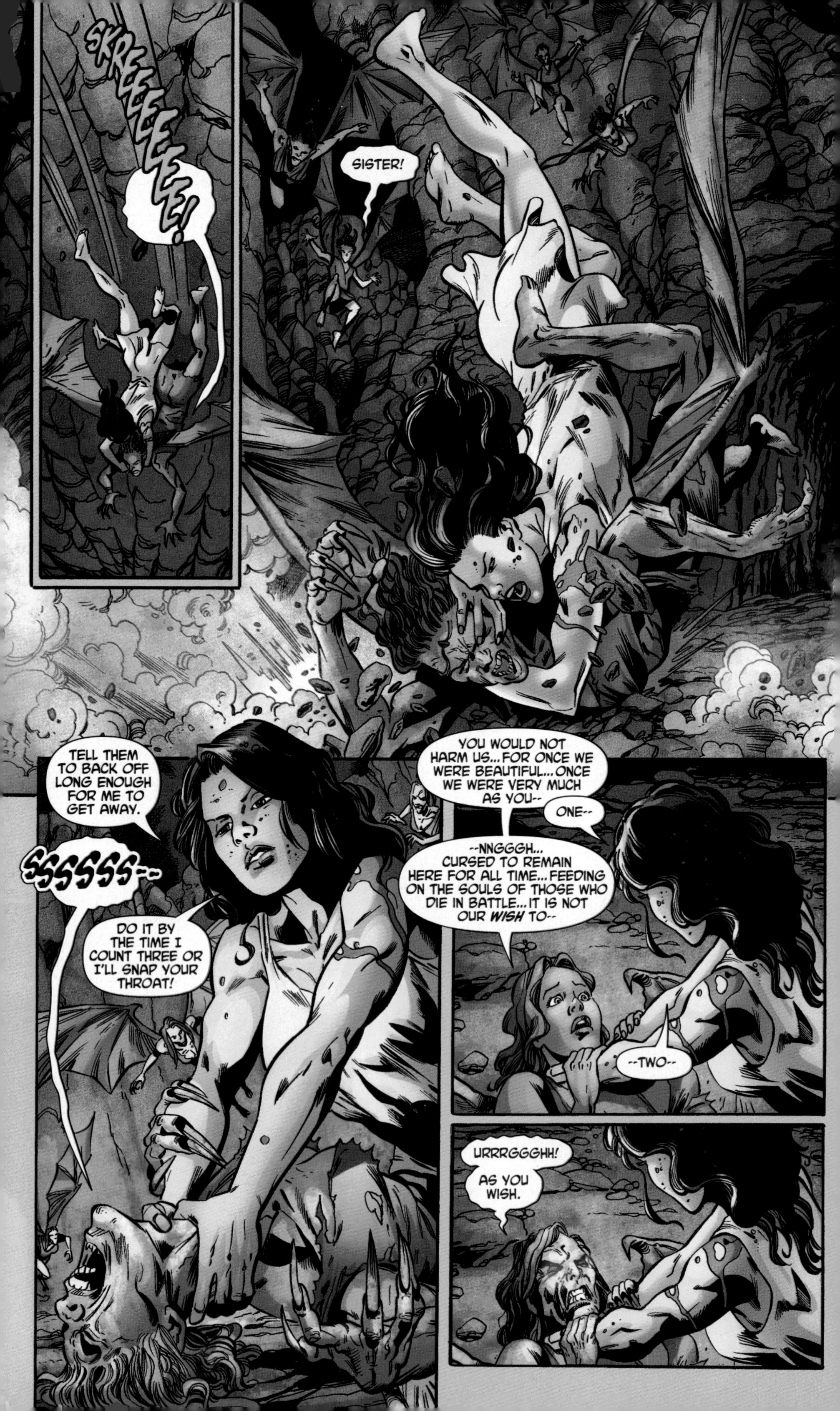
SKREEEEEEE!
SISTER!
TELL THEM TO BACK OFF LONG ENOUGH FOR ME TO GET AWAY.
SSSSSS--
DO IT BY THE TIME I COUNT THREE OR I'LL SNAP YOUR THROAT!
YOU WOULD NOT HARM US... FOR ONCE WE WERE BEAUTIFUL... ONCE WE WERE VERY MUCH AS YOU--
ONE--
--NNGGGH... CURSED TO REMAIN HERE FOR ALL TIME... FEEDING ON THE SOULS OF THOSE WHO DIE IN BATTLE... IT IS NOT OUR WISH TO--
--TWO--
URRRGGGHH!
AS YOU WISH.

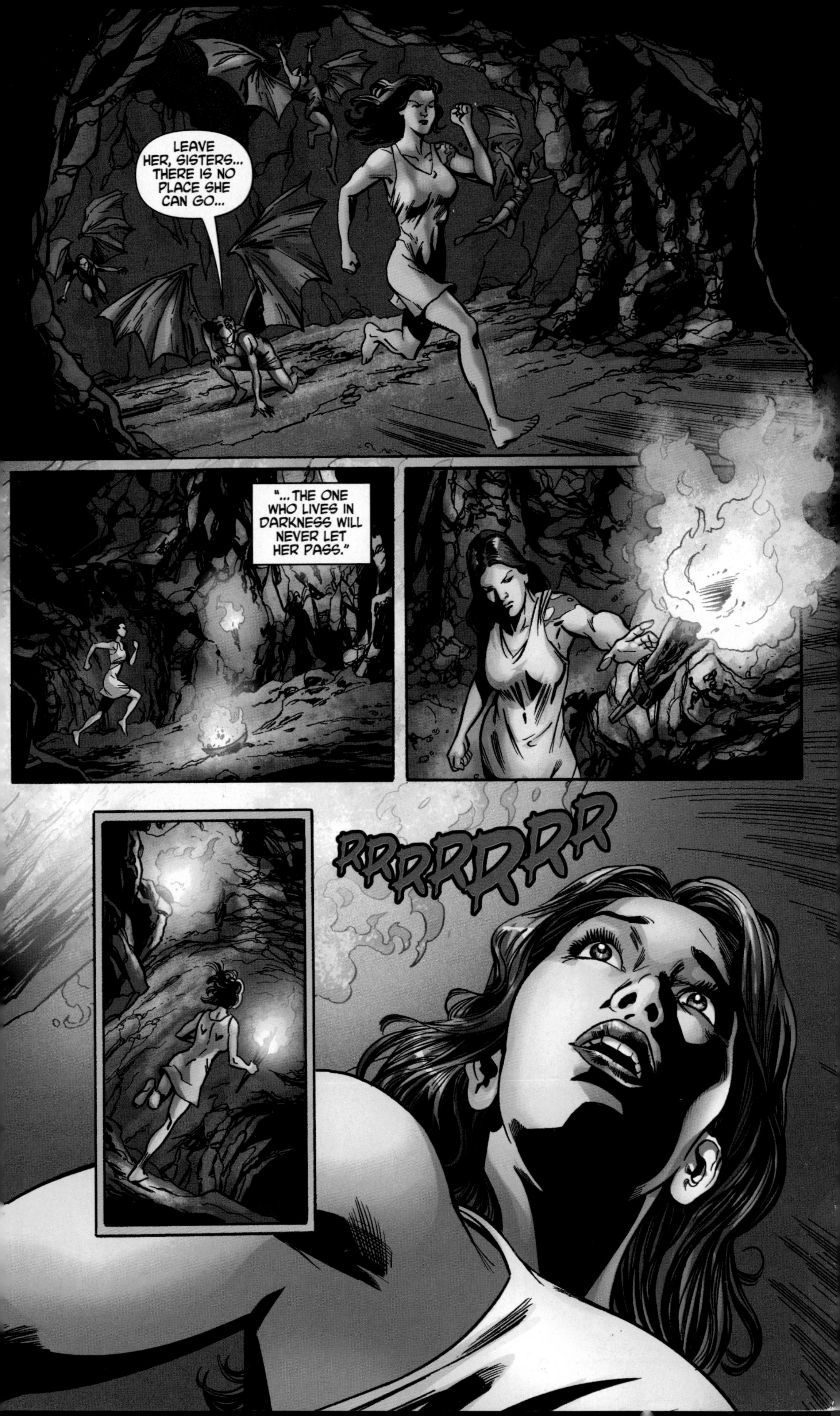
LEAVE HER, SISTERS... THERE IS NO PLACE SHE CAN GO...
"...THE ONE WHO LIVES IN DARKNESS WILL NEVER LET HER PASS."
RRRRRRRR

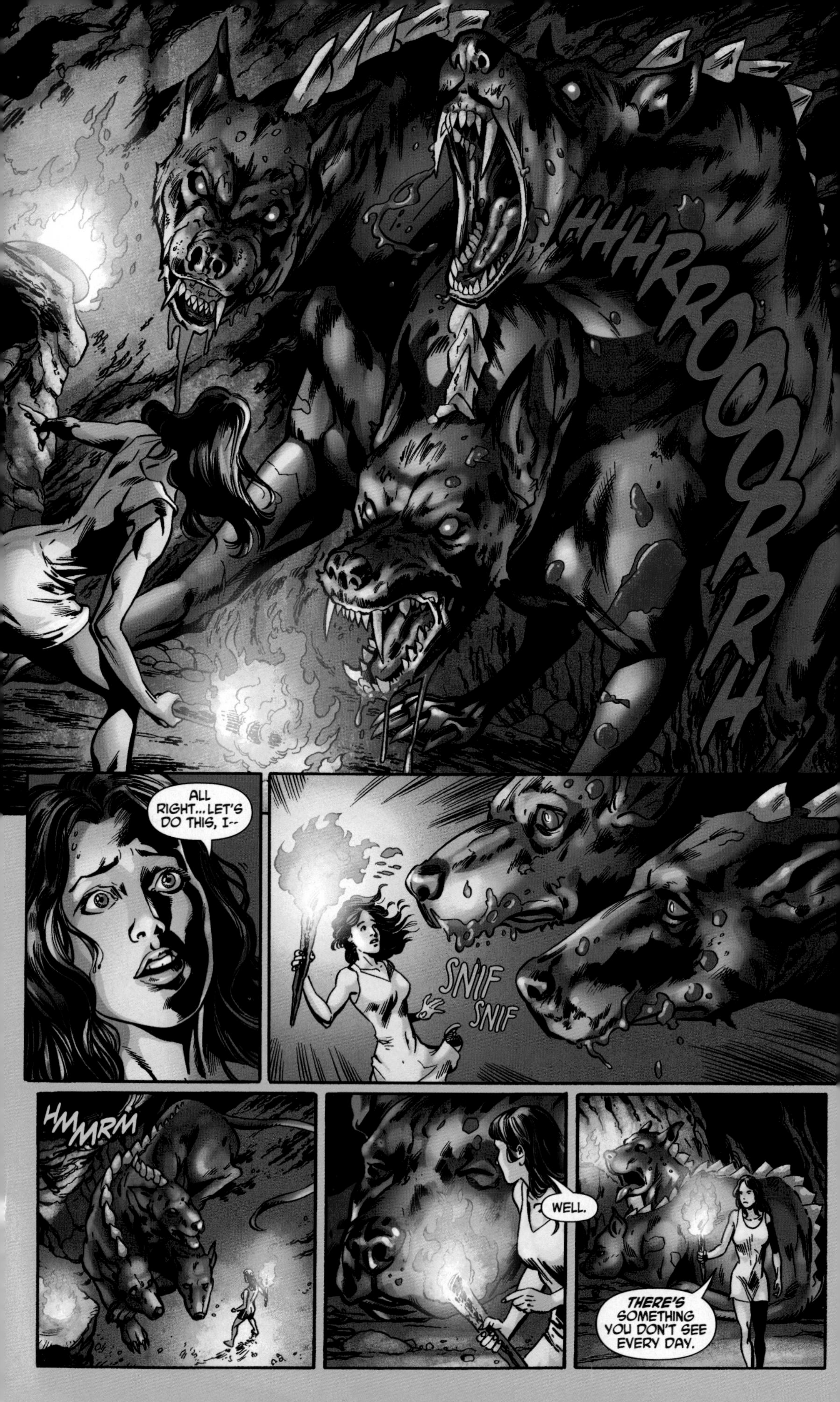
HHHRROOOORRH
ALL RIGHT...LET'S DO THIS, I--
SNIF SNIF
HMMRM
WELL.
THERE'S SOMETHING YOU DON'T SEE EVERY DAY.

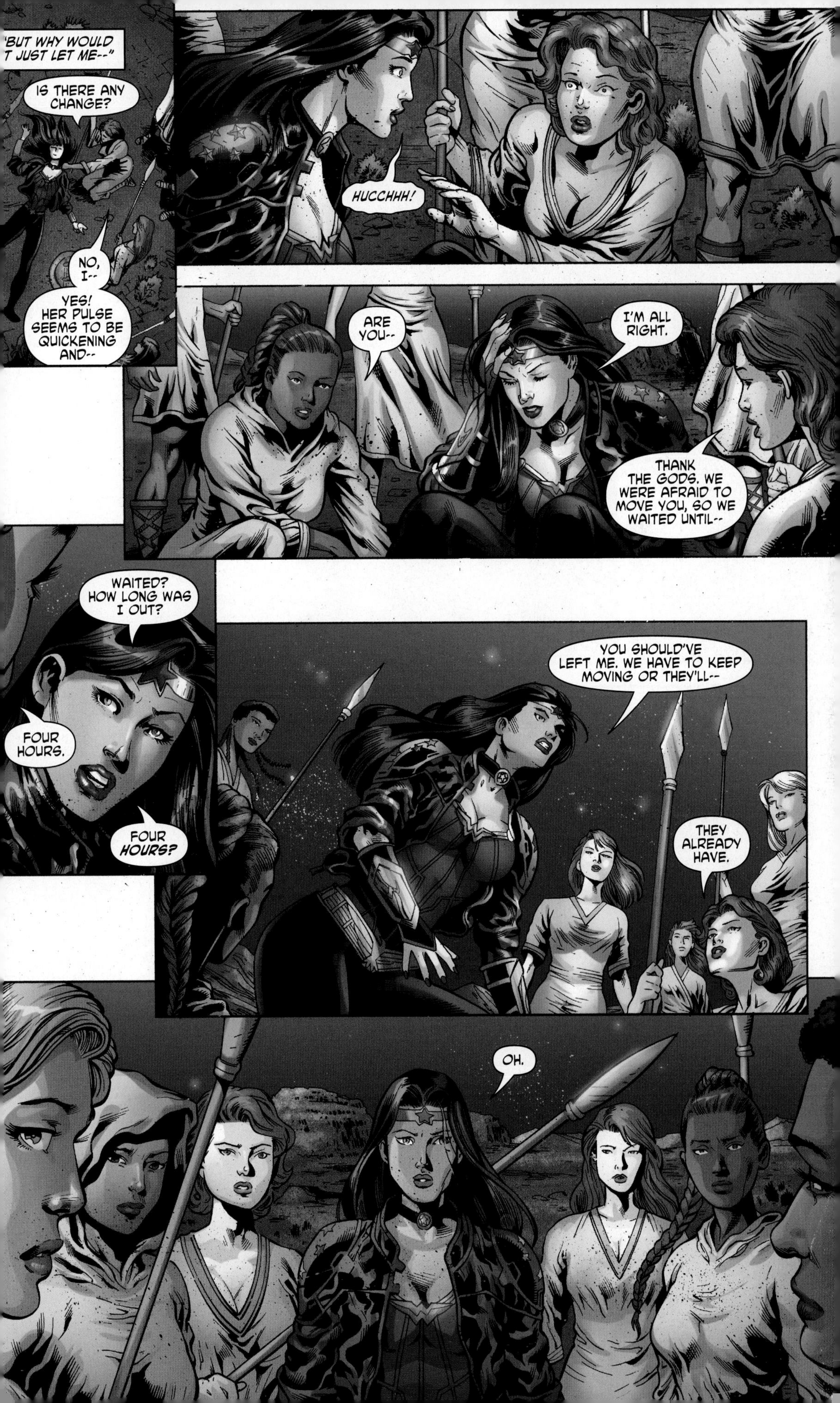
"BUT WHY WOULD
T JUST LET ME--"
IS THERE ANY CHANGE?
HUCCHHH!
NO, I--
YES! HER PULSE SEEMS TO BE QUICKENING AND--
ARE YOU--
I'M ALL RIGHT.
THANK THE GODS. WE WERE AFRAID TO MOVE YOU, SO WE WAITED UNTIL--
WAITED? HOW LONG WAS I OUT?
FOUR HOURS.
FOUR HOURS?
YOU SHOULD'VE LEFT ME. WE HAVE TO KEEP MOVING OR THEY'LL--
THEY ALREADY HAVE.
OH.

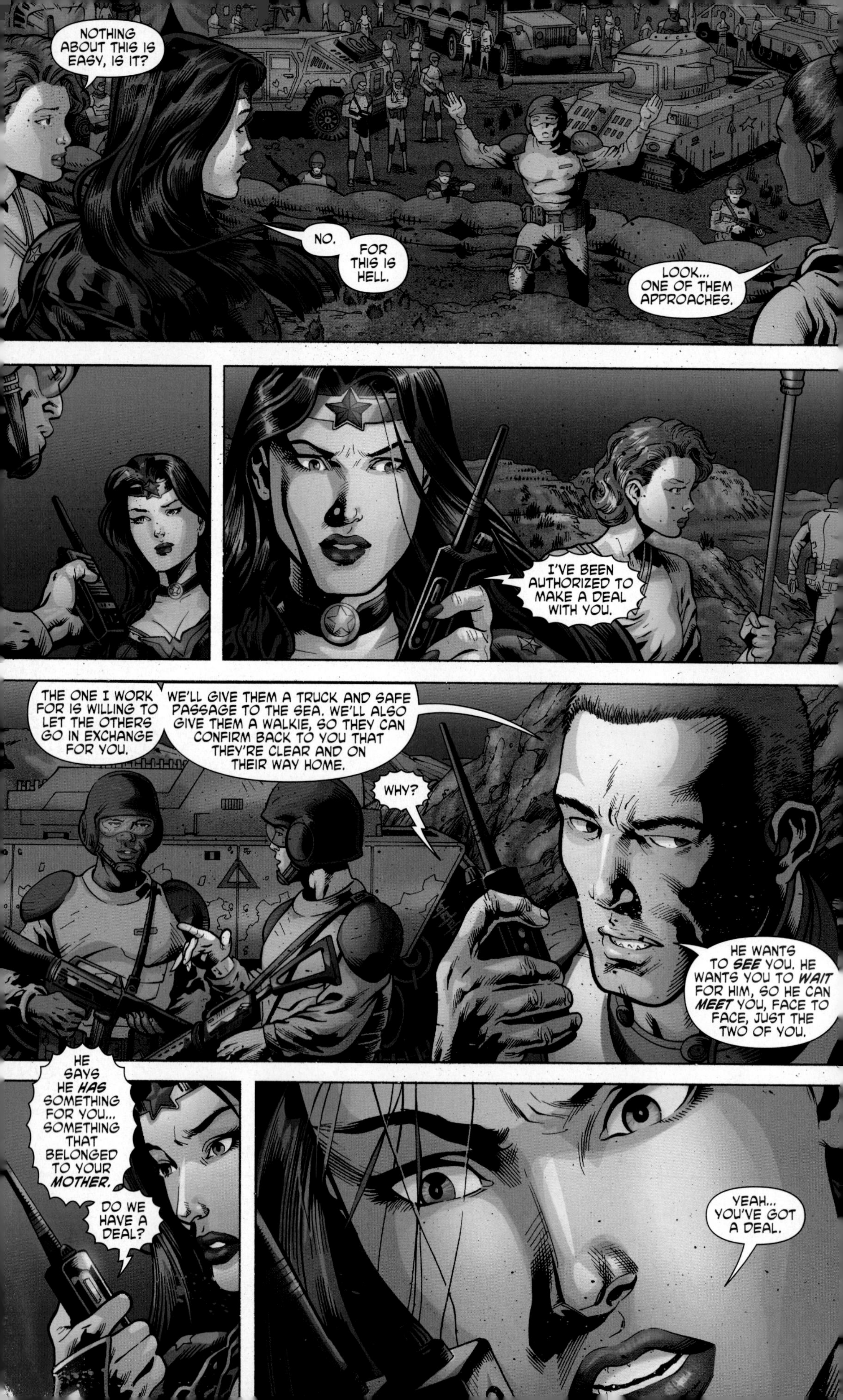

NOTHING ABOUT THIS IS EASY, IS IT?
NO. FOR THIS IS HELL.
LOOK... ONE OF THEM APPROACHES.
I'VE BEEN AUTHORIZED TO MAKE A DEAL WITH YOU.
THE ONE I WORK FOR IS WILLING TO LET THE OTHERS GO IN EXCHANGE FOR YOU.
WE'LL GIVE THEM A TRUCK AND SAFE PASSAGE TO THE SEA. WE'LL ALSO GIVE THEM A WALKIE, SO THEY CAN CONFIRM BACK TO YOU THAT THEY'RE CLEAR AND ON THEIR WAY HOME.
WHY?
HE WANTS TO SEE YOU. HE WANTS YOU TO WAIT FOR HIM, SO HE CAN MEET YOU, FACE TO FACE, JUST THE TWO OF YOU.
HE SAYS HE HAS SOMETHING FOR YOU... SOMETHING THAT BELONGED TO YOUR MOTHER.
DO WE HAVE A DEAL?
YEAH... YOU'VE GOT A DEAL.

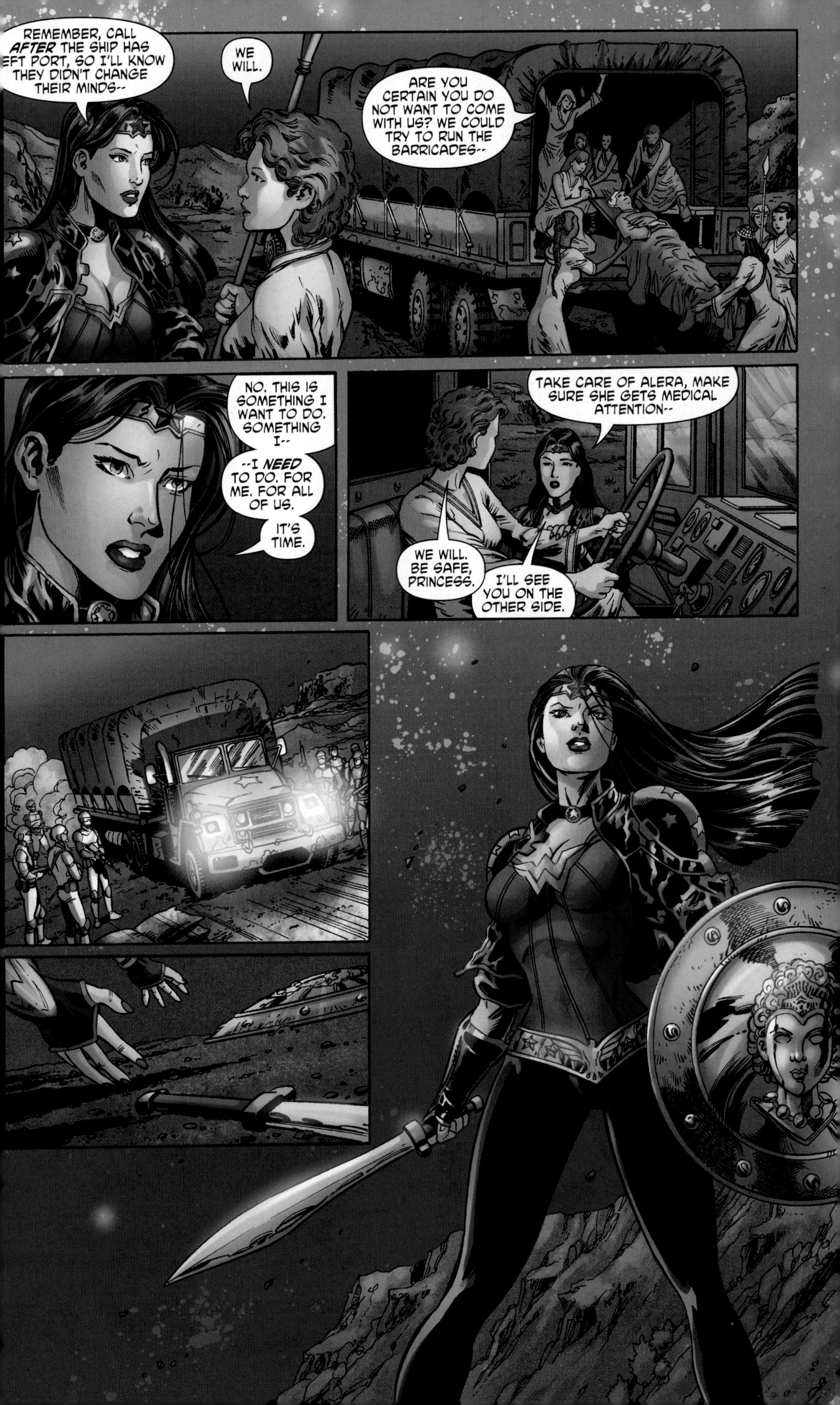

REMEMBER, CALL *AFTER* THE SHIP HAS LEFT PORT, SO I'LL KNOW THEY DIDN'T CHANGE THEIR MINDS--
WE WILL.
ARE YOU CERTAIN YOU DO NOT WANT TO COME WITH US? WE COULD TRY TO RUN THE BARRICADES--
NO. THIS IS SOMETHING I WANT TO DO. SOMETHING I--
--I *NEED* TO DO. FOR ME. FOR ALL OF US.
IT'S TIME.
TAKE CARE OF ALERA, MAKE SURE SHE GETS MEDICAL ATTENTION--
WE WILL. BE SAFE, PRINCESS.
I'LL SEE YOU ON THE OTHER SIDE.

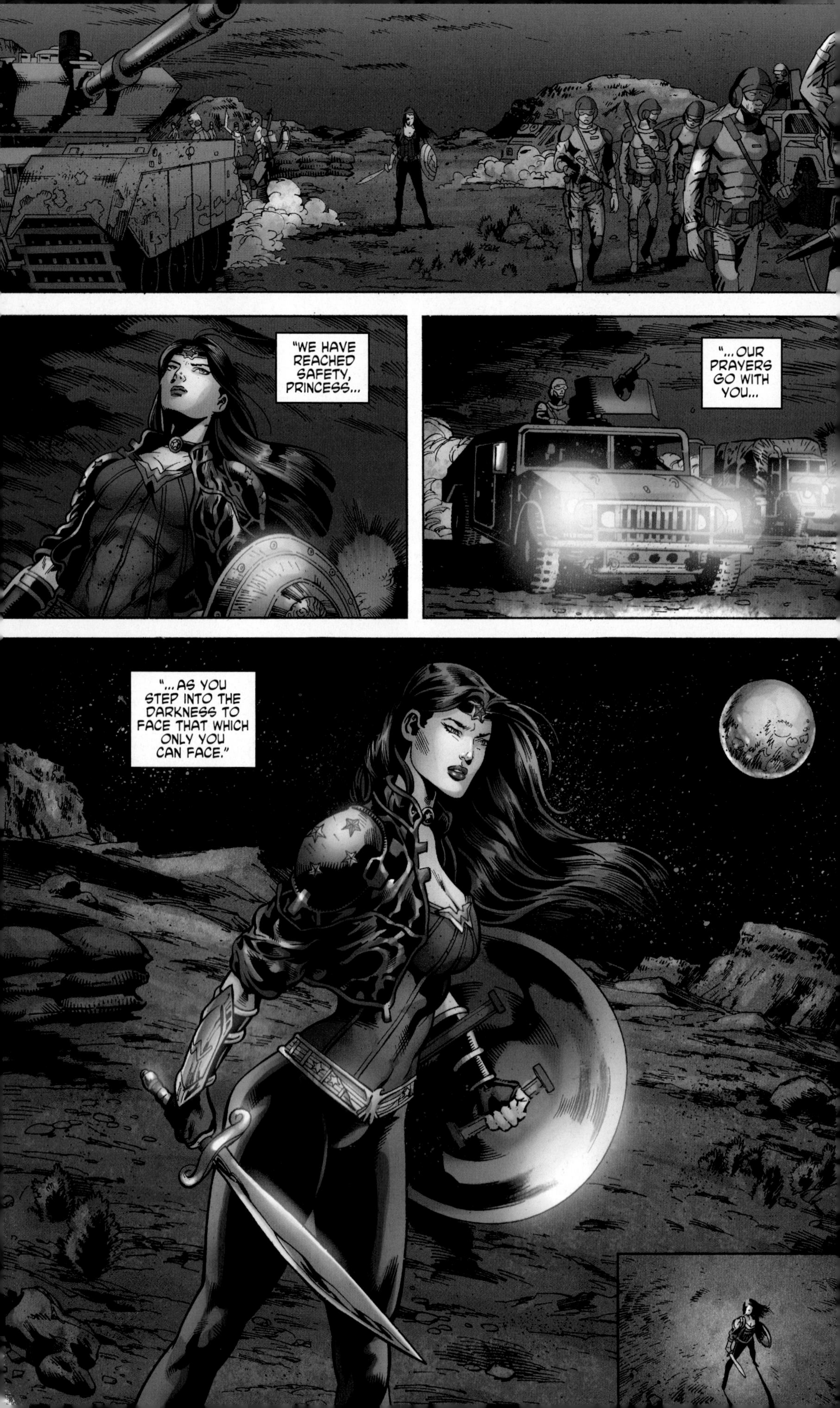
"WE HAVE REACHED SAFETY, PRINCESS...
"...OUR PRAYERS GO WITH YOU...
"...AS YOU STEP INTO THE DARKNESS TO FACE THAT WHICH ONLY YOU CAN FACE."

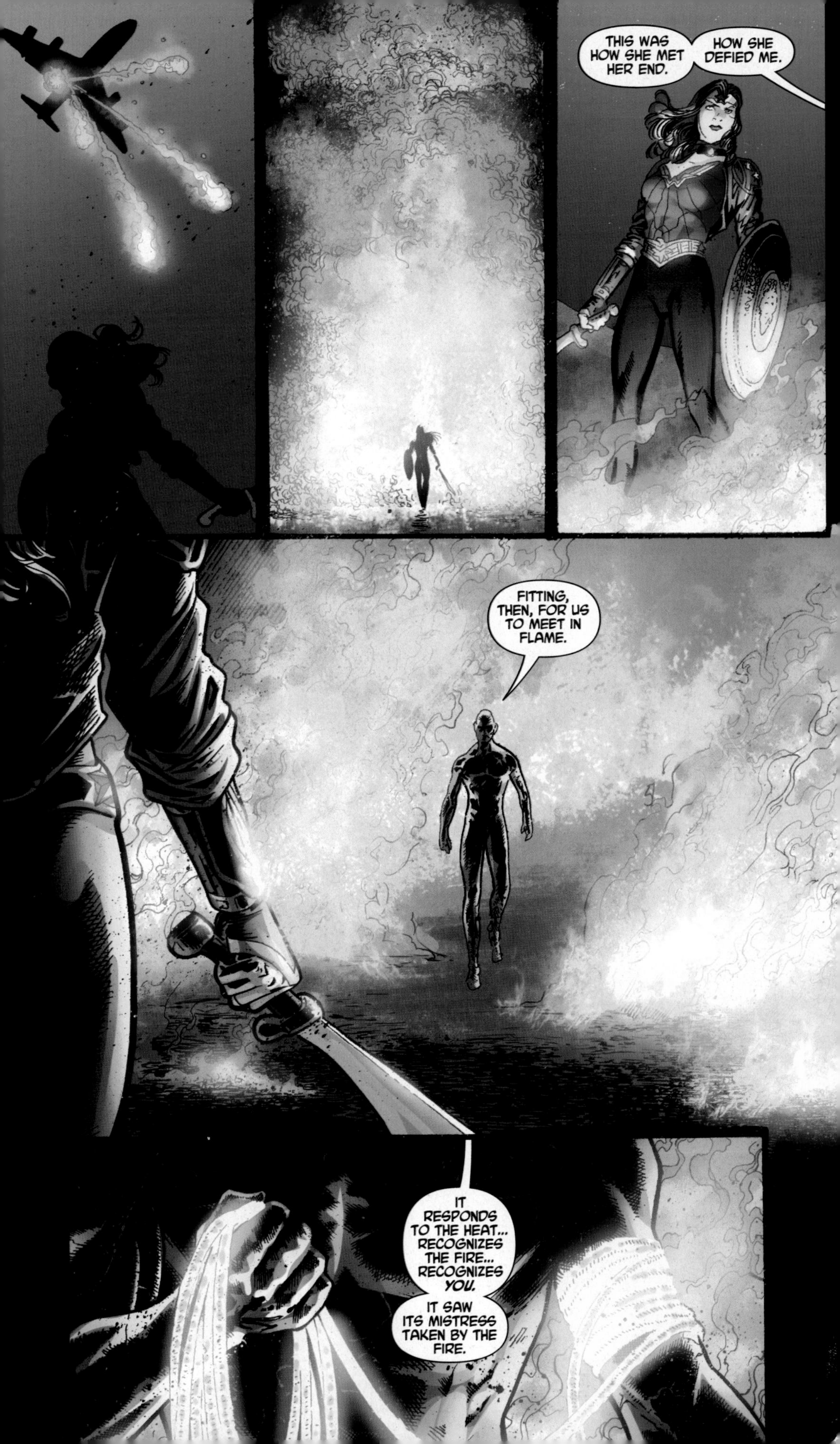
THIS WAS HOW SHE MET HER END.
HOW SHE DEFIED ME.
FITTING, THEN, FOR US TO MEET IN FLAME.
IT RESPONDS TO THE HEAT... RECOGNIZES THE FIRE... RECOGNIZES YOU.
IT SAW ITS MISTRESS TAKEN BY THE FIRE.

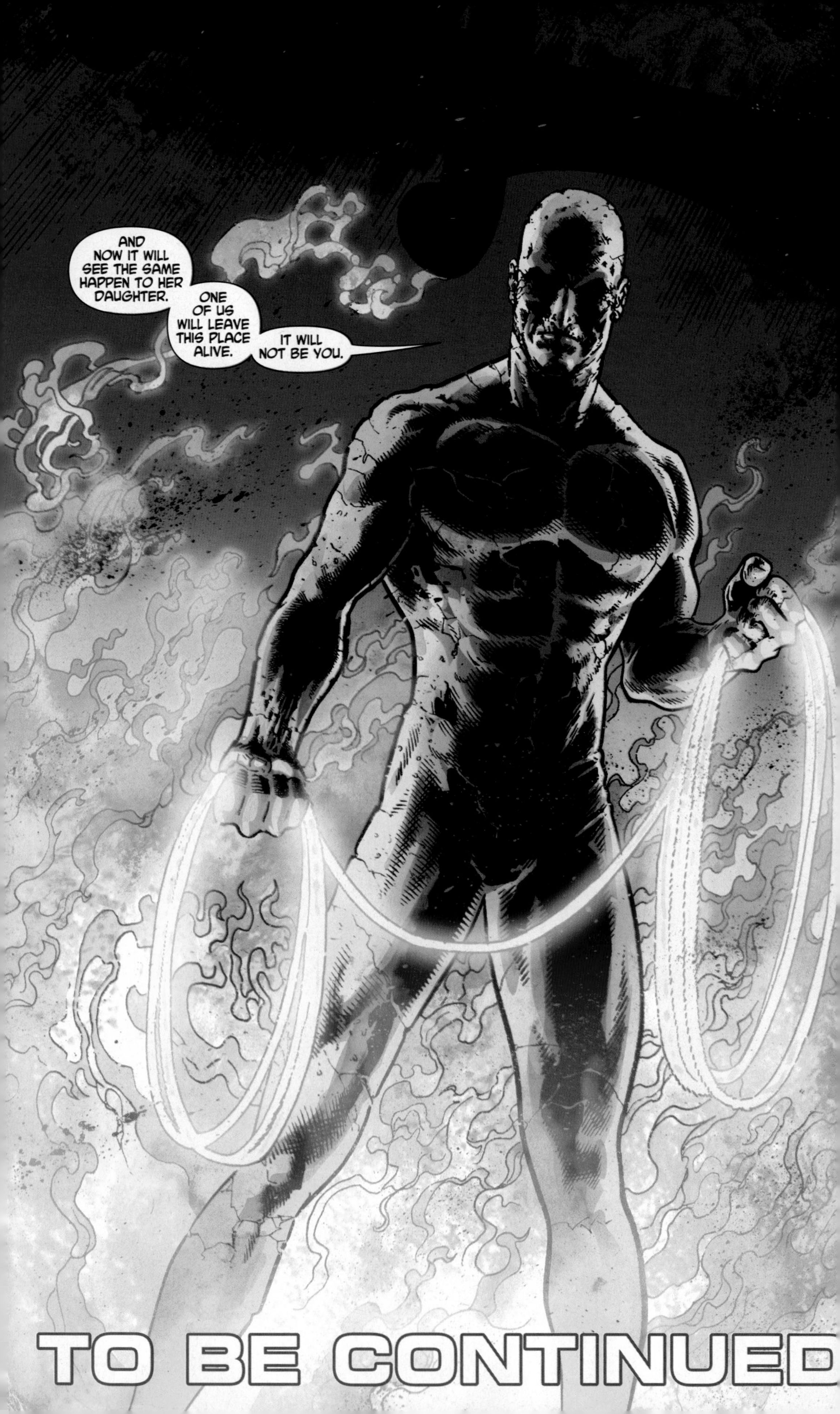
AND NOW IT WILL SEE THE SAME HAPPEN TO HER DAUGHTER.
ONE OF US WILL LEAVE THIS PLACE ALIVE.
IT WILL NOT BE YOU.
TO BE CONTINUED

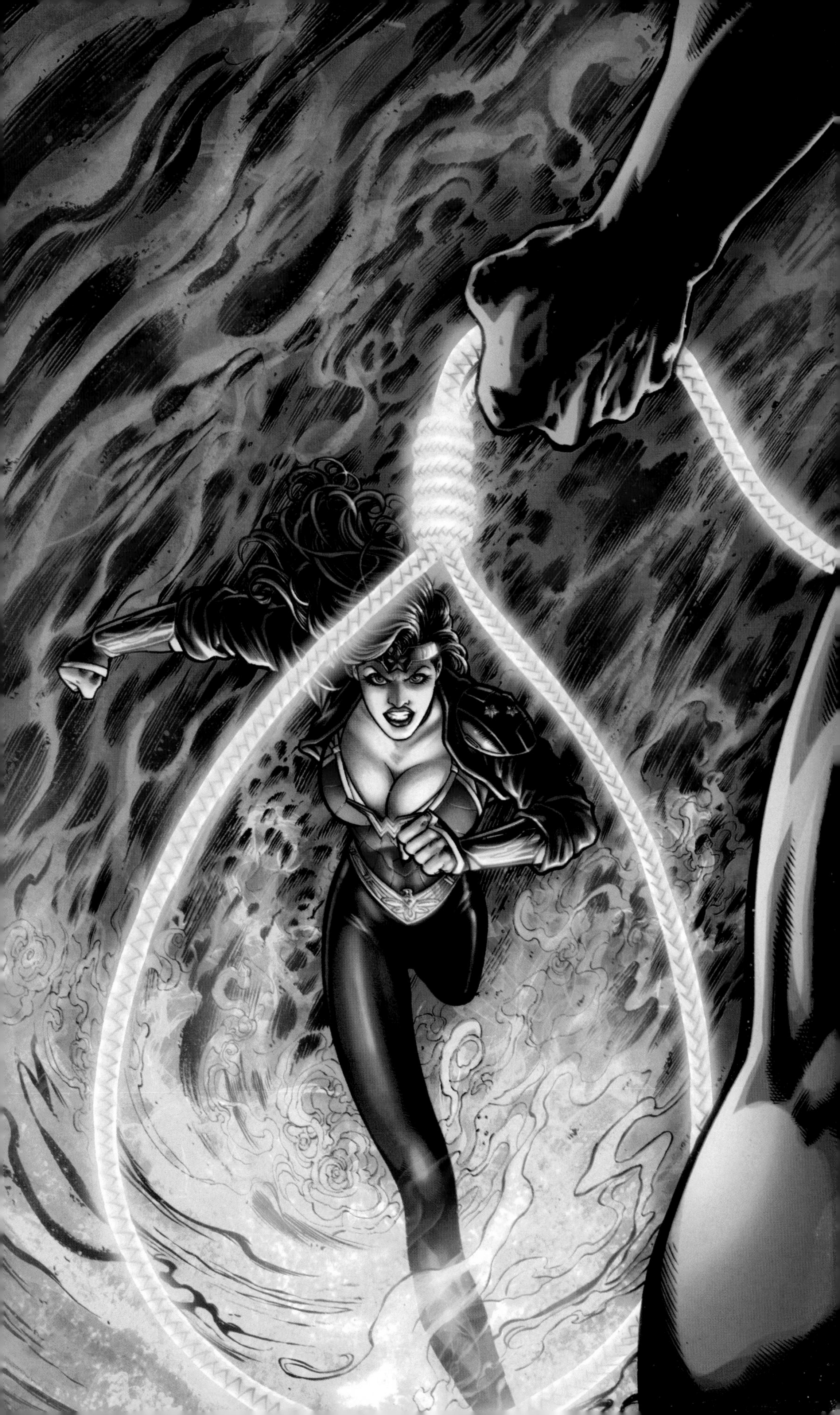

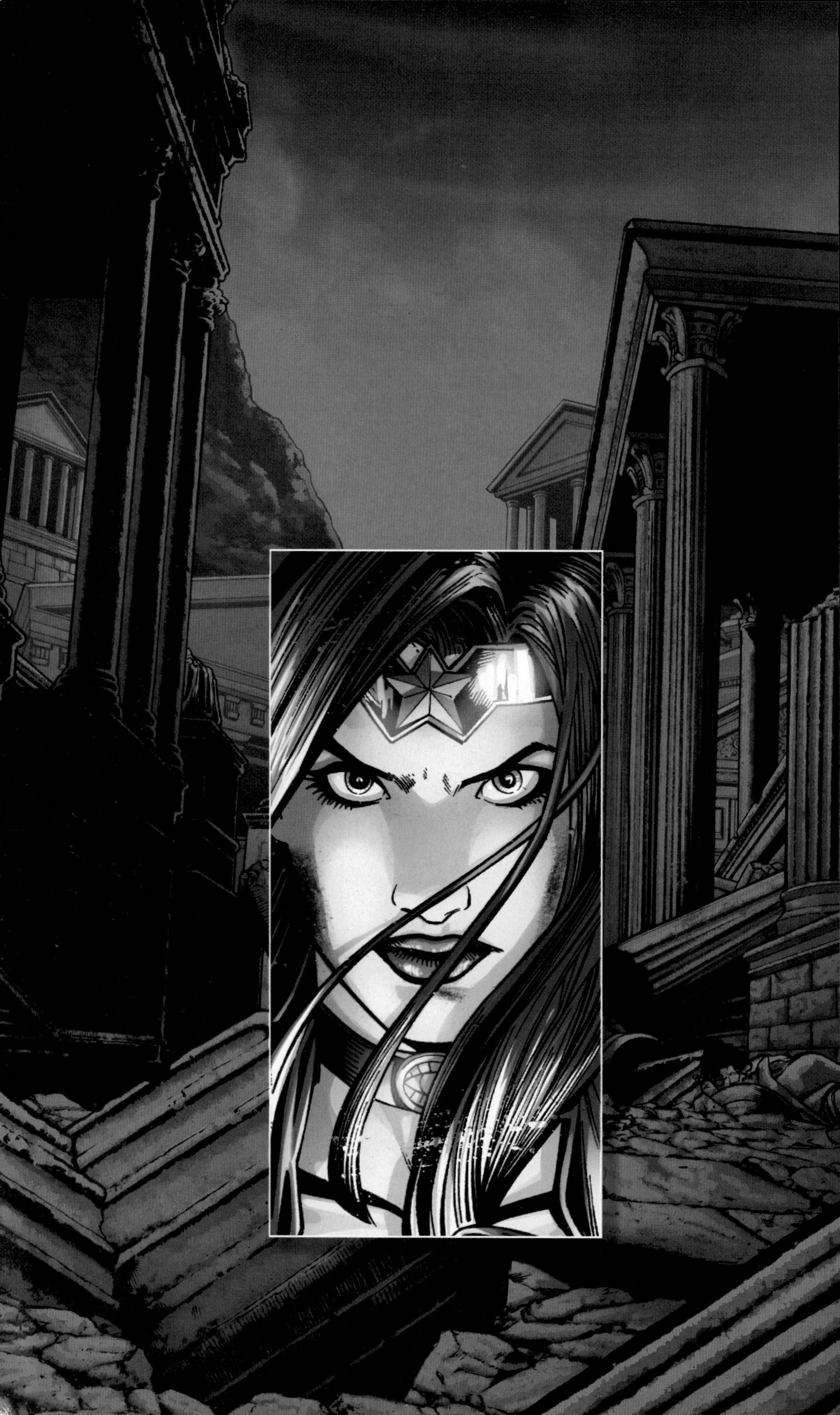

ODYSSEY: PART FOUR

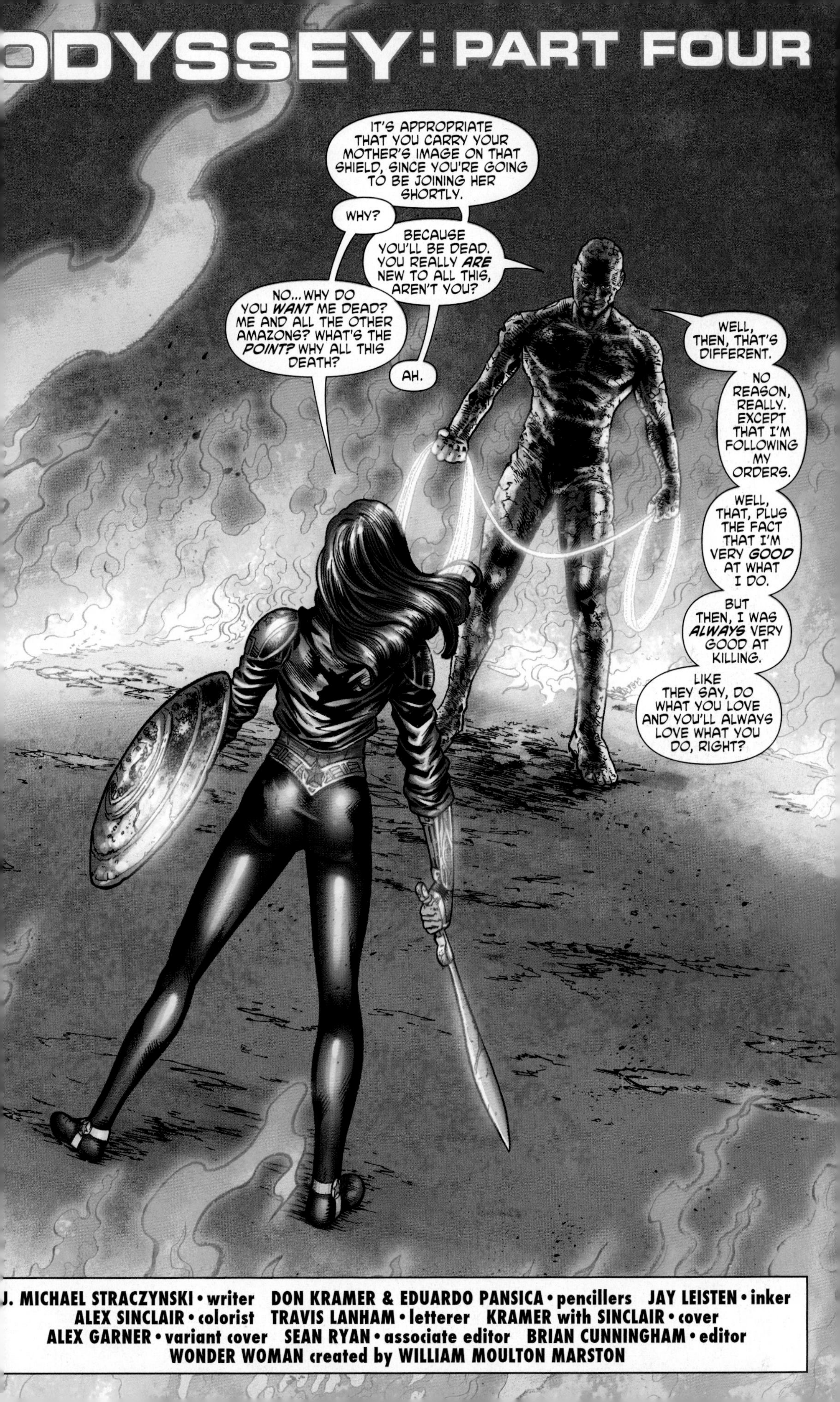

IT'S APPROPRIATE THAT YOU CARRY YOUR MOTHER'S IMAGE ON THAT SHIELD, SINCE YOU'RE GOING TO BE JOINING HER SHORTLY.
WHY?
BECAUSE YOU'LL BE DEAD. YOU REALLY ARE NEW TO ALL THIS, AREN'T YOU?
NO... WHY DO YOU WANT ME DEAD? ME AND ALL THE OTHER AMAZONS? WHAT'S THE POINT? WHY ALL THIS DEATH?
AH.
WELL, THEN, THAT'S DIFFERENT.
NO REASON, REALLY. EXCEPT THAT I'M FOLLOWING MY ORDERS.
WELL, THAT, PLUS THE FACT THAT I'M VERY GOOD AT WHAT I DO.
BUT THEN, I WAS ALWAYS VERY GOOD AT KILLING.
LIKE THEY SAY, DO WHAT YOU LOVE AND YOU'LL ALWAYS LOVE WHAT YOU DO, RIGHT?

J. MICHAEL STRACZYNSKI • writer DON KRAMER & EDUARDO PANSICA • pencillers JAY LEISTEN • inker
ALEX SINCLAIR • colorist TRAVIS LANHAM • letterer KRAMER with SINCLAIR • cover
ALEX GARNER • variant cover SEAN RYAN • associate editor BRIAN CUNNINGHAM • editor
WONDER WOMAN created by WILLIAM MOULTON MARSTON

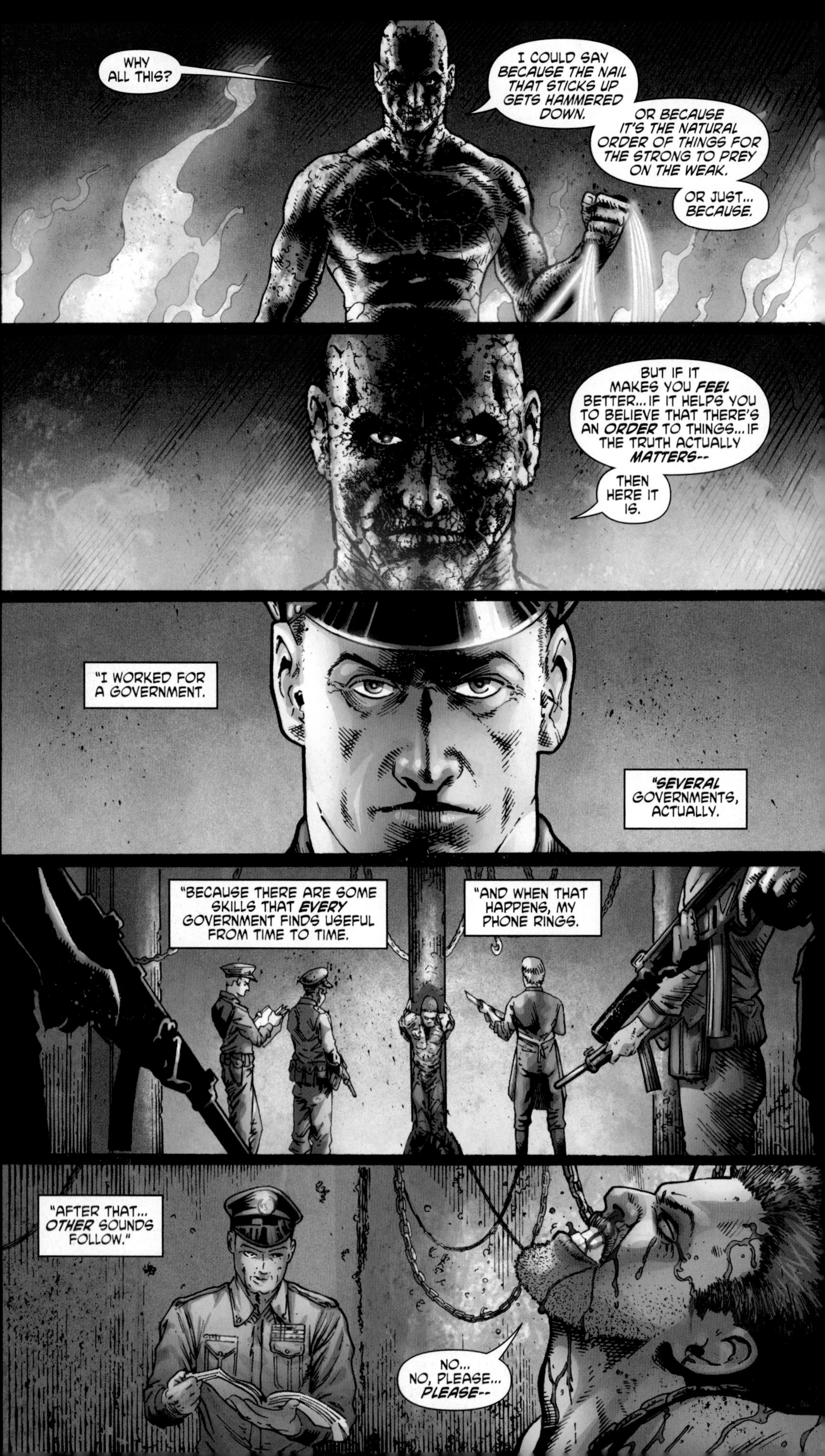
WHY ALL THIS?
I COULD SAY BECAUSE THE NAIL THAT STICKS UP GETS HAMMERED DOWN.
OR BECAUSE IT'S THE NATURAL ORDER OF THINGS FOR THE STRONG TO PREY ON THE WEAK.
OR JUST... BECAUSE.
BUT IF IT MAKES YOU FEEL BETTER... IF IT HELPS YOU TO BELIEVE THAT THERE'S AN ORDER TO THINGS... IF THE TRUTH ACTUALLY MATTERS--
THEN HERE IT IS.
"I WORKED FOR A GOVERNMENT.
"SEVERAL GOVERNMENTS, ACTUALLY.
"BECAUSE THERE ARE SOME SKILLS THAT EVERY GOVERNMENT FINDS USEFUL FROM TIME TO TIME.
"AND WHEN THAT HAPPENS, MY PHONE RINGS.
"AFTER THAT... OTHER SOUNDS FOLLOW."
NO... NO, PLEASE... PLEASE--

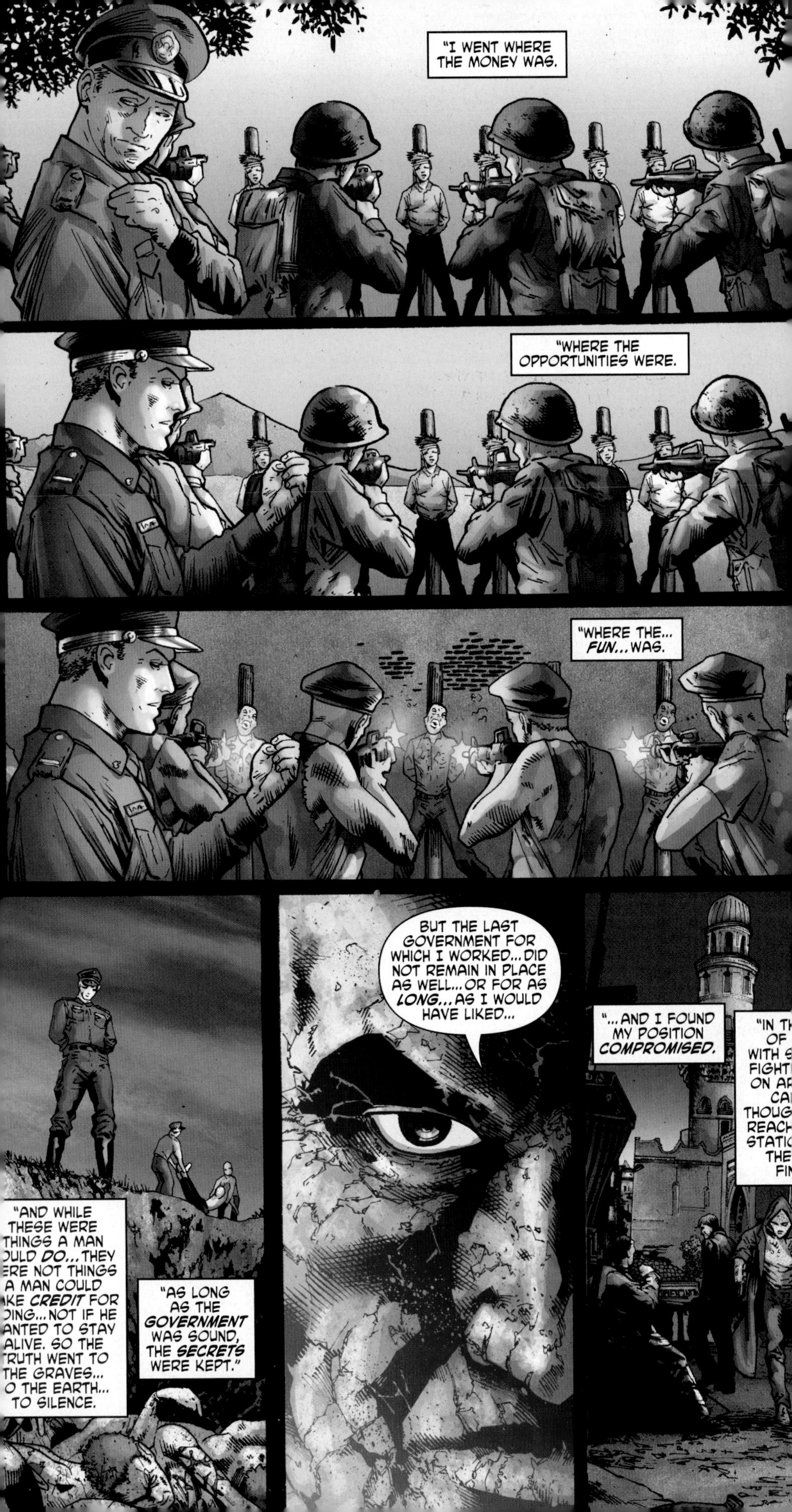
"I WENT WHERE THE MONEY WAS.
"WHERE THE OPPORTUNITIES WERE.
"WHERE THE... *FUN*... WAS.
"AND WHILE THESE WERE THINGS A MAN OULD *DO*... THEY ERE NOT THINGS A MAN COULD AKE *CREDIT* FOR OING... NOT IF HE ANTED TO STAY ALIVE. SO THE TRUTH WENT TO THE GRAVES... O THE EARTH... TO SILENCE.
"AS LONG AS THE *GOVERNMENT* WAS SOUND, THE *SECRETS* WERE KEPT."
BUT THE LAST GOVERNMENT FOR WHICH I WORKED... DID NOT REMAIN IN PLACE AS WELL... OR FOR AS *LONG*... AS I WOULD HAVE LIKED...
"...AND I FOUND MY POSITION *COMPROMISED*.

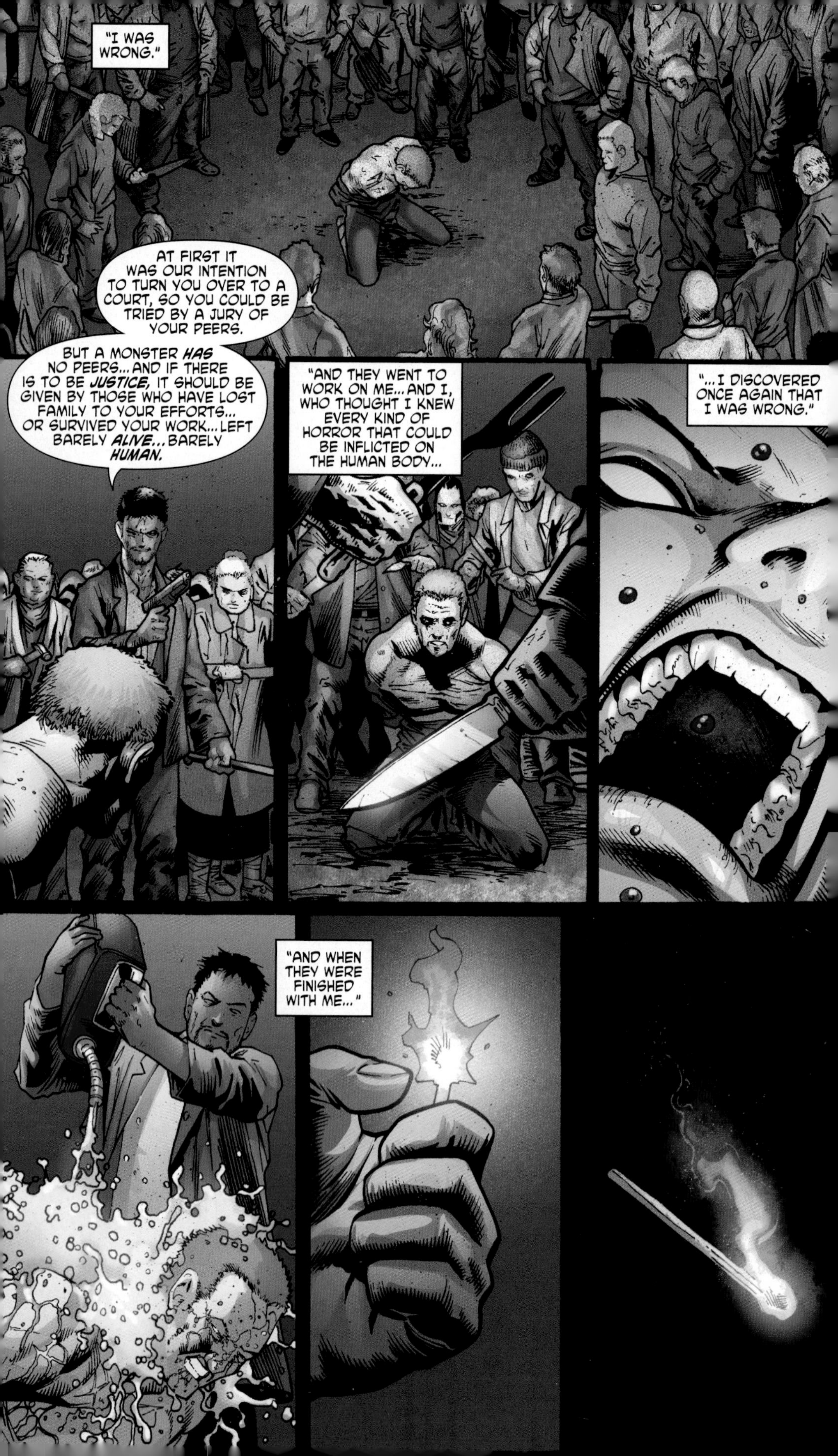
"I WAS WRONG."
AT FIRST IT WAS OUR INTENTION TO TURN YOU OVER TO A COURT, SO YOU COULD BE TRIED BY A JURY OF YOUR PEERS.
BUT A MONSTER *HAS* NO PEERS... AND IF THERE IS TO BE *JUSTICE,* IT SHOULD BE GIVEN BY THOSE WHO HAVE LOST FAMILY TO YOUR EFFORTS... OR SURVIVED YOUR WORK... LEFT BARELY *ALIVE*... BARELY *HUMAN.*
"AND THEY WENT TO WORK ON ME... AND I, WHO THOUGHT I KNEW EVERY KIND OF HORROR THAT COULD BE INFLICTED ON THE HUMAN BODY...
"...I DISCOVERED ONCE AGAIN THAT I WAS WRONG."
"AND WHEN THEY WERE FINISHED WITH ME..."

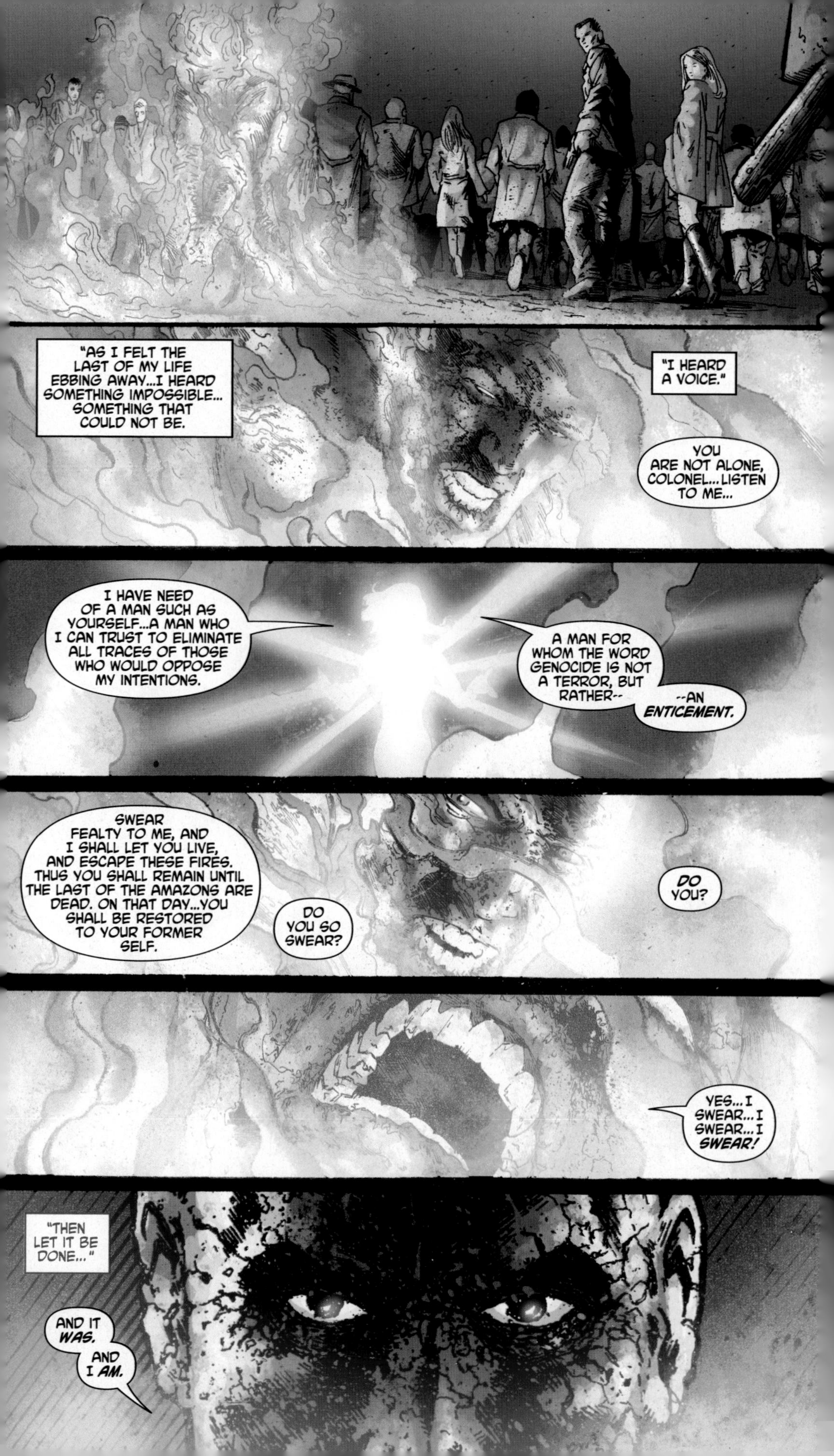

"AS I FELT THE LAST OF MY LIFE EBBING AWAY...I HEARD SOMETHING IMPOSSIBLE... SOMETHING THAT COULD NOT BE.
"I HEARD A VOICE."
YOU ARE NOT ALONE, COLONEL...LISTEN TO ME...
I HAVE NEED OF A MAN SUCH AS YOURSELF...A MAN WHO I CAN TRUST TO ELIMINATE ALL TRACES OF THOSE WHO WOULD OPPOSE MY INTENTIONS.
A MAN FOR WHOM THE WORD GENOCIDE IS NOT A TERROR, BUT RATHER--
--AN ENTICEMENT.
SWEAR FEALTY TO ME, AND I SHALL LET YOU LIVE, AND ESCAPE THESE FIRES. THUS YOU SHALL REMAIN UNTIL THE LAST OF THE AMAZONS ARE DEAD. ON THAT DAY...YOU SHALL BE RESTORED TO YOUR FORMER SELF.
DO YOU SO SWEAR?
DO YOU?
YES...I SWEAR...I SWEAR...I SWEAR!
"THEN LET IT BE DONE..."
AND IT WAS. AND I AM.

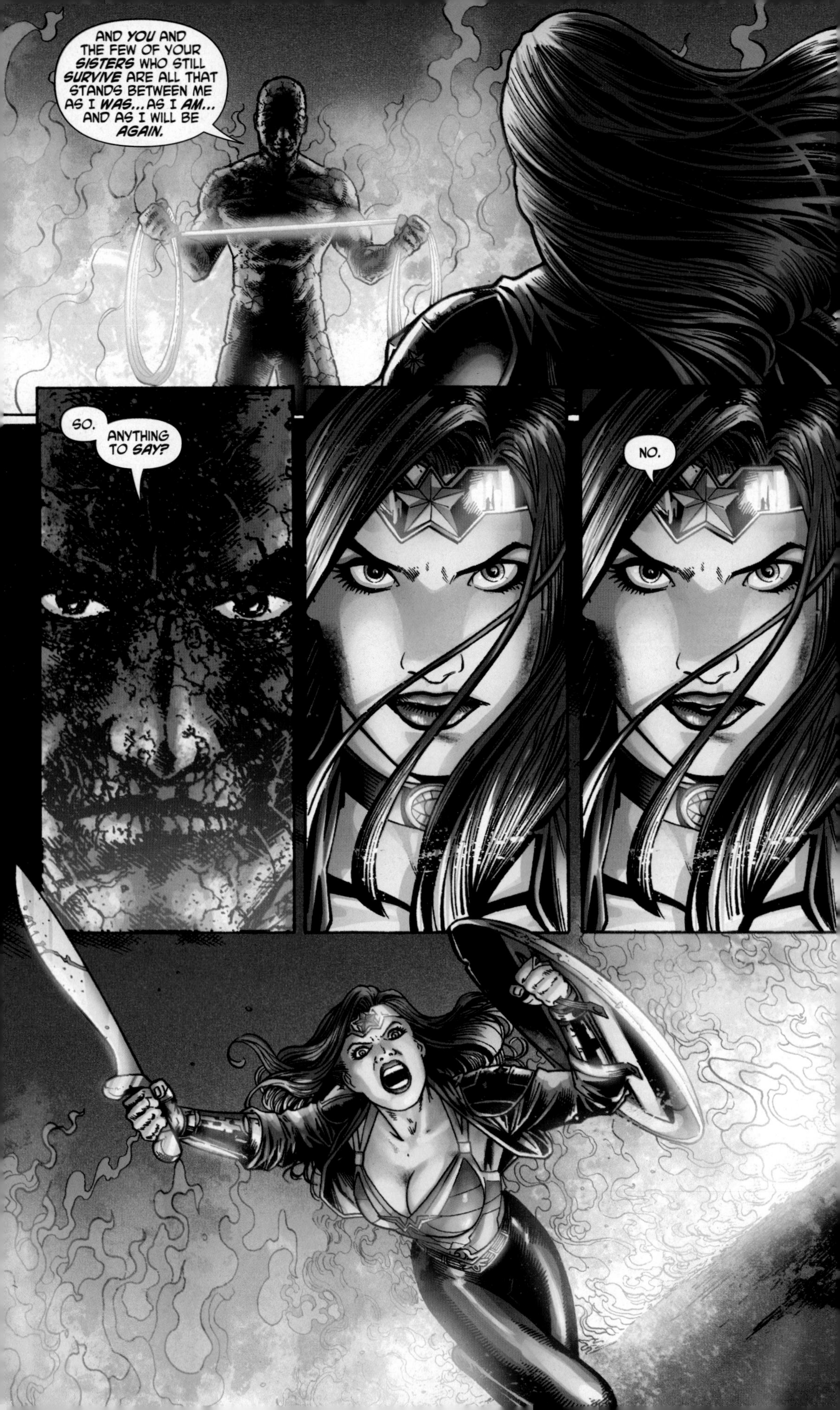
AND YOU AND THE FEW OF YOUR SISTERS WHO STILL SURVIVE ARE ALL THAT STANDS BETWEEN ME AS I WAS...AS I AM... AND AS I WILL BE AGAIN.
SO.
ANYTHING TO SAY?
NO.

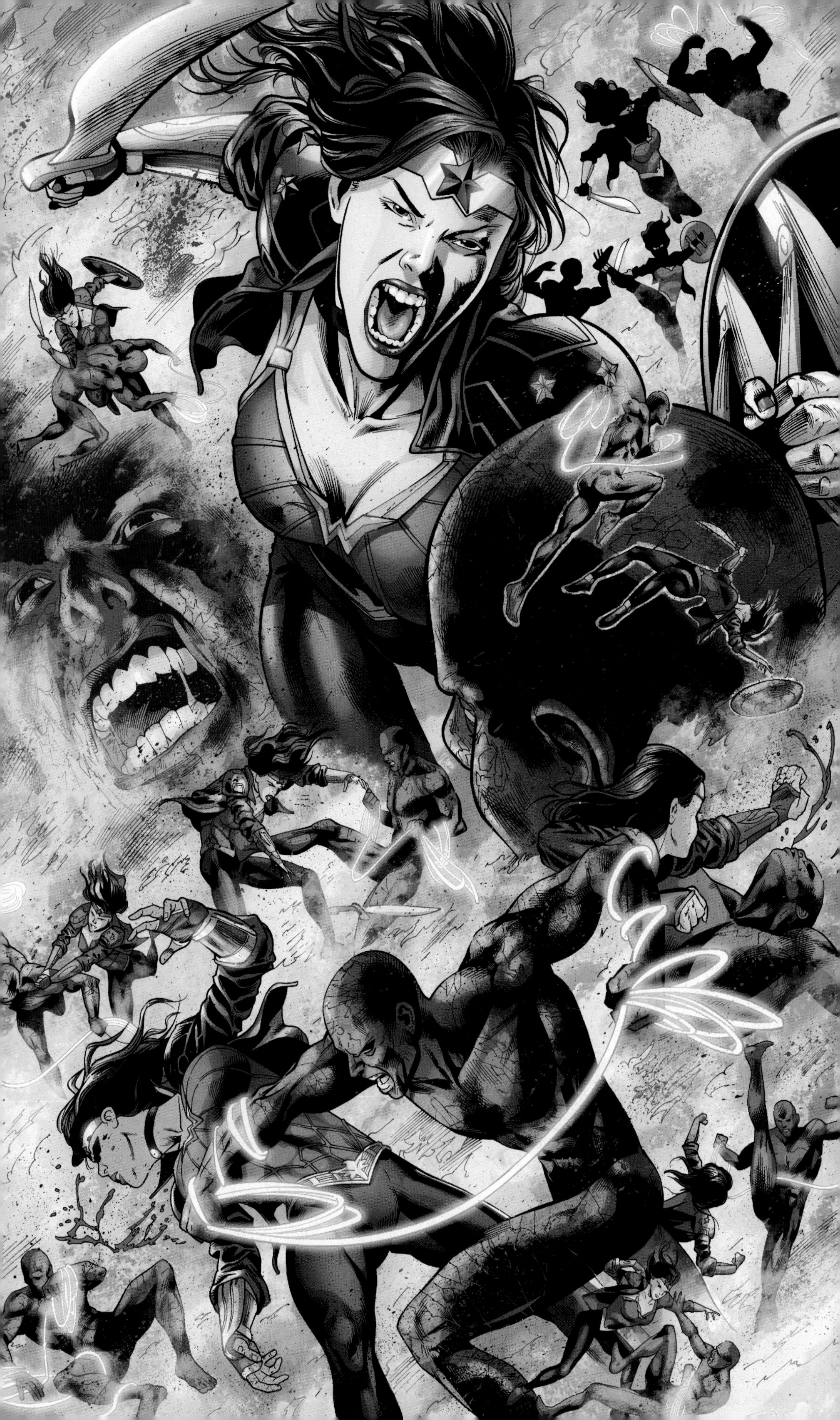

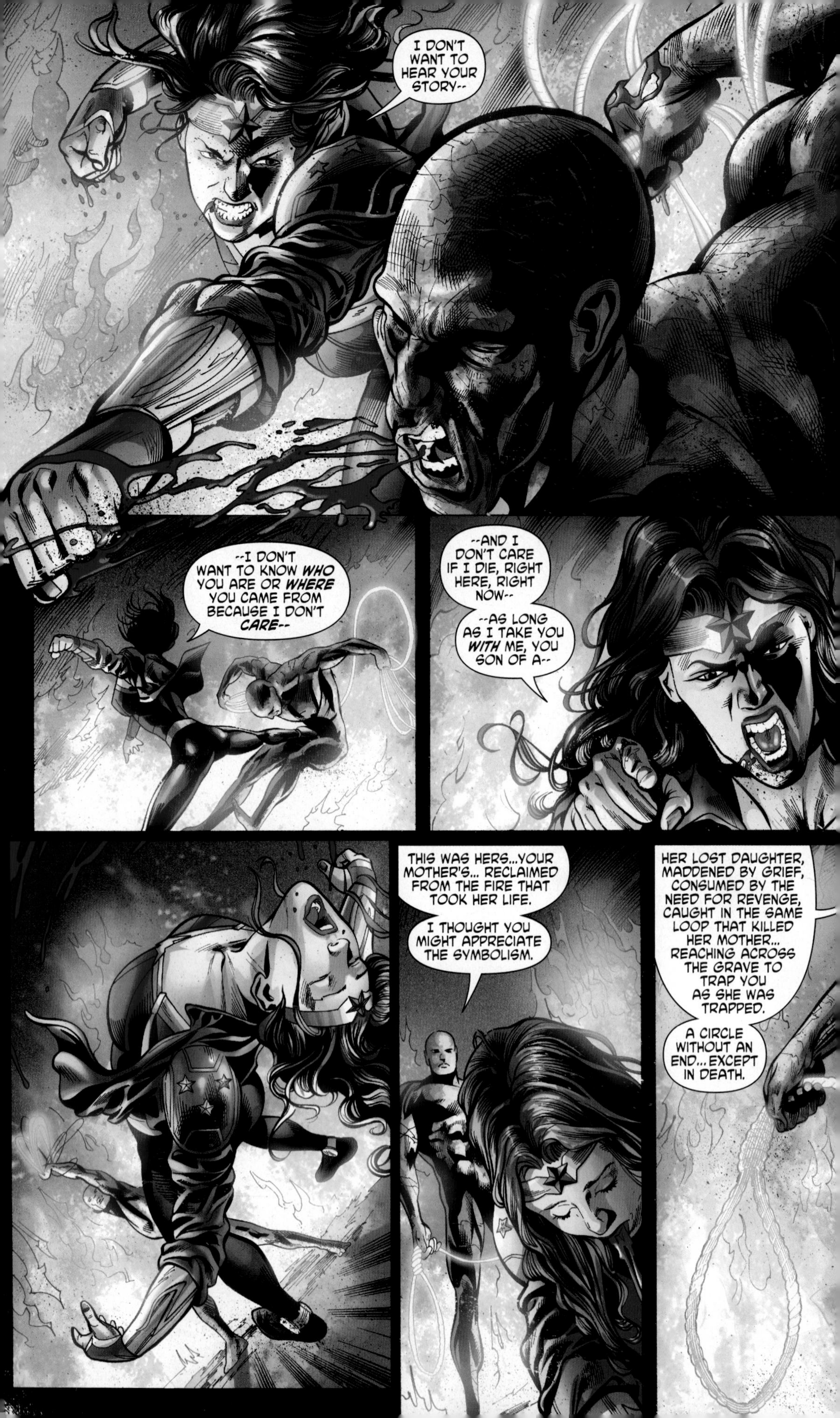
I DON'T WANT TO HEAR YOUR STORY--
--I DON'T WANT TO KNOW WHO YOU ARE OR WHERE YOU CAME FROM BECAUSE I DON'T CARE--
--AND I DON'T CARE IF I DIE, RIGHT HERE, RIGHT NOW--
--AS LONG AS I TAKE YOU WITH ME, YOU SON OF A--
THIS WAS HERS...YOUR MOTHER'S... RECLAIMED FROM THE FIRE THAT TOOK HER LIFE.
I THOUGHT YOU MIGHT APPRECIATE THE SYMBOLISM.
HER LOST DAUGHTER, MADDENED BY GRIEF, CONSUMED BY THE NEED FOR REVENGE, CAUGHT IN THE SAME LOOP THAT KILLED HER MOTHER... REACHING ACROSS THE GRAVE TO TRAP YOU AS SHE WAS TRAPPED.
A CIRCLE WITHOUT AN END...EXCEPT IN DEATH.

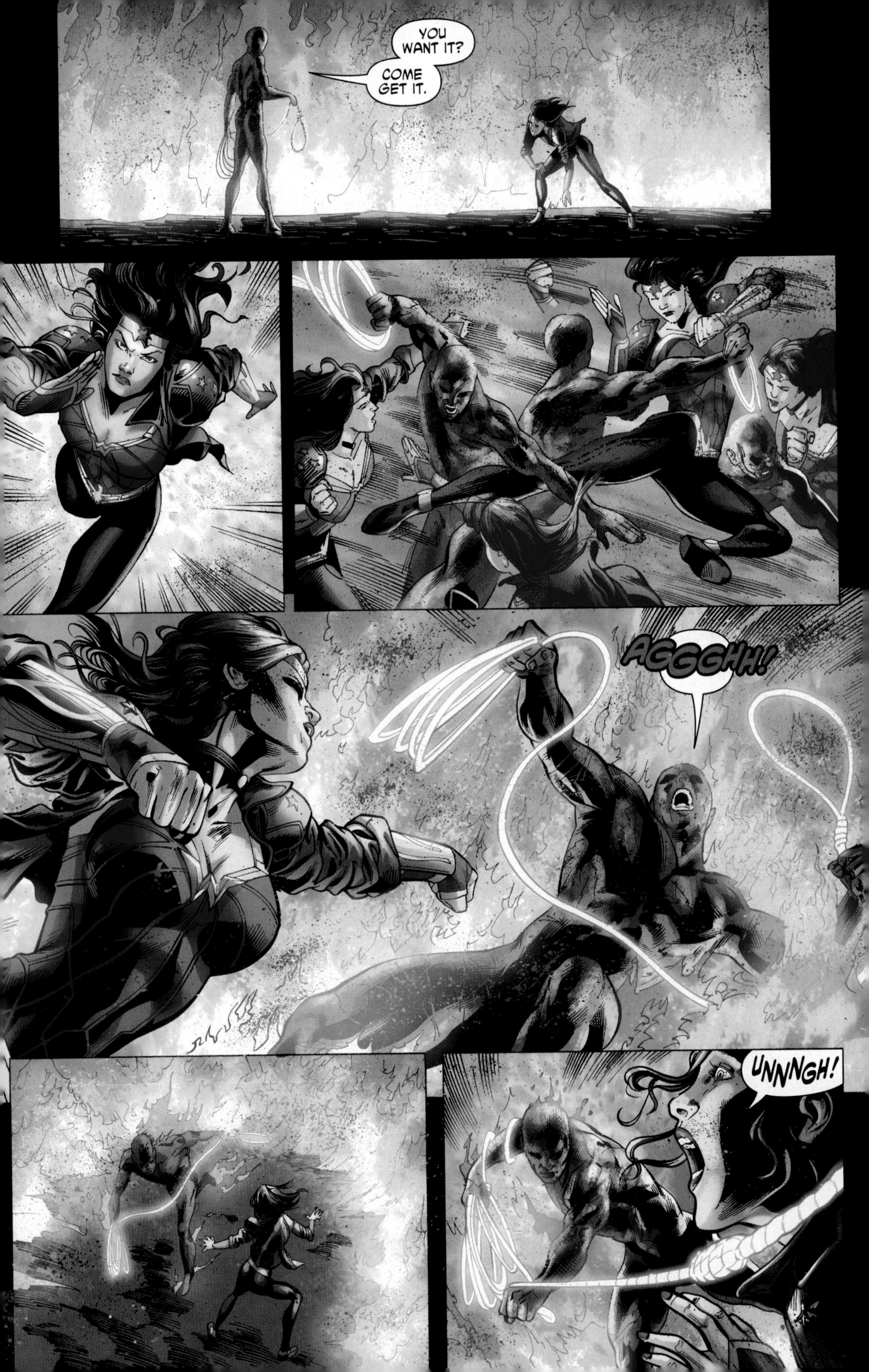
YOU WANT IT?
COME GET IT.
AGGGHH!
UNNNGH!

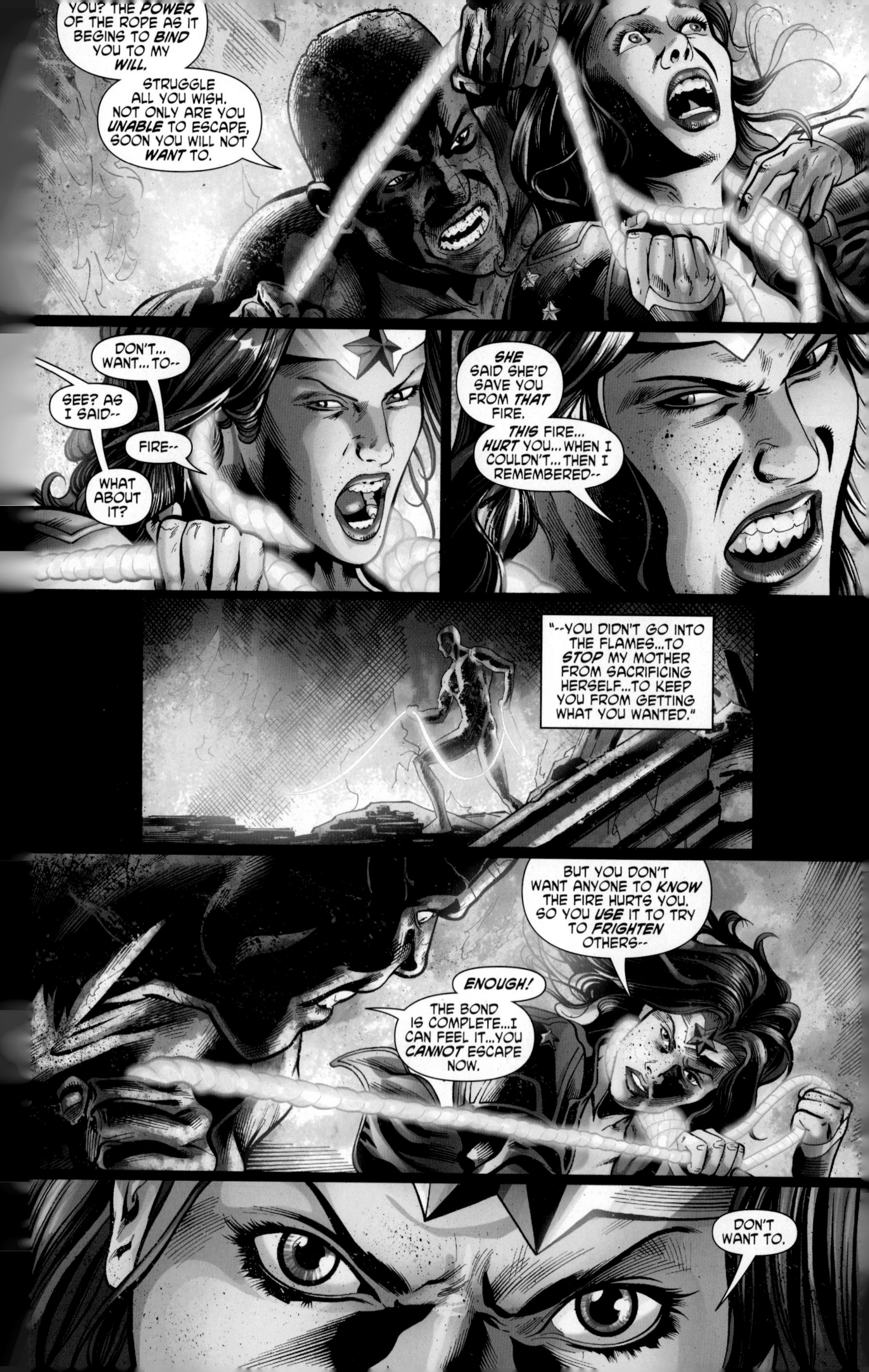
YOU? THE POWER OF THE ROPE AS IT BEGINS TO BIND YOU TO MY WILL.
STRUGGLE ALL YOU WISH. NOT ONLY ARE YOU UNABLE TO ESCAPE, SOON YOU WILL NOT WANT TO.
DON'T... WANT... TO--
SEE? AS I SAID--
FIRE--
WHAT ABOUT IT?
SHE SAID SHE'D SAVE YOU FROM THAT FIRE.
THIS FIRE... HURT YOU... WHEN I COULDN'T... THEN I REMEMBERED--
"--YOU DIDN'T GO INTO THE FLAMES...TO STOP MY MOTHER FROM SACRIFICING HERSELF...TO KEEP YOU FROM GETTING WHAT YOU WANTED."
BUT YOU DON'T WANT ANYONE TO KNOW THE FIRE HURTS YOU. SO YOU USE IT TO TRY TO FRIGHTEN OTHERS--
ENOUGH!
THE BOND IS COMPLETE...I CAN FEEL IT...YOU CANNOT ESCAPE NOW.
DON'T WANT TO.

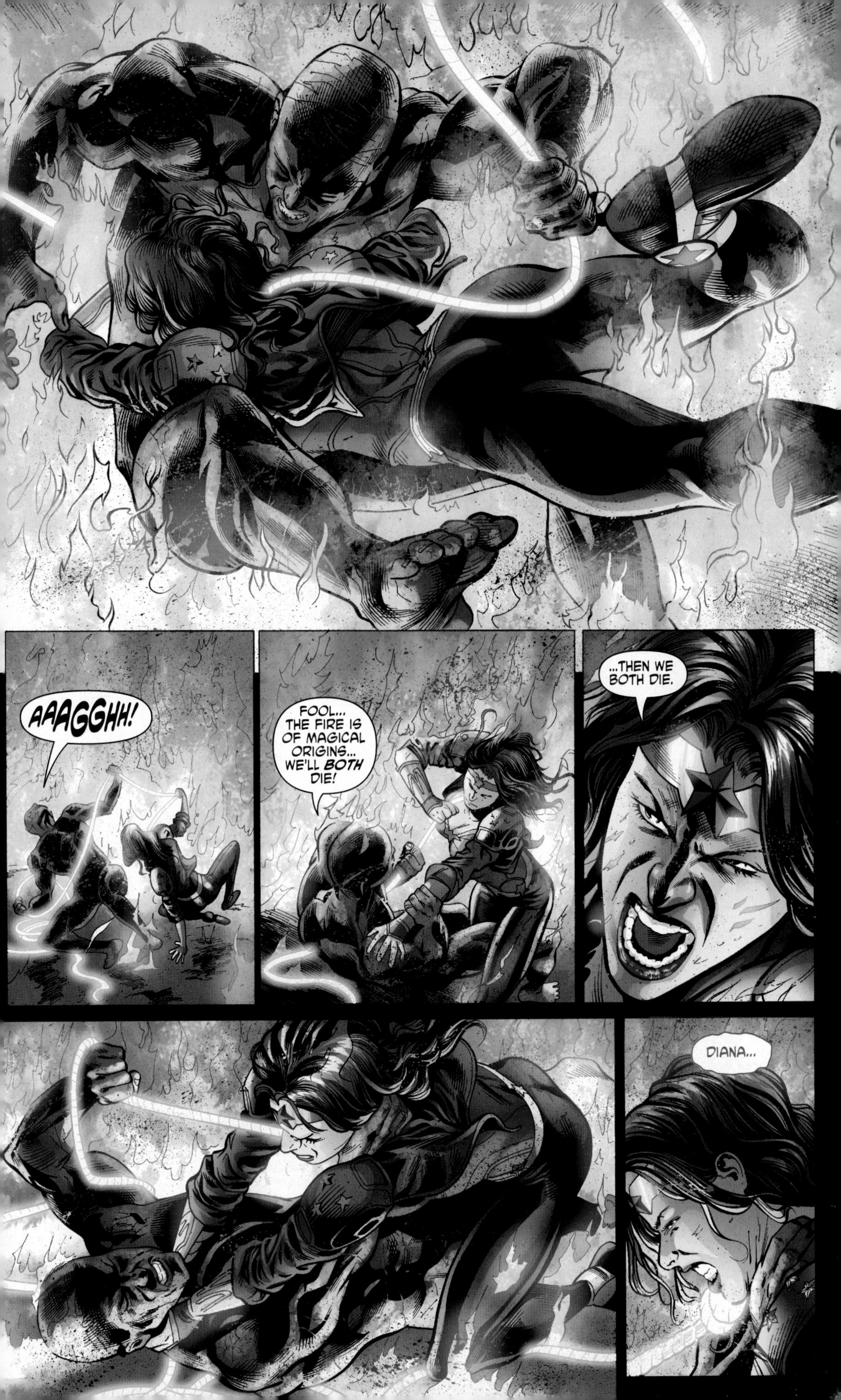
AAAGGHH!
FOOL... THE FIRE IS OF MAGICAL ORIGINS... WE'LL *BOTH* DIE!
...THEN WE BOTH DIE.
DIANA...

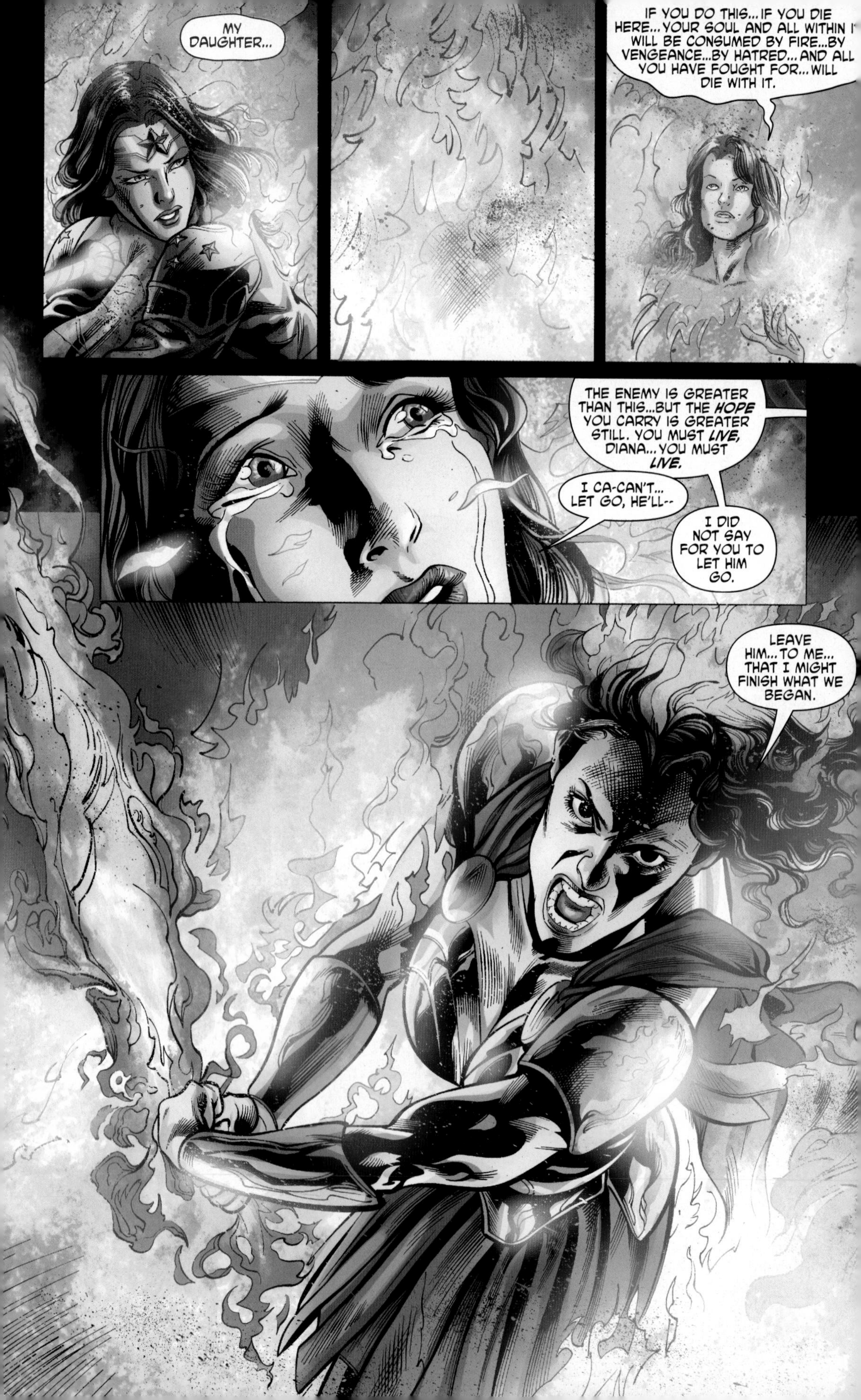
MY DAUGHTER...
IF YOU DO THIS...IF YOU DIE HERE...YOUR SOUL AND ALL WITHIN IT WILL BE CONSUMED BY FIRE...BY VENGEANCE...BY HATRED...AND ALL YOU HAVE FOUGHT FOR...WILL DIE WITH IT.
THE ENEMY IS GREATER THAN THIS...BUT THE *HOPE* YOU CARRY IS GREATER STILL. YOU MUST *LIVE,* DIANA...YOU MUST *LIVE.*
I CA-CAN'T... LET GO, HE'LL--
I DID NOT SAY FOR YOU TO LET HIM GO.
LEAVE HIM...TO ME... THAT I MIGHT FINISH WHAT WE BEGAN.

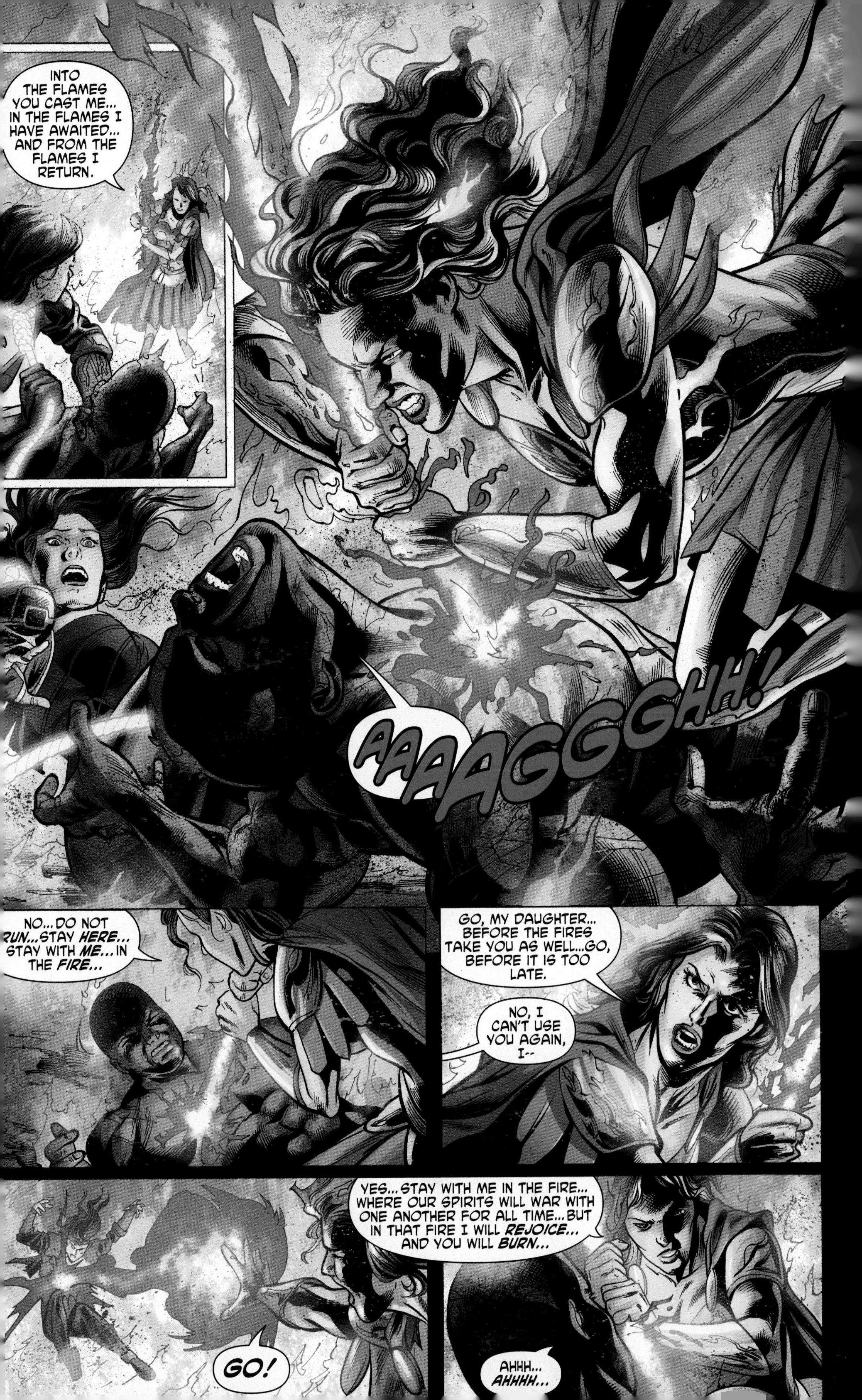
INTO THE FLAMES YOU CAST ME... IN THE FLAMES I HAVE AWAITED... AND FROM THE FLAMES I RETURN.
AAAAGGGGHH!
NO...DO NOT RUN...STAY HERE... STAY WITH ME...IN THE FIRE...
GO, MY DAUGHTER... BEFORE THE FIRES TAKE YOU AS WELL...GO, BEFORE IT IS TOO LATE.
NO, I CAN'T USE YOU AGAIN, I--
YES...STAY WITH ME IN THE FIRE... WHERE OUR SPIRITS WILL WAR WITH ONE ANOTHER FOR ALL TIME...BUT IN THAT FIRE I WILL REJOICE... AND YOU WILL BURN...
GO!
AHHH... AHHHH...

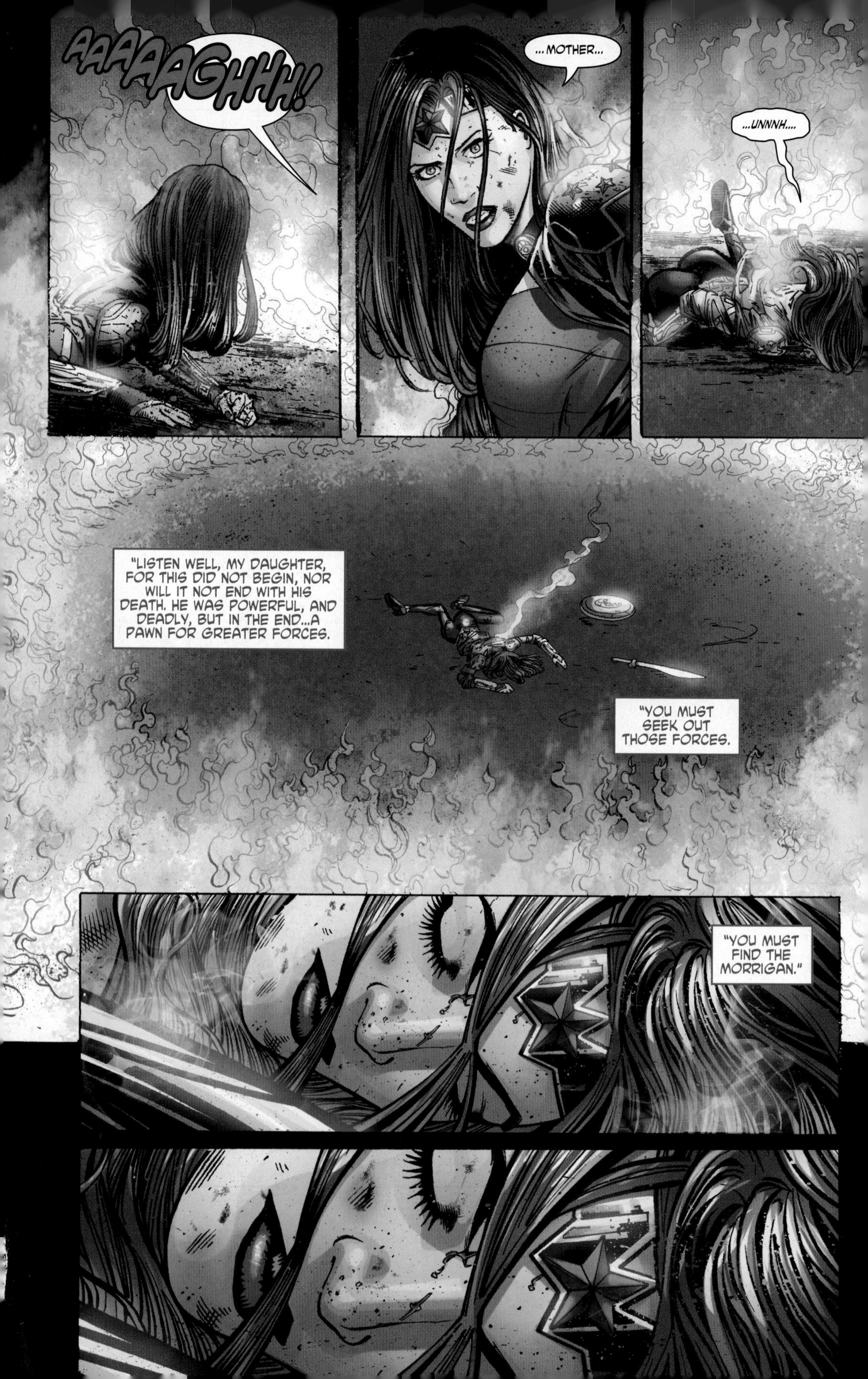
AAAAAAGHHH!
...MOTHER...
...UNNNH....
"LISTEN WELL, MY DAUGHTER, FOR THIS DID NOT BEGIN, NOR WILL IT NOT END WITH HIS DEATH. HE WAS POWERFUL, AND DEADLY, BUT IN THE END...A PAWN FOR GREATER FORCES.
"YOU MUST SEEK OUT THOSE FORCES.
"YOU MUST FIND THE MORRIGAN."

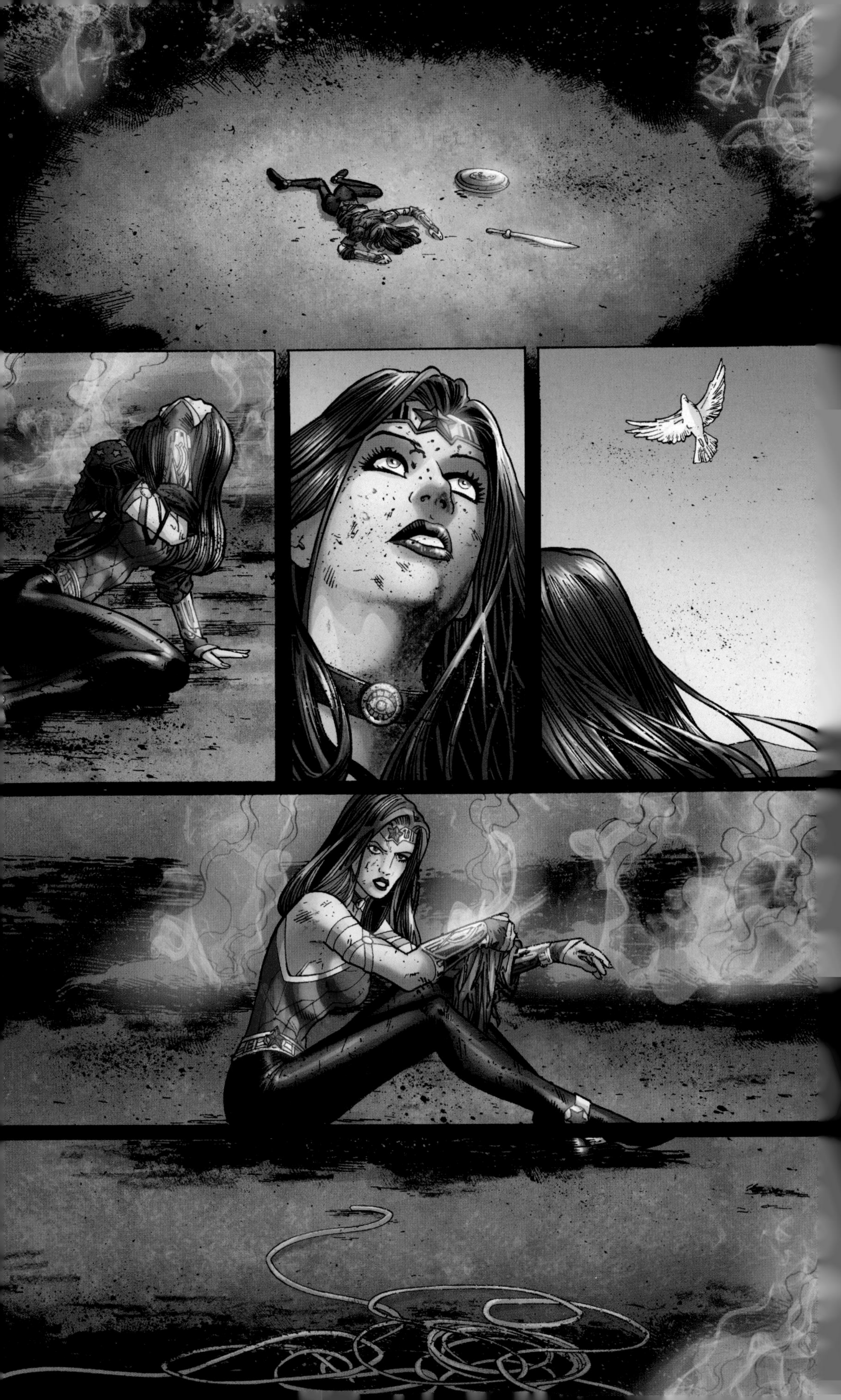

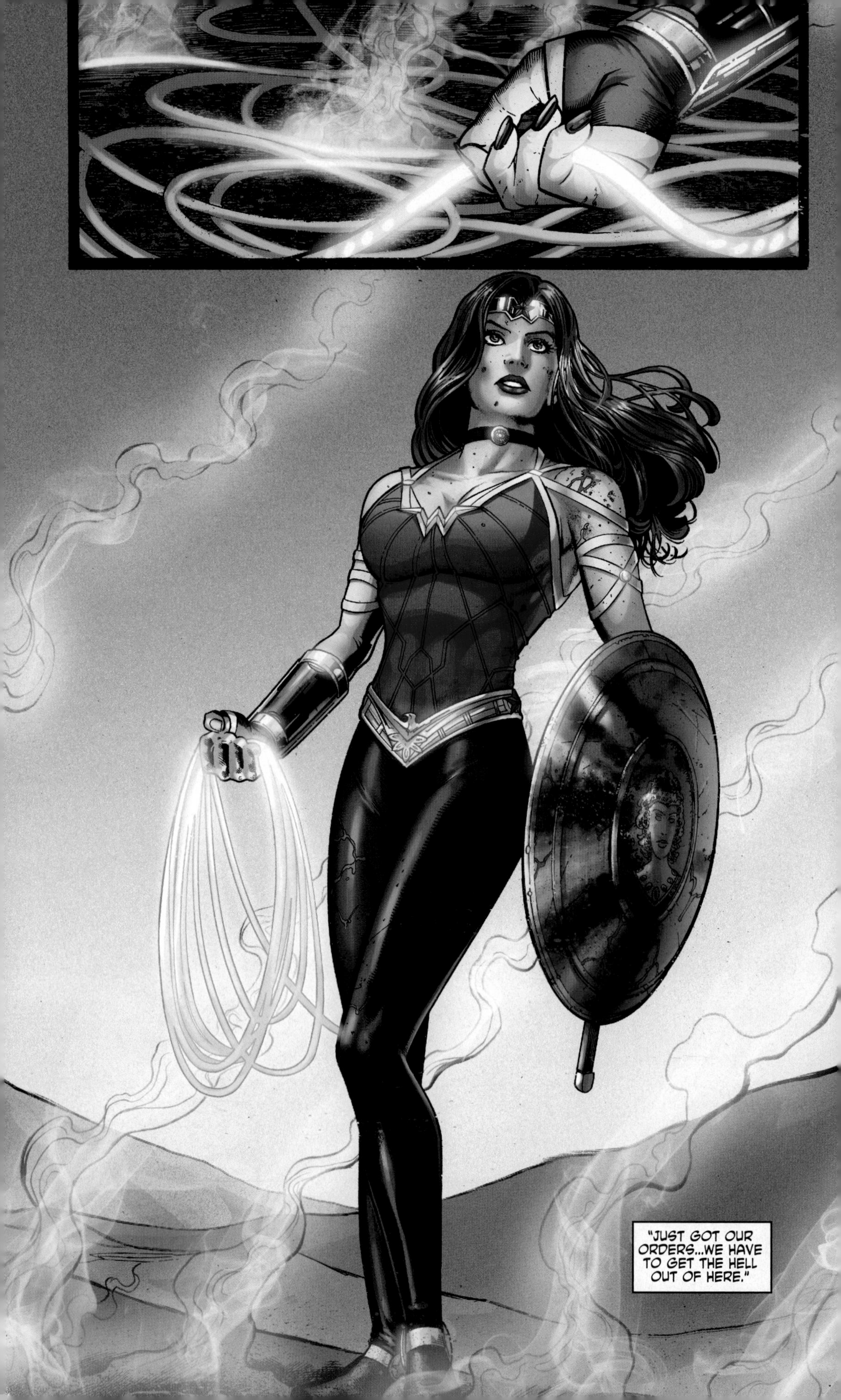
"JUST GOT OUR ORDERS...WE HAVE TO GET THE HELL OUT OF HERE."

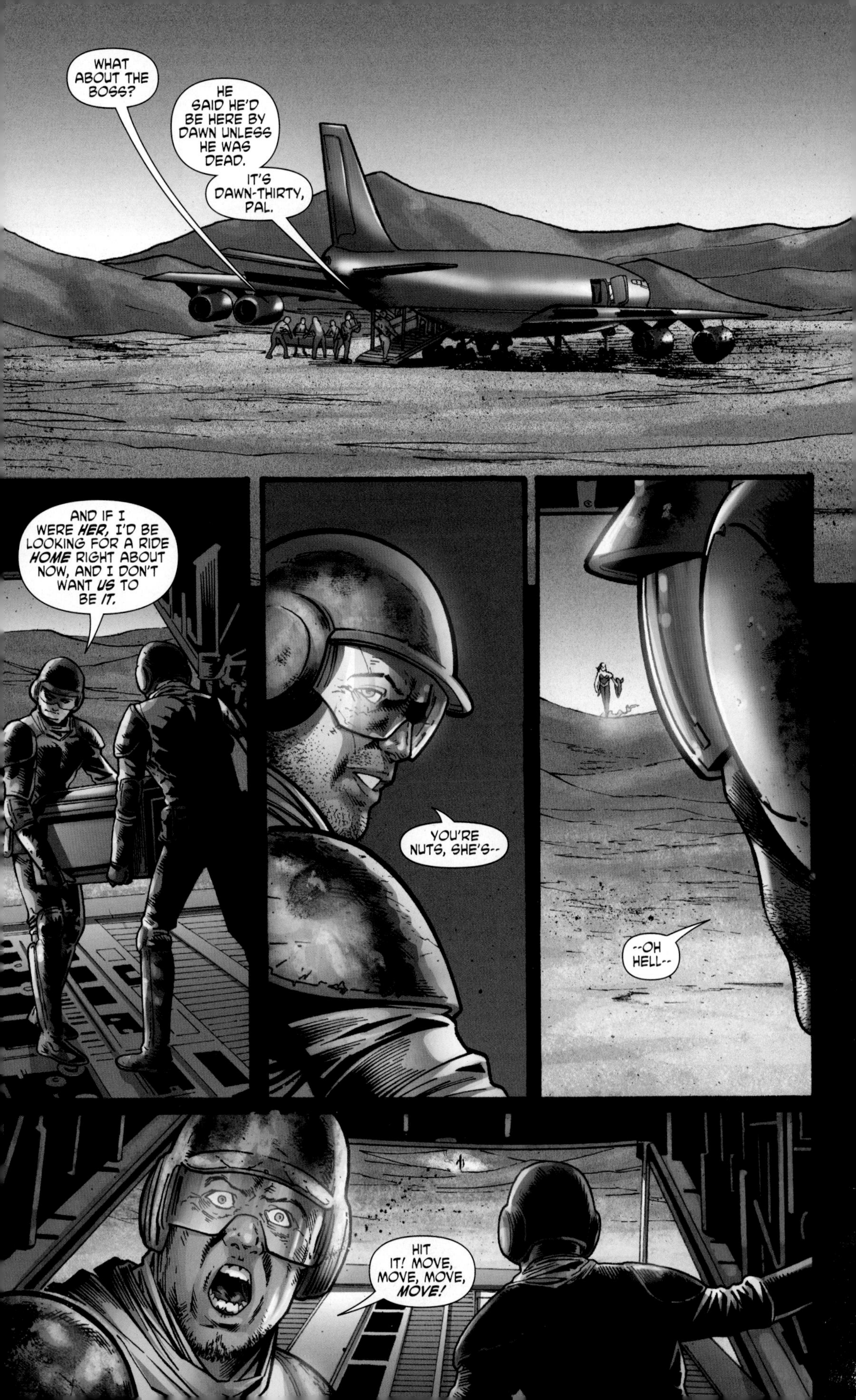

WHAT ABOUT THE BOSS?
HE SAID HE'D BE HERE BY DAWN UNLESS HE WAS DEAD.
IT'S DAWN-THIRTY, PAL.
AND IF I WERE HER, I'D BE LOOKING FOR A RIDE HOME RIGHT ABOUT NOW, AND I DON'T WANT US TO BE IT.
YOU'RE NUTS, SHE'S--
--OH HELL--
HIT IT! MOVE, MOVE, MOVE, MOVE!

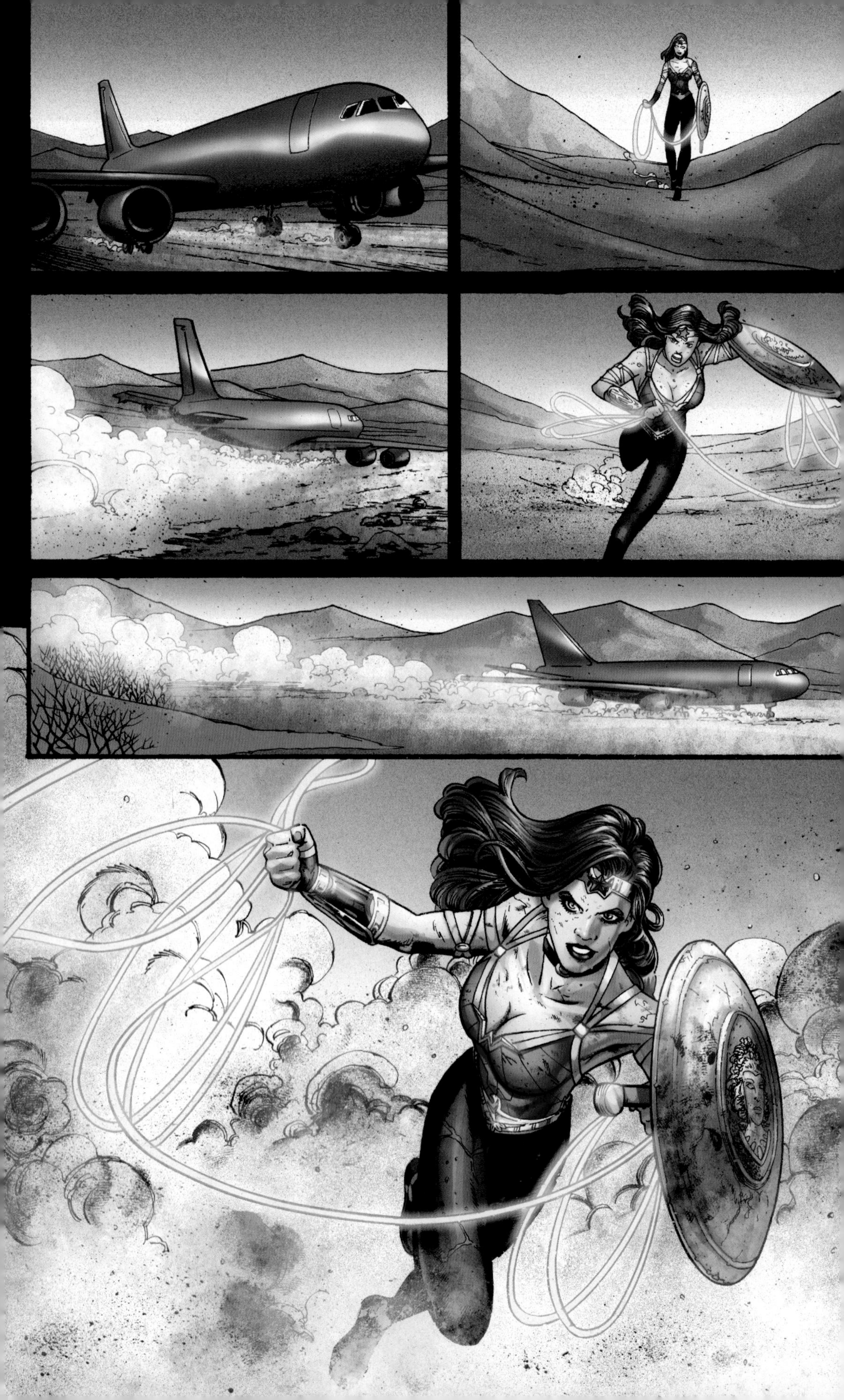

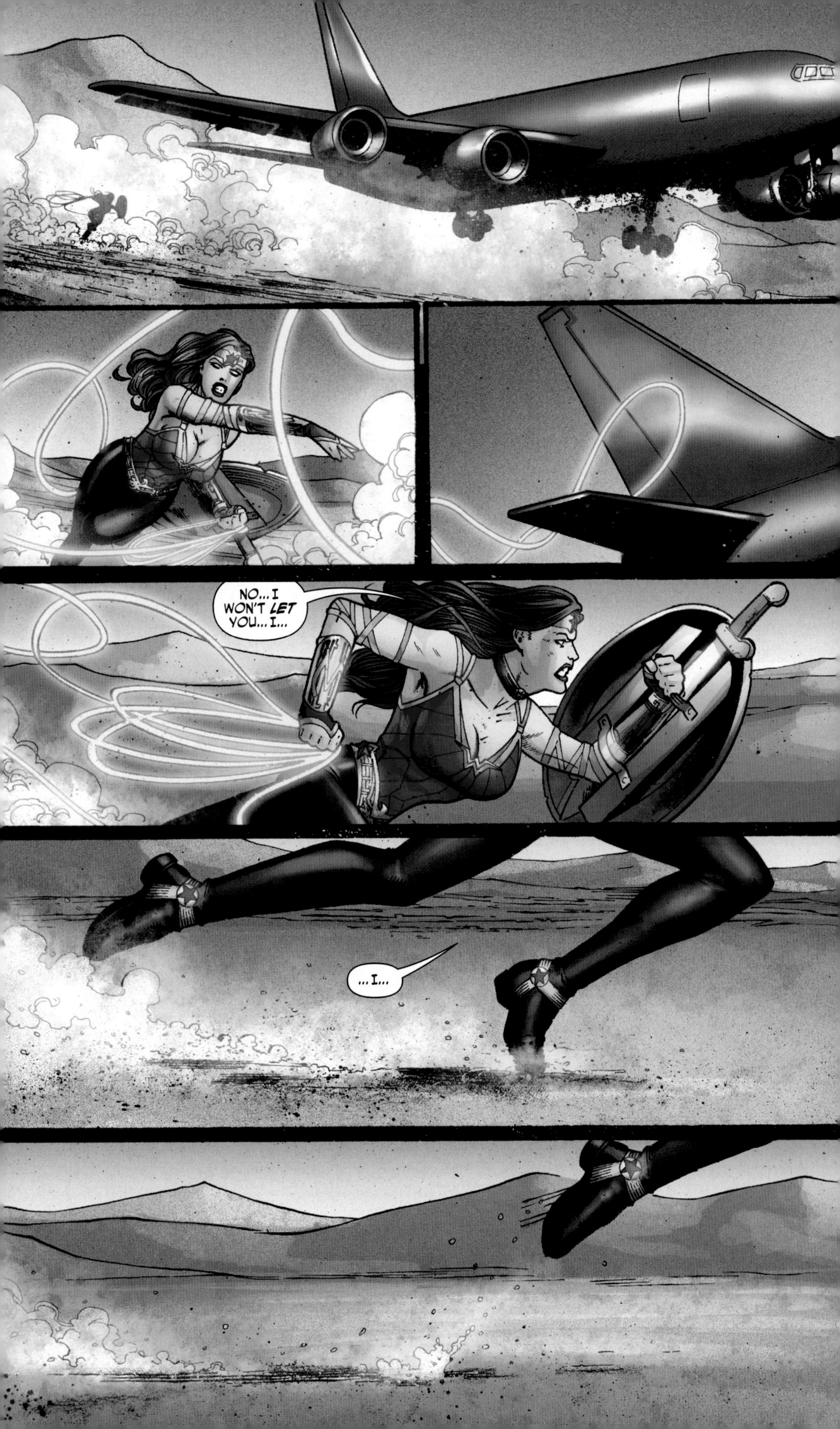
NO... I WON'T LET YOU... I...
...I...

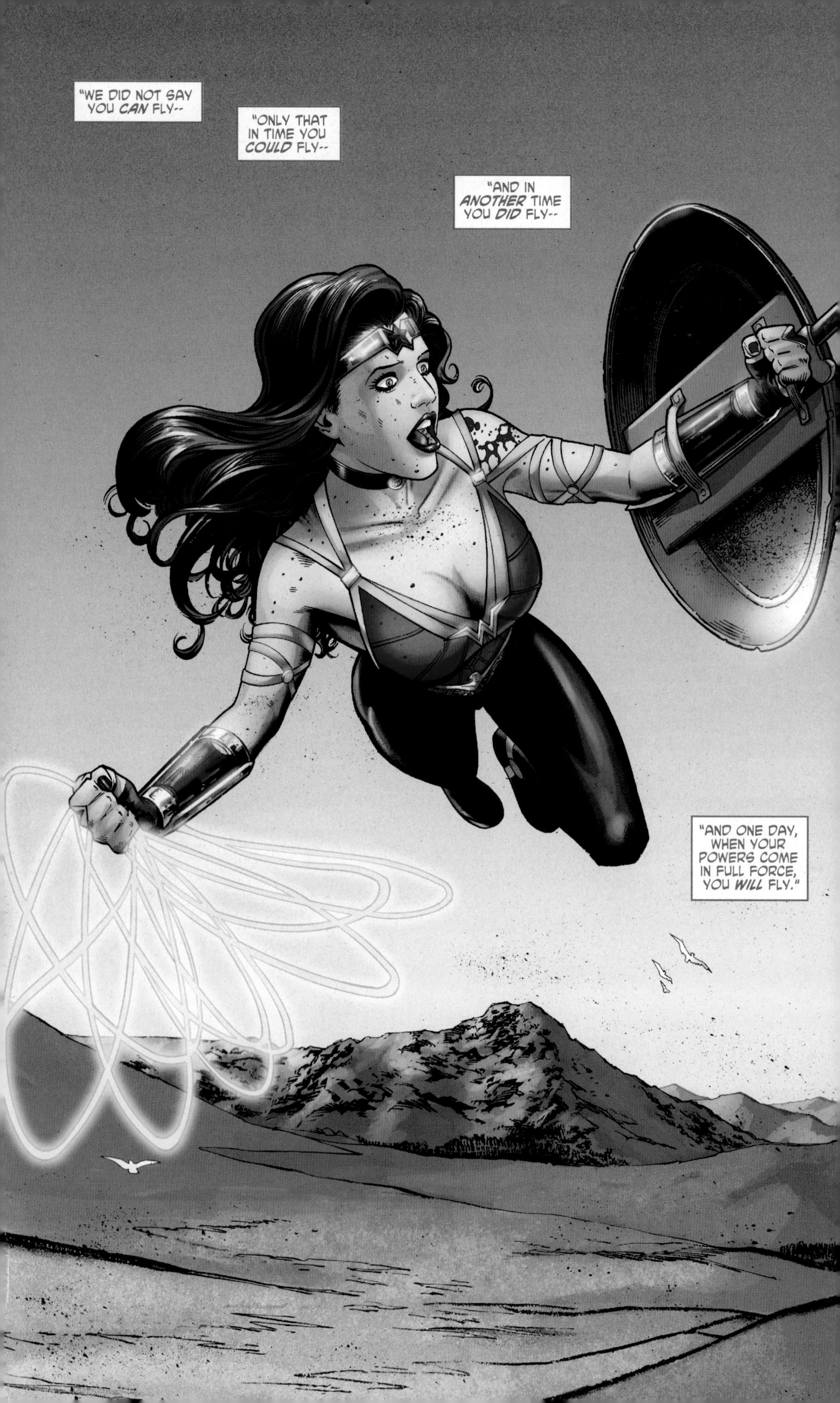
"WE DID NOT SAY YOU *CAN* FLY--
"ONLY THAT IN TIME YOU *COULD* FLY--
"AND IN *ANOTHER* TIME YOU *DID* FLY--
"AND ONE DAY, WHEN YOUR POWERS COME IN FULL FORCE, YOU *WILL* FLY."

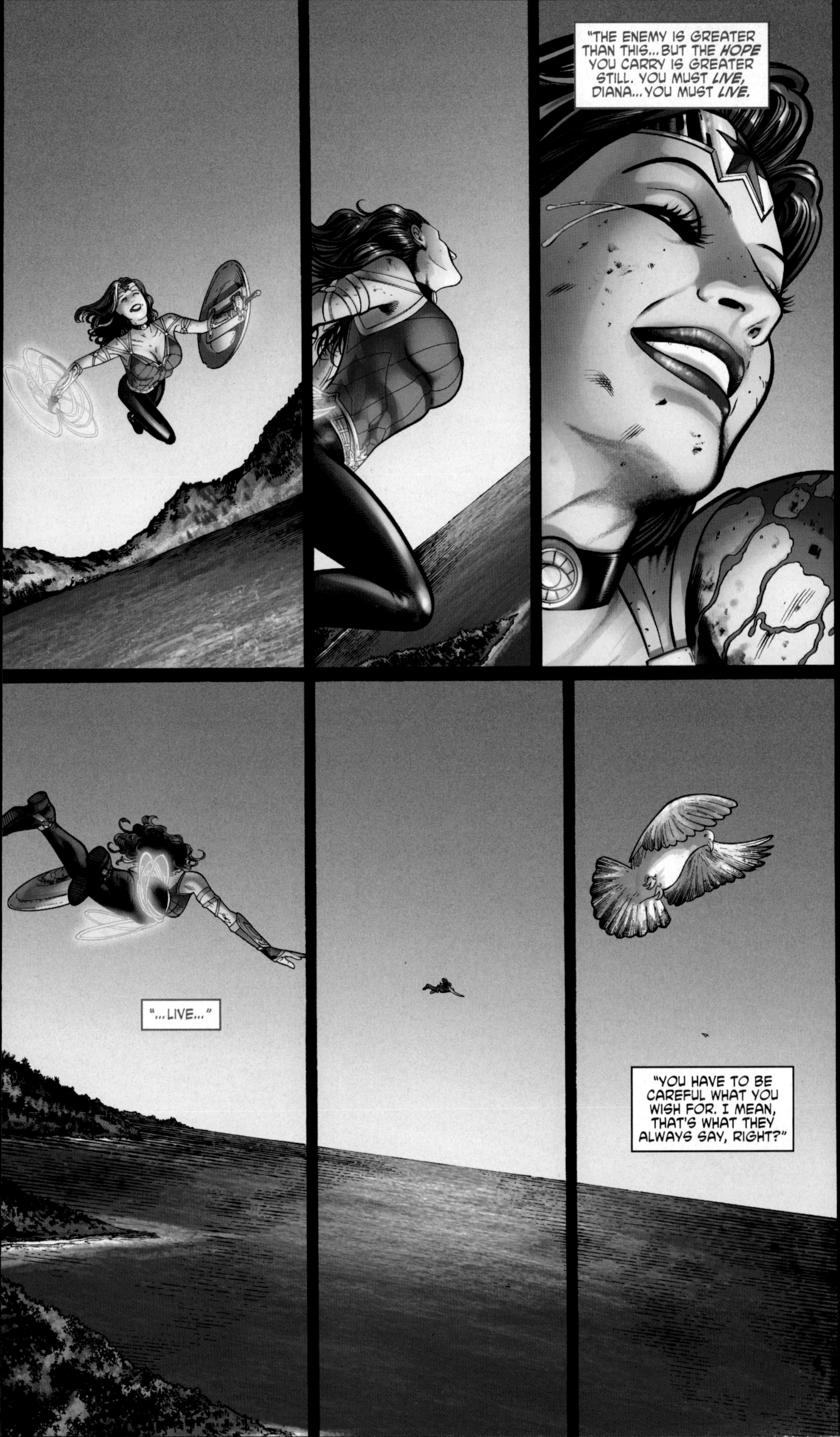
"THE ENEMY IS GREATER THAN THIS... BUT THE *HOPE* YOU CARRY IS GREATER STILL. YOU MUST *LIVE,* DIANA... YOU MUST *LIVE.*
"...LIVE..."
"YOU HAVE TO BE CAREFUL WHAT YOU WISH FOR. I MEAN, THAT'S WHAT THEY ALWAYS SAY, RIGHT?"

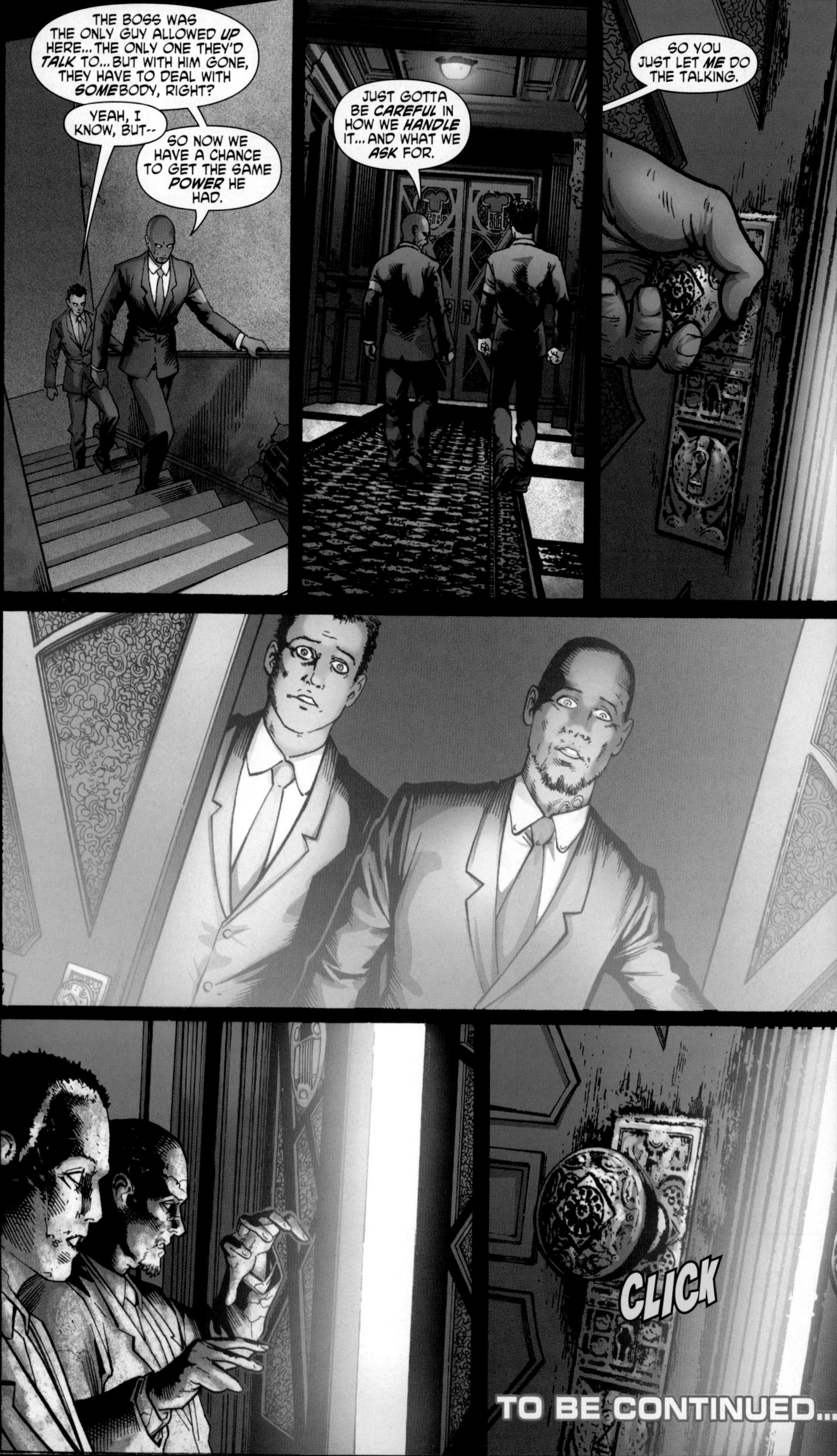
THE BOSS WAS THE ONLY GUY ALLOWED UP HERE... THE ONLY ONE THEY'D TALK TO... BUT WITH HIM GONE, THEY HAVE TO DEAL WITH SOMEBODY, RIGHT?
YEAH, I KNOW, BUT--
SO NOW WE HAVE A CHANCE TO GET THE SAME POWER HE HAD.
JUST GOTTA BE CAREFUL IN HOW WE HANDLE IT... AND WHAT WE ASK FOR.
SO YOU JUST LET ME DO THE TALKING.
CLICK
TO BE CONTINUED...

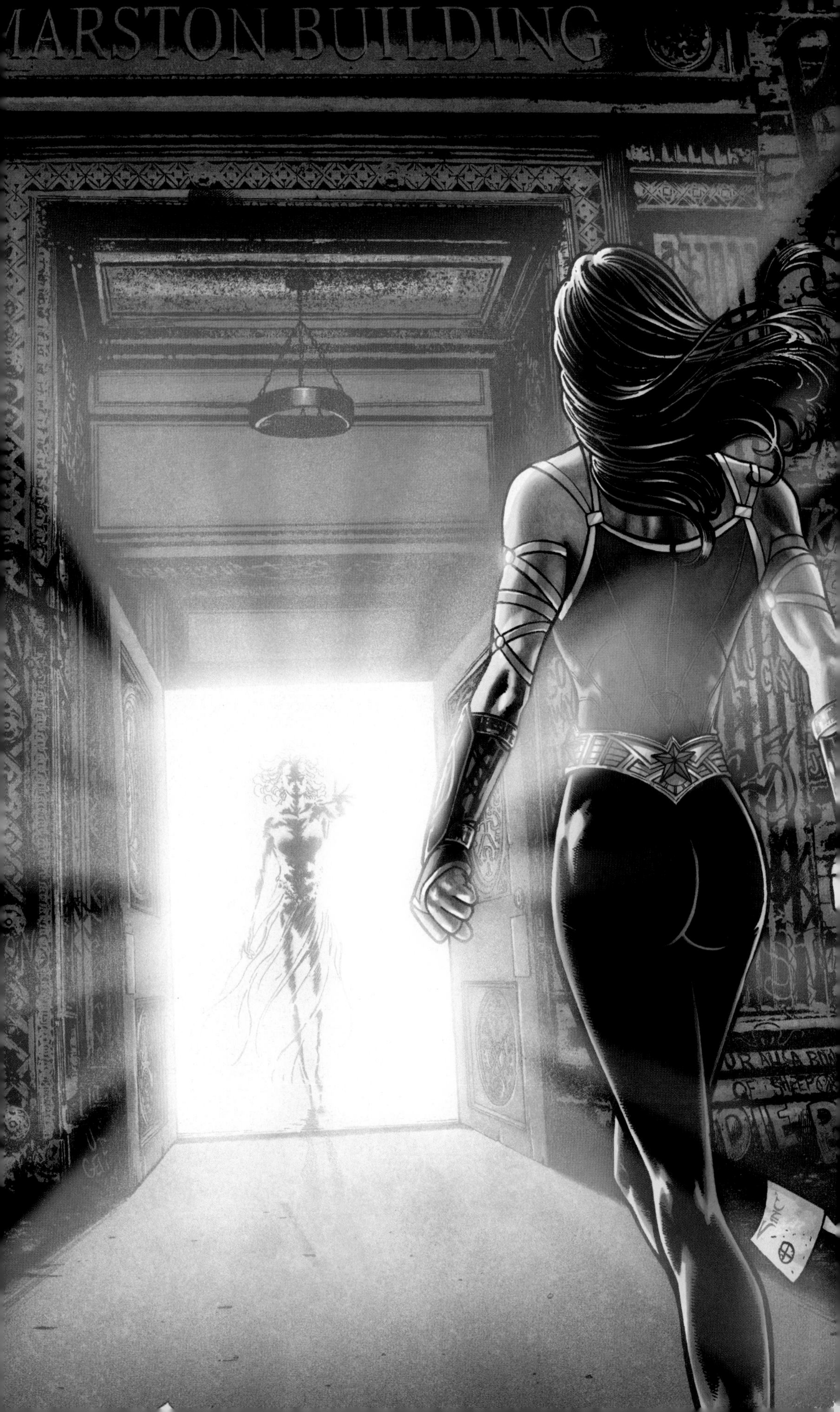
MARSTON BUILDING

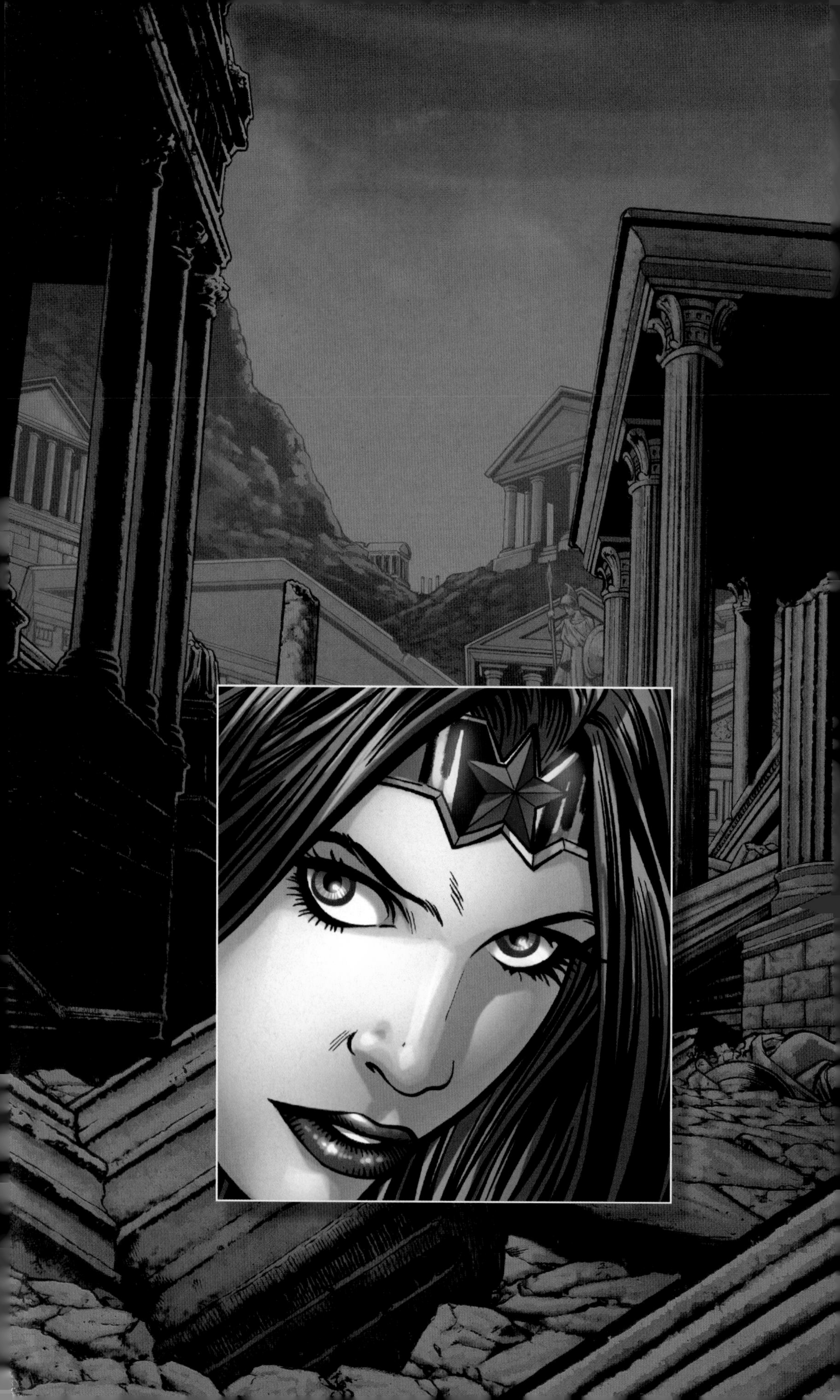

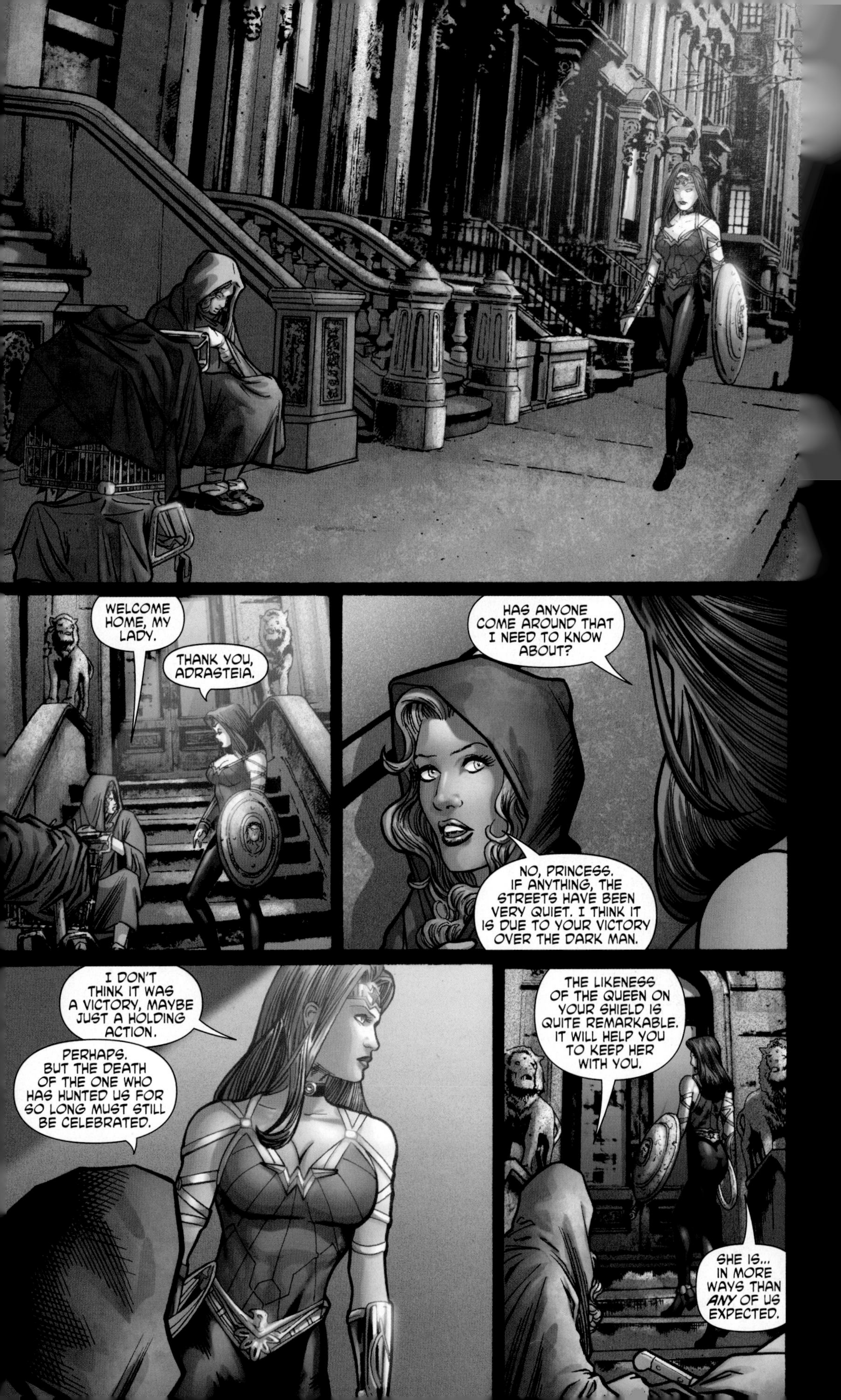
WELCOME HOME, MY LADY.
THANK YOU, ADRASTEIA.
HAS ANYONE COME AROUND THAT I NEED TO KNOW ABOUT?
NO, PRINCESS. IF ANYTHING, THE STREETS HAVE BEEN VERY QUIET. I THINK IT IS DUE TO YOUR VICTORY OVER THE DARK MAN.
I DON'T THINK IT WAS A VICTORY, MAYBE JUST A HOLDING ACTION.
PERHAPS. BUT THE DEATH OF THE ONE WHO HAS HUNTED US FOR SO LONG MUST STILL BE CELEBRATED.
THE LIKENESS OF THE QUEEN ON YOUR SHIELD IS QUITE REMARKABLE. IT WILL HELP YOU TO KEEP HER WITH YOU.
SHE IS... IN MORE WAYS THAN *ANY* OF US EXPECTED.

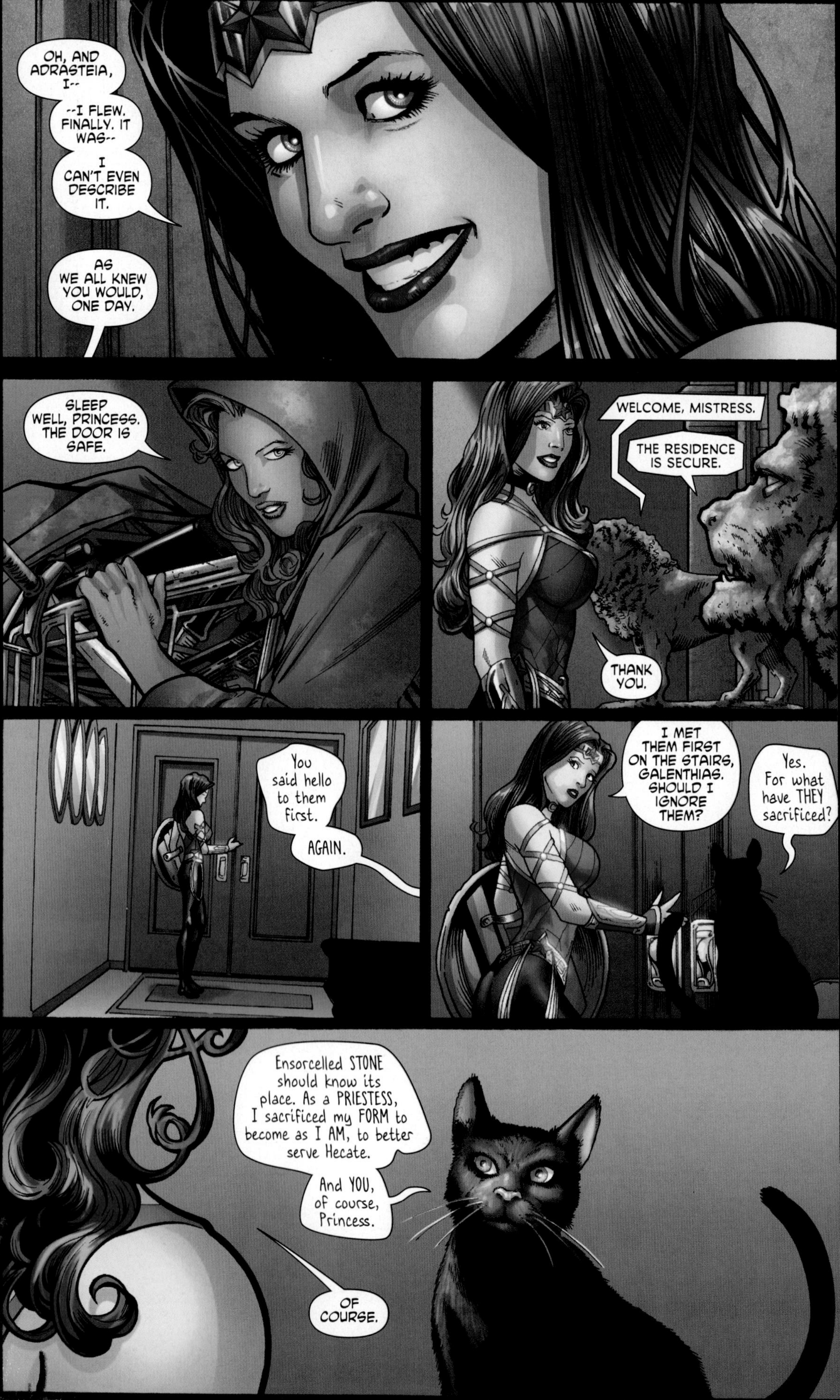
OH, AND ADRASTEIA, I--
--I FLEW. FINALLY. IT WAS--
I CAN'T EVEN DESCRIBE IT.
AS WE ALL KNEW YOU WOULD, ONE DAY.
SLEEP WELL, PRINCESS. THE DOOR IS SAFE.
WELCOME, MISTRESS.
THE RESIDENCE IS SECURE.
THANK YOU.
You said hello to them first.
AGAIN.
I MET THEM FIRST ON THE STAIRS, GALENTHIAS. SHOULD I IGNORE THEM?
Yes. For what have THEY sacrificed?
Ensorcelled STONE should know its place. As a PRIESTESS, I sacrificed my FORM to become as I AM, to better serve Hecate.
And YOU, of course, Princess.
OF COURSE.

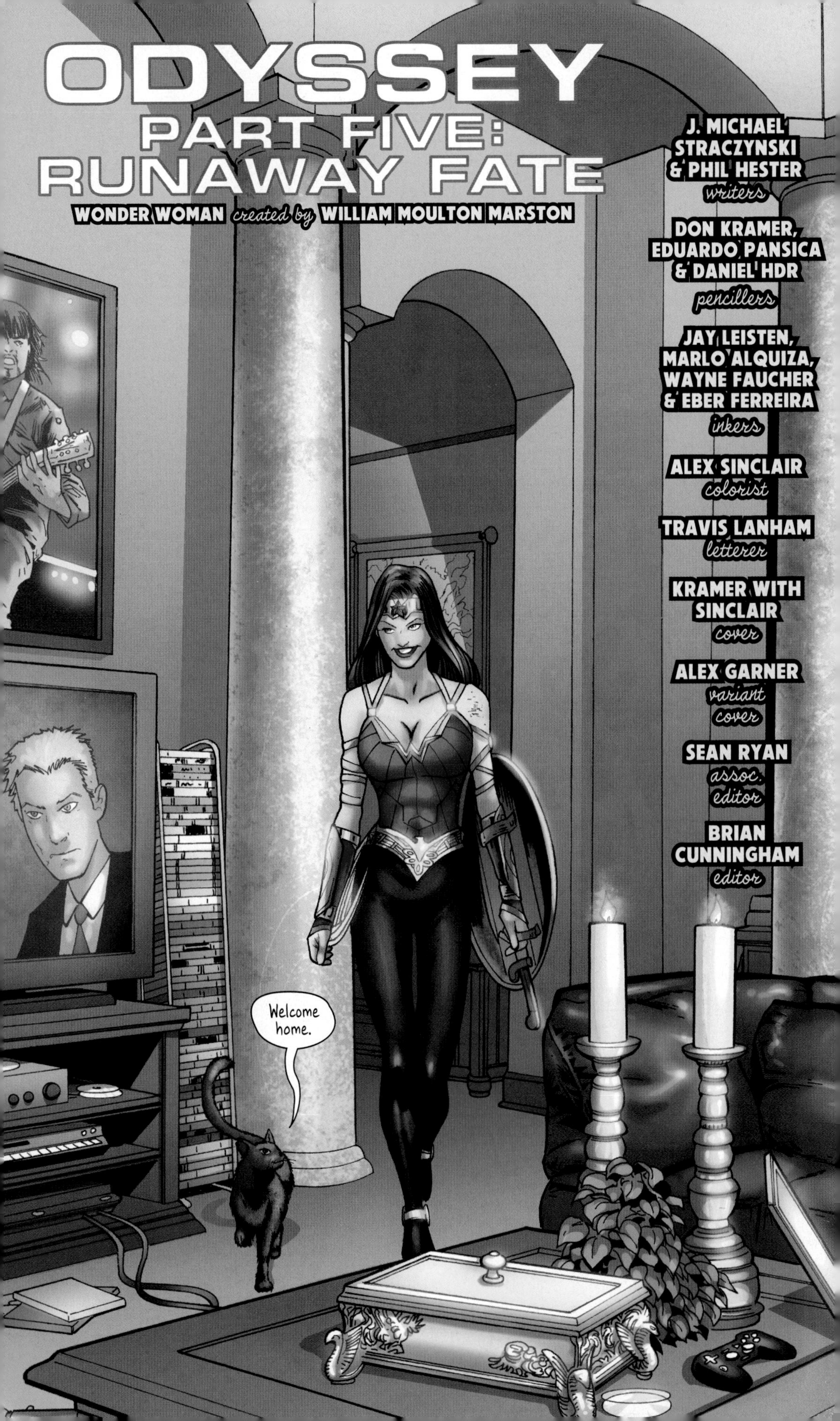
ODYSSEY
PART FIVE: RUNAWAY FATE
WONDER WOMAN created by WILLIAM MOULTON MARSTON
J. MICHAEL STRACZYNSKI & PHIL HESTER writers
DON KRAMER, EDUARDO PANSICA & DANIEL HDR pencillers
JAY LEISTEN, MARLO ALQUIZA, WAYNE FAUCHER & EBER FERREIRA inkers
ALEX SINCLAIR colorist
TRAVIS LANHAM letterer
KRAMER WITH SINCLAIR cover
ALEX GARNER variant cover
SEAN RYAN assoc. editor
BRIAN CUNNINGHAM editor
Welcome home.

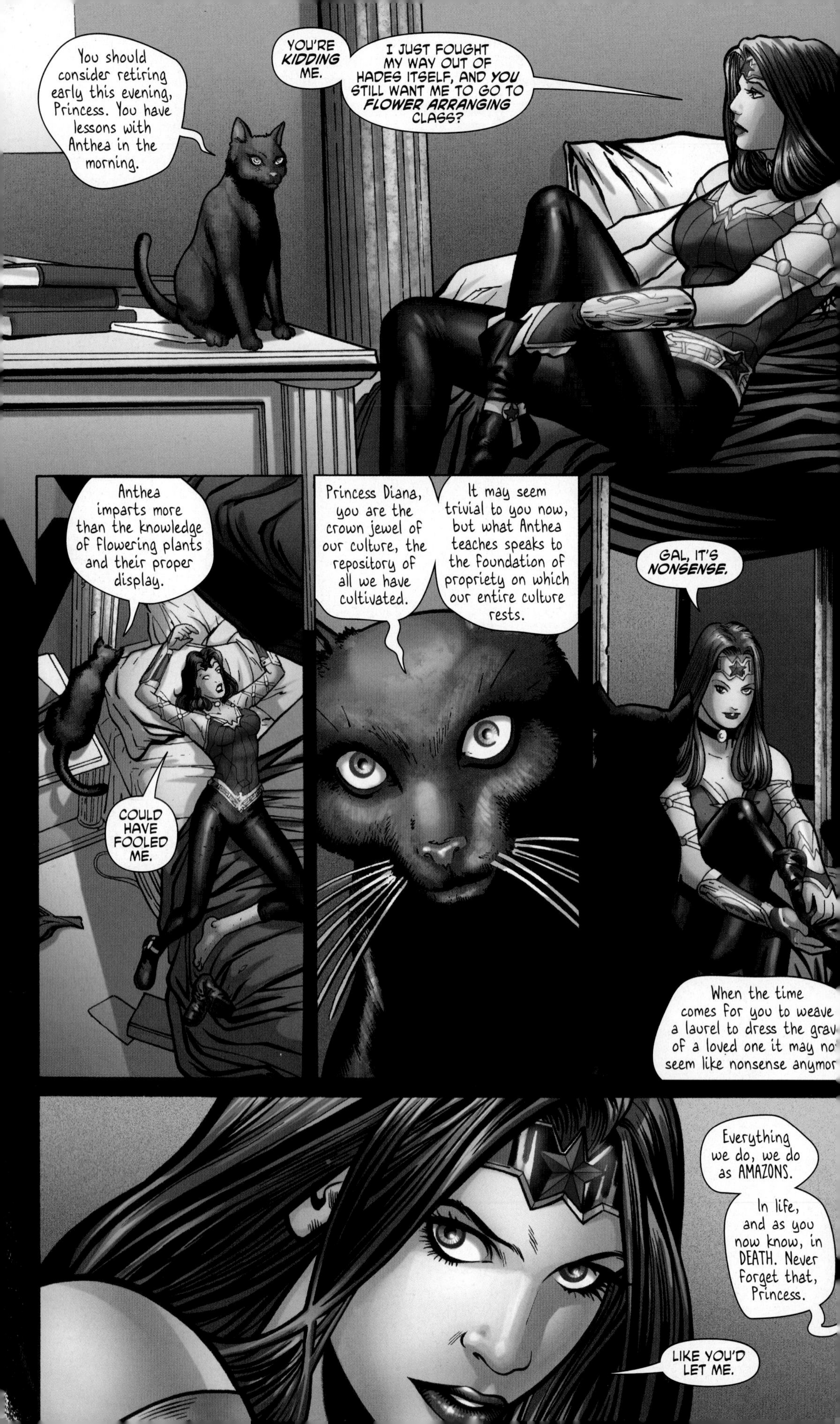
You should consider retiring early this evening, Princess. You have lessons with Anthea in the morning.
YOU'RE KIDDING ME.
I JUST FOUGHT MY WAY OUT OF HADES ITSELF, AND YOU STILL WANT ME TO GO TO FLOWER ARRANGING CLASS?
Anthea imparts more than the knowledge of flowering plants and their proper display.
COULD HAVE FOOLED ME.
Princess Diana, you are the crown jewel of our culture, the repository of all we have cultivated.
It may seem trivial to you now, but what Anthea teaches speaks to the foundation of propriety on which our entire culture rests.
GAL, IT'S NONSENSE.
When the time comes for you to weave a laurel to dress the grav of a loved one it may no seem like nonsense anymor
Everything we do, we do as AMAZONS.
In life, and as you now know, in DEATH. Never forget that, Princess.
LIKE YOU'D LET ME.

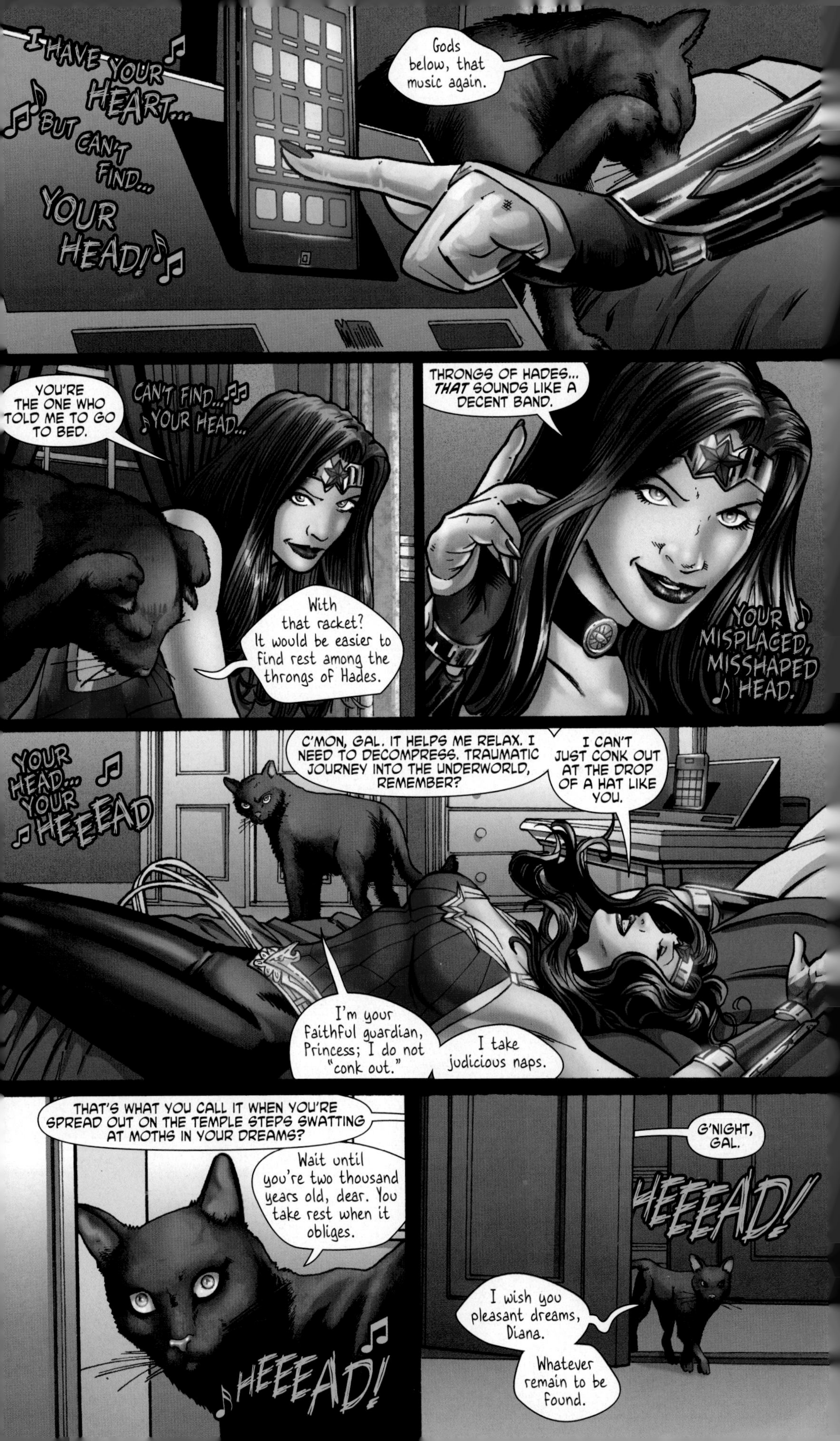
I HAVE YOUR HEART... BUT CAN'T FIND... YOUR HEAD!
Gods below, that music again.
YOU'RE THE ONE WHO TOLD ME TO GO TO BED.
CAN'T FIND... YOUR HEAD...
With that racket? It would be easier to find rest among the throngs of Hades.
THRONGS OF HADES... *THAT* SOUNDS LIKE A DECENT BAND.
YOUR MISPLACED, MISSHAPED HEAD.
YOUR HEAD... YOUR HEEEAD
C'MON, GAL. IT HELPS ME RELAX. I NEED TO DECOMPRESS. TRAUMATIC JOURNEY INTO THE UNDERWORLD, REMEMBER?
I CAN'T JUST CONK OUT AT THE DROP OF A HAT LIKE YOU.
I'm your faithful guardian, Princess; I do not "conk out."
I take judicious naps.
THAT'S WHAT YOU CALL IT WHEN YOU'RE SPREAD OUT ON THE TEMPLE STEPS SWATTING AT MOTHS IN YOUR DREAMS?
Wait until you're two thousand years old, dear. You take rest when it obliges.
HEEEAD!
G'NIGHT, GAL.
HEEEAD!
I wish you pleasant dreams, Diana.
Whatever remain to be found.

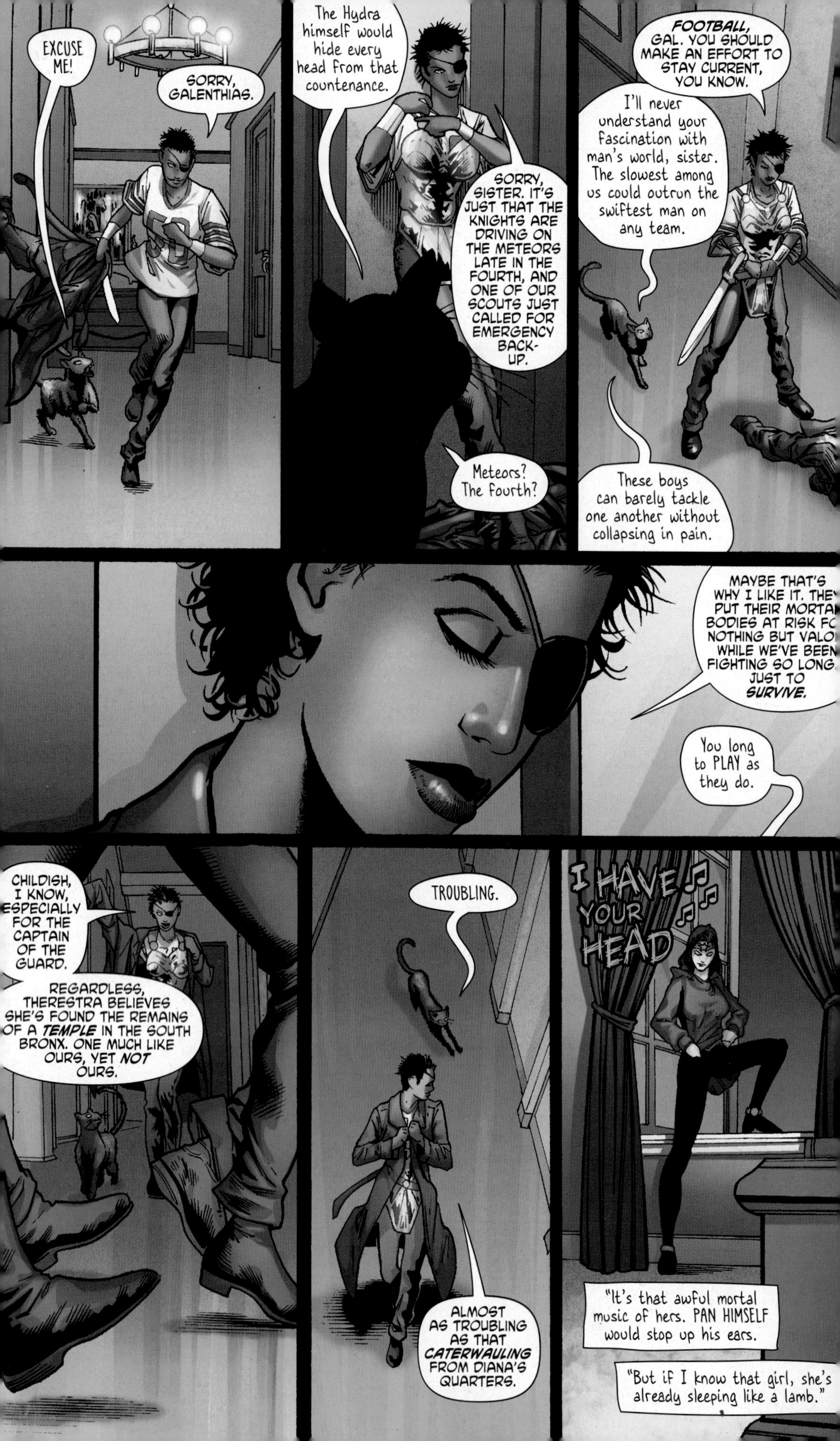
EXCUSE ME!
SORRY, GALENTHIAS.
The Hydra himself would hide every head from that countenance.
SORRY, SISTER. IT'S JUST THAT THE KNIGHTS ARE DRIVING ON THE METEORS LATE IN THE FOURTH, AND ONE OF OUR SCOUTS JUST CALLED FOR EMERGENCY BACK-UP.
Meteors? The Fourth?
FOOTBALL, GAL. YOU SHOULD MAKE AN EFFORT TO STAY CURRENT, YOU KNOW.
I'll never understand your fascination with man's world, sister. The slowest among us could outrun the swiftest man on any team.
These boys can barely tackle one another without collapsing in pain.
MAYBE THAT'S WHY I LIKE IT. THEY PUT THEIR MORTAL BODIES AT RISK FOR NOTHING BUT VALOR WHILE WE'VE BEEN FIGHTING SO LONG, JUST TO SURVIVE.
You long to PLAY as they do.
CHILDISH, I KNOW, ESPECIALLY FOR THE CAPTAIN OF THE GUARD.
REGARDLESS, THERESTRA BELIEVES SHE'S FOUND THE REMAINS OF A TEMPLE IN THE SOUTH BRONX. ONE MUCH LIKE OURS, YET NOT OURS.
TROUBLING.
ALMOST AS TROUBLING AS THAT CATERWAULING FROM DIANA'S QUARTERS.
I HAVE YOUR HEAD
"It's that awful mortal music of hers. PAN HIMSELF would stop up his ears.
"But if I know that girl, she's already sleeping like a lamb."

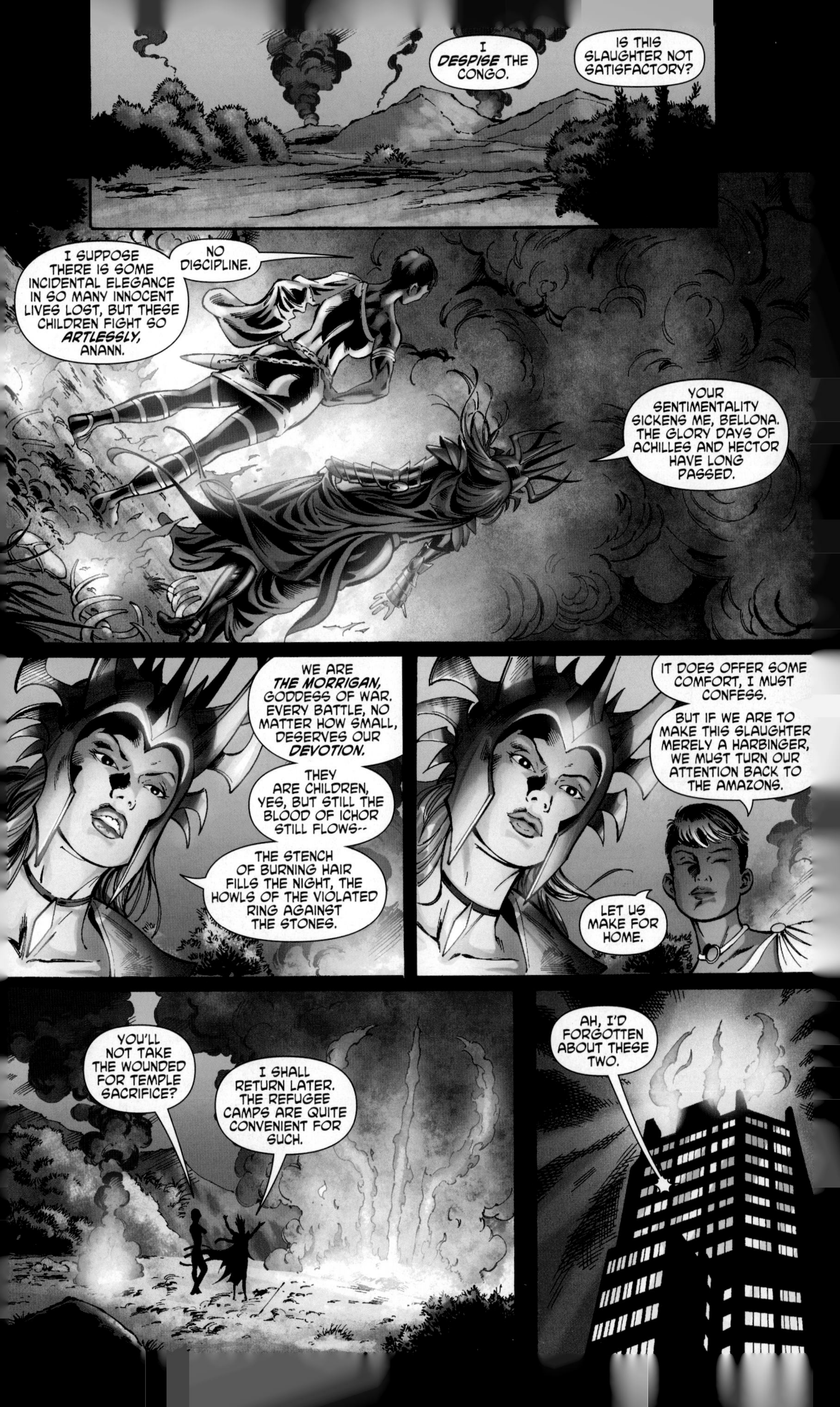

I DESPISE THE CONGO.
IS THIS SLAUGHTER NOT SATISFACTORY?
NO DISCIPLINE.
I SUPPOSE THERE IS SOME INCIDENTAL ELEGANCE IN SO MANY INNOCENT LIVES LOST, BUT THESE CHILDREN FIGHT SO ARTLESSLY, ANANN.
YOUR SENTIMENTALITY SICKENS ME, BELLONA. THE GLORY DAYS OF ACHILLES AND HECTOR HAVE LONG PASSED.
WE ARE THE MORRIGAN, GODDESS OF WAR. EVERY BATTLE, NO MATTER HOW SMALL, DESERVES OUR DEVOTION.
THEY ARE CHILDREN, YES, BUT STILL THE BLOOD OF ICHOR STILL FLOWS--
THE STENCH OF BURNING HAIR FILLS THE NIGHT, THE HOWLS OF THE VIOLATED RING AGAINST THE STONES.
IT DOES OFFER SOME COMFORT, I MUST CONFESS.
BUT IF WE ARE TO MAKE THIS SLAUGHTER MERELY A HARBINGER, WE MUST TURN OUR ATTENTION BACK TO THE AMAZONS.
LET US MAKE FOR HOME.
YOU'LL NOT TAKE THE WOUNDED FOR TEMPLE SACRIFICE?
I SHALL RETURN LATER. THE REFUGEE CAMPS ARE QUITE CONVENIENT FOR SUCH.
AH, I'D FORGOTTEN ABOUT THESE TWO.

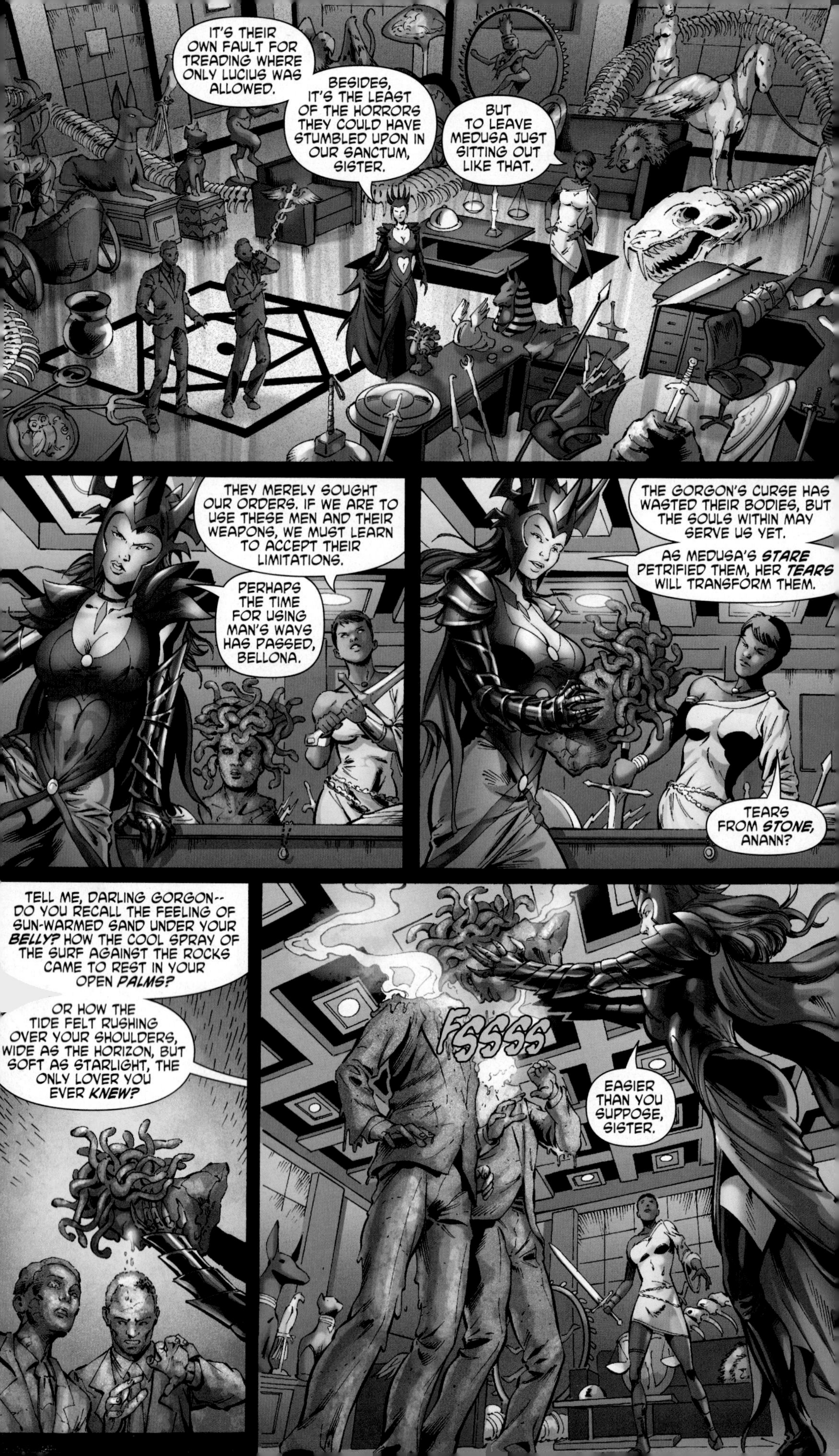
IT'S THEIR OWN FAULT FOR TREADING WHERE ONLY LUCIUS WAS ALLOWED.
BESIDES, IT'S THE LEAST OF THE HORRORS THEY COULD HAVE STUMBLED UPON IN OUR SANCTUM, SISTER.
BUT TO LEAVE MEDUSA JUST SITTING OUT LIKE THAT.
THEY MERELY SOUGHT OUR ORDERS. IF WE ARE TO USE THESE MEN AND THEIR WEAPONS, WE MUST LEARN TO ACCEPT THEIR LIMITATIONS.
PERHAPS THE TIME FOR USING MAN'S WAYS HAS PASSED, BELLONA.
THE GORGON'S CURSE HAS WASTED THEIR BODIES, BUT THE SOULS WITHIN MAY SERVE US YET.
AS MEDUSA'S STARE PETRIFIED THEM, HER TEARS WILL TRANSFORM THEM.
TEARS FROM STONE, ANANN?
TELL ME, DARLING GORGON-- DO YOU RECALL THE FEELING OF SUN-WARMED SAND UNDER YOUR BELLY? HOW THE COOL SPRAY OF THE SURF AGAINST THE ROCKS CAME TO REST IN YOUR OPEN PALMS?
OR HOW THE TIDE FELT RUSHING OVER YOUR SHOULDERS, WIDE AS THE HORIZON, BUT SOFT AS STARLIGHT, THE ONLY LOVER YOU EVER KNEW?
FSSSS
EASIER THAN YOU SUPPOSE, SISTER.

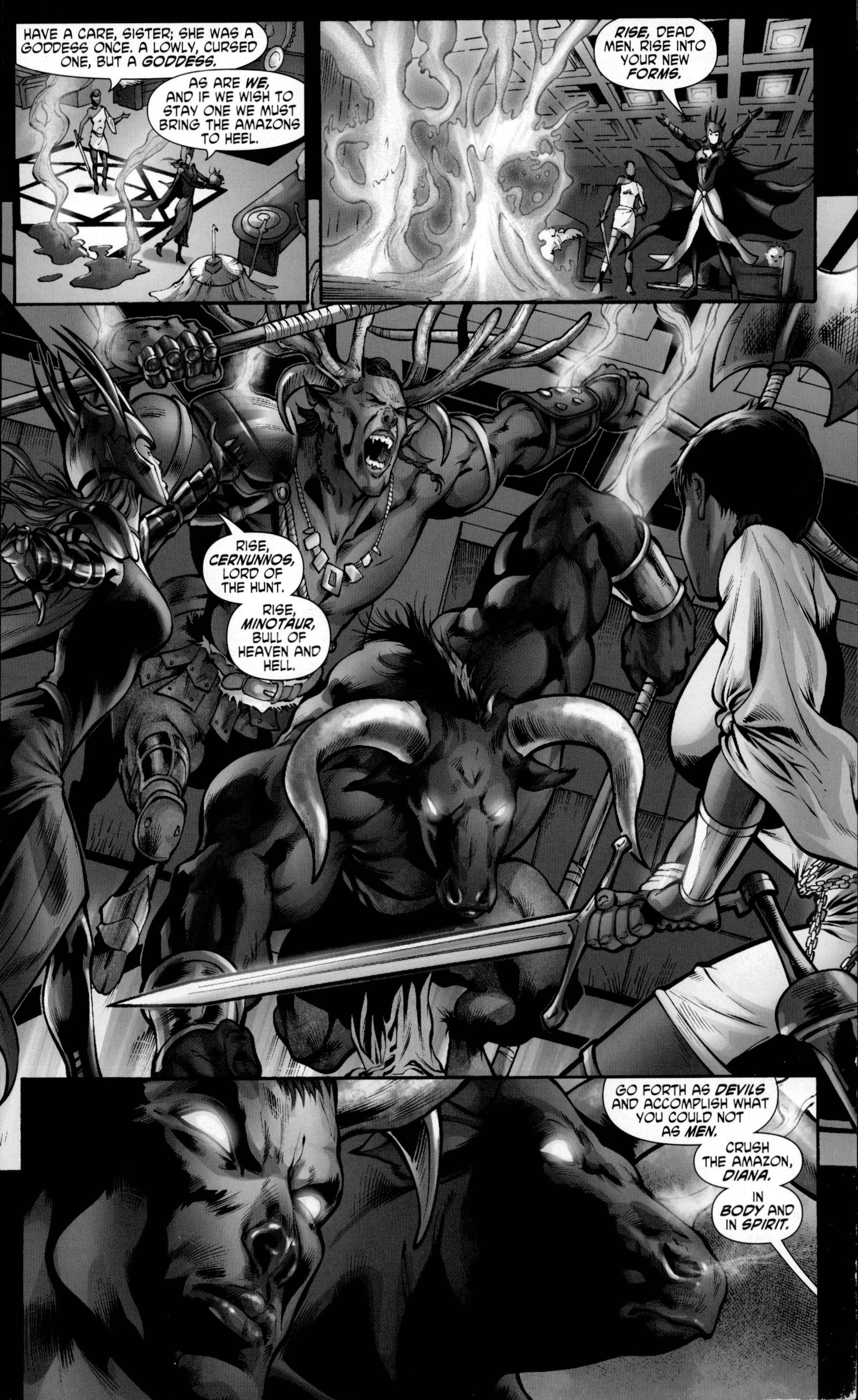
HAVE A CARE, SISTER; SHE WAS A GODDESS ONCE. A LOWLY, CURSED ONE, BUT A GODDESS.
AS ARE WE, AND IF WE WISH TO STAY ONE WE MUST BRING THE AMAZONS TO HEEL.
RISE, DEAD MEN. RISE INTO YOUR NEW FORMS.
RISE, CERNUNNOS, LORD OF THE HUNT.
RISE, MINOTAUR, BULL OF HEAVEN AND HELL.
GO FORTH AS DEVILS AND ACCOMPLISH WHAT YOU COULD NOT AS MEN.
CRUSH THE AMAZON, DIANA.
IN BODY AND IN SPIRIT.

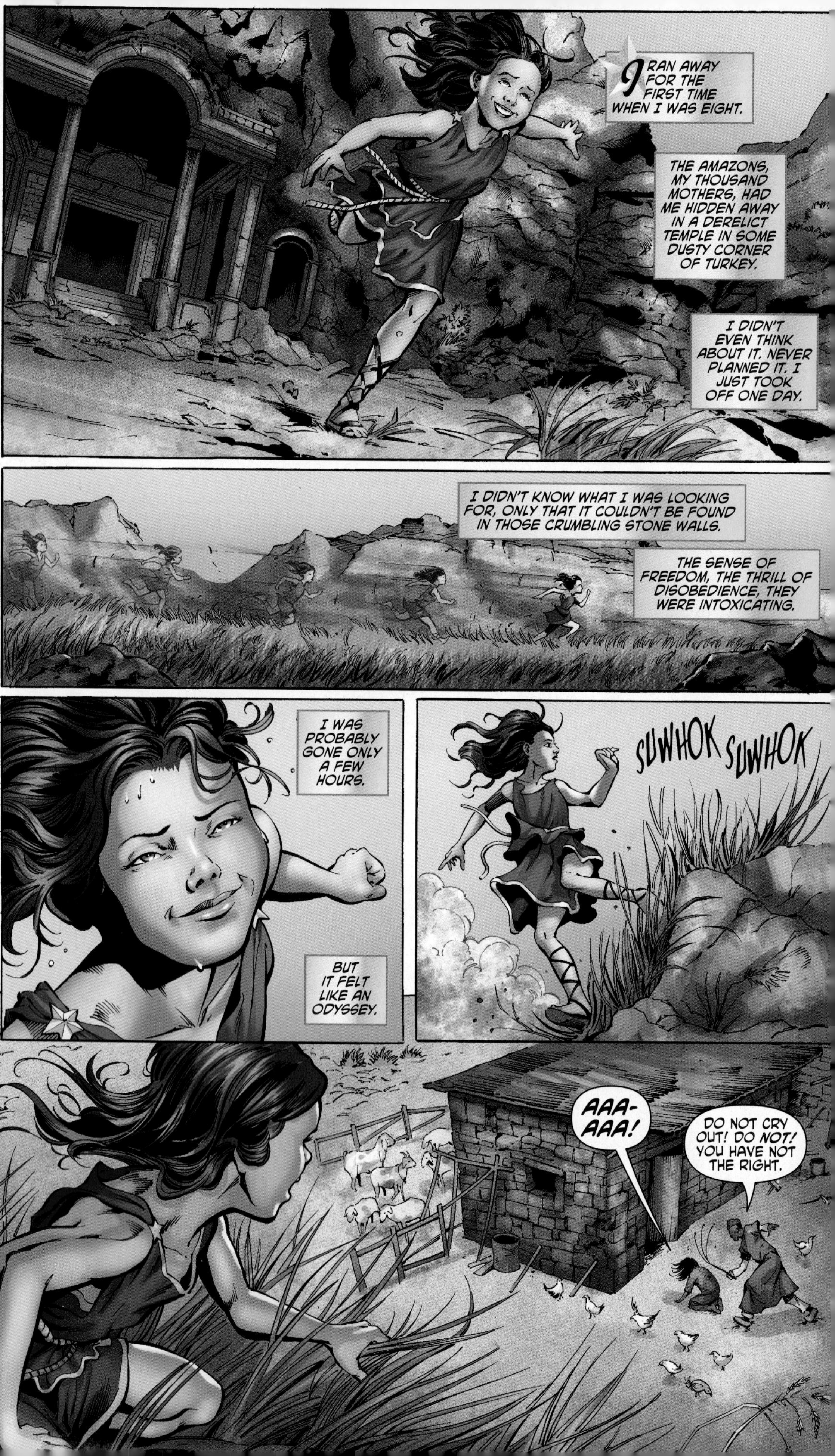
I RAN AWAY FOR THE FIRST TIME WHEN I WAS EIGHT.
THE AMAZONS, MY THOUSAND MOTHERS, HAD ME HIDDEN AWAY IN A DERELICT TEMPLE IN SOME DUSTY CORNER OF TURKEY.
I DIDN'T EVEN THINK ABOUT IT. NEVER PLANNED IT. I JUST TOOK OFF ONE DAY.
I DIDN'T KNOW WHAT I WAS LOOKING FOR, ONLY THAT IT COULDN'T BE FOUND IN THOSE CRUMBLING STONE WALLS.
THE SENSE OF FREEDOM, THE THRILL OF DISOBEDIENCE, THEY WERE INTOXICATING.
I WAS PROBABLY GONE ONLY A FEW HOURS.
BUT IT FELT LIKE AN ODYSSEY.
SUWHOK SUWHOK
AAA-AAA!
DO NOT CRY OUT! DO NOT! YOU HAVE NOT THE RIGHT.

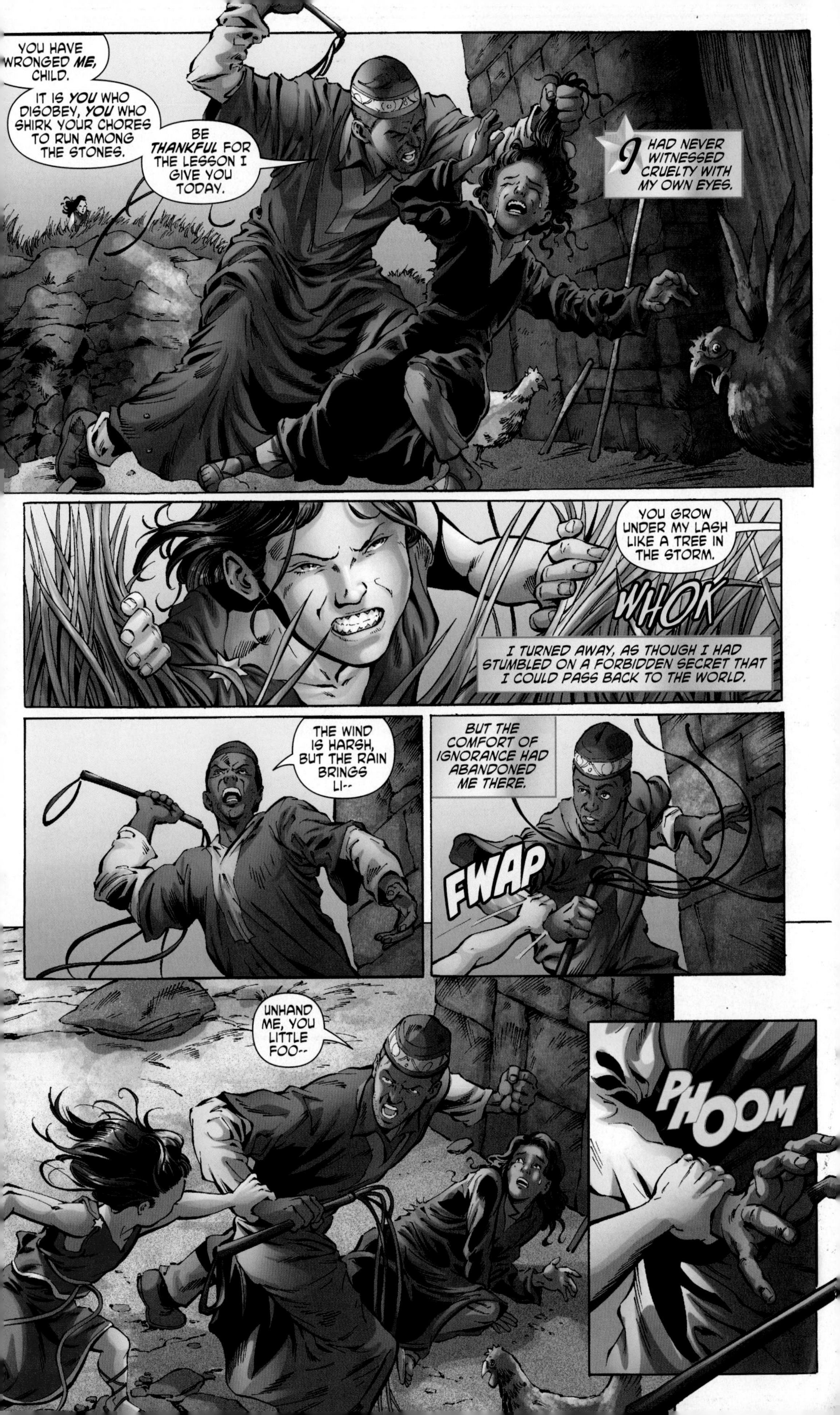
YOU HAVE WRONGED ME, CHILD.
IT IS YOU WHO DISOBEY, YOU WHO SHIRK YOUR CHORES TO RUN AMONG THE STONES.
BE THANKFUL FOR THE LESSON I GIVE YOU TODAY.
I HAD NEVER WITNESSED CRUELTY WITH MY OWN EYES.
YOU GROW UNDER MY LASH LIKE A TREE IN THE STORM.
WHOK
I TURNED AWAY, AS THOUGH I HAD STUMBLED ON A FORBIDDEN SECRET THAT I COULD PASS BACK TO THE WORLD.
THE WIND IS HARSH, BUT THE RAIN BRINGS LI--
BUT THE COMFORT OF IGNORANCE HAD ABANDONED ME THERE.
FWAP
UNHAND ME, YOU LITTLE FOO--
PHOOM

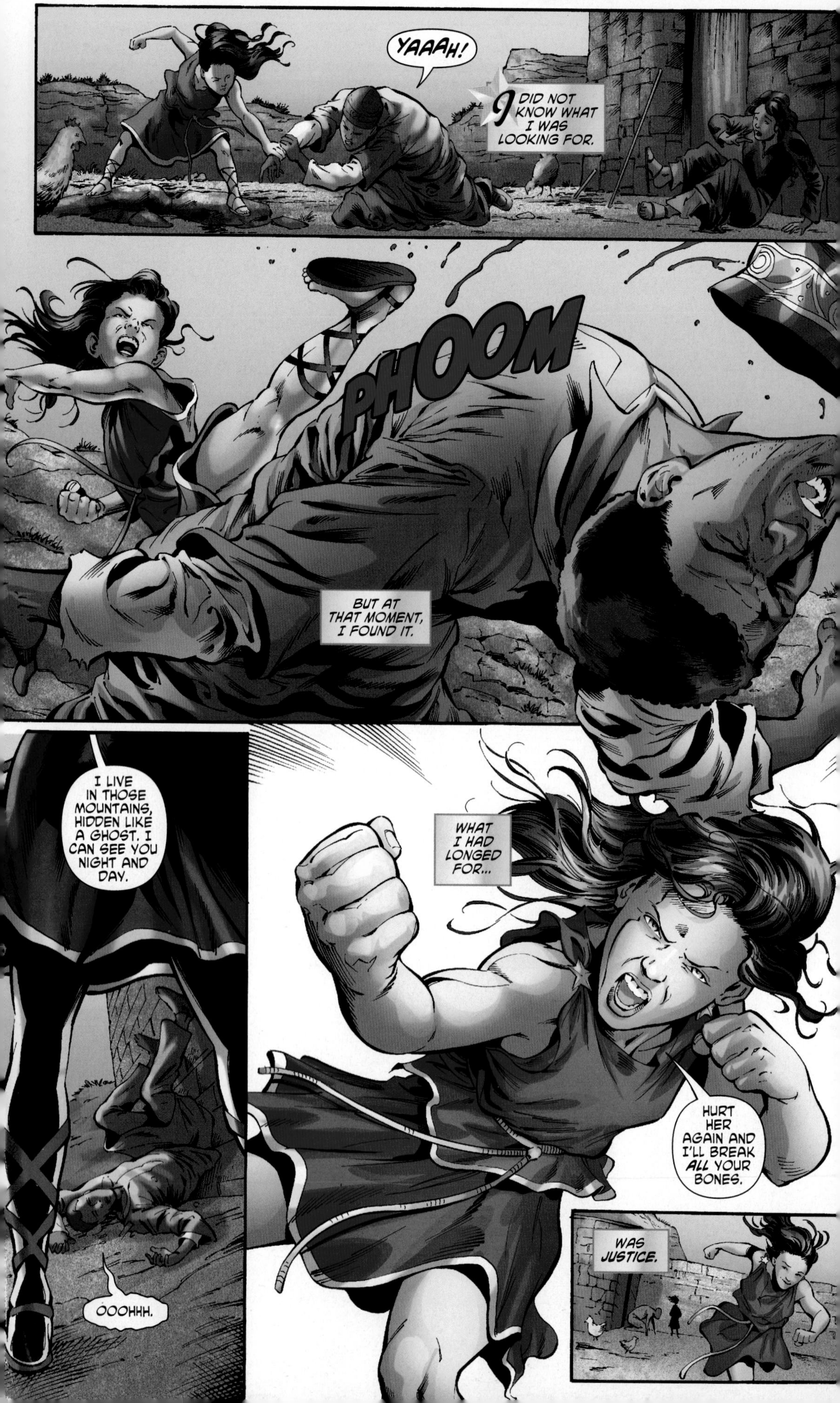
YAAAH!
I DID NOT KNOW WHAT I WAS LOOKING FOR.
PHOOM
BUT AT THAT MOMENT, I FOUND IT.
I LIVE IN THOSE MOUNTAINS, HIDDEN LIKE A GHOST. I CAN SEE YOU NIGHT AND DAY.
OOOHHH.
WHAT I HAD LONGED FOR...
HURT HER AGAIN AND I'LL BREAK ALL YOUR BONES.
WAS JUSTICE.

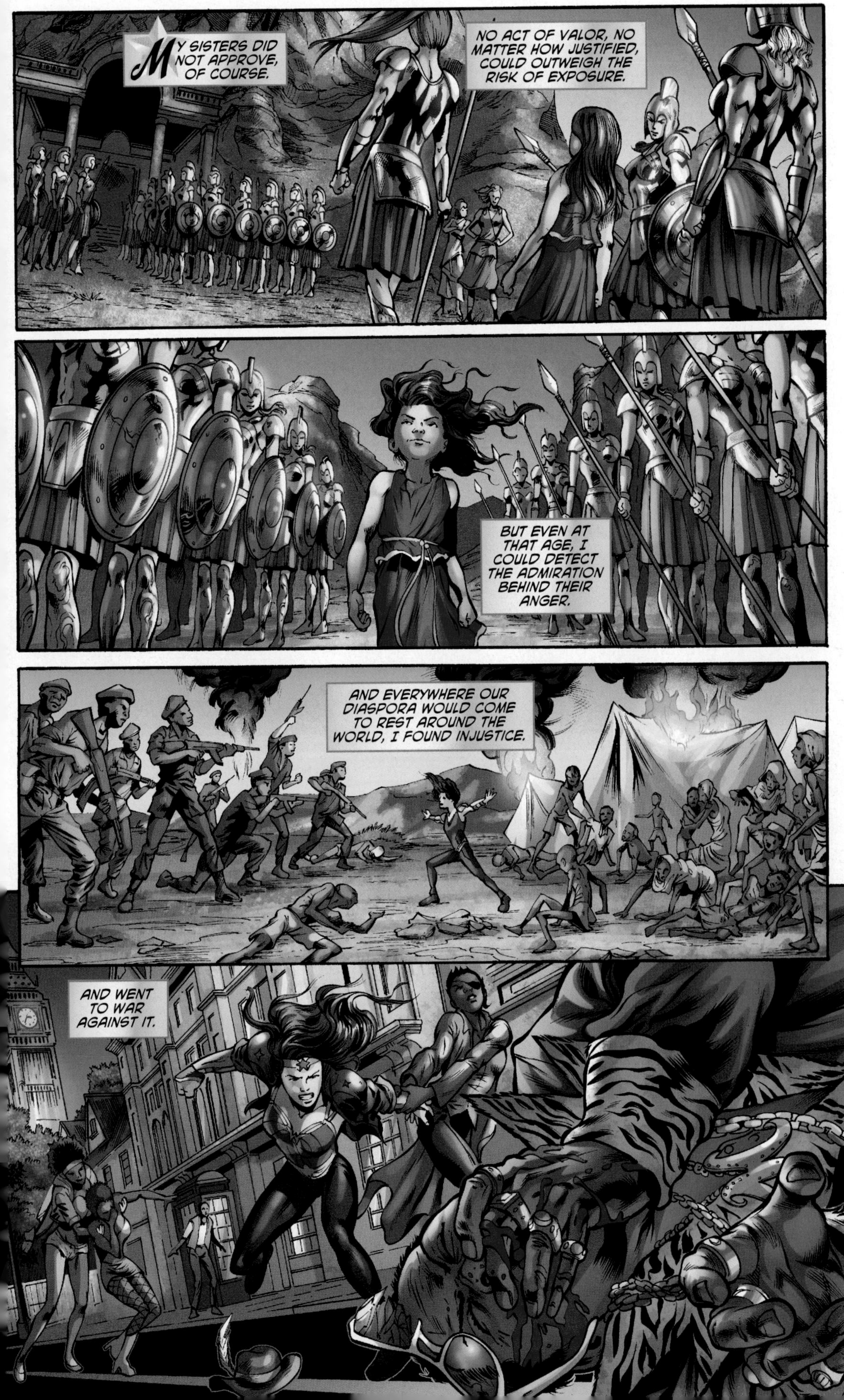
MY SISTERS DID NOT APPROVE, OF COURSE.
NO ACT OF VALOR, NO MATTER HOW JUSTIFIED, COULD OUTWEIGH THE RISK OF EXPOSURE.
BUT EVEN AT THAT AGE, I COULD DETECT THE ADMIRATION BEHIND THEIR ANGER.
AND EVERYWHERE OUR DIASPORA WOULD COME TO REST AROUND THE WORLD, I FOUND INJUSTICE.
AND WENT TO WAR AGAINST IT.

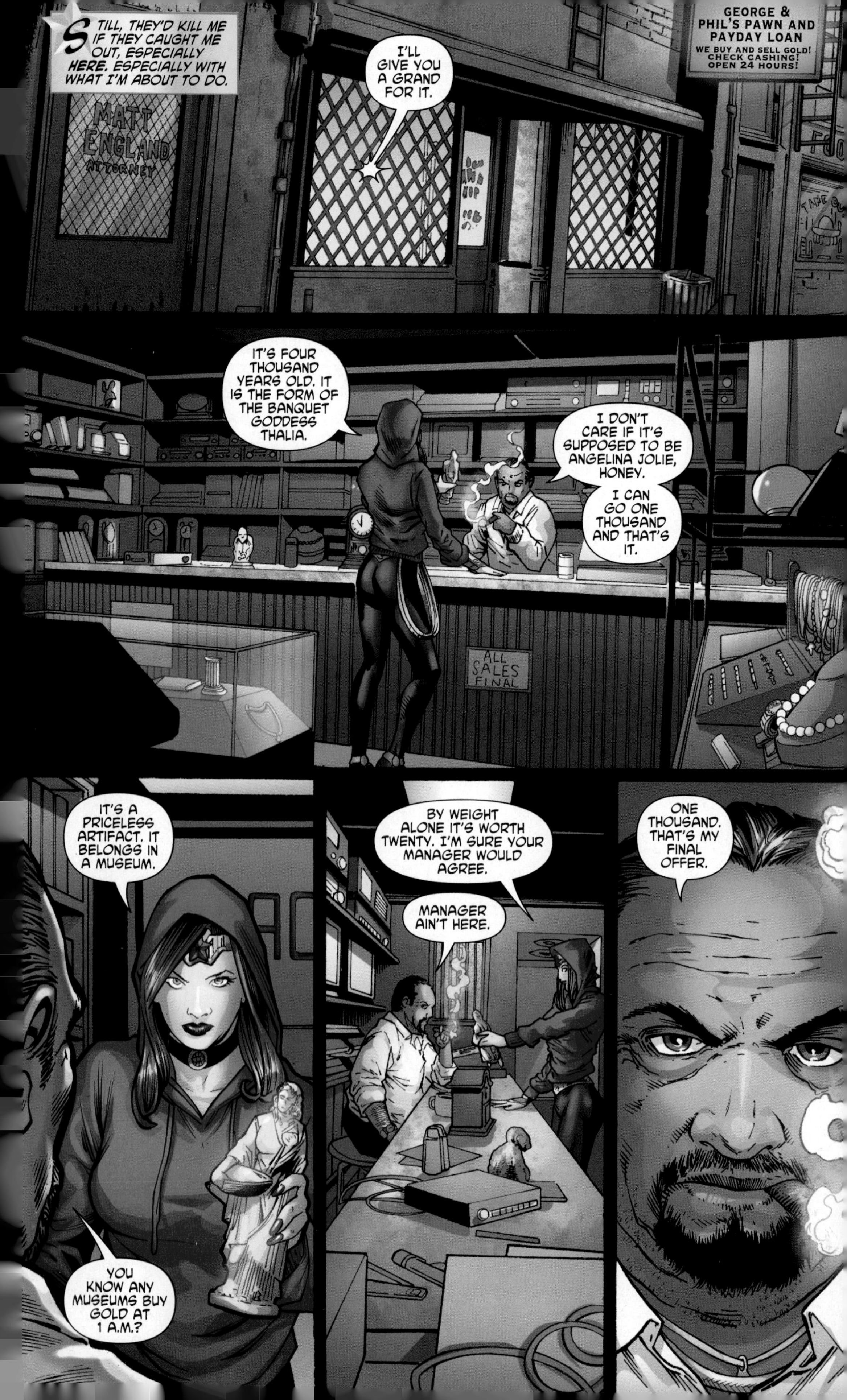
STILL, THEY'D KILL ME IF THEY CAUGHT ME OUT, ESPECIALLY HERE. ESPECIALLY WITH WHAT I'M ABOUT TO DO.
MATT ENGLAND ATTORNEY
I'LL GIVE YOU A GRAND FOR IT.
GEORGE & PHIL'S PAWN AND PAYDAY LOAN
WE BUY AND SELL GOLD! CHECK CASHING! OPEN 24 HOURS!
IT'S FOUR THOUSAND YEARS OLD. IT IS THE FORM OF THE BANQUET GODDESS THALIA.
I DON'T CARE IF IT'S SUPPOSED TO BE ANGELINA JOLIE, HONEY.
I CAN GO ONE THOUSAND AND THAT'S IT.
ALL SALES FINAL
IT'S A PRICELESS ARTIFACT. IT BELONGS IN A MUSEUM.
YOU KNOW ANY MUSEUMS BUY GOLD AT 1 A.M.?
BY WEIGHT ALONE IT'S WORTH TWENTY. I'M SURE YOUR MANAGER WOULD AGREE.
MANAGER AIN'T HERE.
ONE THOUSAND. THAT'S MY FINAL OFFER.

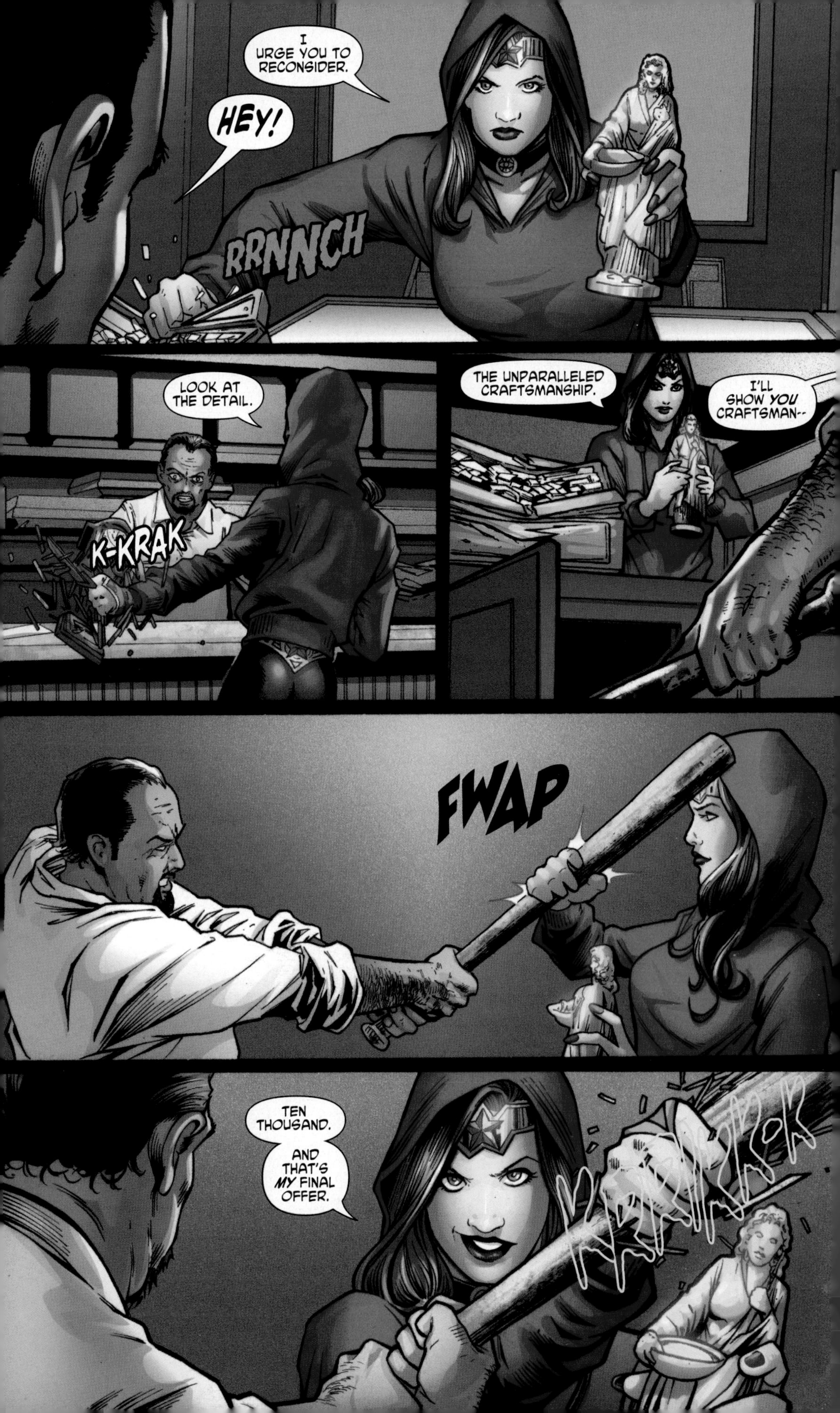
I URGE YOU TO RECONSIDER.
HEY!
RRNNCH
LOOK AT THE DETAIL.
K-KRAK
THE UNPARALLELED CRAFTSMANSHIP.
I'LL SHOW YOU CRAFTSMAN--
FWAP
TEN THOUSAND.
AND THAT'S MY FINAL OFFER.

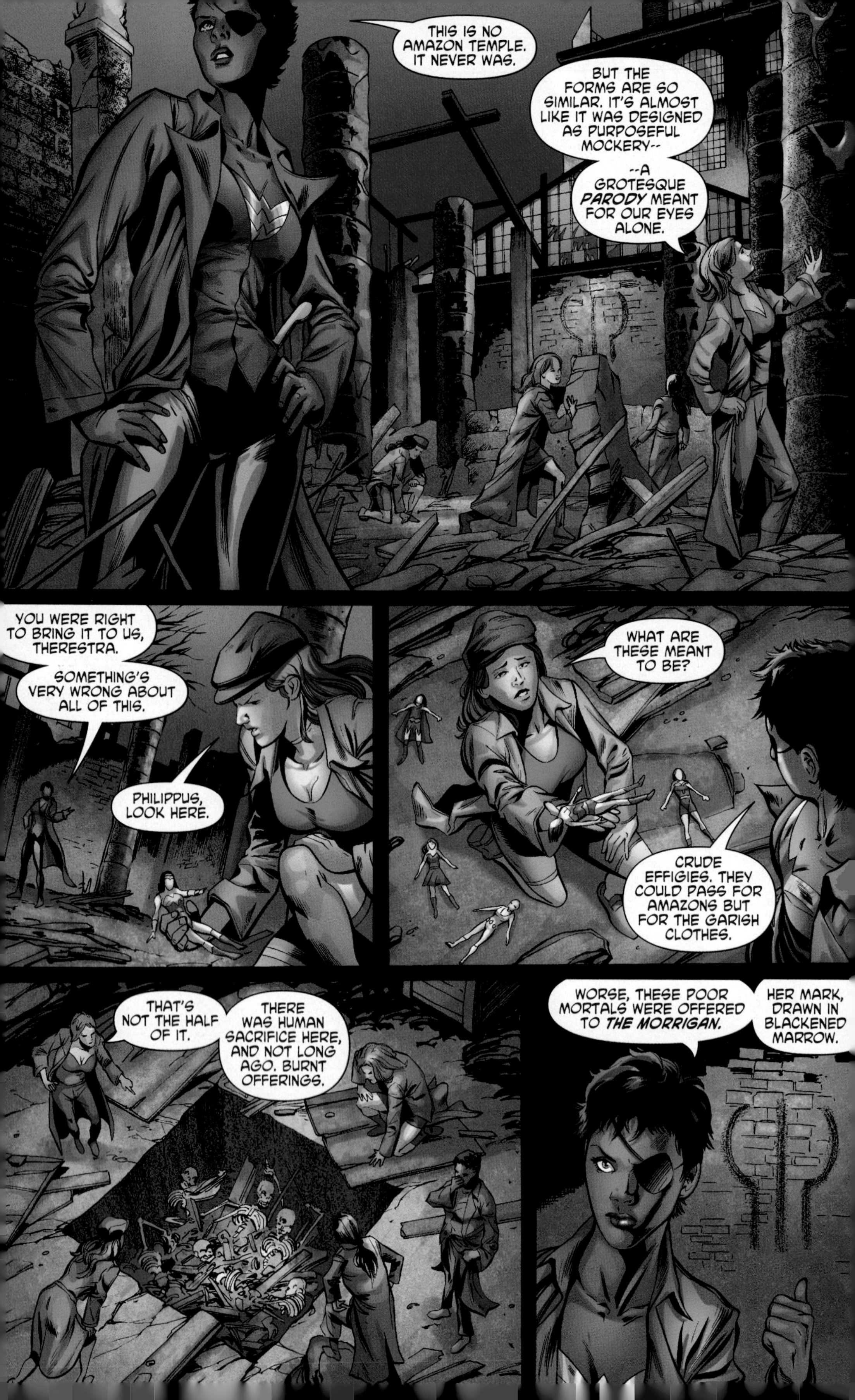
THIS IS NO AMAZON TEMPLE. IT NEVER WAS.
BUT THE FORMS ARE SO SIMILAR. IT'S ALMOST LIKE IT WAS DESIGNED AS PURPOSEFUL MOCKERY--
--A GROTESQUE *PARODY* MEANT FOR OUR EYES ALONE.
YOU WERE RIGHT TO BRING IT TO US, THERESTRA.
SOMETHING'S VERY WRONG ABOUT ALL OF THIS.
PHILIPPUS, LOOK HERE.
WHAT ARE THESE MEANT TO BE?
CRUDE EFFIGIES. THEY COULD PASS FOR AMAZONS BUT FOR THE GARISH CLOTHES.
THAT'S NOT THE HALF OF IT.
THERE WAS HUMAN SACRIFICE HERE, AND NOT LONG AGO. BURNT OFFERINGS.
WORSE, THESE POOR MORTALS WERE OFFERED TO *THE MORRIGAN.*
HER MARK, DRAWN IN BLACKENED MARROW.

THE MORRIGAN?

BROADEN YOUR STUDIES, ORITHIA, NOT ALL GODS ARE OF AMAZON KEN.

SHE WAS ORIGINALLY A GODDESS OF THE CELTS, A SHRIEKING GHOUL-QUEEN WHO DANCED AMONG THE CORPSES AFTER WAR.

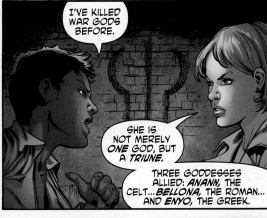

I'VE KILLED WAR GODS BEFORE.

SHE IS NOT MERELY *ONE* GOD, BUT A *TRIUNE*.

THREE GODDESSES ALLIED: *ANANN*, THE CELT...*BELLONA*, THE ROMAN... AND *ENYO*, THE GREEK.

THEY FEED ON THE HORROR OF WAR, GROW FAT ON THE BLOOD OF THE INNOCENT DEAD.

IMAGINE THEIR STRENGTH IN THESE TIMES.

I REMEMBER THE ORACLE SAYING SOMETHING ABOUT THE DEATH OF ENYO.

BUT AS WITH ALL THINGS REGARDING GODS OR ORACLES, I'LL BELIEVE IT WHEN I SEE--

MEEP MEEP

We have an emergency.

IT *MUST* BE FOR YOU TO USE A CELL PHONE, GALENTHIAS.

Philippus, Diana is MISSING!

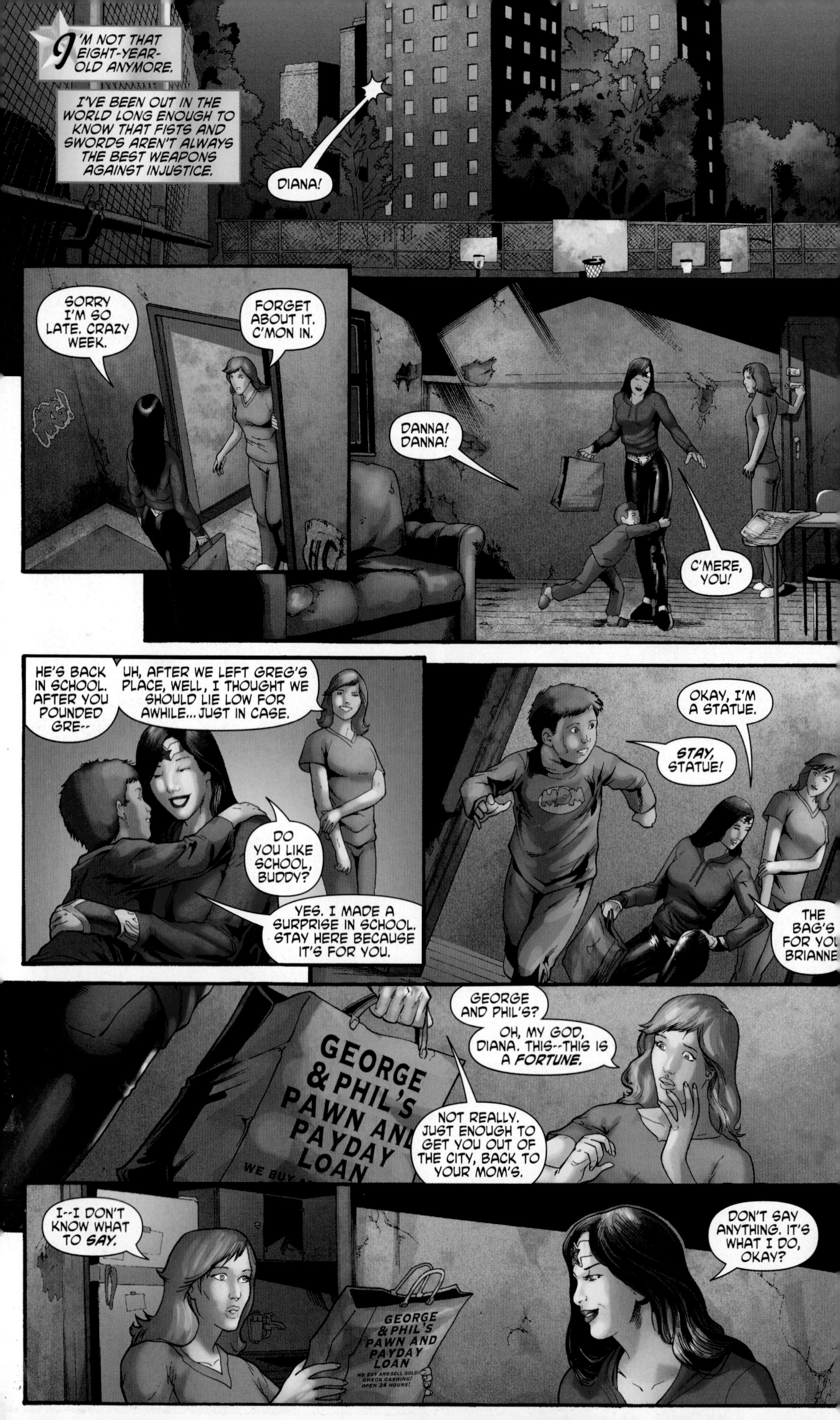
I'M NOT THAT EIGHT-YEAR-OLD ANYMORE.
I'VE BEEN OUT IN THE WORLD LONG ENOUGH TO KNOW THAT FISTS AND SWORDS AREN'T ALWAYS THE BEST WEAPONS AGAINST INJUSTICE.
DIANA!
SORRY I'M SO LATE. CRAZY WEEK.
FORGET ABOUT IT. C'MON IN.
DANNA! DANNA!
C'MERE, YOU!
HE'S BACK IN SCHOOL. AFTER YOU POUNDED GRE--
UH, AFTER WE LEFT GREG'S PLACE, WELL, I THOUGHT WE SHOULD LIE LOW FOR AWHILE... JUST IN CASE.
DO YOU LIKE SCHOOL, BUDDY?
YES. I MADE A SURPRISE IN SCHOOL. STAY HERE BECAUSE IT'S FOR YOU.
OKAY, I'M A STATUE.
STAY, STATUE!
THE BAG'S FOR YOU BRIANNE
GEORGE AND PHIL'S?
OH, MY GOD, DIANA. THIS--THIS IS A FORTUNE.
GEORGE & PHIL'S PAWN AND PAYDAY LOAN
NOT REALLY. JUST ENOUGH TO GET YOU OUT OF THE CITY, BACK TO YOUR MOM'S.
I--I DON'T KNOW WHAT TO SAY.
GEORGE & PHIL'S PAWN AND PAYDAY LOAN
WE BUY AND SELL GOLD! CHECK CASHING! OPEN 24 HOURS!
DON'T SAY ANYTHING. IT'S WHAT I DO, OKAY?

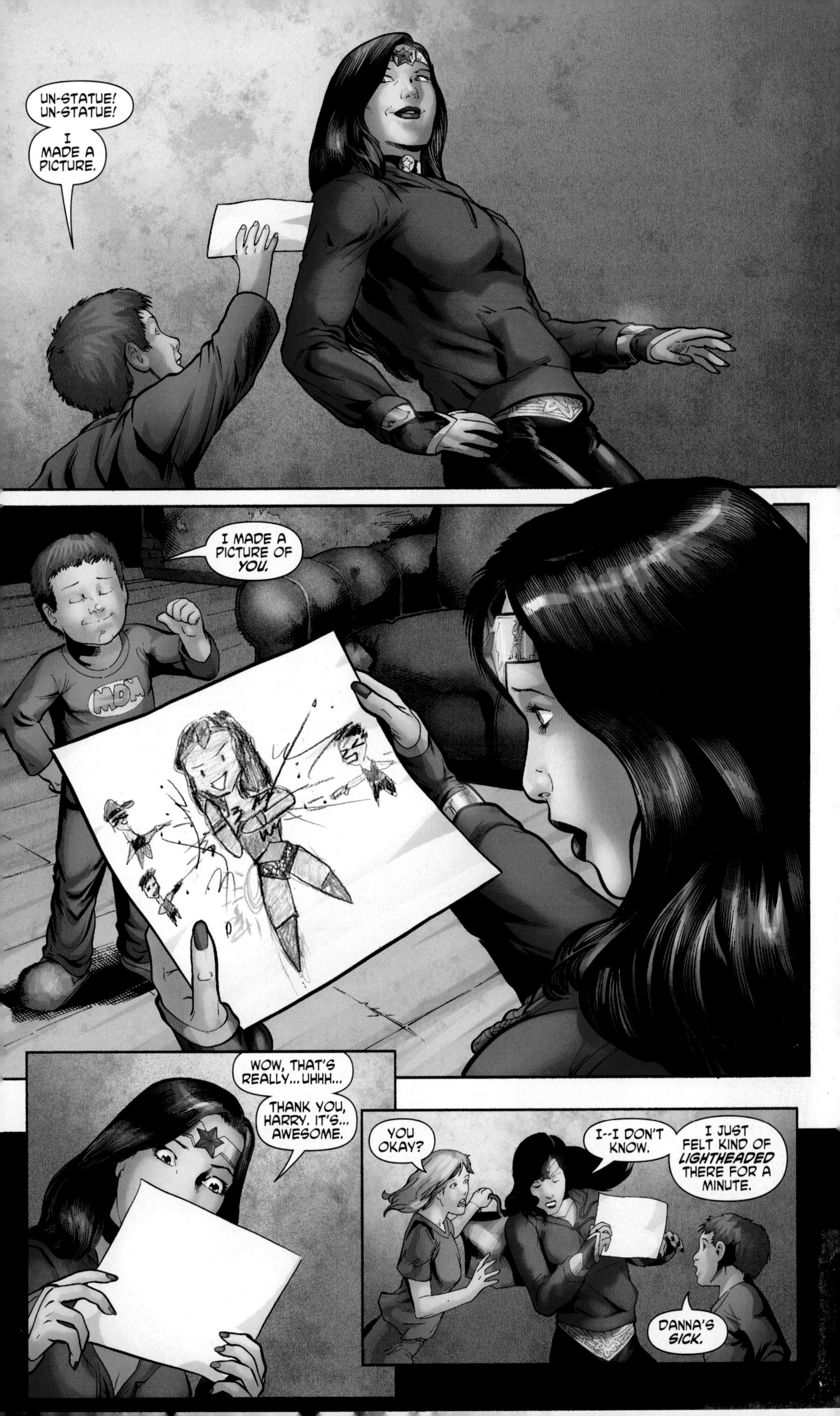
UN-STATUE! UN-STATUE!
I MADE A PICTURE.
I MADE A PICTURE OF *YOU.*
WOW, THAT'S REALLY... UHHH...
THANK YOU, HARRY. IT'S... AWESOME.
YOU OKAY?
I--I DON'T KNOW.
I JUST FELT KIND OF *LIGHTHEADED* THERE FOR A MINUTE.
DANNA'S *SICK.*

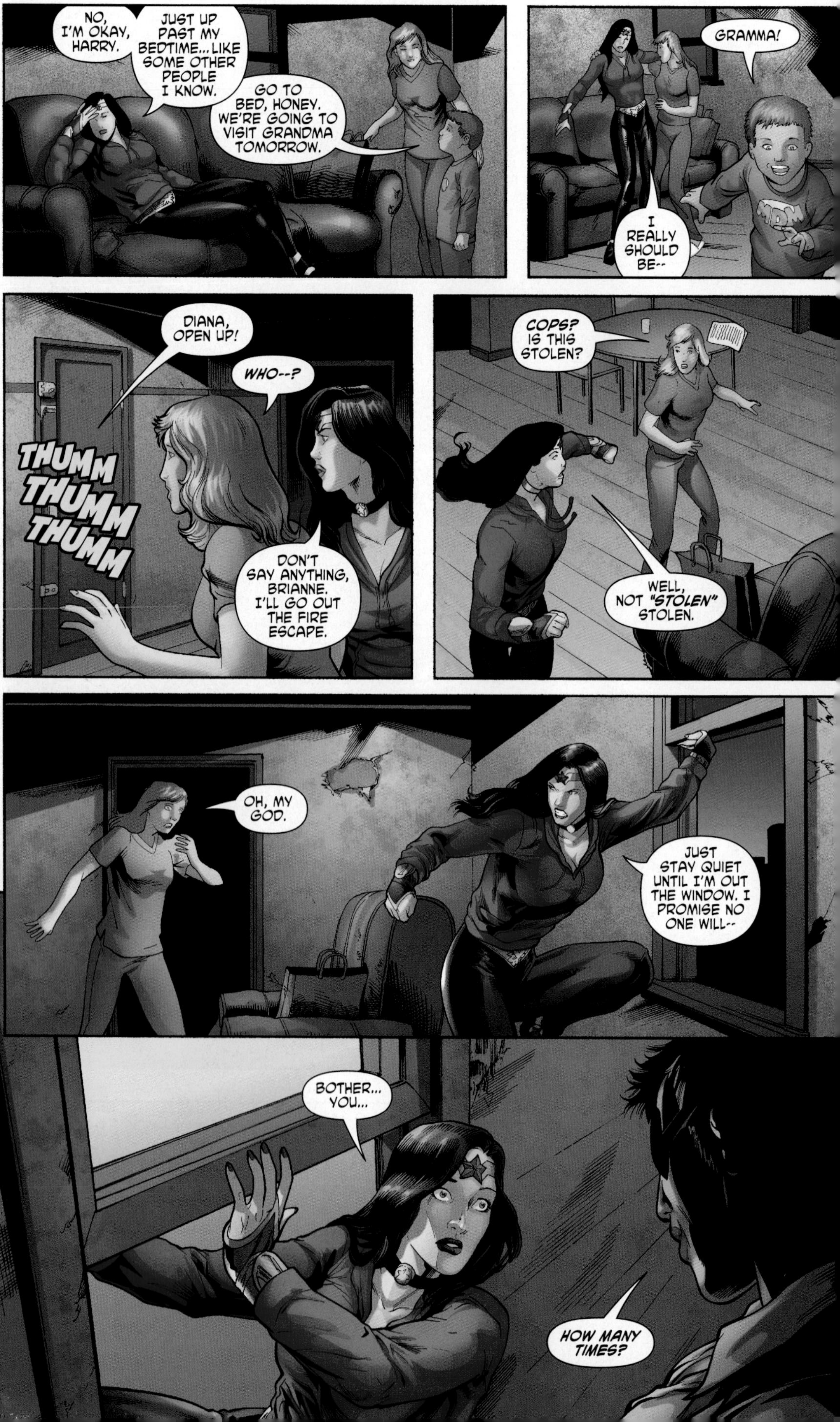
NO, I'M OKAY, HARRY.
JUST UP PAST MY BEDTIME... LIKE SOME OTHER PEOPLE I KNOW.
GO TO BED, HONEY. WE'RE GOING TO VISIT GRANDMA TOMORROW.
GRAMMA!
I REALLY SHOULD BE--
DIANA, OPEN UP!
WHO--?
THUMM THUMM THUMM
DON'T SAY ANYTHING, BRIANNE. I'LL GO OUT THE FIRE ESCAPE.
COPS? IS THIS STOLEN?
WELL, NOT "STOLEN" STOLEN.
OH, MY GOD.
JUST STAY QUIET UNTIL I'M OUT THE WINDOW. I PROMISE NO ONE WILL--
BOTHER... YOU...
HOW MANY TIMES?

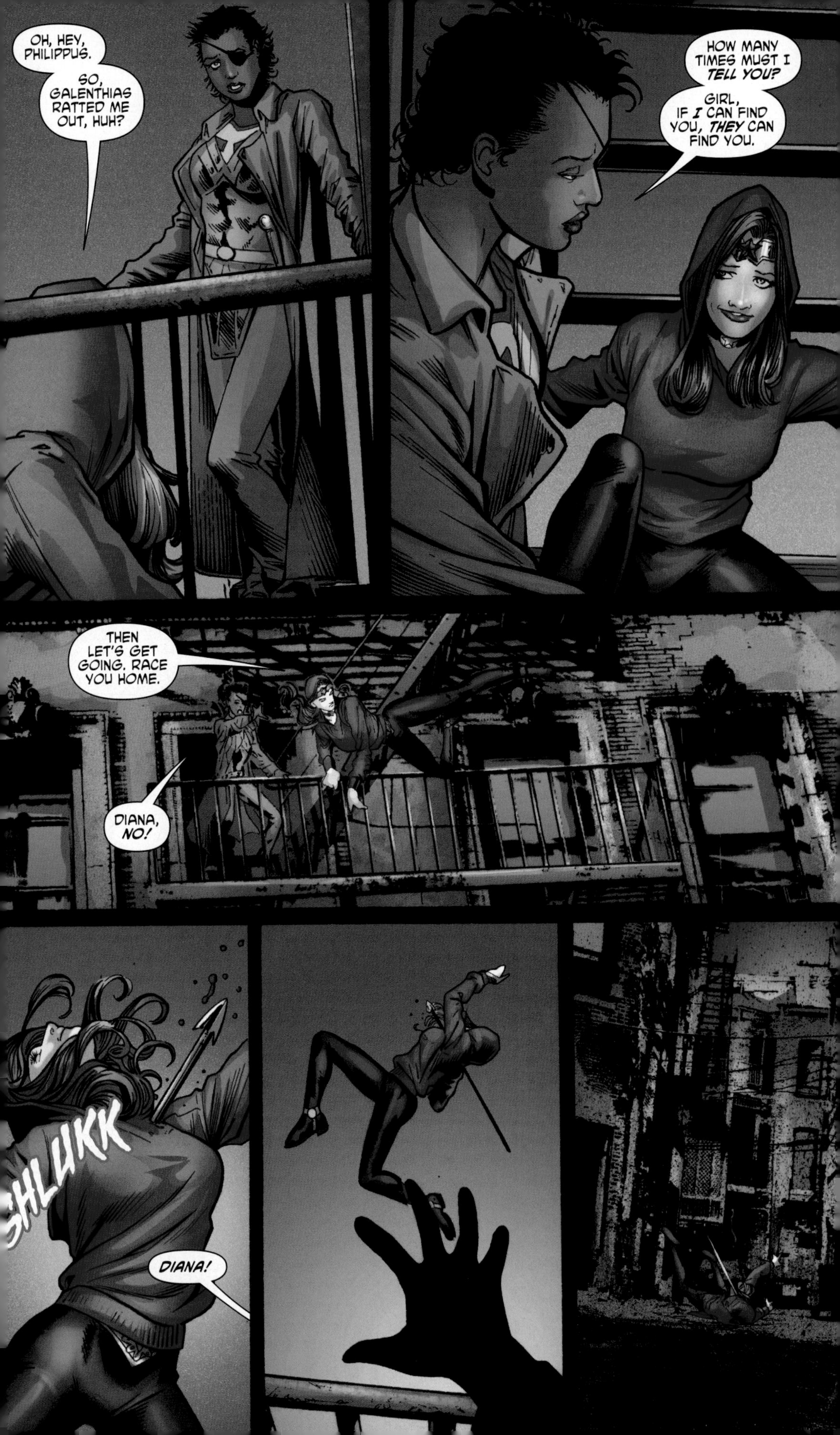
OH, HEY, PHILIPPUS.
SO, GALENTHIAS RATTED ME OUT, HUH?
HOW MANY TIMES MUST I *TELL YOU?*
GIRL, IF *I* CAN FIND YOU, *THEY* CAN FIND YOU.
THEN LET'S GET GOING. RACE YOU HOME.
DIANA, *NO!*
SHLUKK
DIANA!

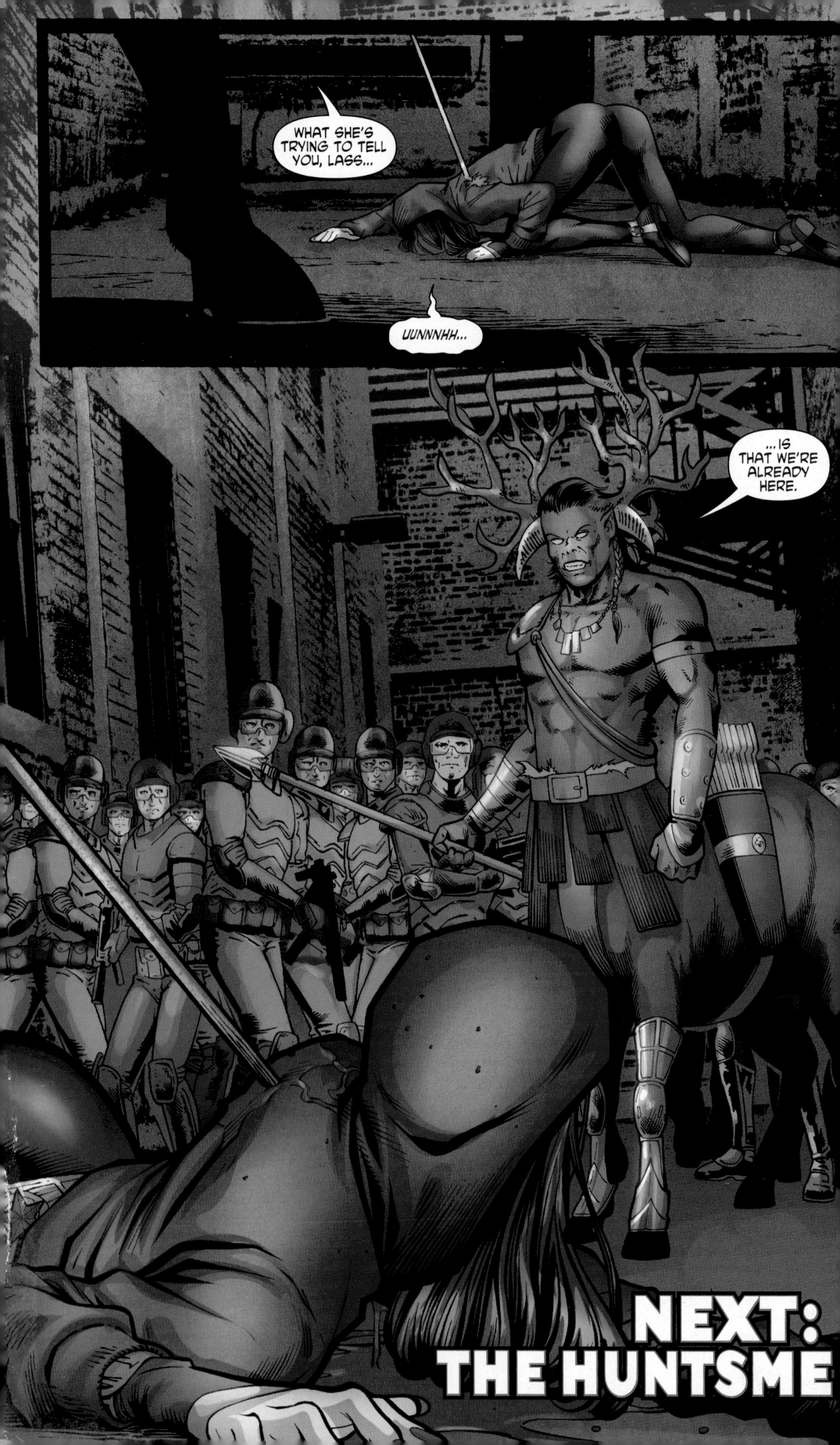
WHAT SHE'S TRYING TO TELL YOU, LASS...
UUNNNHH...
...IS THAT WE'RE ALREADY HERE.
NEXT: THE HUNTSME

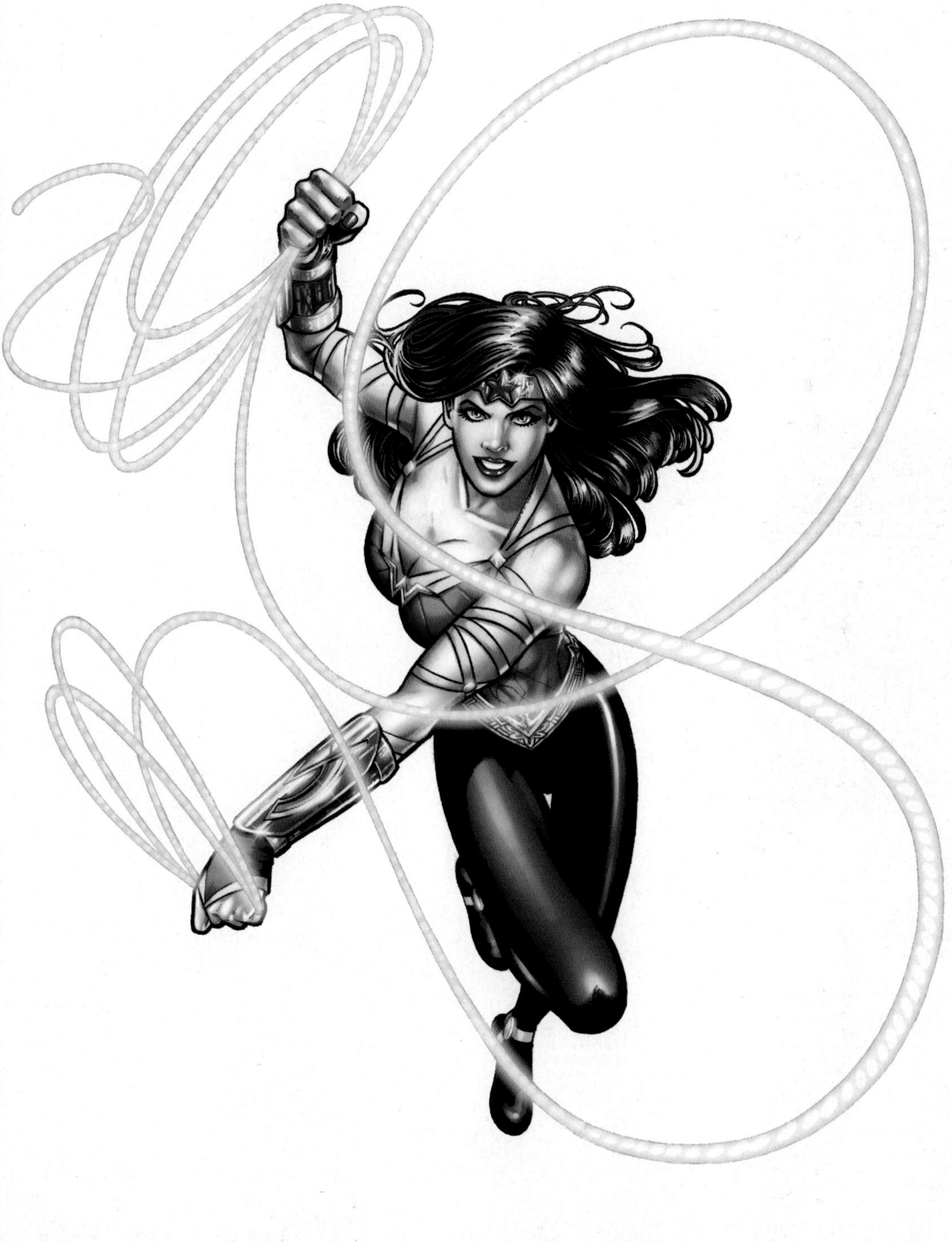

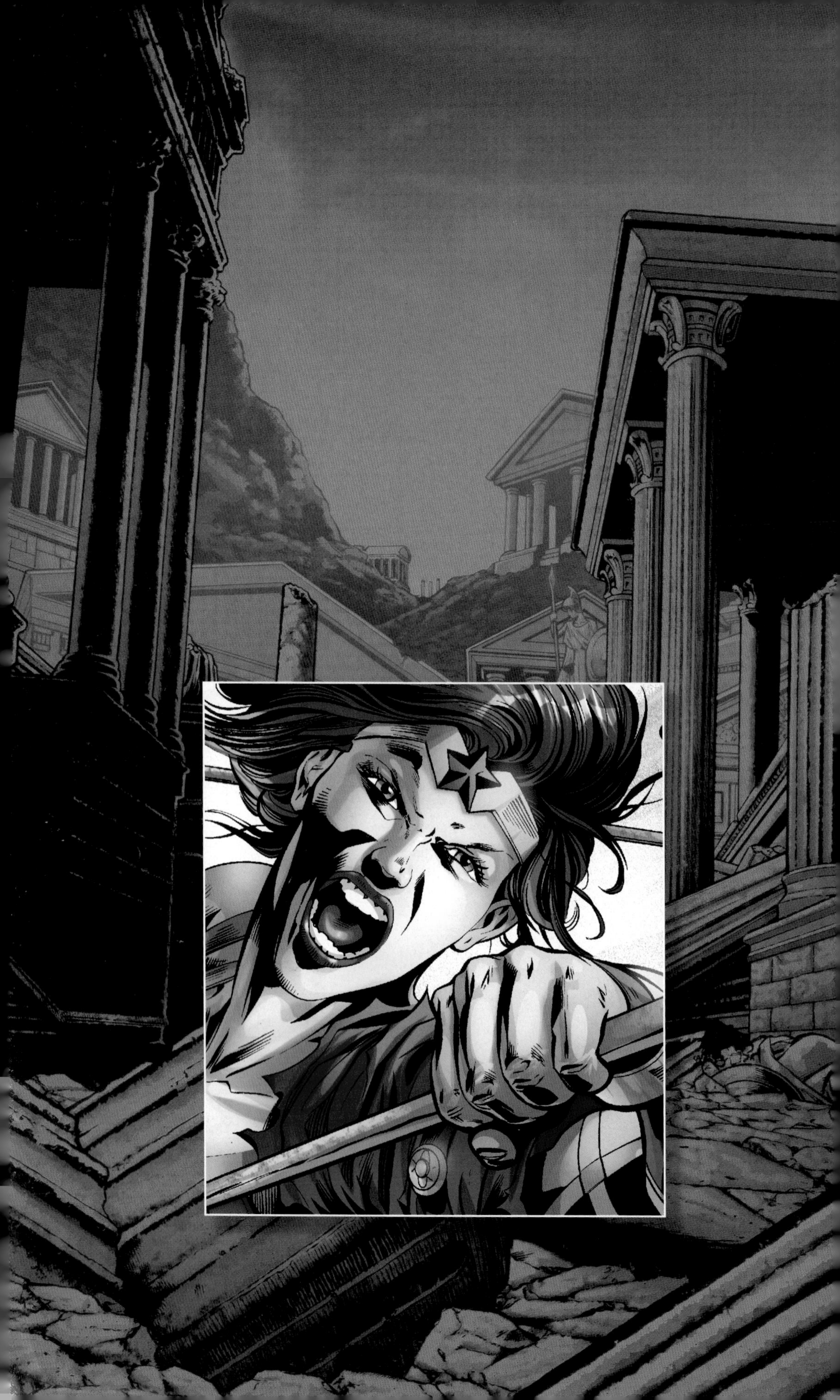

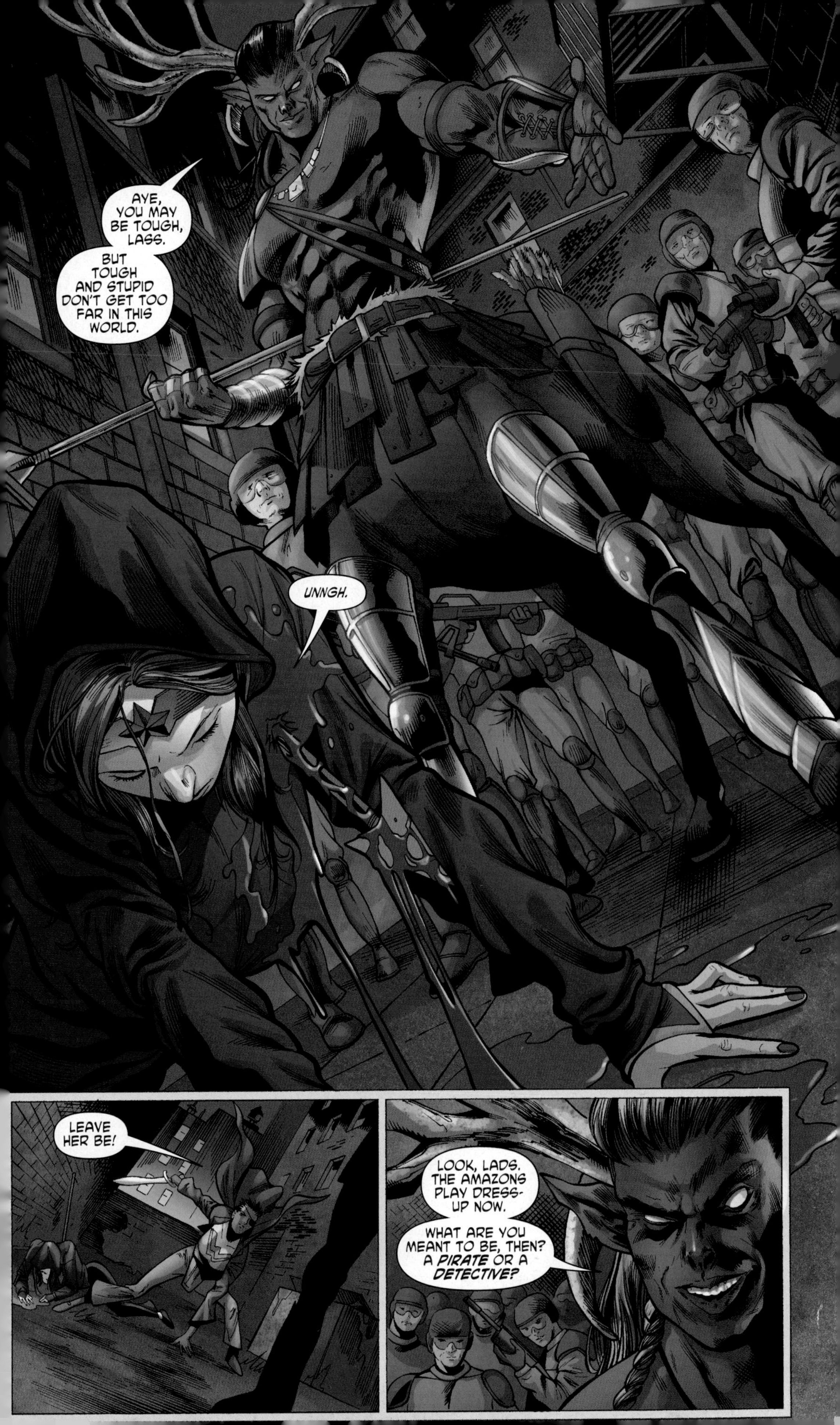
AYE, YOU MAY BE TOUGH, LASS.
BUT TOUGH AND STUPID DON'T GET TOO FAR IN THIS WORLD.
UNNGH.
LEAVE HER BE!
LOOK, LADS. THE AMAZONS PLAY DRESS-UP NOW.
WHAT ARE YOU MEANT TO BE, THEN? A PIRATE OR A DETECTIVE?

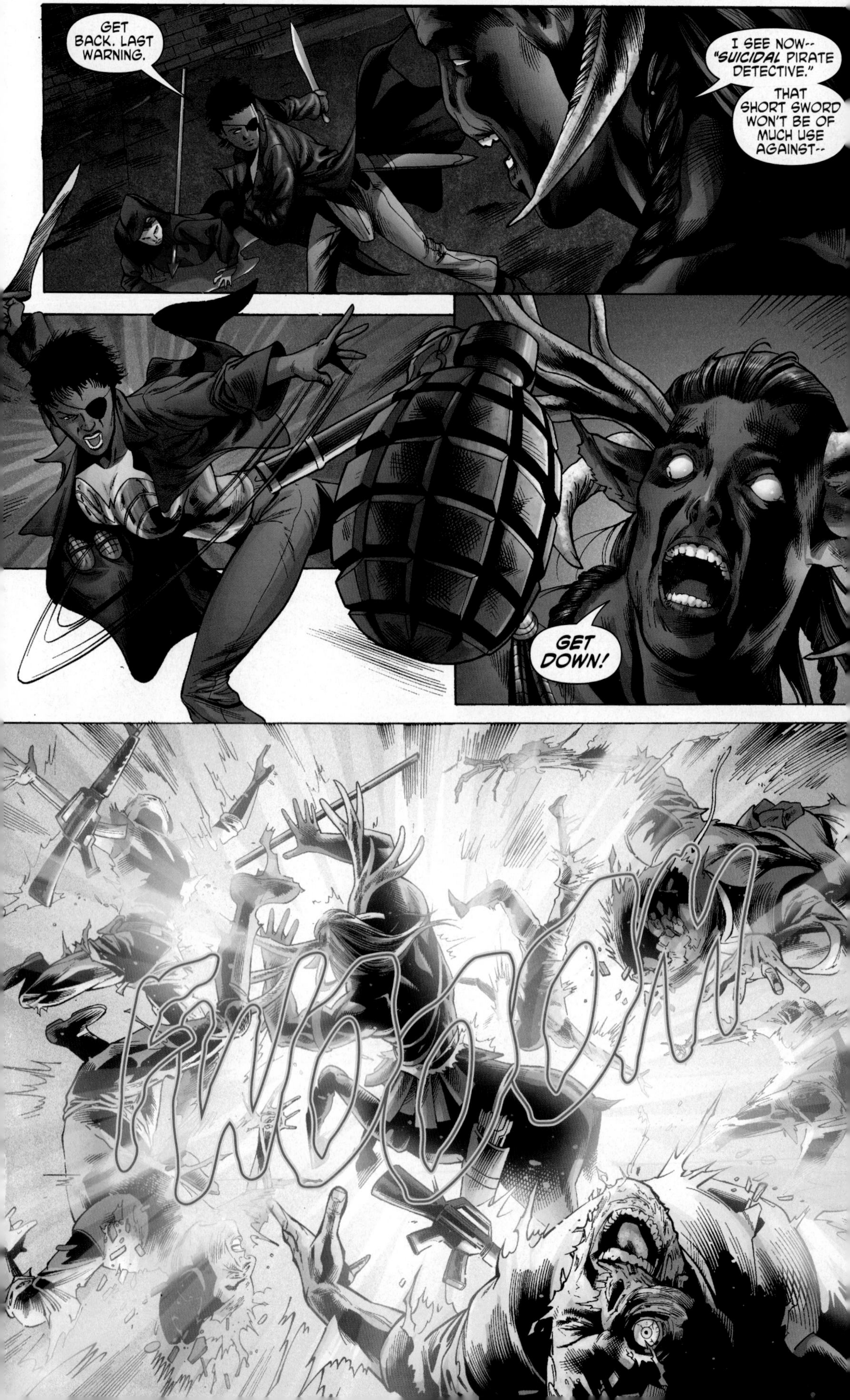
GET BACK. LAST WARNING.
I SEE NOW-- "SUICIDAL PIRATE DETECTIVE."
THAT SHORT SWORD WON'T BE OF MUCH USE AGAINST--
GET DOWN!
FWOOOOM

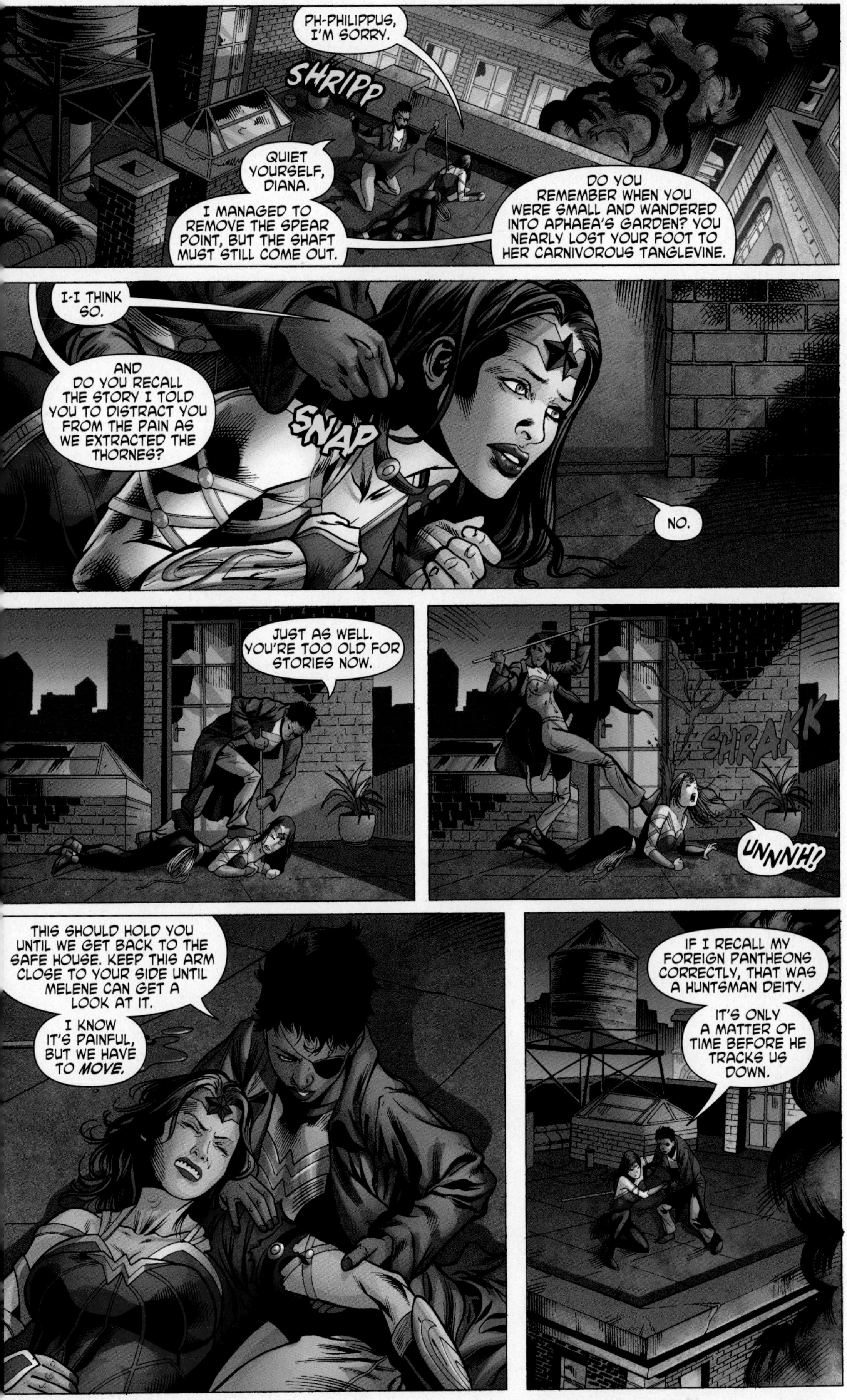
PH-PHILIPPUS, I'M SORRY.
SHRIPP
QUIET YOURSELF, DIANA.
I MANAGED TO REMOVE THE SPEAR POINT, BUT THE SHAFT MUST STILL COME OUT.
DO YOU REMEMBER WHEN YOU WERE SMALL AND WANDERED INTO APHAEA'S GARDEN? YOU NEARLY LOST YOUR FOOT TO HER CARNIVOROUS TANGLEVINE.
I-I THINK SO.
AND DO YOU RECALL THE STORY I TOLD YOU TO DISTRACT YOU FROM THE PAIN AS WE EXTRACTED THE THORNES?
SNAP
NO.
JUST AS WELL. YOU'RE TOO OLD FOR STORIES NOW.
SHRAKK
UNNNH!
THIS SHOULD HOLD YOU UNTIL WE GET BACK TO THE SAFE HOUSE. KEEP THIS ARM CLOSE TO YOUR SIDE UNTIL MELENE CAN GET A LOOK AT IT.
I KNOW IT'S PAINFUL, BUT WE HAVE TO MOVE.
IF I RECALL MY FOREIGN PANTHEONS CORRECTLY, THAT WAS A HUNTSMAN DEITY.
IT'S ONLY A MATTER OF TIME BEFORE HE TRACKS US DOWN.

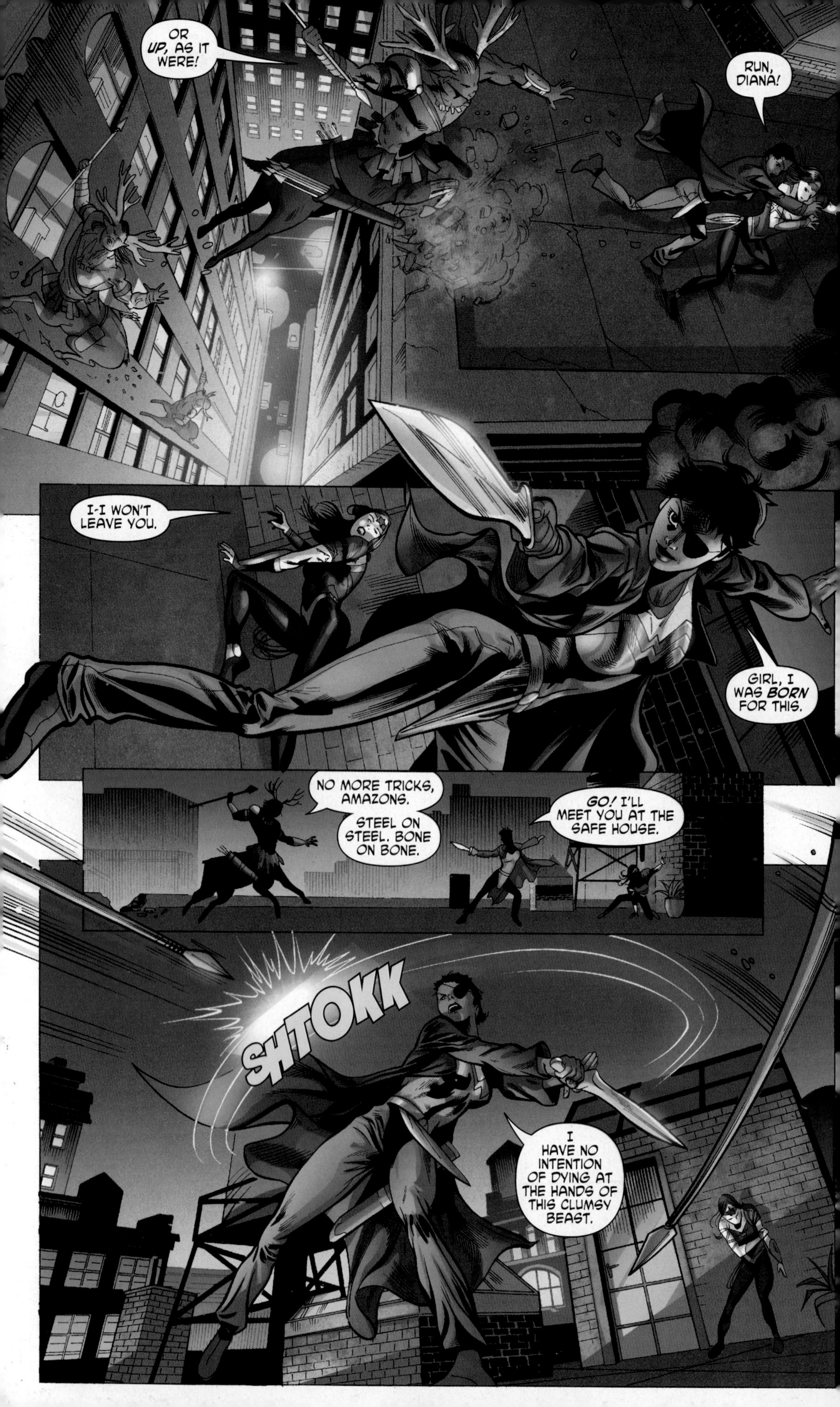

OR UP, AS IT WERE!
RUN, DIANA!
I-I WON'T LEAVE YOU.
GIRL, I WAS BORN FOR THIS.
NO MORE TRICKS, AMAZONS.
STEEL ON STEEL. BONE ON BONE.
GO! I'LL MEET YOU AT THE SAFE HOUSE.
SHTOKK
I HAVE NO INTENTION OF DYING AT THE HANDS OF THIS CLUMSY BEAST.

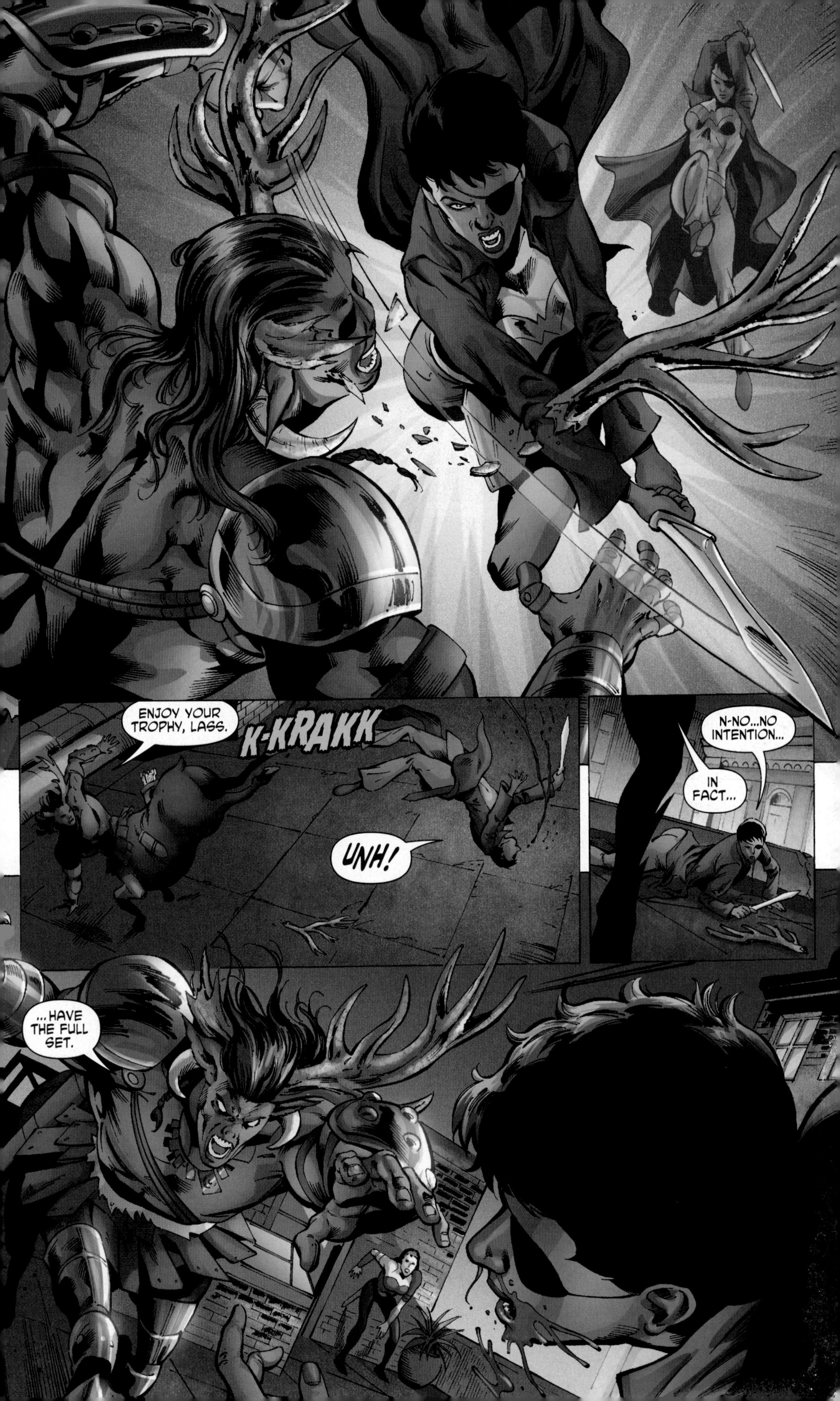
ENJOY YOUR TROPHY, LASS.
K-KRAKK
UNH!
N-NO...NO INTENTION...
IN FACT...
...HAVE THE FULL SET.

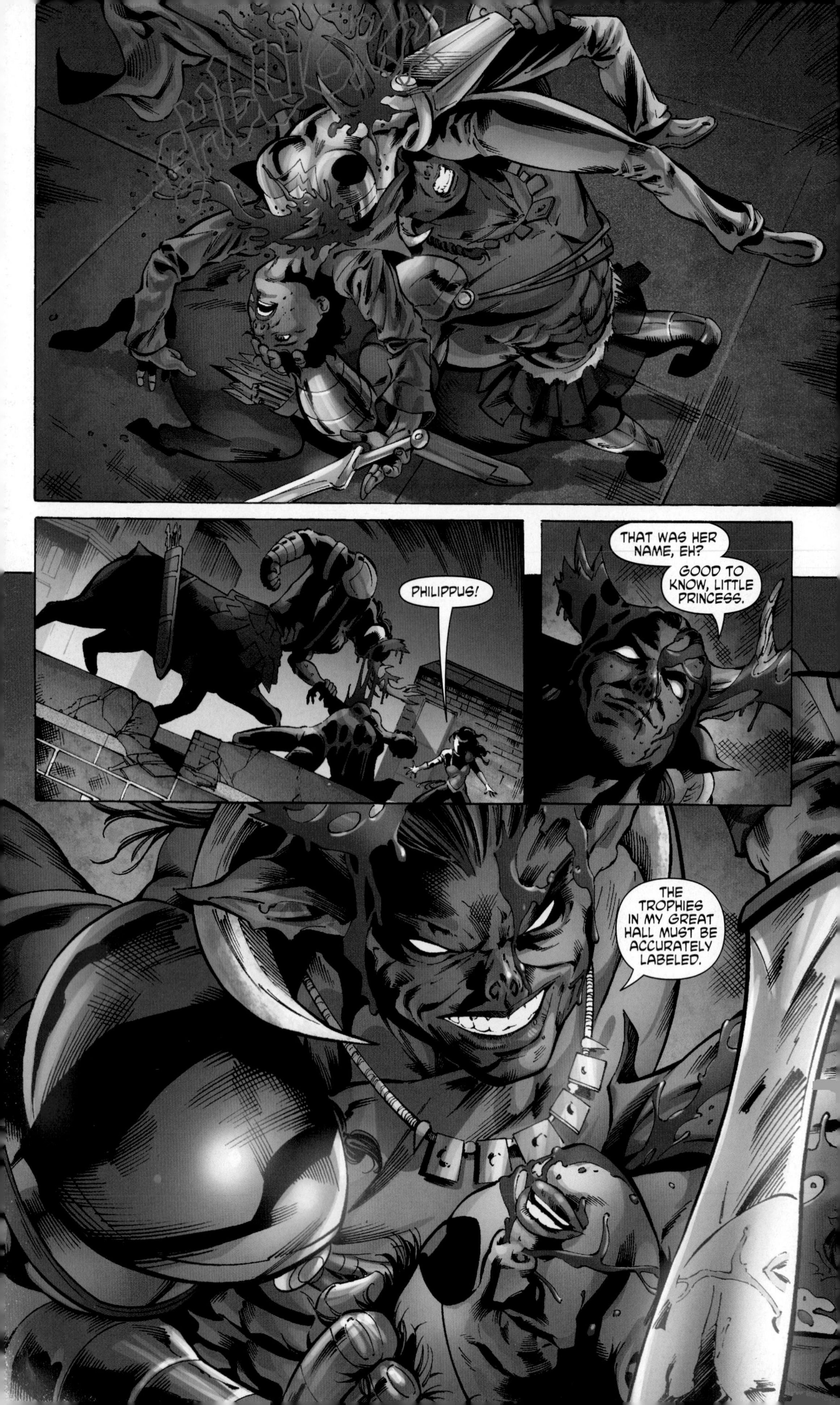
PHILIPPUS!
THAT WAS HER NAME, EH?
GOOD TO KNOW, LITTLE PRINCESS.
THE TROPHIES IN MY GREAT HALL MUST BE ACCURATELY LABELED.

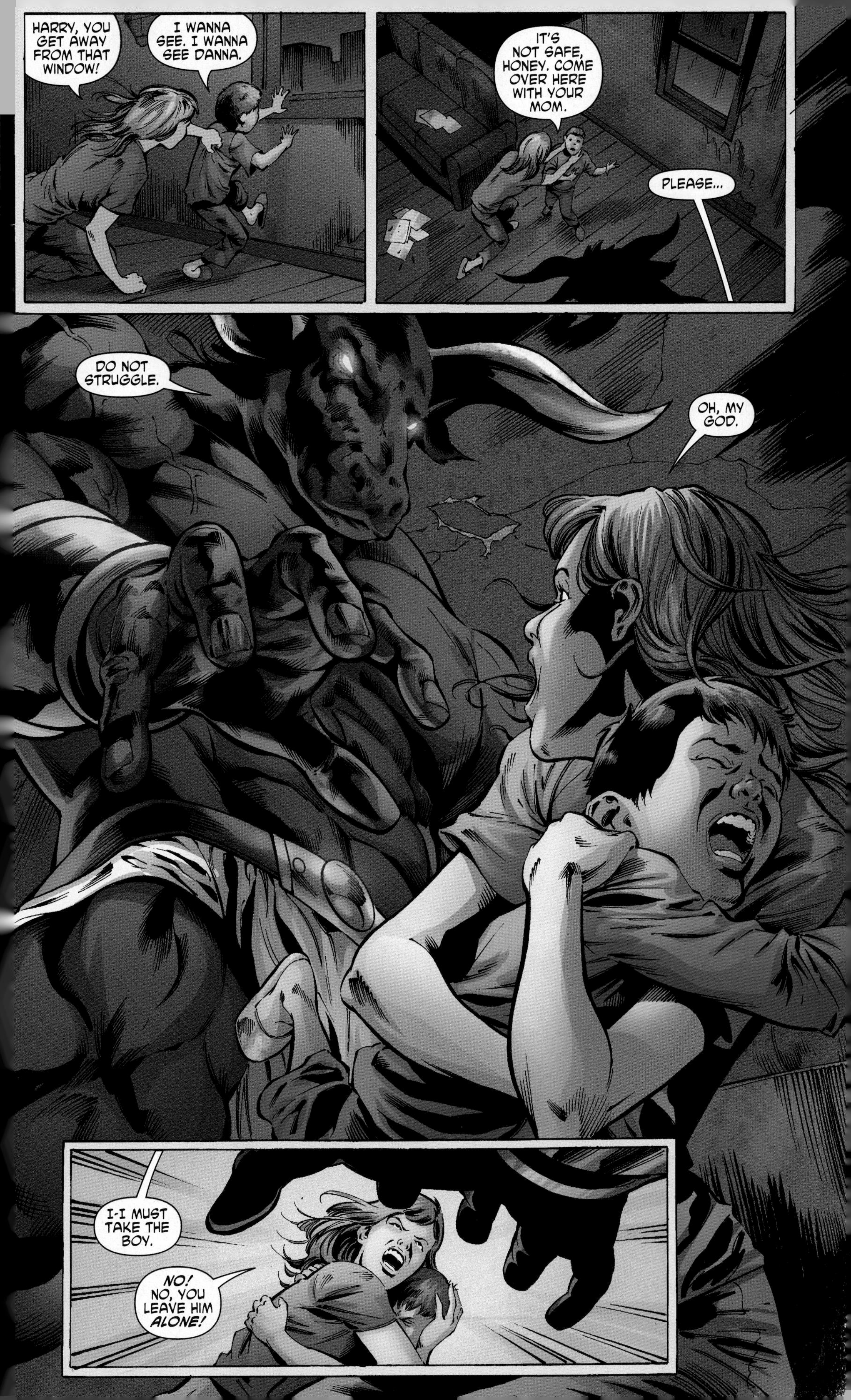
HARRY, YOU GET AWAY FROM THAT WINDOW!
I WANNA SEE. I WANNA SEE DANNA.
IT'S NOT SAFE, HONEY. COME OVER HERE WITH YOUR MOM.
PLEASE...
DO NOT STRUGGLE.
OH, MY GOD.
I-I MUST TAKE THE BOY.
NO! NO, YOU LEAVE HIM *ALONE!*

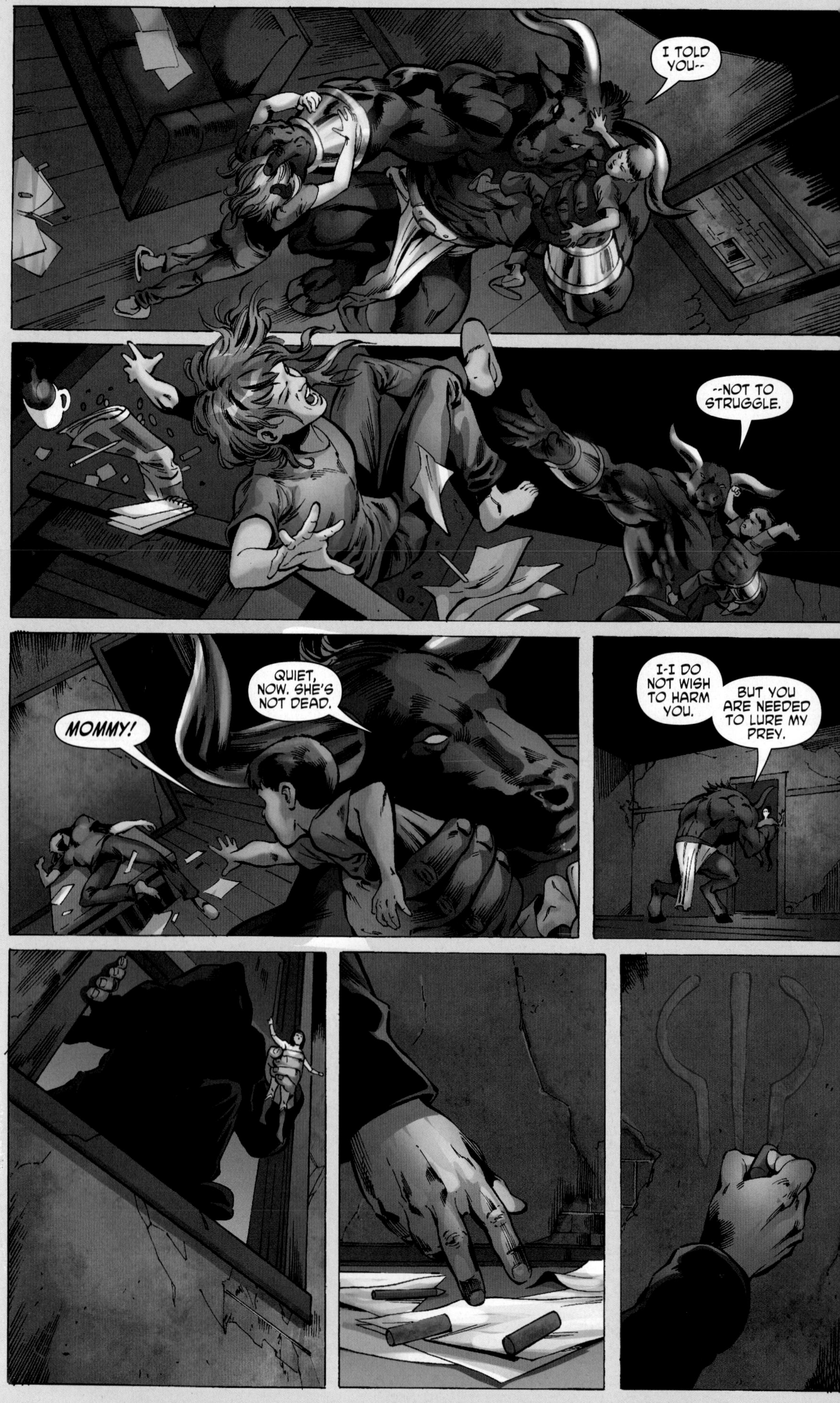
I TOLD YOU--
--NOT TO STRUGGLE.
MOMMY!
QUIET, NOW. SHE'S NOT DEAD.
I-I DO NOT WISH TO HARM YOU.
BUT YOU ARE NEEDED TO LURE MY PREY.

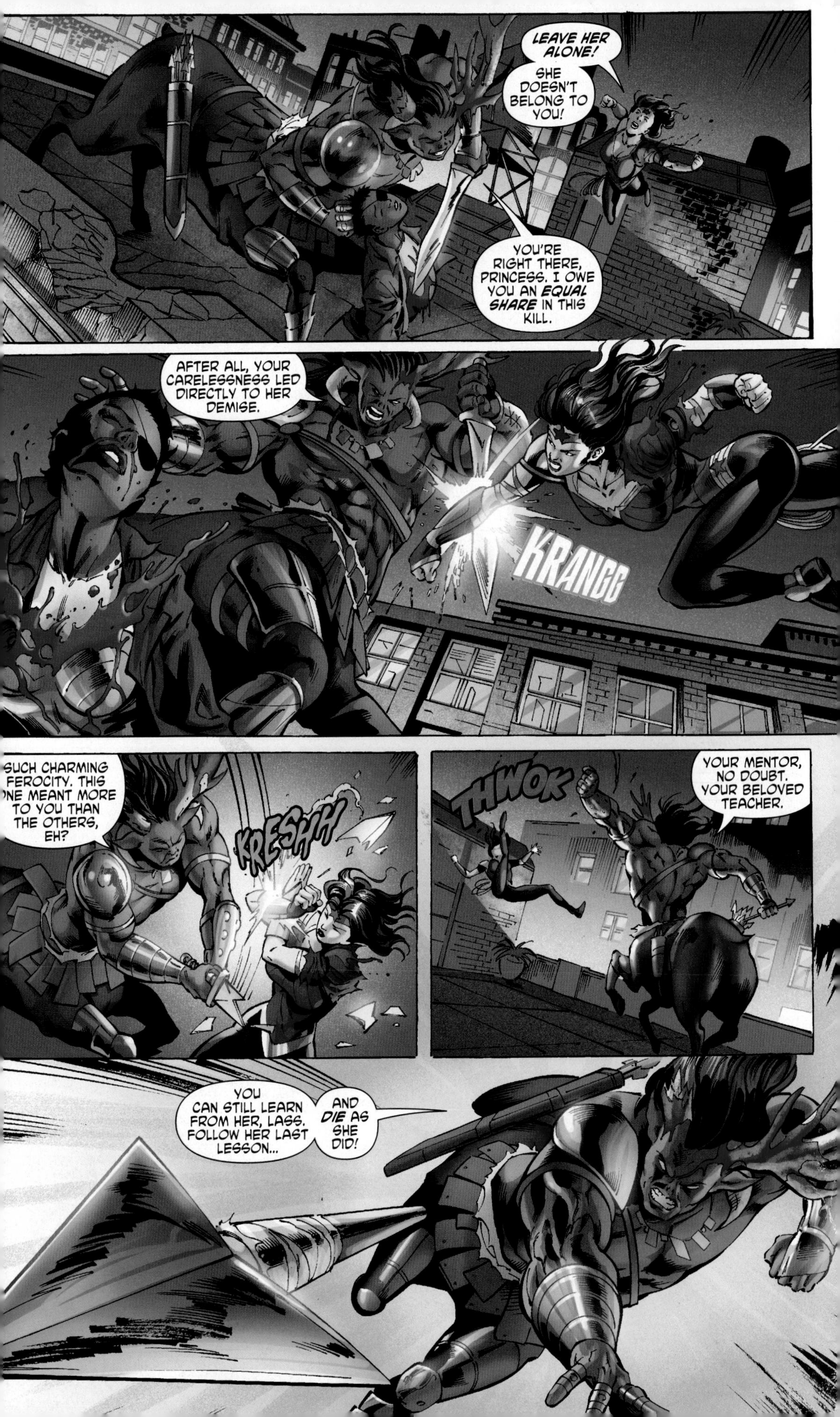
LEAVE HER ALONE!
SHE DOESN'T BELONG TO YOU!
YOU'RE RIGHT THERE, PRINCESS. I OWE YOU AN EQUAL SHARE IN THIS KILL.
AFTER ALL, YOUR CARELESSNESS LED DIRECTLY TO HER DEMISE.
KRANGG
SUCH CHARMING FEROCITY. THIS ONE MEANT MORE TO YOU THAN THE OTHERS, EH?
KRESHH
THWOK
YOUR MENTOR, NO DOUBT. YOUR BELOVED TEACHER.
YOU CAN STILL LEARN FROM HER, LASS. FOLLOW HER LAST LESSON...
AND DIE AS SHE DID!

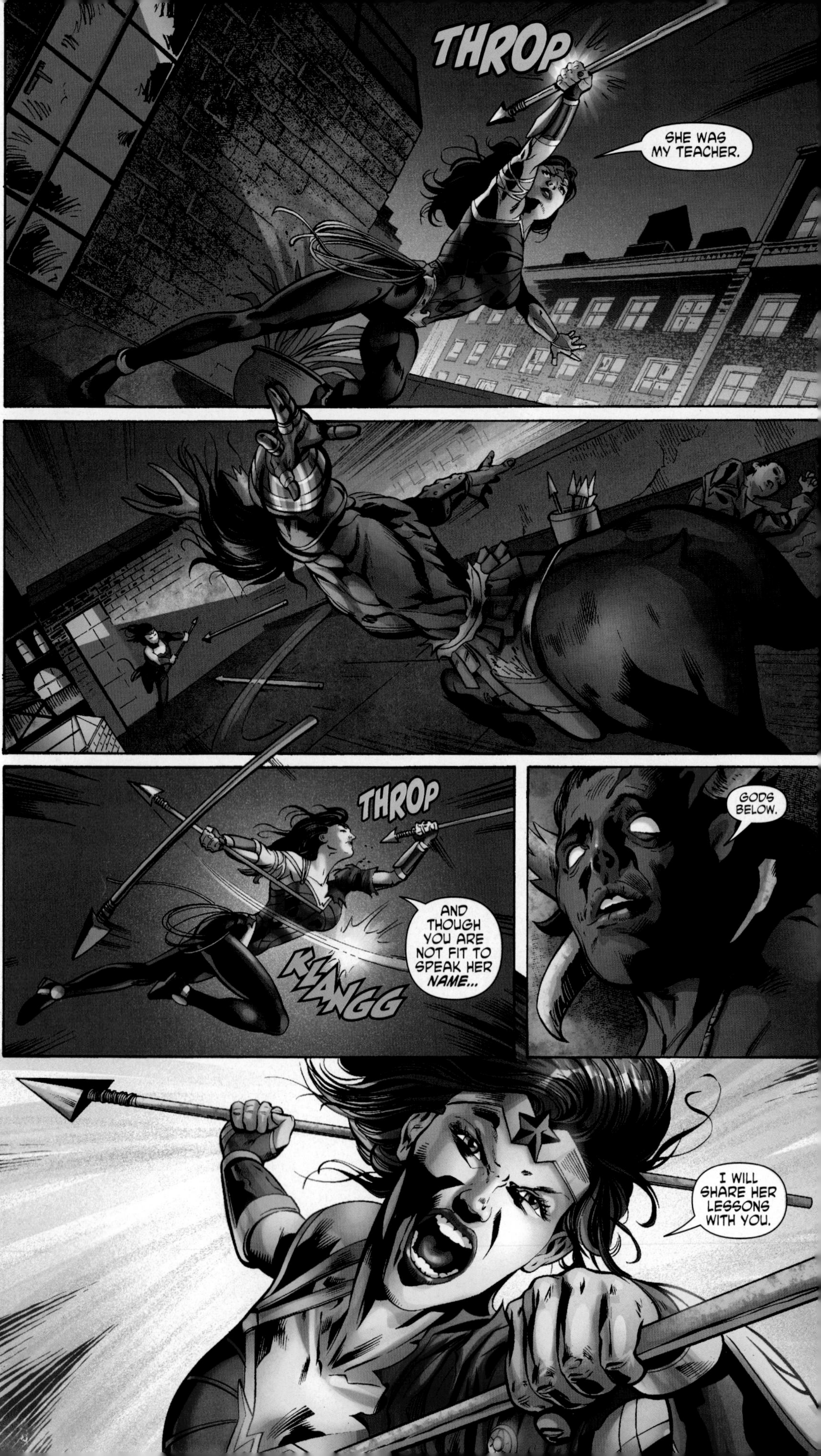
THROP
SHE WAS MY TEACHER.
THROP
AND THOUGH YOU ARE NOT FIT TO SPEAK HER *NAME*...
KLANGG
GODS BELOW.
I WILL SHARE HER LESSONS WITH YOU.

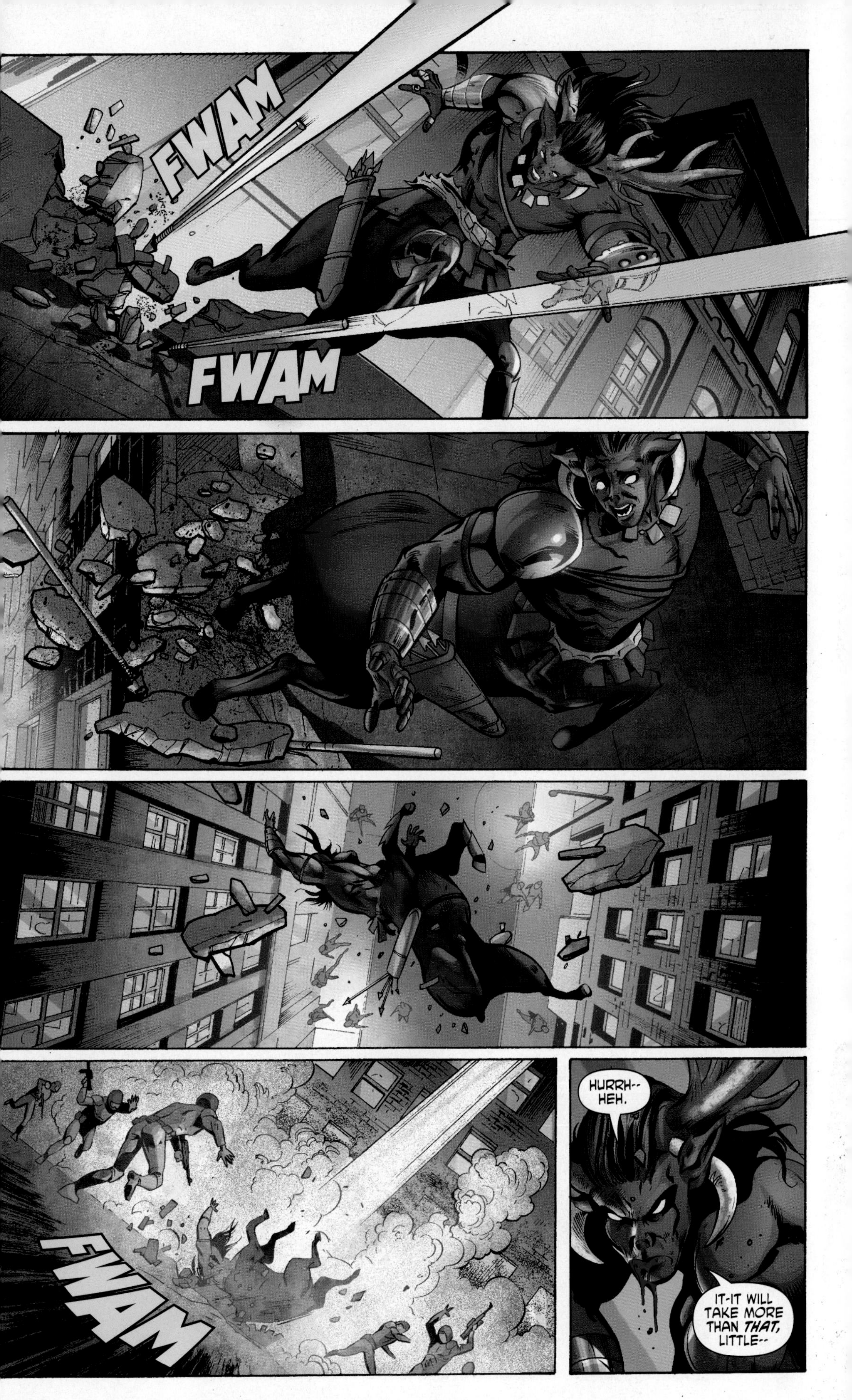
FWAM
FWAM
FWAM
HURRH--
HEH.
IT-IT WILL
TAKE MORE
THAN *THAT,*
LITTLE--

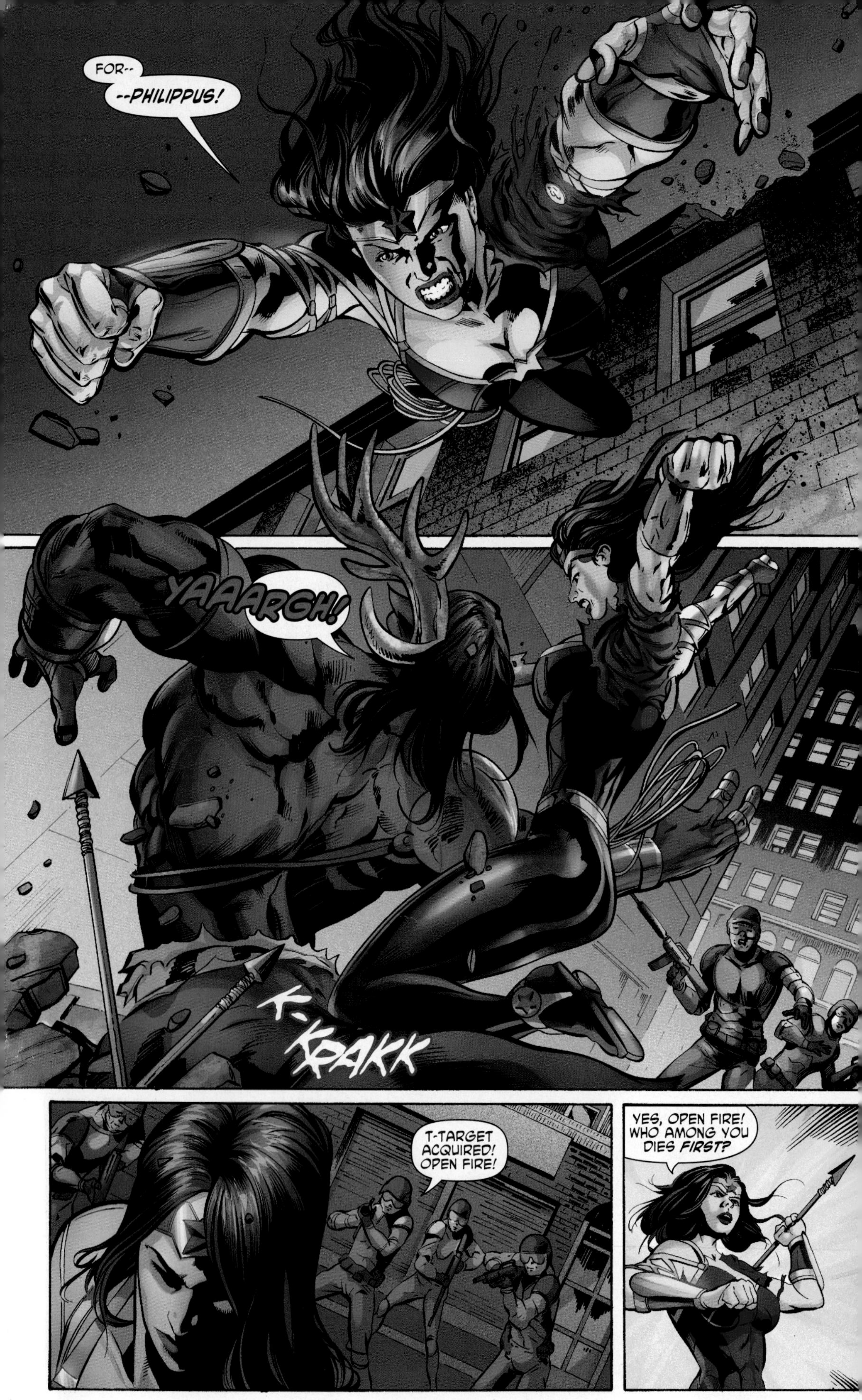
FOR--
--PHILIPPUS!
YAAARGH!
K-KRAKK
T-TARGET ACQUIRED! OPEN FIRE!
YES, OPEN FIRE! WHO AMONG YOU DIES FIRST?

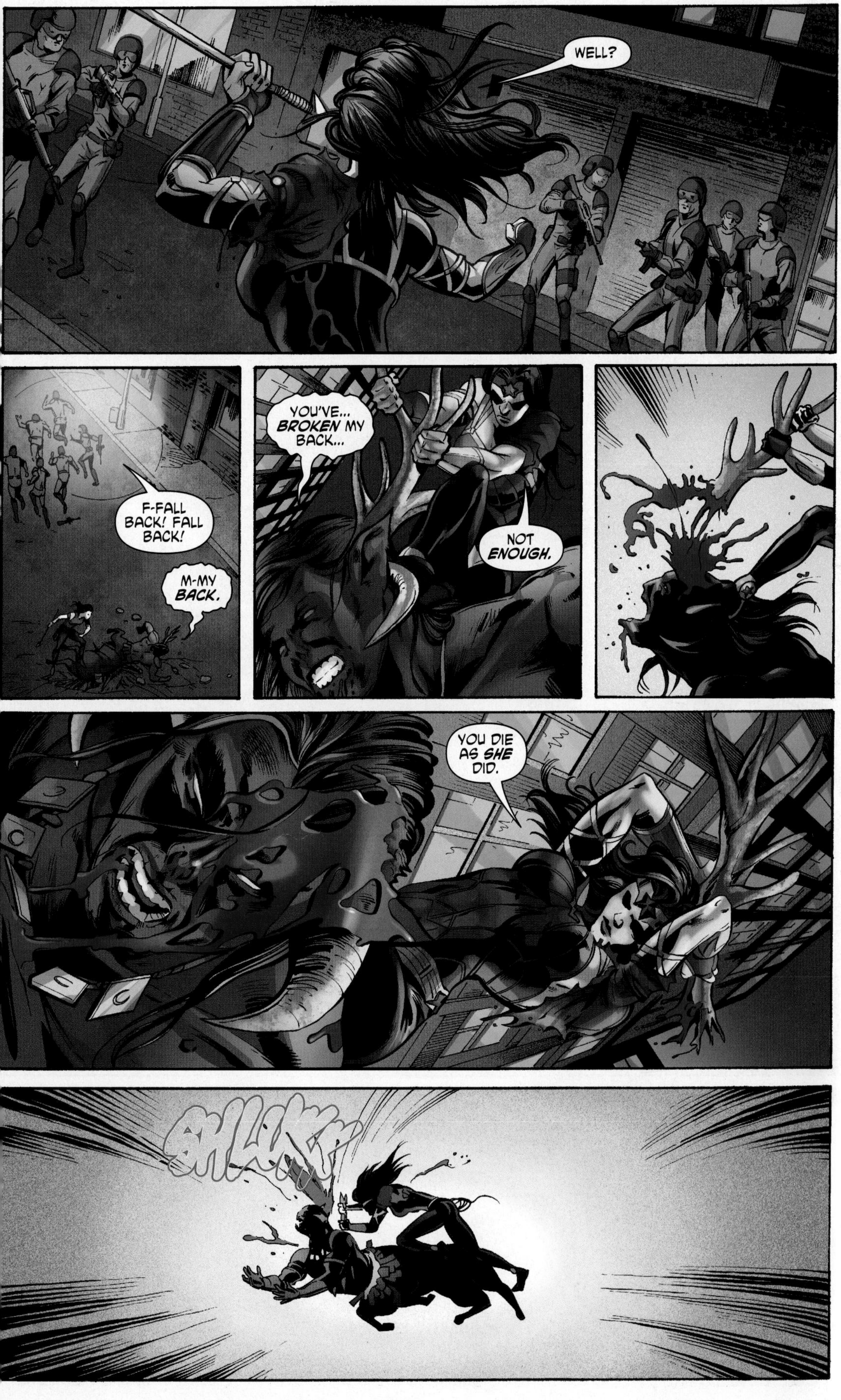
WELL?
F-FALL BACK! FALL BACK!
M-MY BACK.
YOU'VE... BROKEN MY BACK...
NOT ENOUGH.
YOU DIE AS SHE DID.

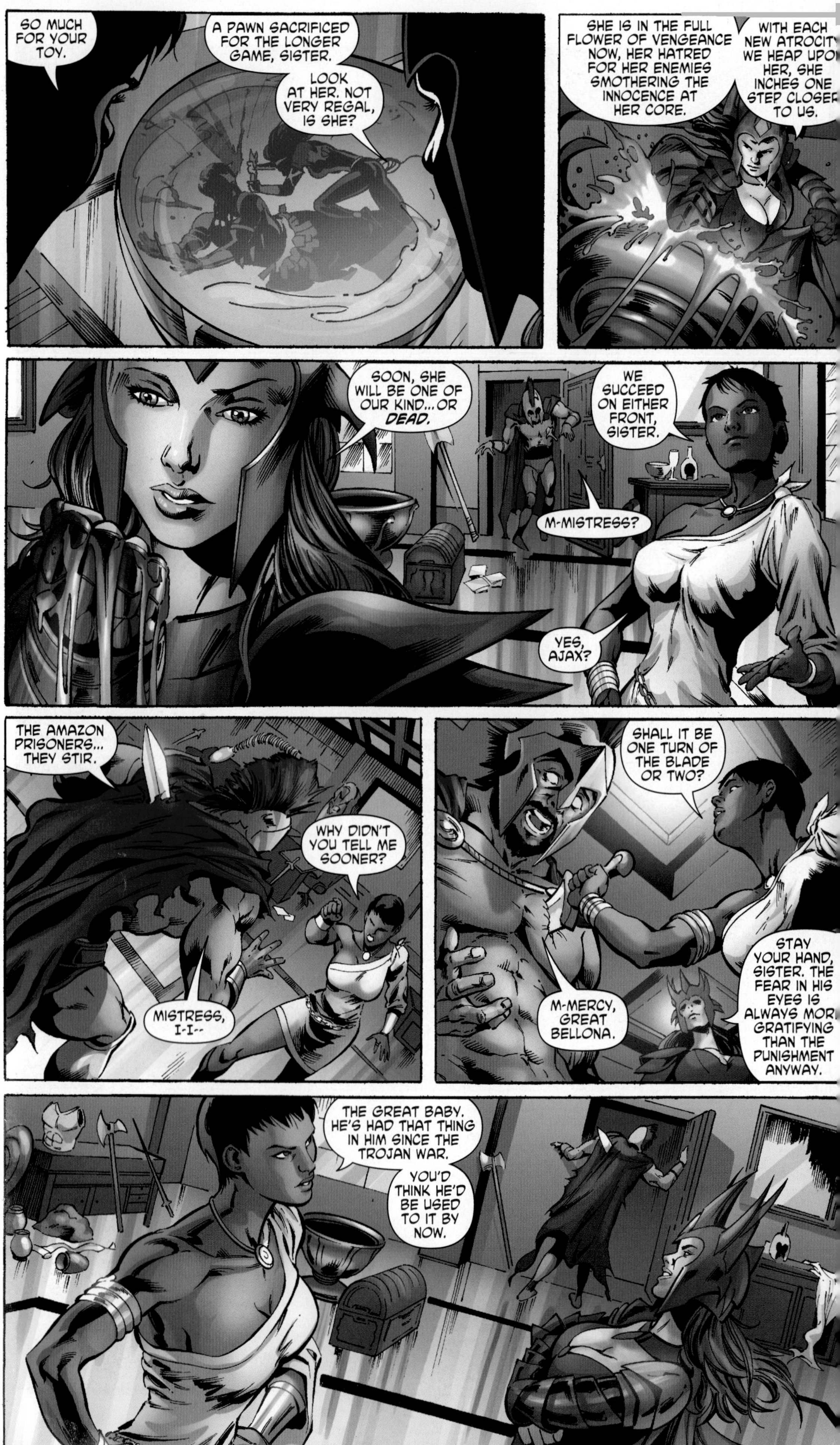
SO MUCH FOR YOUR TOY.
A PAWN SACRIFICED FOR THE LONGER GAME, SISTER.
LOOK AT HER. NOT VERY REGAL, IS SHE?
SHE IS IN THE FULL FLOWER OF VENGEANCE NOW, HER HATRED FOR HER ENEMIES SMOTHERING THE INNOCENCE AT HER CORE.
WITH EACH NEW ATROCIT WE HEAP UPO HER, SHE INCHES ONE STEP CLOSER TO US.
SOON, SHE WILL BE ONE OF OUR KIND...OR *DEAD.*
WE SUCCEED ON EITHER FRONT, SISTER.
M-MISTRESS?
YES, AJAX?
THE AMAZON PRISONERS... THEY STIR.
WHY DIDN'T YOU TELL ME SOONER?
MISTRESS, I-I--
SHALL IT BE ONE TURN OF THE BLADE OR TWO?
M-MERCY, GREAT BELLONA.
STAY YOUR HAND, SISTER. THE FEAR IN HIS EYES IS ALWAYS MOR GRATIFYING THAN THE PUNISHMENT ANYWAY.
THE GREAT BABY. HE'S HAD THAT THING IN HIM SINCE THE TROJAN WAR.
YOU'D THINK HE'D BE USED TO IT BY NOW.

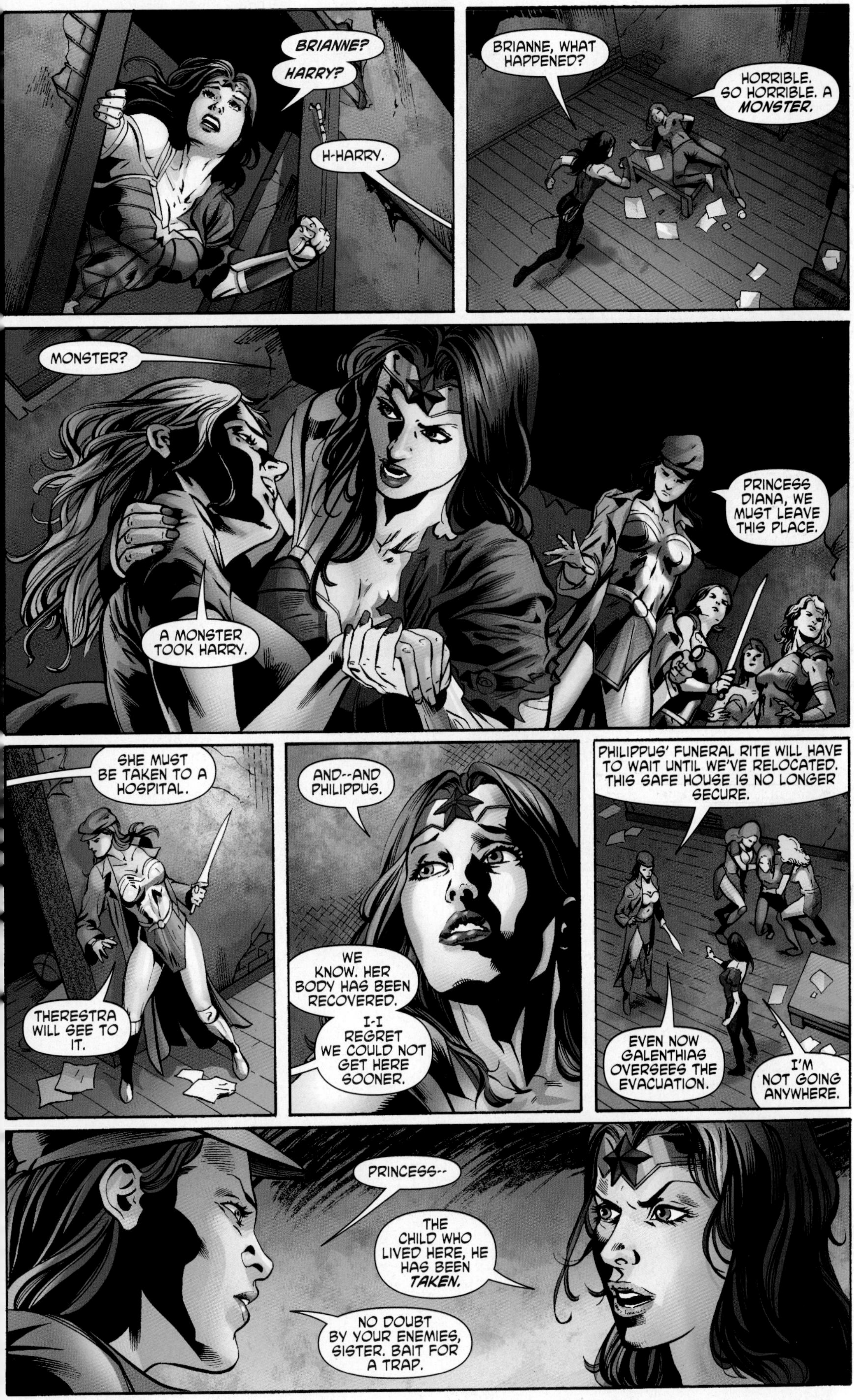
BRIANNE?
HARRY?
H-HARRY.
BRIANNE, WHAT HAPPENED?
HORRIBLE. SO HORRIBLE. A MONSTER.
MONSTER?
A MONSTER TOOK HARRY.
PRINCESS DIANA, WE MUST LEAVE THIS PLACE.
SHE MUST BE TAKEN TO A HOSPITAL.
THERESTRA WILL SEE TO IT.
AND--AND PHILIPPUS.
WE KNOW. HER BODY HAS BEEN RECOVERED.
I-I REGRET WE COULD NOT GET HERE SOONER.
PHILIPPUS' FUNERAL RITE WILL HAVE TO WAIT UNTIL WE'VE RELOCATED. THIS SAFE HOUSE IS NO LONGER SECURE.
EVEN NOW GALENTHIAS OVERSEES THE EVACUATION.
I'M NOT GOING ANYWHERE.
PRINCESS--
THE CHILD WHO LIVED HERE, HE HAS BEEN TAKEN.
NO DOUBT BY YOUR ENEMIES, SISTER. BAIT FOR A TRAP.

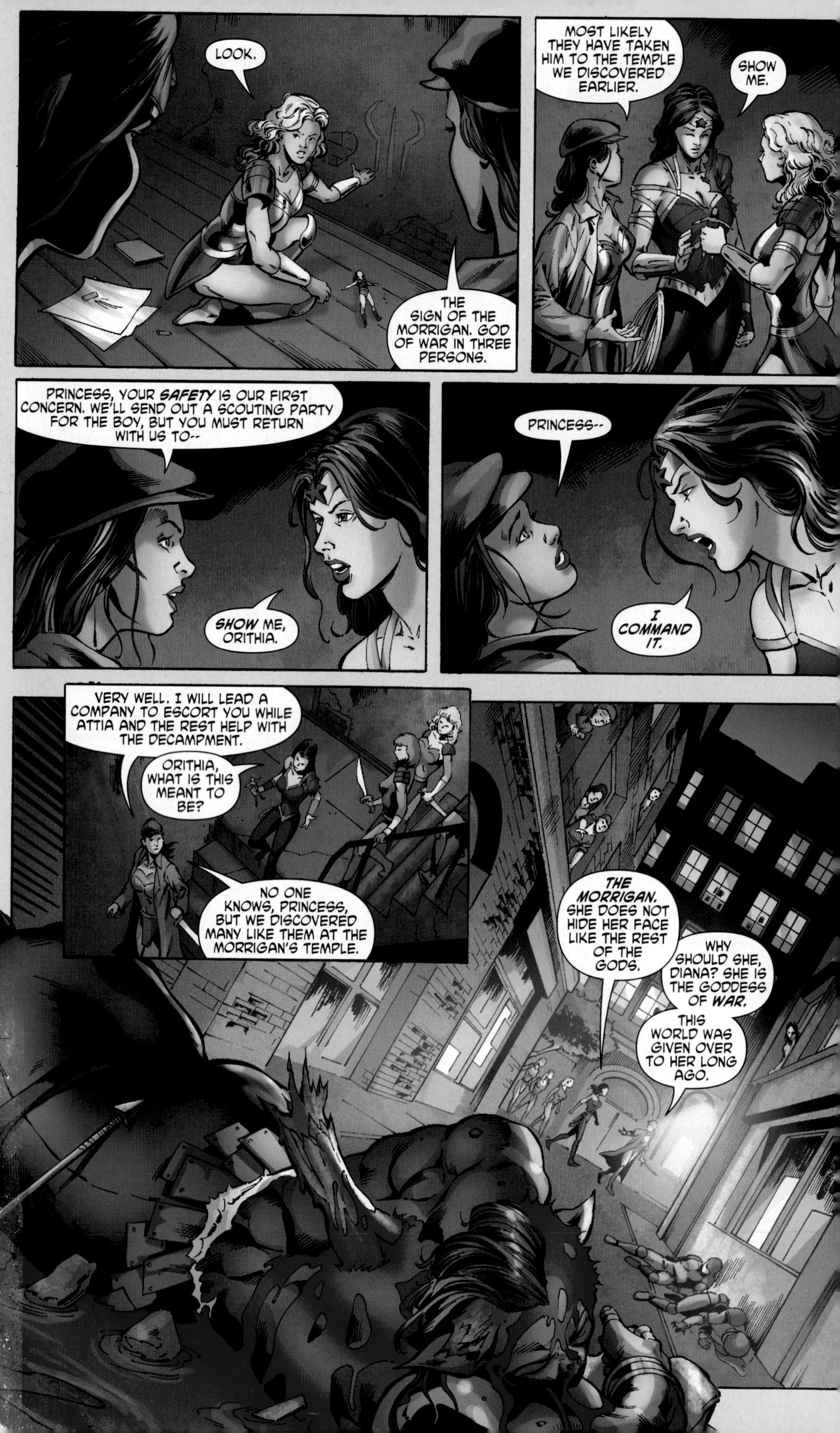
LOOK.
THE SIGN OF THE MORRIGAN. GOD OF WAR IN THREE PERSONS.
MOST LIKELY THEY HAVE TAKEN HIM TO THE TEMPLE WE DISCOVERED EARLIER.
SHOW ME.
PRINCESS, YOUR SAFETY IS OUR FIRST CONCERN. WE'LL SEND OUT A SCOUTING PARTY FOR THE BOY, BUT YOU MUST RETURN WITH US TO--
SHOW ME, ORITHIA.
PRINCESS--
I COMMAND IT.
VERY WELL. I WILL LEAD A COMPANY TO ESCORT YOU WHILE ATTIA AND THE REST HELP WITH THE DECAMPMENT.
ORITHIA, WHAT IS THIS MEANT TO BE?
NO ONE KNOWS, PRINCESS, BUT WE DISCOVERED MANY LIKE THEM AT THE MORRIGAN'S TEMPLE.
THE MORRIGAN. SHE DOES NOT HIDE HER FACE LIKE THE REST OF THE GODS.
WHY SHOULD SHE, DIANA? SHE IS THE GODDESS OF WAR.
THIS WORLD WAS GIVEN OVER TO HER LONG AGO.

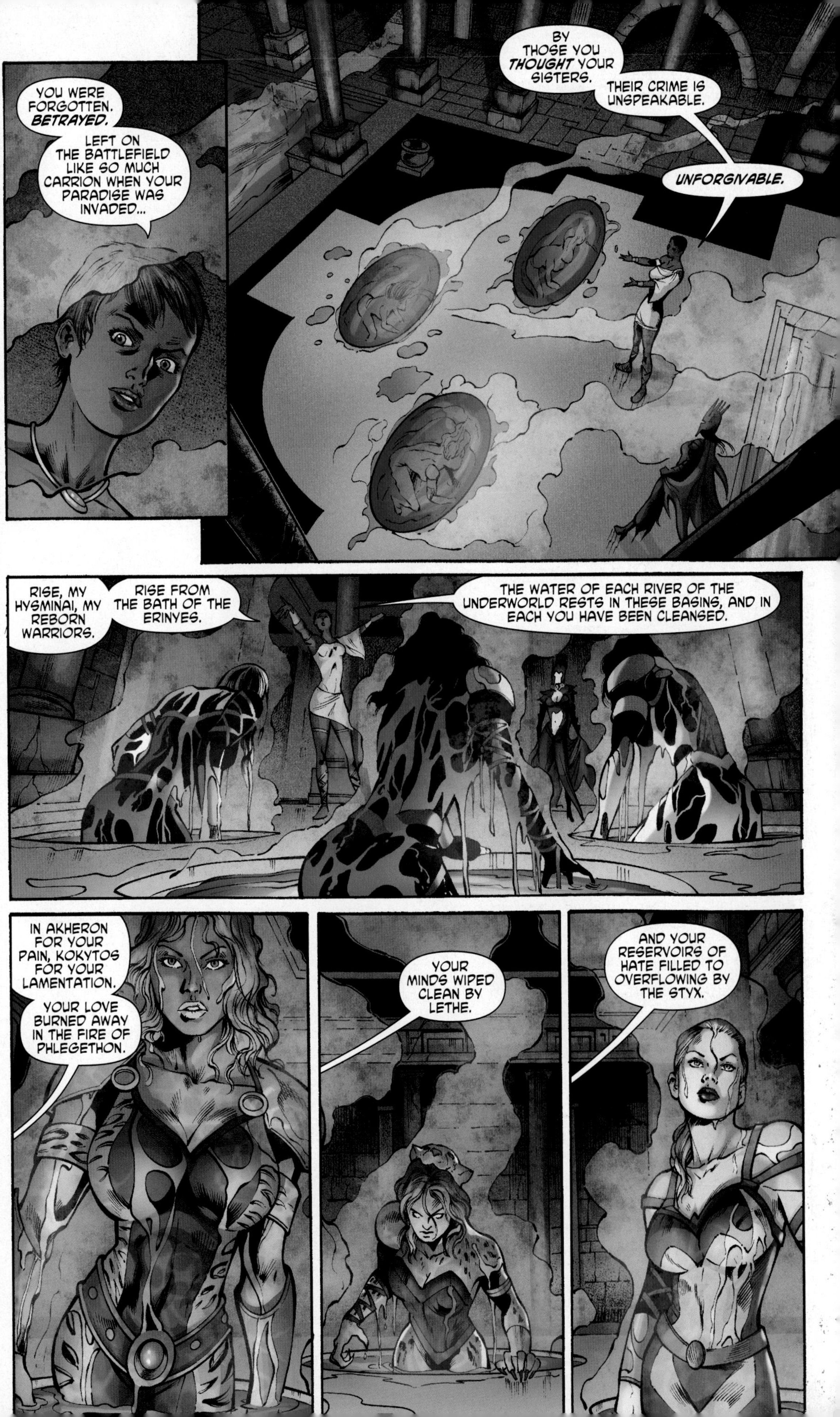
YOU WERE FORGOTTEN. *BETRAYED.*
LEFT ON THE BATTLEFIELD LIKE SO MUCH CARRION WHEN YOUR PARADISE WAS INVADED...
BY THOSE YOU *THOUGHT* YOUR SISTERS.
THEIR CRIME IS UNSPEAKABLE.
UNFORGIVABLE.
RISE, MY HYSMINAI, MY REBORN WARRIORS.
RISE FROM THE BATH OF THE ERINYES.
THE WATER OF EACH RIVER OF THE UNDERWORLD RESTS IN THESE BASINS, AND IN EACH YOU HAVE BEEN CLEANSED.
IN AKHERON FOR YOUR PAIN, KOKYTOS FOR YOUR LAMENTATION.
YOUR LOVE BURNED AWAY IN THE FIRE OF PHLEGETHON.
YOUR MINDS WIPED CLEAN BY LETHE.
AND YOUR RESERVOIRS OF HATE FILLED TO OVERFLOWING BY THE STYX.

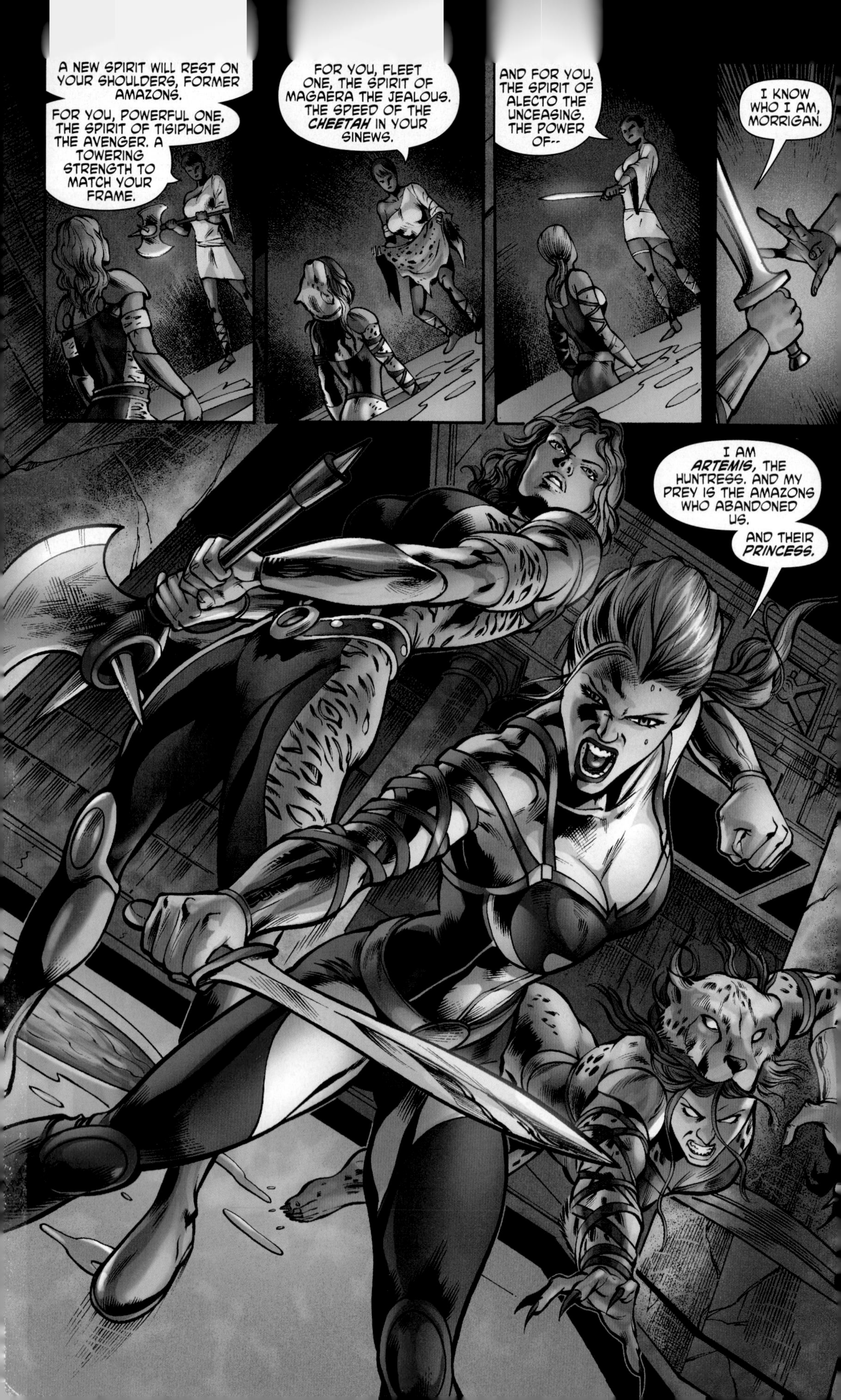
A NEW SPIRIT WILL REST ON YOUR SHOULDERS, FORMER AMAZONS.
FOR YOU, POWERFUL ONE, THE SPIRIT OF TISIPHONE THE AVENGER. A TOWERING STRENGTH TO MATCH YOUR FRAME.
FOR YOU, FLEET ONE, THE SPIRIT OF MAGAERA THE JEALOUS. THE SPEED OF THE CHEETAH IN YOUR SINEWS.
AND FOR YOU, THE SPIRIT OF ALECTO THE UNCEASING. THE POWER OF--
I KNOW WHO I AM, MORRIGAN.
I AM ARTEMIS, THE HUNTRESS. AND MY PREY IS THE AMAZONS WHO ABANDONED US.
AND THEIR PRINCESS.

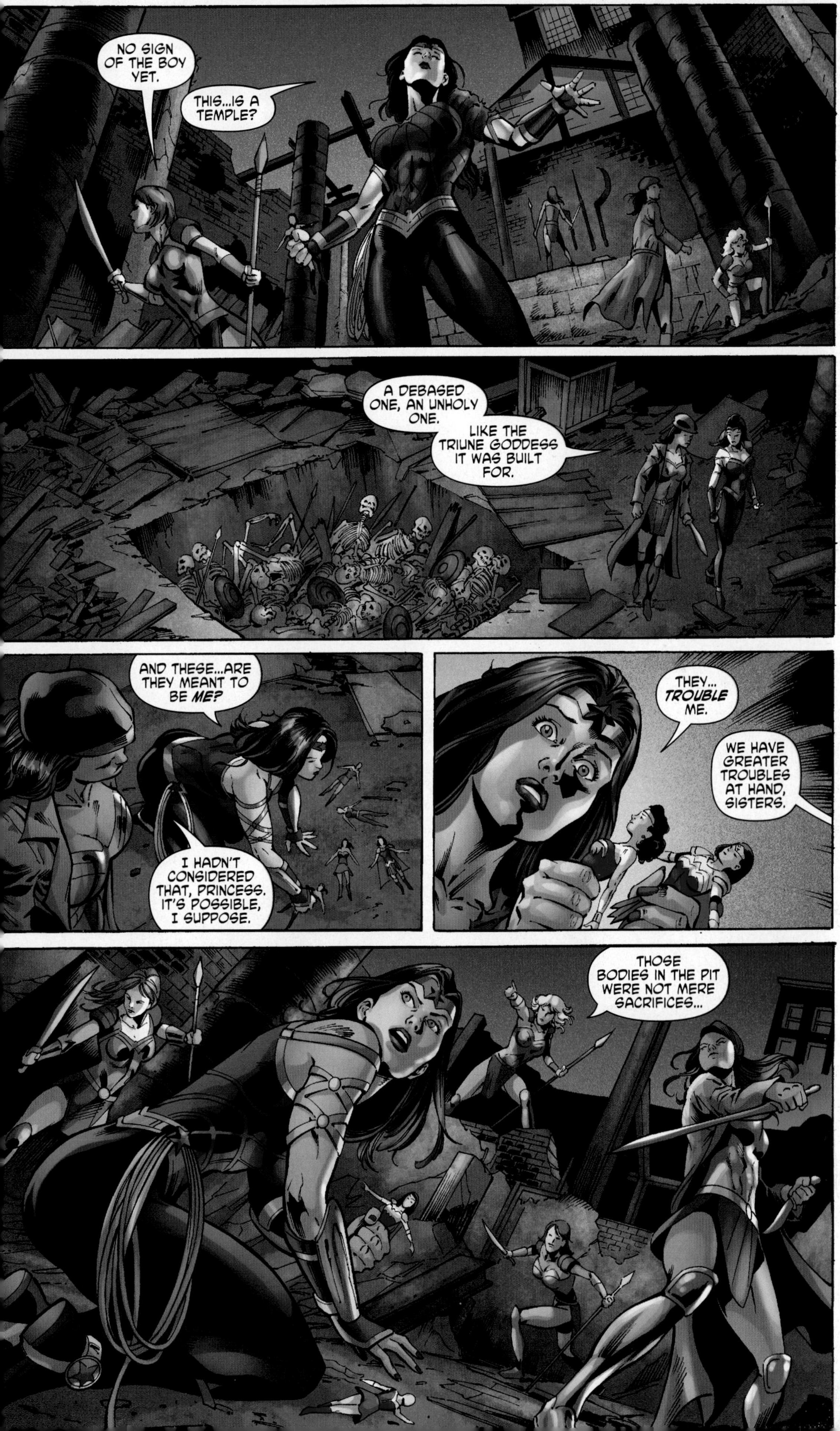
NO SIGN OF THE BOY YET.
THIS...IS A TEMPLE?
A DEBASED ONE, AN UNHOLY ONE.
LIKE THE TRIUNE GODDESS IT WAS BUILT FOR.
AND THESE...ARE THEY MEANT TO BE *ME?*
I HADN'T CONSIDERED THAT, PRINCESS. IT'S POSSIBLE, I SUPPOSE.
THEY... *TROUBLE* ME.
WE HAVE GREATER TROUBLES AT HAND, SISTERS.
THOSE BODIES IN THE PIT WERE NOT MERE SACRIFICES...

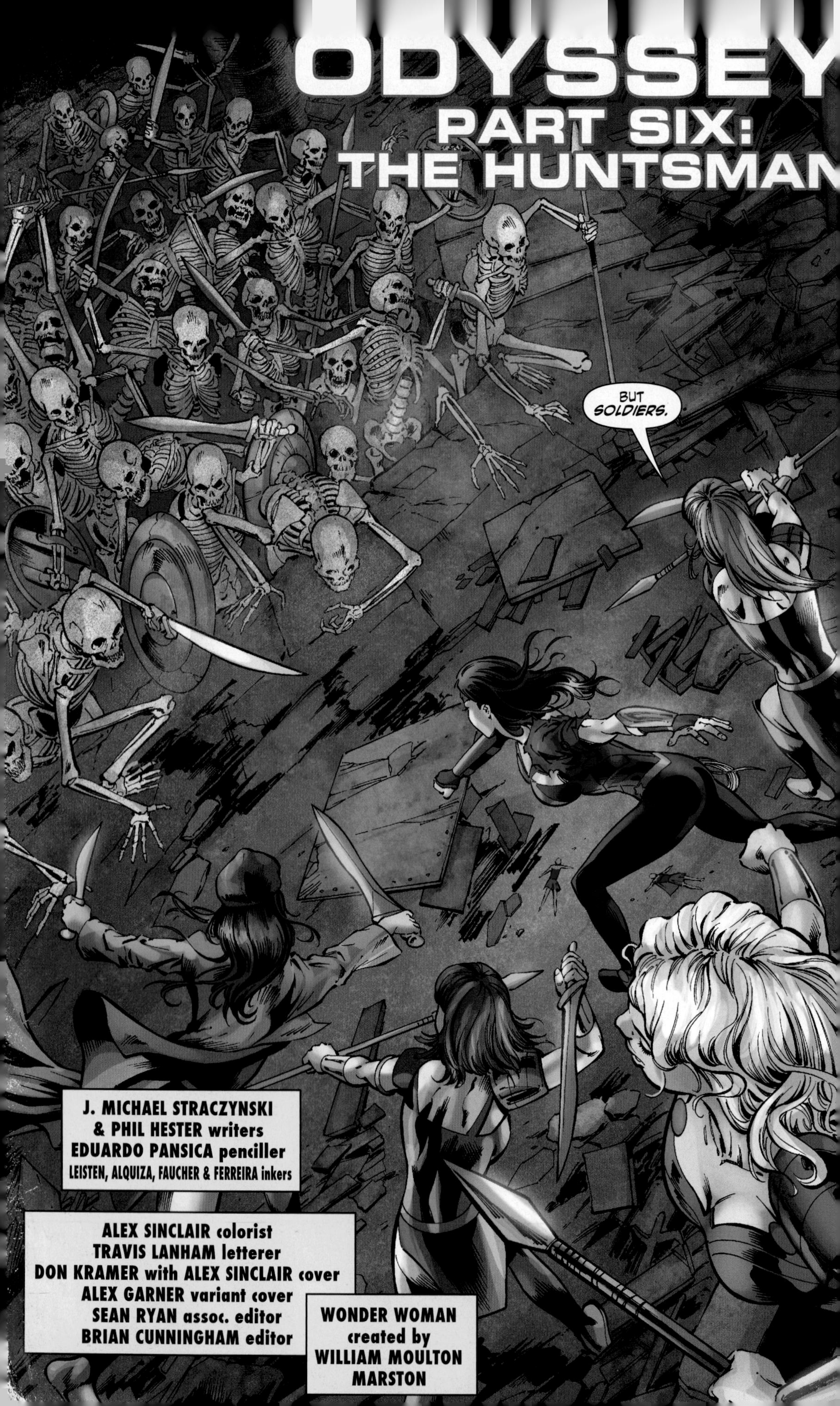

ODYSSEY
PART SIX:
THE HUNTSMAN
BUT SOLDIERS.
J. MICHAEL STRACZYNSKI & PHIL HESTER writers
EDUARDO PANSICA penciller
LEISTEN, ALQUIZA, FAUCHER & FERREIRA inkers
ALEX SINCLAIR colorist
TRAVIS LANHAM letterer
DON KRAMER with ALEX SINCLAIR cover
ALEX GARNER variant cover
SEAN RYAN assoc. editor
BRIAN CUNNINGHAM editor
WONDER WOMAN created by WILLIAM MOULTON MARSTON

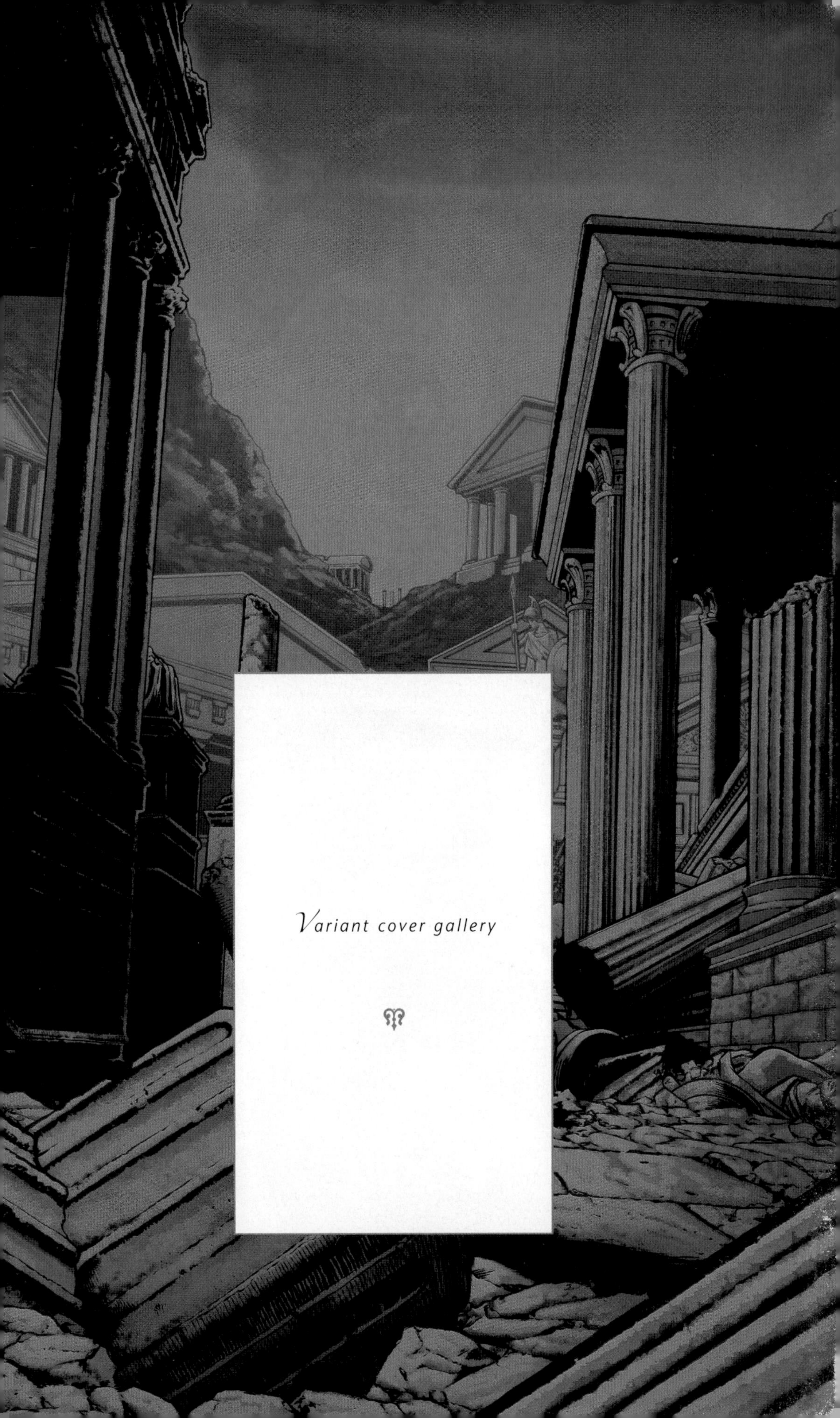

Variant cover gallery

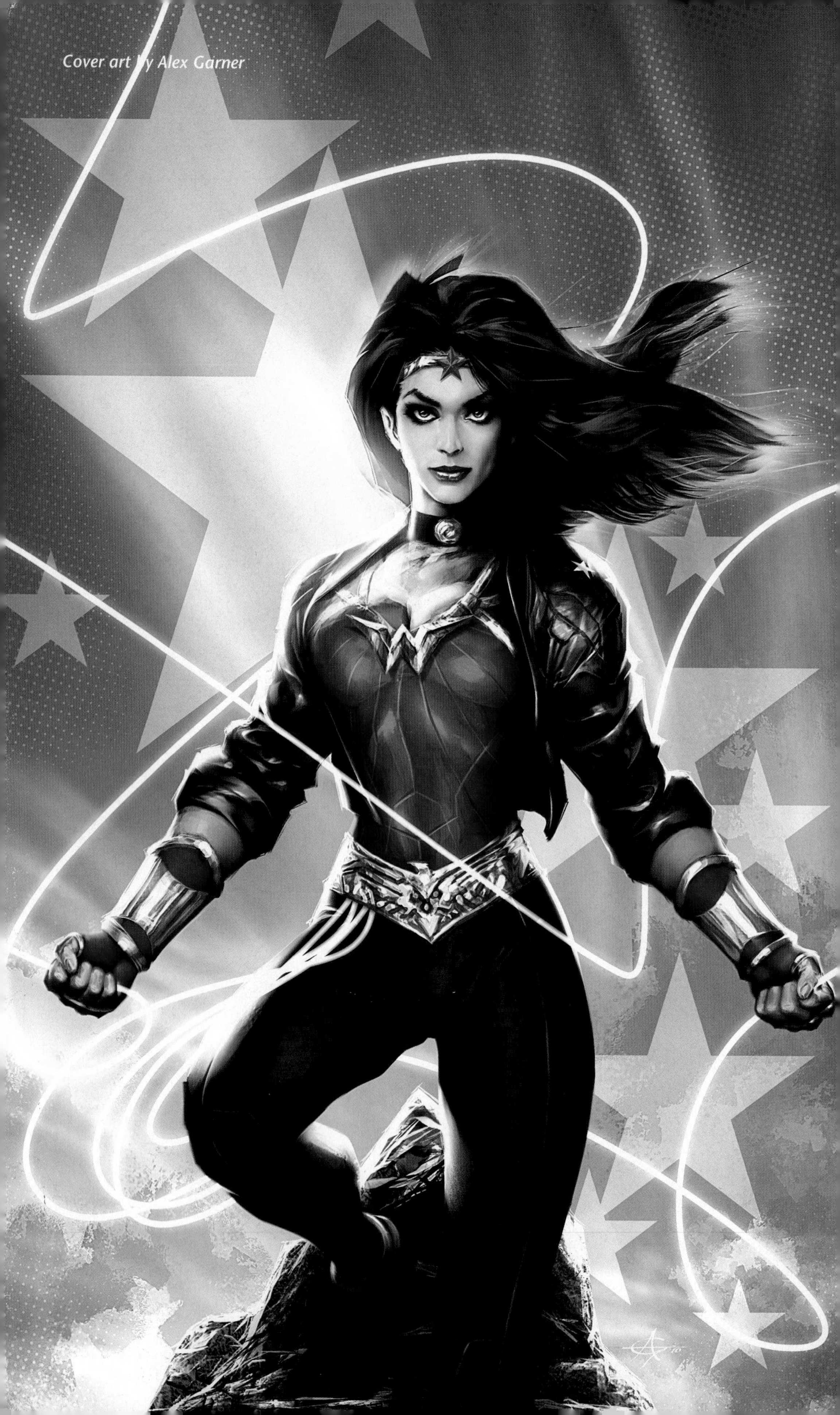

Cover art by Alex Garner

Cover art by Alex Garner

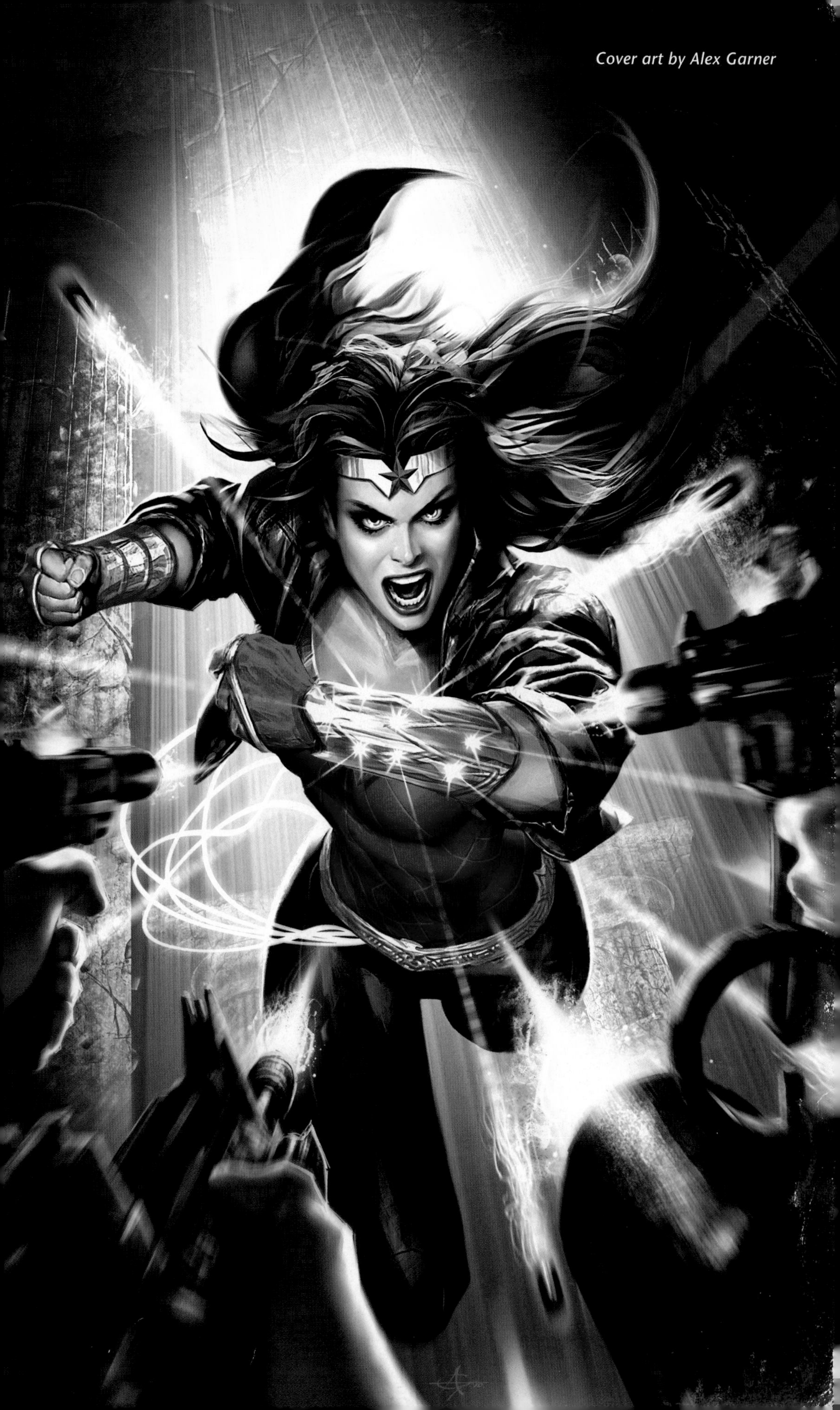

Cover art by J.H. Williams III after H.G. Peter. Cover color by Dave Stewart.

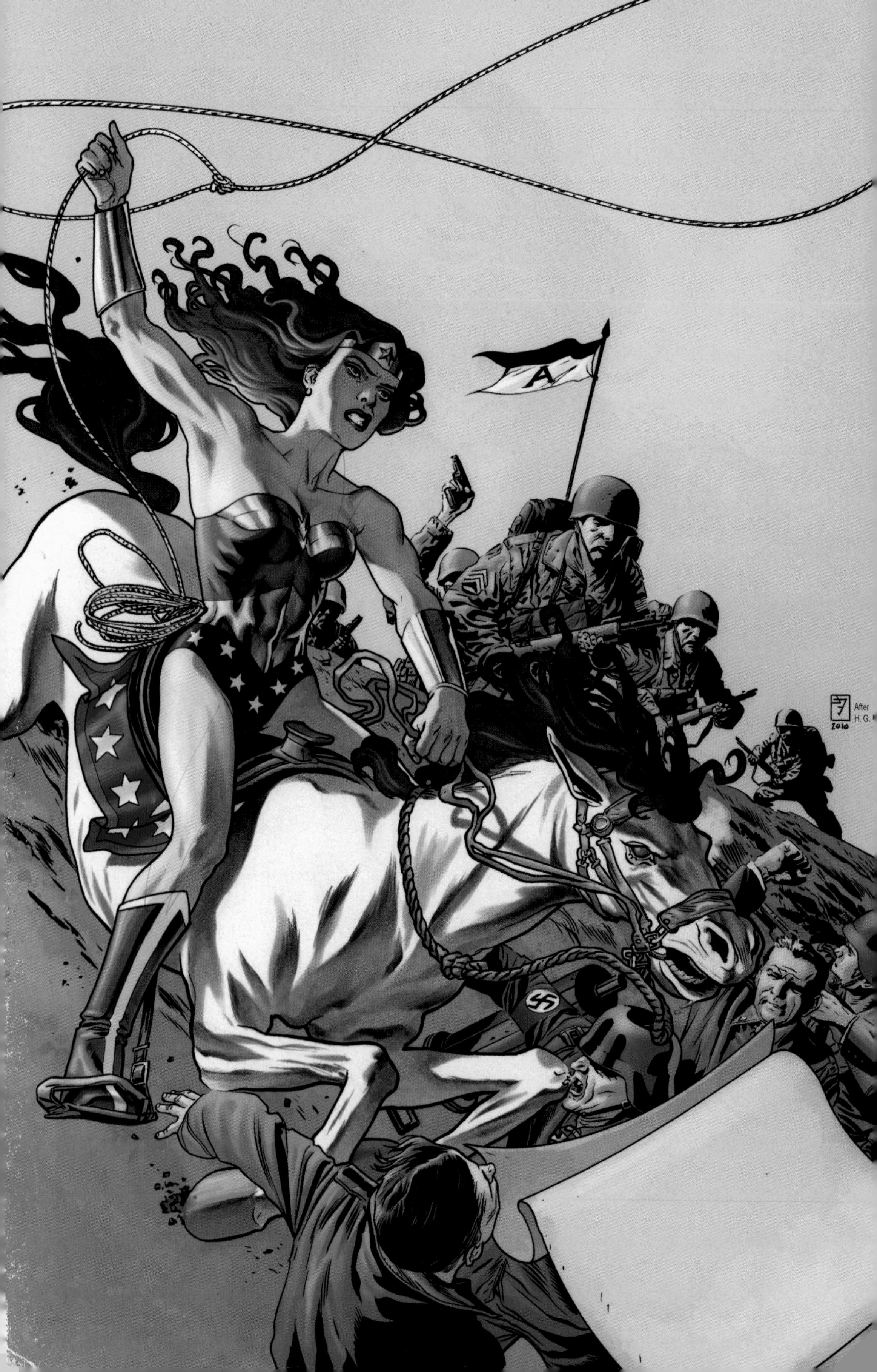
A
After
H.G.

Cover art by Alex Garner

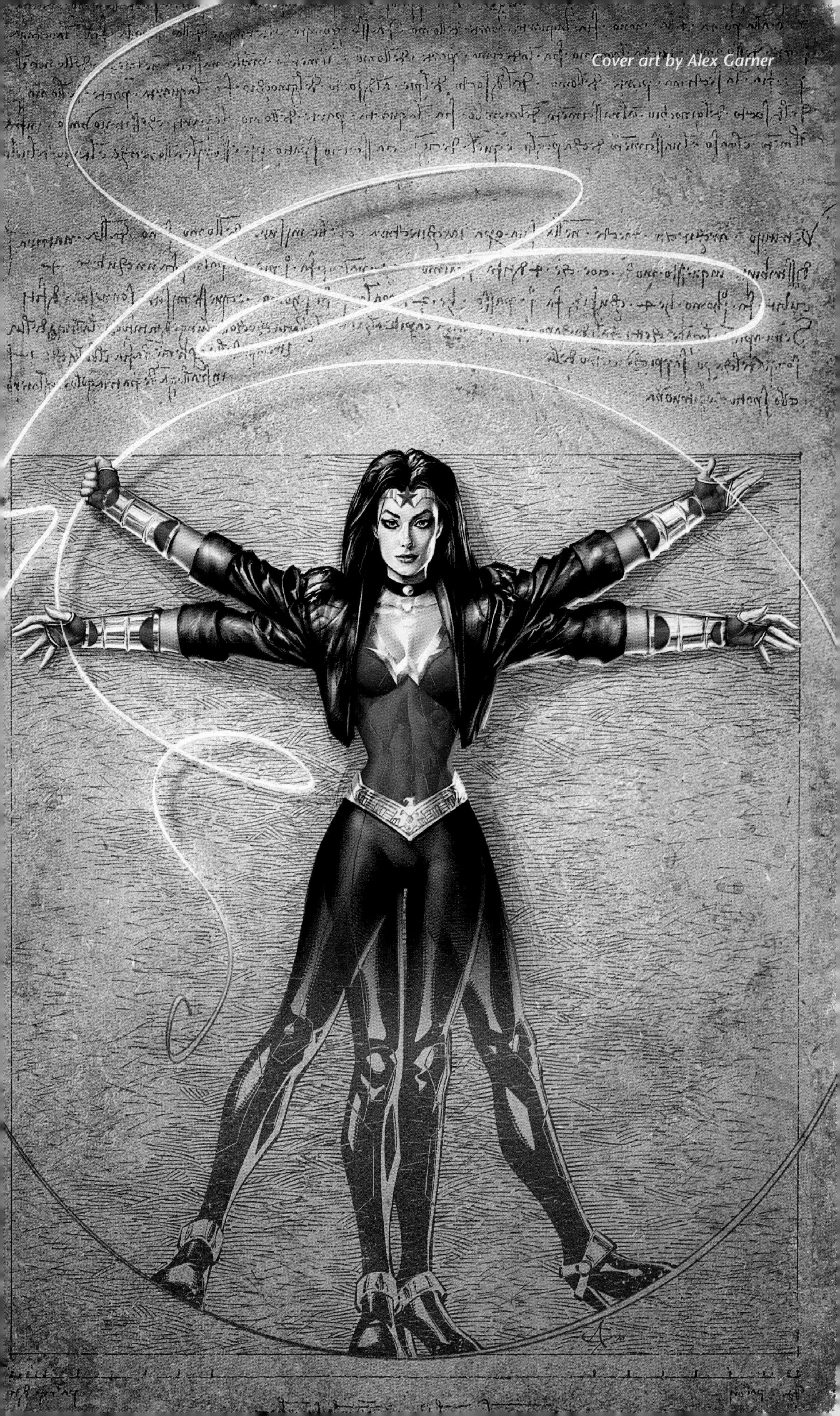

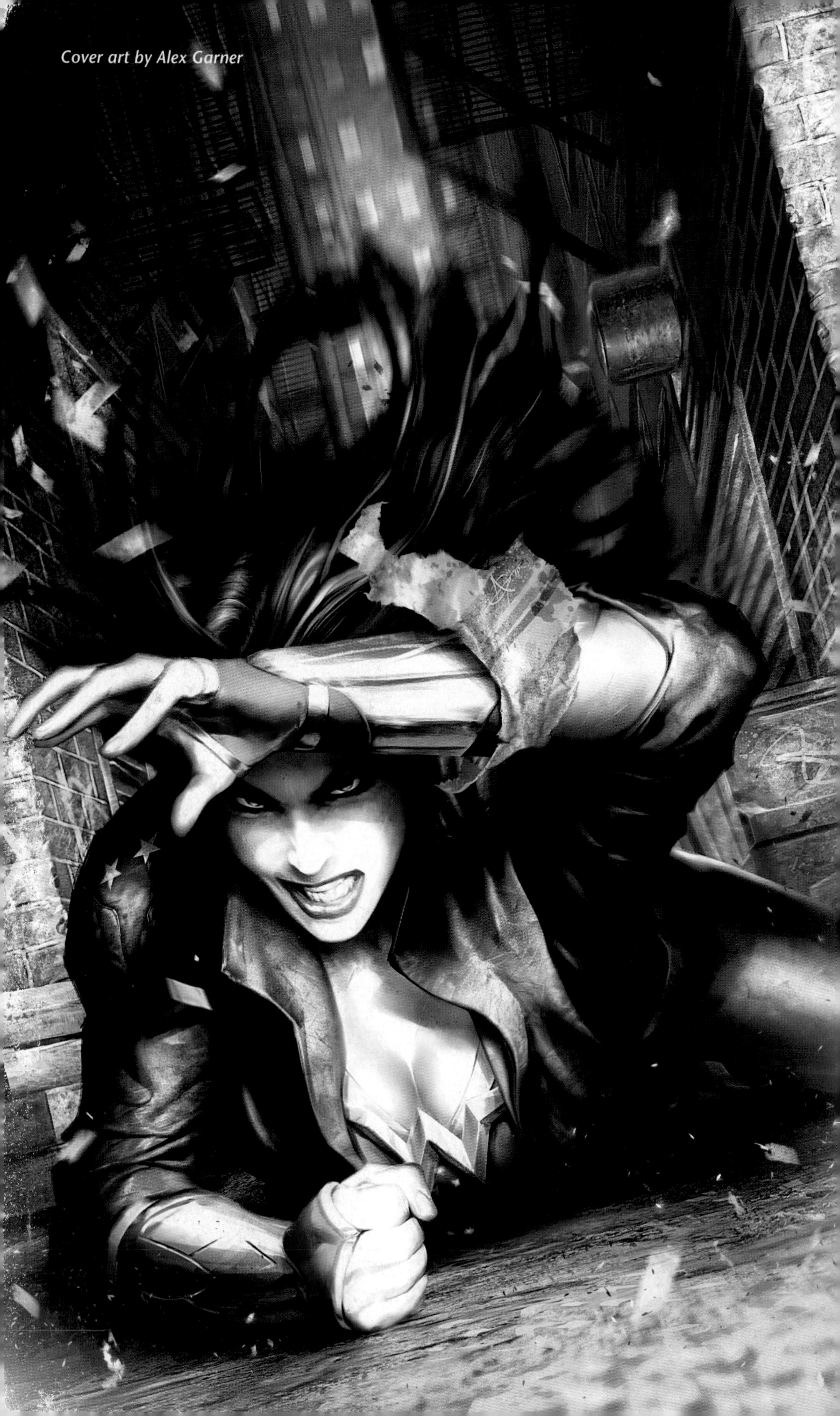
Cover art by Alex Garner

Cover art by Alex Garner

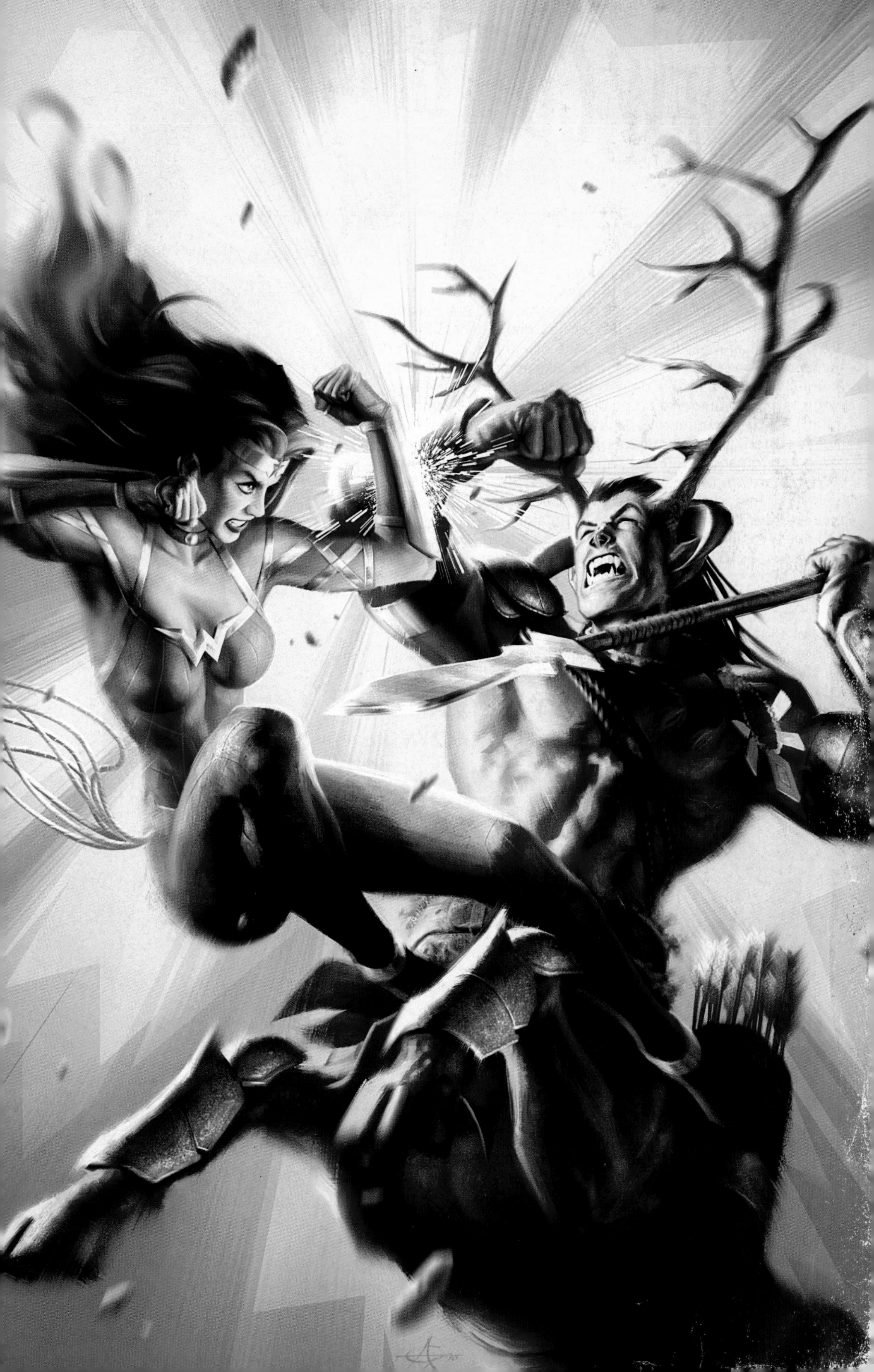

BEHIND THE SCENES: THE NEW COSTUME

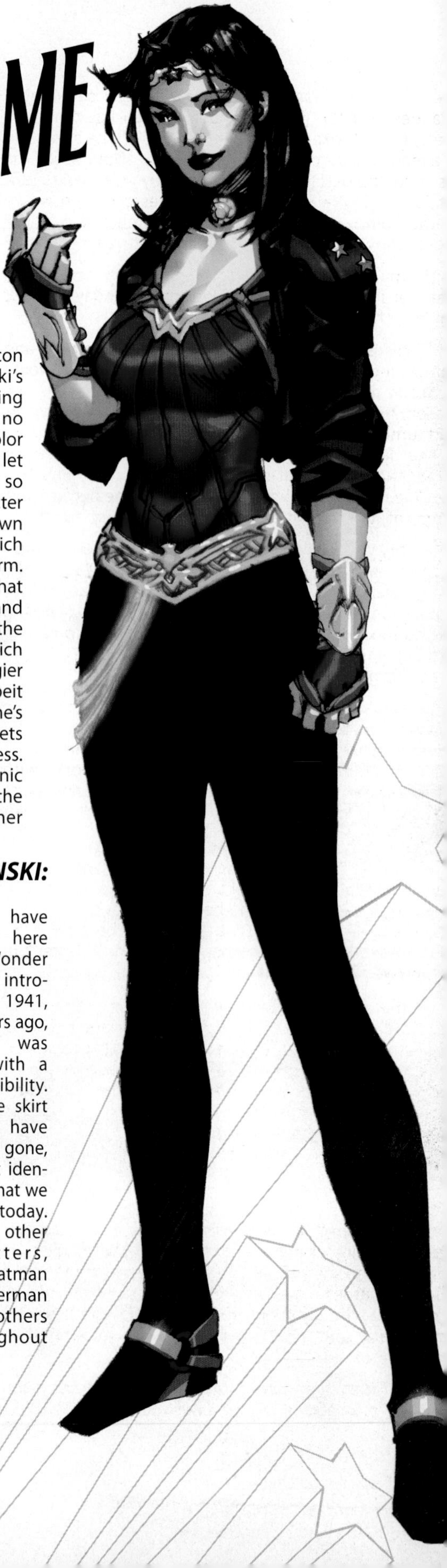

JIM LEE ON HIS DESIGN:

"There's nothing more daunting than re-designing an icon but what was refreshing and novel in Joe Straczynski's directive to be bold in our choices was that we were starting with no preconceptions. This was no mere tweaking, no change of half-measures like haircuts or alterations of color schemes. We decided to go for broke, take no prisoners, and let me tell you—it was difficult. Wonder Woman's costume is so infused into our understanding of the identity of the character that it took many numerous back and forths 'til we broke down what existed, got back metaphorically to the clay from which Wonder Woman started and something new started to form. A design worthy of the mantle of Wonder Woman but one that didn't scream classic superhero! So we played down and scaled back the iconic elements—the stars, the eagles, the double WW's, lightened up the motifs and added armor which could pass as street gear. Visually, the character seems edgier than before but stylish enough to warrant a second, albeit cautious, glance. The jacket and boots confirm the costume's functionality and the open, thinner tiara and shaped bracelets reveal a lighter, even youthful, bent to the Amazonian Princess. All in all, a difficult but rewarding reworking of an iconic costume to usher in a new age; a fresh look worthy of the character defining journey JMS has in store for her ultimate rebirth!"

J. MICHAEL STRACZYNSKI:

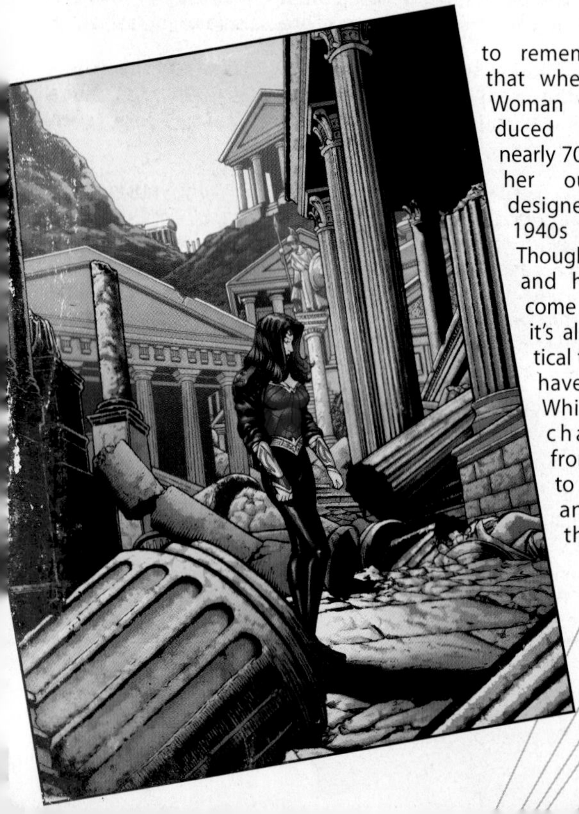

"We have to remember here that when Wonder Woman was introduced in 1941, nearly 70 years ago, her outfit was designed with a 1940s sensibility. Though the skirt and heels have come and gone, it's almost identical to what we have today. While other characters, from Batman to Superman and others throughout e DC Universe, have undergone substantial ﾑanges over the years, Wonder Woman has remained ﾟetty much the same in appearance. (With the exception ￦a mod look used briefly in the 1960s…about which the ﾟss said, the better.) What woman only wears one outfit ﾗr 70 years? What woman doesn't accessorize? And more ﾑ the point, as many women have lamented over the ﾟars…how does she fight in that thing?

"So my mission statement going into Wonder Woman ﾑs real simple: If we were to design her today, without ﾑy prior history…what would she look like?

"This is a character that is interesting enough and ﾗmpelling enough to merit being in the top twenty ﾗoks at minimum…so why was she languishing? The ﾟason, I felt, was that she'd concretized over the years, ﾑd turned into this really cool Porsche that people kept ﾑ the garage because they were afraid of denting it ﾟther than going flat-out on the open road. She had ﾟcome, for lack of a better word, stuffy. She became the ﾗom of the girl next door you wanted to date.

"This was really underscored to me when I used ﾦonder Woman in Brave and the Bold #33, and ﾑany were appalled that Wonder Woman told ﾑ joke…that she flirted…that she was relaxed and ﾑving fun. One podcaster said that Wonder Woman ﾑd become like his grandmother, and he didn't like ﾟ see his grandmother being flirty.

"It seemed to me that the only way to address the ﾑtuation and turn the character around was to go in pre-ﾟared to make massive changes in how we think about ﾦonder Woman. It wasn't going to work with ﾑalf-measures. We had to be willing to go the extra ﾑile. We had to be bold.

"So we came at this from a 21st century perspective. ﾑsually, I wanted her to look strong and tough but still ﾑuite beautiful. Let's give her clothes that she can fight in, ﾑat add to her presence and her strength and her power. ﾑ took a while for us to get there, precisely because we've ﾑl become so locked-in to how we see her character, but ﾑ time we came to a final design.

"Rather than have the W symbol all over the place on ﾟr wardrobe, I wanted to highlight it in one area and ﾑake that our statement, letting everything else feel ﾑore youthful and street-wise. The exception would be ﾑe bracelets, which would be solid on the outer side, ﾟith a stylized, almost handwritten W symbol there so ﾑat when she crosses her arms you get the full effect. ﾑnd if she hits you with it, it leaves a W mark. She signs ﾟr work.

"None of this would work, however, without a strong ﾑaracter behind it. I wanted to free her up from the ﾦeight of a lot of her supporting universe so that we ﾗuld see who she was. Guys tend to see women in terms ﾗf what role they play—mother, girlfriend, wife—instead ﾗf who they are on their own terms. But I didn't simply ﾦant to eradicate all of it and destroy the work of those ﾦho came before me.

"So the solution was to tweak time: at some point ﾑbout 20 years ago or so, the time stream was changed.

Paradise Island was destroyed, and Diana as an infant was smuggled out before her mother was killed along with most of the others. She was raised by guardians sent with her, and some surviving Amazons, so she has a foot in two worlds, the urban world and the world of her people, which still exists in the shadows, underground. So we keep what makes her an Amazon but mix it up with a more modern perspective.

"Those who can see those two worlds know that something has changed, and they try to get Diana to see that, but she only knows what she's seen and experienced.

"To solve the problem before them she must a) find out who attacked Paradise Island and why, b) stop those who are trying to kill the remaining Amazons now, c) rescue any more surviving Amazons, and d) find some way to straighten out the timeline and reconcile what was to what is. So we continue to get glimpses of Wonder Woman as she was juxtaposed against Diana as she is.

"The result—storywise and visually—is a character who is fiery, dynamic, a bit more vulnerable (she's still working her way up to her full set of powers), tough, determined and smart and, due to her background, tragic. She keeps her roots in the Amazonian universe while growing up in a more modern setting. The result will, we hope, be a redesign that is as current with the zeitgeist of the 21st century as the original was with 1941."

DC COMICS™

FLASHPOINT
GEOFF JOHNS with ANDY KUBERT

FLASHPOINT: THE WORLD OF FLASHPOINT FEATURING BATMAN

FLASHPOINT: THE WORLD OF FLASHPOINT FEATURING GREEN LANTERN

Read the Entire Epic!

Flashpoint

Flashpoint: The World of Flashpoint Featuring Batman

Flashpoint: The World of Flashpoint Featuring The Flash

Flashpoint: The World of Flashpoint Featuring Green Lantern

Flashpoint: The World of Flashpoint Featuring Superman

Flashpoint: The World of Flashpoint Featuring Wonder Woman

"Heroic comic-book art at its finest" - ENTERTAINMENT WEEKLY / SHELF LIFE

GEOFF JOHNS · ANDY KUBERT · SANDRA HOPE

FLASHPOINT

"A soaring, if radical, tale that uses superheroes in ways that may surprise both first-time readers and long-time fans."
– THE ASSOCIATED PRESS